CONCENTRATION CAMPS ON THE HOME FRONT

1. Two boys at the Rohwer concentration camp, May 1944. 97.292.11I, MC, JANM.

CONCENTRATION CAMPS ON THE HOME FRONT

JAPANESE AMERICANS IN THE HOUSE OF JIM CROW

JOHN HOWARD

THE UNIVERSITY OF CHICAGO PRESS CHICAGO AND LONDON

JOHN HOWARD is professor of American studies at King's College London. He is the author of *Men Like That: A Southern Queer History*, also published by the University of Chicago Press, and the editor of three volumes in social and literary history.

The University of Chicago Press, Chicago 60637
The University of Chicago Press, Ltd., London

Printed in the United States of America

17 16 15 14 13 12 11 10 09 08 1 2 3 4 5
ISBN-13: 978-0-226-35476-7 (cloth)
ISBN-10: 0-226-35476-8 (cloth)

Library of Congress Cataloging-in-Publication Data
Howard, John, 1962–
Concentration camps on the home front: Japanese Americans in the house of Jim Crow / John Howard.
p. cm.
Includes bibliographical references and index.
ISBN-13: 978-0-226-35476-7 (cloth: alk. paper)
ISBN-10: 0-226-35476-8 (cloth: alk. paper) 1. Japanese Americans—Evacuation and relocation, 1942–1945. 2. World War, 1939–1945—Concentration camps—Arkansas—Jerome. 3. World War, 1939–1945—Concentration camps—Arkansas—Rohwer. 4. Japanese Americans—Arkansas—Biography. 5. Japanese Americans—Arkansas—Social conditions—20th century. 6. Community life—Arkansas—History—20th century. 7. Imprisonment—Social aspects—Arkansas—History—20th century. 8. Arkansas—Race relations—History—20th century. 9. Southern states—Race relations—Case studies. I. Title.
D769.8.A6H69 2008
940.53'17767—dc22 2007050680

∞ The paper used in this publication meets the minimum requirements of the American National Standard for Information Sciences—Permanence of Paper for Printed Library Materials, ANSI Z39.48-1992.

To the Memory of
John DeVelling Howard Sr.

HECTOR [AN ENGLISH TEACHER]: So, thrown into a common grave though he may be, he is still Hodge the drummer. Lost boy though he is on the other side of the world, he still has a name.

POSNER [A STUDENT]: How old was he?

HECTOR: If he's a drummer he would be a young soldier, younger than you probably.

POSNER: No. Hardy.

HECTOR: Oh, how old was Hardy? When he wrote this, about sixty. My age, I suppose.

Saddish life, though not unappreciated.

"Uncoffined" is a typical Hardy usage.

A compound adjective, formed by putting "un-" in front of the noun. Or verb, of course.

Un-kissed. Un-rejoicing. Un-confessed. Un-embraced.

It's a turn of phrase he has bequeathed to Larkin, who liked Hardy, apparently.

He does the same.

Un-spent. Un-fingermarked.

And with both of them it brings a sense of not sharing, of being out of it.

Whether because of diffidence or shyness, but a holding back. Not being in the swim. Can you see that?

POSNER: Yes, sir. I felt that a bit.

HECTOR: The best moments in reading are when you come across something—a thought, a feeling, a way of looking at things—which you had thought special and particular to you. Now here it is, set down by someone else, a person you have never met, someone even who is long dead. And it is as if a hand has come out and taken yours.

Alan Bennett, *The History Boys* (2004)

Racism, . . . if by that is meant white supremacism and its accompanying mystique, is not un-American in the historical sense. It is despicable—but there we go. . . .

William F. Buckley Jr., *The Committee and Its Critics* (1962)

Contents

CONCENTRATION CAMPS
ON THE HOME FRONT

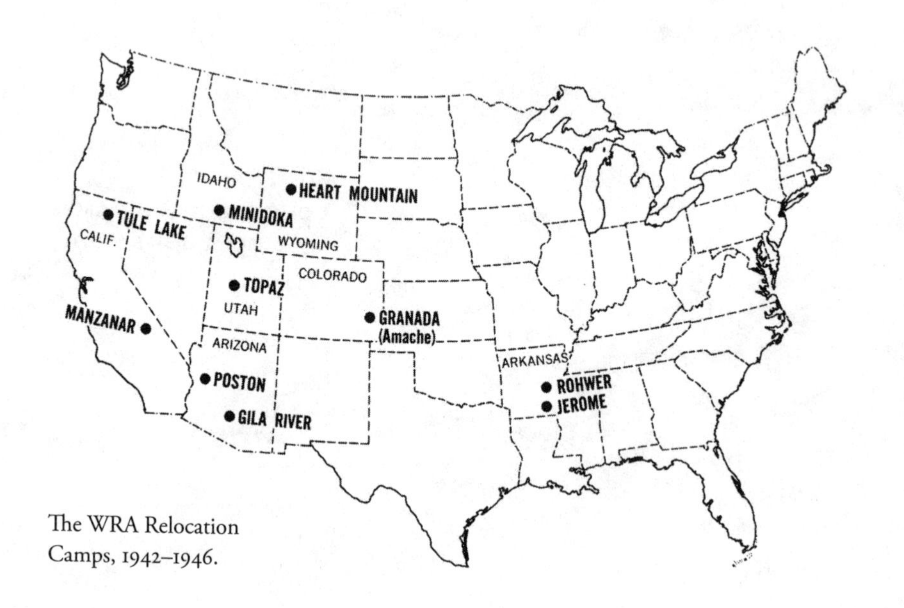

The WRA Relocation Camps, 1942–1946.

Introduction

NEITHER A MILITARY HERO nor sports figure, neither an elected official nor popular entertainer, Earl Finch cultivated a unique celebrity in mid-twentieth-century America. Raised poor in rural Mississippi, Finch was known only to his family and a small circle of peers as of 1943. By 1945 he would meet with President Truman; he would be spotlighted in press accounts and magazine features; and he would go on to be warmly remembered in innumerable memoirs of the war years. His friends and acquaintances would span the globe. Neither a Carnegie nor a Rockefeller, Earl Finch was a philanthropist of limited means, a do-gooder with what seemed a single cause.[1]

Prone to immoderate gift-giving, Finch embodied the most prominent symbols of openhandedness. He was Santa Claus, turning up at Christmastime and doling out presents to youngsters. He was the Easter bunny, securing thousands of decorated eggs for hunts in the spring. He was the Christian servant, a disciplined Southern Baptist who followed Jesus' parable on eternal life: he fed the hungry; he visited the sick; he went to those in prison; he welcomed the strangers. The strangers to the Deep South during World War II, those most in need, as Earl Finch saw it, were Americans of Japanese descent. Finch's altruism was focused on the victims of U.S. concentration camps, the 120,000 Japanese American citizens and longtime residents forced from their homes on the West Coast and indiscriminately incarcerated in the interior, particularly those locked up in the two camps in nearby Arkansas. And he was especially concerned with the second-generation (or Nisei) men who, despite all this, had volunteered to serve in the war effort, those soldiers training in the segregated 442nd Regimental Combat Team at Camp Shelby, Mississippi, just down the road from Finch's hometown.[2]

According to the legend, corroborated by veteran Keiso Nakagawa and others, Finch first met one or two of the "lonely" soldier boys—names are rarely mentioned—on the streets of Hattiesburg, gazing "forlornly" into a store window. He extended an invitation to dinner. Alerted to their plight, Finch went to work wholeheartedly on behalf of Japanese Americans. When told about the children of Jerome and Rohwer, Arkansas, he sent toys and candy by the truckload. When informed of the dietary dilemmas resulting from displacement, he arranged shipments of rice, soy, and tofu. When he heard about racial segregation at the local USOs—the United Service Organizations clubs for the off-duty entertainment of troops—he helped form a new Aloha Center, and he contributed furnishings to USO clubrooms within the Arkansas concentration camps. Finch threw dinners and parties; he organized rodeos and road trips for the servicemen. After they left for combat in the European theater, he kept up correspondence. After they returned home—some on stretchers, some in coffins—he made hospital calls and paid visits to the next of kin.[3]

There was ceaseless speculation about Earl Finch. To some, the lanky white Mississippian seemed too good to be true. Behind the selfless humanitarianism surely lurked self-serving impulses, perhaps even sinister machinations. For one thing, Finch had an uncanny ability to procure those delicacies that, in World War II America, were in shortest supply. Might he be connected to the underworld? Or, worse still, the enemy? At the least, Finch's style raised alarm. In practicing his piety, he didn't always manage the quiet humility required by the Gospels. In its glowing feature on Earl Finch, the *Saturday Evening Post*—that profit-minded purveyor of white American wholesomeness—spoke these worries, but only through the skeptical voice of a jaded New Yorker. The "smooth, fast-talking" owner of "the lavish Broadway night club" frequented by Finch and company bluntly posed the question no one else seemed willing to enunciate: "What's his angle, anyway?" Taking the query as a framing device for his article, writer Maurice Zolotow examined Finch's murky motivations, which many found "perplexing in the extreme." Zolotow reached the happiest of conclusions: "Spontaneously, and with all the fullness of his heart, [Finch] became a friend of an unjustly persecuted and cruelly misunderstood minority. . . . Finch [wa]s that rare being, a man without an angle." Zolotow believed Finch, who succinctly stated his reasons for helping the 442nd, including the recently incorporated 100th Infantry Battalion from Hawaii: "I do it because I like these boys."[4]

Well, I believe Finch too. Indeed, I've discovered that Finch took a special liking to a series of young men of Japanese descent. I want to take Earl Finch at his word; or more to the point, I want to explore how his words—"I like these boys"—could be variously interpreted, both then and now. I don't want to suggest that, armed with a heat-sensitive twentieth-first-century night vision, a technologically superior post-Stonewall gaydar, we can now clearly see in retrospect the homoeroticism that mainstream midcentury media refused to acknowledge. Quite the contrary, I propose that queer implications in Finch's activities were right on the surface, fully perceptible at the time. More interesting, in my view, are the ways in which those implications were negotiated by Earl Finch and his many Japanese American friends. More interesting still—or, rather, more available to historical inquiry—are the ways in which queer implications were largely tamed and contained in media representations. Like the dangerous parallels repeatedly evoked between the moral culpabilities of American racism and European fascism, any comparisons between Earl Finch's peculiarities and a subversive nonconformity required vigilant if subtle denunciation. In a period of intense international conflict, fraught with countless ethical ambiguities, Finch's eccentric homespun generosity was normalized and valorized; it was made to comport with a mythical American goodness born of the rural heartland.

If I begin this book by examining Finch's angle, his incentive for stepping outside the bounds of race and gender privilege to help members of one persecuted minority—while apparently overlooking another, African Americans—it's because I think it can provide us with a new angle of vision on to Japanese American incarceration and twentieth-century racial formation: historical phenomena made increasingly visible in American cultural production, but from a persistently skewed perspective. As we write ever more histories of such injustices, as we continue to look anew at the past, we can rely on the insights of feminist scholarship, critical race studies, and socioeconomic analysis in a Marxist tradition—all of which this study attempts. We further can benefit from developments in queer theory, stressing as it does the centrality of power differentials in culture, the intricate interconnectedness of, the reciprocal relationships between, the self and the other, normal and deviant, mainstream and margin. If we proceed under the assumption that categories of human difference are historically produced or constructed over time—that is, they are made as much as found—then the inequalities that have tended to accompany those differences we can more clearly *observe* both then and now. And perhaps *undo* in the future. A key vector of difference and dominance, whether one is American or "foreign"—or un-American, whatever that means—might also be reconsidered. It might prove less worrisome than it seems.[5]

UNNATURAL BUT NOT UN-AMERICAN

Born in 1915 on a farm outside the village of Ovett, Mississippi, Earl Finch was only twenty-seven years old when he first became acquainted with Nisei in Hattiesburg. Thus, of the thousands of Japanese Americans who trained at Camp Shelby, he was scarcely older than most and was younger than many. At six feet two inches tall, however, he stood above almost all. And in the symbolically rich world of masculine privilege, size mattered. Already effeminized in midcentury popular film, as Gina Marchetti has shown, Nisei men short of stature guarded against further aspersions. For example, when stock-depleted quartermasters sent them outerwear and underwear appropriately sized but originally intended for the Women's Army Corps, the men of the 442nd chose the WAC garments with care: "The raincoats were handed out, but not the panties. We didn't want our men to be known as being 'mahu' (gay)."[6]

Earl Finch stood tall, and he stood out. Photographs of dinners show the fair-complected Finch seated at the center or the patriarchal head of the table, wearing a suit and tie, surrounded by unnamed Nisei in uniform. In a largely biracial South, where interracial friendships rarely survived childhood and where, in adulthood, they were countenanced only in hierarchical work environments, Finch might have been called anything but a companion to Japanese Americans. Rather, with extraordinary frequency and consistency, the prematurely bald Finch was referred to—and subsequently has been remembered—as "the godfather of the 442nd."[7]

But why not comrade? As would be asked of any able-bodied twenty-seven-year-old male in 1943, why wasn't Finch also enlisted in the armed services? As the *Saturday Evening Post* was quick to point out, whereas Finch's brother Brownie had signed up for the U.S. Navy, Earl "was turned down as 4-F"—unsuitable for military service. More precisely, Finch volunteered for the prestigious Officer Candidate School in late October 1942, but his application was denied. He requested regular induction in early 1944 but was rejected due to flat feet and a heart ailment. Thus, as a white civilian seemingly advanced beyond his years, Finch took on the popular wartime mantle of booster, "a sort of guardian," particularly as board member for the USO. If his references to his charges, to "my boys," mirrored the racist infantilizing of black southern men, they also resonated with the prevalent if ambivalent American depictions of soldier boys, sailor boys, and flyboys sent overseas to kill. The pseudo-intergenerational relationship between Finch and the press's representative Nisei soldier was further manufactured through the latter's reference to Earl as "Mistuh Finch," as white writers rendered the ostensibly accented English. After a fatal injury in Italy, for example, one Japanese American "boy"—again, unnamed—reportedly offered these last dying words: "Just say good-by to Mr. Finch for me." A year older and, in some sense, a man of greater professional distinction, Protestant minister and 442nd chaplain George Aki insists, "I always called him *Mr.* Finch."[8]

White military leaders and concentration camp officials helped cast Earl Finch as a "mentor" to the 442nd by relying on a common narrative of American success ideology. Finch's personal history, they suggested, was an admirable and imitable tale of class ascendancy. Failing to finish high school, Finch nonetheless had brushed the dirt off his work boots and, with gumption and industry, had become proprietor of any number of local enterprises: a bowling alley, a furniture store, a clothing shop, and—important in the iconography of southern aristocracy—a farming operation or ranch. In truth, Finch was solidly middle class, seldom generating balances of more than $2,000 in his personal or commercial bank accounts. Locals gossiped about the way he seemed to spend well beyond his earnings. In fact, he often simply brokered deals for his Japanese American friends, particularly those from the territory of Hawaii who had been spared incarceration and thus had not lost their assets in distress sales, as had most from the mainland. Moreover, the 442nd took pride as a regiment of successful gamblers: their newsletter masthead spelled out 442 with three correspondingly arranged dice, and as their regimental slogan, they chose the crapshooter's phrase "Go for broke." These were men with money to spend. But in the South, Finch had entrée where Japanese Americans were subject to racial discrimination. It was Finch's whiteness as much as his business acumen that facilitated his ironic title—second only to godfather—of "benefactor" of the 442nd.[9]

Earl Finch's involvements with the 442nd were not merely financial but also social, perhaps sexual. If the *Saturday Evening Post* was loath to explore this, J. Edgar Hoover's Federal Bureau of Investigation was eager. The former readily explained away Finch's lack of interest in young women: he lived with and cared for his disabled mother, confined as she was to a wheelchair. The latter viewed Finch's bachelor status, the fact that he had never married, as a worrying sign of something deeper. The FBI inquiry was solicited by an intelligence officer at Camp Fannin, Texas, after Finch visited Japanese American soldiers there and promised to "pay for all the ice cream [they] wanted." Agents intercepted Finch's voluminous incoming mail; they interrogated Hattiesburg residents and confidential informants. As suspected, many locals "considered Finch to be peculiar in that he never associates with girls." According to one former schoolmate, Finch "always exhibited more or less of an abnormal attitude toward the opposite sex [and was] unnatural in this respect." As another pointed out, Finch had once used his clout to help purchase "a home so a Japanese officer could live in it." The FBI interpreted these actions and character traits as inherent in Finch's "extreme egotism," a narcissism shot through contemporaneous psychiatric accounts of homosexuality, the physical self desiring its mirror image. Whereas the *Saturday Evening Post* sympathetically portrayed Finch as a humble loner, "not much of a joiner," the FBI by contrast viewed him as a "mentally unstable" headline-grabber. In sum, "his association with the Japanese [American] soldiers who in turn pay him a great deal of attention and cause him to be publicized apparently satisfies his personal desires."[10]

And yet in closing its investigation, the FBI had to concede that Finch generally enjoyed a "good reputation." To a person, neighbors and acquaintances absolved him of any wrongdoing. Speaking a common refrain, a reporter for the local paper told the FBI agent that he had "known Finch personally for many years and [wa]s positive that [he had] no un-American motive." The banker likewise "had known [the] subject for many years and . . . [the] subject's family," and he had "never observed any un-American tendencies." Even as the armed forces attempted to cleanse its homosocial ranks by purging its homosexual comrades, as Allan Bérubé has demonstrated, even as Second World War and soon Cold War rhetoric would entangle homosexuality with espionage and sedition, Earl Finch emerged in popular representations as a heroic American with peculiar habits. Indeed, as I've shown elsewhere, rural queers successfully negotiated an environment of quiet accommodation not so much because they were invisible or undercover; but rather—to repeat the words of Finch's neighbors—because they were *known*. Embedded in local communities, bound by relations of kinship and familiarity, sexual nonconformists often were *known* as queer but not as subversive. *Because* their queerness was known or assumed, it could thereby safely be disregarded.[11]

In broader fields of cultural production, in mainstream representations aimed at national audiences, rurality vindicated sexual nonconformity. Critical to Earl Finch's acceptance was the focus on his more authentically rural and thus masculine experiences. "Finch never traveled more than 100 miles," the *Evening Post* told its readers, "until he became involved in the Nisei problem." The magazine accentuated not those high times in the big cities—New Orleans, Chicago, New York. Rather, along with the *Hattiesburg American*, it emphasized the regular Sunday gatherings at Finch's Rolfin Stock Farm, the 542-acre compound replete with chickens, mustangs, sheep, and free-ranging cattle, photographed while being branded. Writers mentioned Finch's grandfather, who first farmed the soil, but rarely his father—who, as a janitor at the Hattiesburg Public Library, was an archetypal victim of agricultural decline, the mass economic exodus from field to town. Finch liked to hunt and ride, as evidenced by pictures astride his horse, oddly reminiscent of heroic military statuary; his more lucrative but gender-suspect profession as haberdasher received scant attention, even though shared by Harry Truman. Similarly, of Finch's Japanese American guests—three hundred attended one rodeo—journalists noticed not the many urban Californians in the 442nd, known for their relative sophistication, the occasional zoot suit, and flair for dance. Instead, they harped on the barefoot Hawaiians of the 100th Battalion—the plainspoken farm folk who, as in racist depictions of African Americans, exhibited culinary preferences for watermelon, lemonade, and fried chicken. Although these imagined island field hands seemed a bit rough around the edges, their crude masculinity would reach appropriate refinement, not defilement, under the tutelage of so-called patron saint and country gentleman, Earl M. Finch.[12]

Utilizing dialect and depicting comic scenarios, white reporters often infantilized Japanese American men. They homogenized the men of the 442nd, whose words rarely were attributed to them by name in print. Such racial grouping further served to deflect the possibility of sexual relations between Earl Finch and any one (or more) of them. That is, a racist understanding of Asian Americans as a homogenous mass—as all looking alike, especially in uniform, and thus uniformly heterosexual—helped defuse the prospect of individual nonnormative desires. And yet we might speculate that some queer readers of the day would recognize Finch as the definitive "rice queen"—a white man whose same-sex desires were structured by a depersonalizing, dehumanizing racial fetish, an exclusive attraction to men of Asian descent. Without the testimony of Earl Finch, however, and without complete sexual candor from the Japanese American men who joined the U.S. Army, we should not rush to conclusions about the egalitarianism of their intimate relationships.[13]

During and particularly after the war, Japanese American men documented their experiences in their own words. In memoirs, Daniel Inouye and many others described their military service as proof of their loyalty, as evidence of their worth as Americans. They wrote very fondly of Earl Finch, as if implicitly sharing a quest to shed outsider status—in his case sexual, in their case racial—by becoming the consummate insider, the superpatriot. Or, by supporting the ultimate insider, Uncle Sam. Perhaps to some Japanese Americans, Earl Finch evoked Uncle Sam: paternalistic, nationalistic, well-intentioned, and asexual. According to veteran Chester Tanaka, who apparently thought of the nation in terms of the "opposite" gender, Earl Finch was "the man who symbolized America at *her* finest."[14]

Many Nisei writers rhetorically overlooked Finch's queerness, even as it seemed to draw him closer after the war. As superpatriot Mike Masaoka explained, Nisei from Hawaii felt obliged to repay Finch's hospitality, and so they invited him to visit them on the islands. One or two ever so subtly expanded the invitation: "You come to Hawaii." Finch came all right. And stayed. He relocated to Hawaii in 1949 and lived there until his death in 1965. Though he never married, in the 1950s he "adopted" two sons around the age of twenty from Japan—first Seiji Naya and, later, Hideo Sakamoto. As Sakamoto explained his arrival in Honolulu: "In the beginning, I was thinking that this was my guardian, my sponsor. He paid for my school. But a couple of weeks later, Seiji told me I had to act like a son. The next day, I called him 'Daddy.' That's the way he needed it, I found out. It was a real close bond."[15]

Related forms of humanitarian international adoption, transferring children from poorer to wealthier countries, from poorer to wealthier parents and guardians, have been criticized as a malign by-product of Western imperial expansion, which generates, exacerbates, and benefits from such inequities. However, adoption within Japan historically has been accepted as a means—not unlike arranged marriages—for shifting the social and economic responsibility for a young person from one house, household, or family registry to another. Boys in particular have been passed into apprenticeship roles designed to enhance future prospects. Thus, adoptions for what was perceived to be better schooling and training overseas became viable options before and after the war.[16]

Meanwhile back in postwar Mississippi, Finch's friend Herbert Sasaki married white local Arnice Dyer and took up residence in Hattiesburg, around the corner from Finch's mother and father. Sasaki sang Finch's praises, though he harbored doubts about his departure: "It was kind of bad, you know, leaving his parents." Afterward Sasaki would take Earl's folks out for drives in the country, since "they liked it so much." I asked Herbert Sasaki the question posed by so many over the years, "What motivated Earl Finch?" He responded either with incomprehension or, much more likely, discretion: "It's very hard to say."[17]

If early twenty-first-century theories privilege the metropolis as the key site of queer sexualities, similarly many mid-twentieth-century representations cast the city as the logical home for sexual difference. For rural Americans negotiating their own sexual and gender nonconforming desires, behaviors, and identities, such biases of understanding could be manipulated to circumvent oppressive forces and carve out enabling social and physical spaces. In his dealings with locals and in his interviews with the press, Earl Finch seemed particularly adept at such negotiation. When Daniel Inouye, Mike Masaoka, Keiso Nakagawa, Herb Sasaki, Chester Tanaka, and hundreds of other Nisei soldiers joined in the all-male rodeos, road trips, and rural recreations organized by Finch, they assented to and participated in official and mainstream media discourses that largely normalized the activities. By emphasizing those second-generation Japanese Americans from the agricultural regions of Hawaii over those from the Little Tokyos of California, by highlighting Finch's career as a rancher as opposed to a merchant, and—crucially—by crafting their interactions not as egalitarian interracial friendship but as hierarchical humanitarian mentorship, the highly publicized 442nd Regimental Combat Team would not be implicated in criminalized queer acts with the unmarried, un-enlisted southerner known to the FBI as "unnatural." Capitalizing upon the productive vagaries of queer innuendo, euphemism, and double entendre, Finch likewise did not demonstrate an underlying gay self but rather circulated narratives open to varied interpretations. Thus, when asked "What's your angle?" Finch could cagily proliferate a multitude of meanings, then as now, by responding, "I like these boys."

Like Earl Finch, the wartime concentration camps for Japanese Americans seemed unnatural to many, the living arrangements inhumane and unjust, as will become all too apparent. But as this book further attempts to demonstrate, the camps yielded mixed results, including—against all intuition—an affirmation and empowerment of many Japanese Americans, based upon a human inclination to work together, to share burdens and benefits, to cooperate. Certainly, the camps were not un-American. United States history is filled with compelling analogies, if brought to light for comparison. Following in an impressive historiography of Japanese American incarceration, described below, *Concentration Camps on the Home Front* attempts to illuminate some of the unflattering precedents for incarceration, as well as noble models for overcoming it. With the help of theorists and interpreters of human difference, the book endeavors to take us beyond American contexts to see if one or two broader hypotheses can be hazarded about the nature of human conflict and resolution.

NOT AMERICAN, NOT AGAIN

As Erica Harth notes, "The mass detention of Japanese Americans may well be the most documented and the least known miscarriage of justice in [American] history." How, she asks, "has all the material on incarceration so long available to the general public managed not to penetrate the national consciousness? Certainly it is a story that we would rather not hear." It is, she suggests, a story of national shame. "Not only does it tarnish the image of our victory in World War II; it also clashes head on with fundamental and enduring American values: the rule of fairness and equality, which allows you to remain innocent until proven guilty; the crowning of hard work by success. The Japanese Americans incarcerated in 1942 were held guilty until proven innocent, and the hard-won success of the older generation was smashed to bits by years behind barbed wire." So, she concludes, it is "a nasty story . . . that we must continue to retell."[18]

Inevitably, to retell any story, to recount any history, is to tell it in a particular way. My principal objective is to understand the powerful and less powerful, those dominant and subordinate cultural groups and their material inequalities during the first half of the twentieth century, particularly World War II. I would like to analyze the ways in which international conflict and imperial expansion shaped and reflected structures of inequity on the home front. Specifically, I hope to illuminate changes in racial hierarchies, sexual normalcy and deviancy, and gender categorization—all through the experiences of incarcerated Japanese Americans, their supporters and detractors. In the process, my aim is to construct a thorough social history, accessible to both academic and popular readerships, of the two most under-evaluated of America's ten concentration camps, Jerome and Rohwer, in Arkansas. The two camps were different from one other and different from all the others, a fact recognized at the time. The facilities were "not ten peas in a pod," as a War Relocation Authority official put it, "but ten separate pea plants." "The conditions existing in the ten centers," he told the Jerome camp newspaper, "cannot be generalized." Thus, this project not only provides the first book-length community study of these southern compounds of nearly ten thousand residents each, but also tracks, within national and international contexts, the local practices—the regional specificity—of human differentiation.[19]

How did the injustice of indiscriminate incarceration reflect continuing equivocation in the United States—ostensibly a nation of immigrants—over varied racial and ethnic minorities? In what ways were imprisoned Japanese Americans, most of them birthright citizens, likewise ambivalent about notions of home and nation, as well as gender and sexuality? How did the camps' daily and weekend leave programs—largely unexamined in the literature—put so-called evacuees into contact with local populations? What impact did these interactions have on the South's and America's seemingly biracial "color line"? Were divided national loyalties—in particular, the renunciation of American citizenship, as was more common at Jerome—a plausible and historically understandable outcome for some? How did gender shape the experience of camp life? In particular, how did a highly concentrated, overwhelmingly Japanese American community, with shifting conceptions of leisure, provide expanded opportunities for women, both in the workplace and as leaders of women's organizations? In what ways was sexuality a key factor in the establishment (fears of miscegenation), maintenance (charges of "overpopulating"), and lived experience (state-sanctioned and oppositional courtship rituals) of the camps? Finally, how did incarceration fit within the broader imperial legacy of the United States in the Pacific, from the annexation of Hawaii in 1898 to the end of the occupation of Japan in 1952?

Surprisingly, these questions often have been overlooked in the vast but partial historical literature on Japanese American "internment," as it has been erroneously labeled. The principal surveys—within a liberal democratic tradition—effectively critiqued official rationales for the mass incarceration and probed the constitutional implications. Along with the government's own study, *Personal Justice Denied*, they cemented support for the landmark congressional restitution of 1988. Like these studies, a number of very useful biographies, autobiographies, and monographs employed broad, male-dominated, top-down approaches, whether about government officials or recognized Japanese American leaders. Moreover, some of the latter works and their authors came to be criticized as too reflective of accommodationist/assimilationist strategies. Studies of the 442nd Regimental Combat Team of Japanese American soldiers, most of whom trained in Mississippi, were almost always celebratory accounts. They trumpeted the unit's European combat successes, coined the description "most decorated unit in American military history," and thereby attempted to demonstrate and solidify nationalist allegiances.[20]

Those few female prisoners whose personal writings reached large audiences tended to come from the same western camps. Academic works that thoroughly analyzed the lived experience of confinement were focused exclusively on camps in the West, even the officially endorsed, cross-camp, *comparative* anthropological study. Manzanar, California, attracted the most attention—as one of the larger camps; as the only facility that served as both "assembly center" and "relocation camp"; as the site for the first National Historic Landmark; and as the location geographically nearest to major Japanese American enclaves, thus making it a logical destination for pilgrimage. Further, Manzanar has been overrepresented in still photography and motion pictures. Along with Dorothea Lange, the renowned Ansel Adams took hundreds of images there, which in turn spawned several illustrated volumes on the camp. Of the mere five major Hollywood films to deal with Japanese American incarceration, the two most recent, 1990's *Come See the Paradise* and 1999's *Snow Falling on Cedars*, were partially set there. With few exceptions, cross-camp thematic works—on poetry, painting, educational systems—ignored the southern camps, seemingly due to regional bias and economies of research. Studies of family life in the camps, particularly Broom and Kitsuse's illustratively titled *The Managed Casualty*, stressed the disruption of Japanese cultural "tradition," monolithically described. They lamented, without critically assessing, contemporaneous accounts of increased "juvenile delinquency," lesser parental control, and, in particular, "emasculated" patriarchs whose wives and children no longer obeyed them. Though several historians since the 1970s have illuminated resistance to incarceration, at camps such as Manzanar, Tule Lake, and Heart Mountain, the extent of discontent across other camps has awaited further elucidation.[21]

In sum, the enormous literature on Japanese American incarceration has overrepresented, among other things, male leaders and their concerns; loyal Nisei citizens and their patriotism; camps in the West and their symbolic imagery; "traditional" notions of the family and their unquestioned validity. As a result, there is a pressing need for studies balanced by women's experiences; the voices of first-generation (or Issei) immigrants and radical voices of dissent; southern episodes, particularly the interactions with racially diverse local populations; and the sophisticated insights of a new field, the history of sexuality. In these ways, easy dichotomies of white oppressors and Japanese American victims can be complicated, at minimum, by demonstrating important cultural differences *within* Japanese American populations: entrepreneurial/laboring classes, mainland/Hawaiian, urban/rural, Protestant/Buddhist, West/South, men/women, Nisei/Issei, English speakers/Japanese speakers, heterosexual/homosexual, loyalists/renunciants. We can further move beyond these binary categorizations to account for the distinctive circumstances of Sansei children, atheists, bilingual and multilingual persons, bisexuals, and individuals with complex, multiple national affiliations and disidentifications.

For obvious important reasons, writing to date on incarceration has stressed that not a single Japanese American was ever convicted of espionage against the United States during the war years, signaling the national and nationalist contexts for scholarly production on the topic. Whether critiquing and bemoaning hypocritical national ideals or honoring Japanese Americans who clung to them and, in the end, purportedly redeemed them, tellers of the incarceration story, almost without exception, describe it as an *American* story. Even as the circle is slowly expanded to take in Japanese and Japanese Americans highly critical of U.S. government policies, their protests—newly cast as heroism—are framed as *American* heroism. Such is the case in Eric Muller's otherwise insightful study of Japanese American draft resisters, those who, previously forbidden from volunteering, were urged to sign up and then were conscripted from behind barbed wire to participate in the fight for American "freedom." As Muller happily concludes, "Good citizenship was not the preserve solely of the obedient." He compares Japanese American draft resisters to Thomas Jefferson, Patrick Henry, and the colonists behind the Boston Tea Party, and he closes his book by crediting these latter-day "patriots" with "the construction of a truly American identity." Muller's "story of untold patriotism" along with so many other stories told about this time do *not* strike me as tales of failure—"failure in the most elemental process[es] of American life" or, as Erica Harth puts it, failure in "fundamental and enduring American values." Rather, they seem to me narratives that bear out and confirm many continuing elements at the core of the American national project, dating to the founding and the conquest before it: violence and brutality, differentiation and domination, exclusion and inequality, greed and corruption, duplicity and degradation. Those who renounced America and *these* American values seem to me equally worthy of study.[22]

It remains an American story, too, because so many historians of the United States, myself included, do not speak Japanese. Still, with the aid of translators and interpreters, I've attempted a few tentative steps toward further internationalizing the study of incarceration, an effort to untether it from what Brian Masaru Hayashi describes as its "domestic sphere." Late nineteenth- and twentieth-century movements of people, voluntary and coerced, throughout the Pacific would have us consider competing American and Japanese empires—or, in Eiichiro Azuma's words, their "respective project[s] of nation-building, racial supremacy, and colonial expansion"—and would have us contextualize our investigations with reference to even broader European and Asian interactions. At minimum, incarceration should be understood in relationship to ongoing American expansionism before and after the war, in pre- and post-statehood Hawaii and in pre- and post-occupation Japan. Whether or not the Pacific War of the 1940s is accepted as a race war, a concept U.S. officials repeatedly, revealingly disavowed, a thorough understanding of Japanese American incarceration pivots not only on Pearl Harbor but also on Hiroshima.[23]

Our understanding also requires an attentiveness to euphemism, the mollifying and obfuscating effects of official discourse. As a result of Executive Order 9066 signed by President Franklin Delano Roosevelt on 19 February 1942, Japanese Americans along the West Coast of the United States faced *eviction* from their homes and *expulsion* from the area—what the War Relocation Authority (WRA) called "evacuation," falsely implying rescue. Far from delivering Japanese Americans from danger, the WRA put them into one hazardous situation after another. Under the leadership of Milton Eisenhower, from 18 March to 17 June 1943, the WRA first confined Japanese Americans at sixteen sites; thirteen in California, one each in Arizona, Oregon, and Washington. Officially labeled "assembly centers," they were, in fact, *detention camps*, with barbed-wire fences, guard towers, and peak populations averaging 5,500. The largest was set up at Santa Anita Race Track (18,719), where horse stables were converted into living quarters and straw was used to stuff mattresses. Then under director Dillon S. Myer, prisoners were forced into ten longer-term facilities constructed on undesirable federal lands across the West and South. Referred to as "relocation centers," they had an average capacity of over 10,000, with two each in Arizona, Arkansas, and California, and one each in Colorado, Idaho, Utah, and Wyoming. Though obviously quite different from Nazi death camps, these compounds for the forced, indiscriminate incarceration of an entire ethnic minority population have earned the designation *concentration camps* from many scholars of Asian American history. The phrase was also widely used by political figures at the time, including Arkansas Governor Homer M. Adkins and President Roosevelt. At the camps, as we shall see, inmates were subjected to *indoctrination* ("rehabilitation") through Americanization and Christianization campaigns and *inquisition* ("registration") via lengthy questionnaires and loyalty hearings. For over 18,000 ruled to be disloyal or un-American, the Tule Lake concentration camp was reconfigured for *isolation* ("segregation"), and inmates were offered *renunciation* of citizenship ("denaturalization"), with 4,724 expatriating or repatriating to Japan: roughly 4 percent of the total 120,313 who came into WRA custody during the war years. More followed from Justice Department camps, bringing the total to 8,000. In a calculated program of *dispersal* ("resettlement"), only half or so (54,127) returned to the West Coast after the war, with the other half (52,798) impelled, if not compelled, to take up new residences in other sections of the United States. Thus, it is not only inaccurate to call this lengthy set of processes "internment," a concept recognized in international law for the treatment of citizens of "enemy nations" during wartime. It is also, in my view, inadequate, for the term fails to capture the great range and magnitude of these injustices, the lasting repercussions for the individuals and groups involved, as well as their descendants.[24]

As with all historical projects, whose stories get told are a function of the historian's methods, the types of people and sources consulted. My history doesn't purport to offer the reader "the truth," a term implying a god's-eye view, a totality, a completeness, an ability to account for it all. My history doesn't claim to be complete. Nor should any. But my project does seek—by giving the floor to many previously left out—to make the field as a whole more encompassing, to leave it a bit better informed by more varied perspectives.

HUMAN DIFFERENCES, HUMAN RIGHTS

Early portions of the book set the stage, in four distinctive corners of America: the nation's capital, the Deep South, the West Coast, and the territory of Hawaii. The story expands outward even further, as U.S. influence takes on global proportions, the roots of which are explored in chapters 1 and 2. Major characters are introduced, including the customary figures of history, elected officials. U.S. Representative John Rankin was a small-time Mississippi politician, eclipsed by bombastic racist Dixiecrats such as Theodore Bilbo and Strom Thurmond. But he bolstered his undistinguished career by exploiting anti-Asian sentiment in the way Martin Dies, of the House Un-American Activities Committee, and later Joseph McCarthy would use anticommunism. On the floor of Congress, Rankin declared, "I'm for catching every Japanese in America, Alaska, and Hawaii now and putting them in concentration camps. . . . Damn them! Let's get rid of them now!" In doing so, he echoed the sentiments of many white Americans, not just white southerners. As we've seen, another white Mississippian, Earl Finch, was a striking variation on the typical American rags-to-riches narrative. Though known to the FBI as unnatural, especially in his support for Japanese Americans and his affection for Japanese American men, he was never convincingly branded un-American.[25]

Two of the most committed Americans of Japanese descent were Mary Nakahara and Mary Tsukamoto, both born and raised in California. Nakahara headed up a number of girls groups in the camps and helped support the troops of the 442nd. Introduced in chapter 3, Tsukamoto was a dutiful housewife who also managed service organizations and, of necessity, became a teacher in the camps. Most instructors were white Arkansans looking for better-paid work or, like Virginia Tidball, any work at all, after being laid off at the war's outset. As we discover in chapter 4, she sold her horse to buy a train ticket to the concentration camp, and she became a great friend to Japanese American inmates. Tidball never married and, like Tsukamoto, she became a lifelong teacher. Still, as role models, their lessons weren't always creditable. Some called Tsukamoto a collaborator, and even the most liberal of white teachers such as Tidball could get only so far outside their American prejudices. But other Japanese Americans and white administrators participated in a daring series of social and economic experiments, which often seemed counter to expressed American aims. If democracy took on distorted forms, as in suspect camp elections, collective endeavors such as the cooperative stores—and camp life, generally—made some socialist ventures an attractive alternative.

Violet Matsuda's relationship to the United States was much more conflicted. As a girl, her first name had been changed from Kazue when a white plantation mistress saw her picking flowers. Matsuda—along with her brother Tokio Yamane—would grow up to resist such enforced Americanization. As we see over the course of the book, she also balanced varied gender roles. A devoted mother who looked after her frail children as well as her elderly in-laws, she denounced the incarceration, was ejected from the Jerome camp, and sent to the isolation center at Tule Lake, California. By war's end, she would turn her back on the country of her birth and face the painful choice of leaving her children behind in the so-called land of opportunity.

Irony of ironies, many a young Japanese American enlisted in the fight for American democracy, as we've already seen. If the 442nd were the most decorated unit in U.S. military history, as we are repeatedly told, then in many ways they were destined to be. Like their families and friends in the concentration camps, Japanese American soldiers were the subject of constant, careful publicity. Though their exploits in the European theater indeed demonstrated great courage, they had help. For heroes are not born; they're made. They're made, in part, by reporters who write about their achievements, historians who record their deeds in books, and boosters—like Earl Finch—who make sure their stories are not forgotten. If a young man's decision over enlistment often tore his family apart, a young woman's choices could cause even more distress. Surprisingly, incarceration helped Japanese American women move up the economic ladder. As never before, in a camp labor market without racial stratification, they held responsible positions as teachers, clerks, writers, and manufacturers. They were paid the same wages as men. And they grew ever more independent of their fathers and husbands, who along with white experts warned of "family breakdown." Some women took up leadership positions in the war effort, while more still refused to participate in the entertainment of Japanese American soldiers. As we see in chapter 5, since the 442nd trained in neighboring Mississippi, Japanese American women were regularly bused across the state line, for wholesome, racially partitioned dating and matrimony, signaling a new era of state-sanctioned courtship and institutionalized heterosexuality. These USO-sponsored events crystallized the paradox of incarceration and military service. And most women resisted.

Visual artifacts such as photographs and drawings are crucial tools for historians. Pictures of incarceration, however, often mislead; they tend to depict happy campers. Still, these images can and should be read against the grain. When Washington photographers showed up, mess hall menus improved dramatically. When they took pictures of the one-room apartments, it was only in the homes of Japanese American patriots, as subtly evidenced by the tabletop portrait of a son or cousin serving in the army. The table itself, the furnishings, were always of the highest quality, although the government only provided rickety beds. Official cameramen found the homes of the best woodworkers, whereas one Japanese American photographer snapped a sign that threatened jail time for those caught taking scrap lumber. Semi-weekly camp newspapers, vital sources of information, were edited by Japanese Americans in the service of the administration. George Akimoto's comic strip *Lil Dan'l* demonstrates the lengths to which some would go. Clinging fiercely to the American dream, it depicts a Japanese American boy with round glasses and a coonskin cap. Like Daniel Boone, Lil Dan'l is a pioneer—though, as the strip rarely references, his migration was eastward, at gunpoint. His Arkansas hardships—snakes, cold, deprivation—are recast as humorous adventures. Through an analysis of such Pollyanna iconography, we see that administrators attempted to quash dissent and that many "loyal" middle-class Japanese

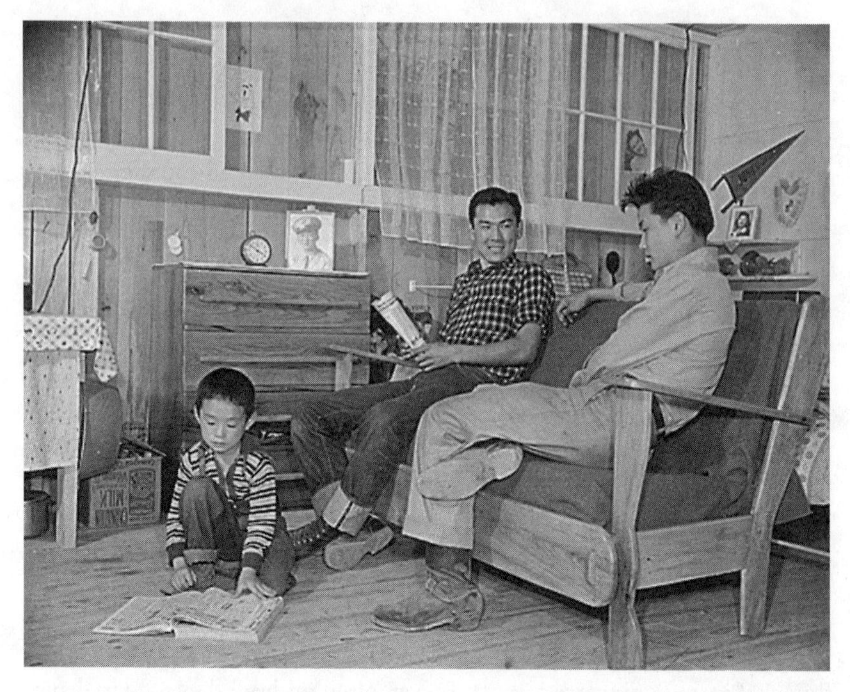

2. Fred Hayarki, at left on a settee he built, along with the chest of drawers. Block 7, Jerome concentration camp, November 1942. Tom Parker, photographer. NWDNS-210-G-E290, WRAR, SPB, NA.

Americans such as Akimoto failed to convince their neighbors of incarceration's benign necessity.

In the concentration camps, Japanese Americans also were subjected to aggressive Americanization campaigns, examined in chapter 6. Elders were urged to learn English, and tots were told how to honor the flag. Unlike ordinary primary and secondary education in the United States, which was administered at the local level, camp school policies were dictated from Washington. And white officials viewed it as a unique opportunity for indoctrination. Furthermore, though the vast majority of inmates were Buddhist, authorities invited Protestant evangelists into the camps to conduct crusades. E. Stanley Jones and other Christian luminaries led workshops, sing-alongs, and revivals as part of their missionary campaigns. Still, as chapter 7 reveals, resistance to incarceration and its indignities was more widespread than we've been led to believe. In Arkansas, work crews in the fields refused to eat the paltry lunches they were given; timber cutters protested dangerous conditions, as one after another was injured or killed on the job; and despite official threats to terminate visits outside the camp, mechanics and other workers walked out in protest over white bigotry. Though *inu* or "dogs" were said to control the camp newspapers and to inform on fellow inmates in attempts to quell discontent—indeed, one columnist is unmasked here as the confidential informant "Mr. C"—resisters somehow managed to mimeograph strike notices, which mysteriously appeared on latrine walls. Try as they might, government officials could not suppress hostilities. And Arkansas resisters at Jerome were transferred to the isolation center at Tule Lake at levels higher than any other camp.

As we see in chapter 8, authorities insisted that the WRA's registration program was "neither a trial nor inquisition." Yet they demanded unambiguous answers to their highly ambiguous loyalty questions. Like racial categories and gender roles, national allegiances for most Japanese Americans were ambivalently held, especially after the trauma of incarceration. Though Japanese American patriots tell us their nonconforming neighbors were "confused" by the registration program, it was rather the program—and U.S. policy—that was muddled and often incompetently administered. One edict, however, was well-enforced: those who expressed doubts had their freedoms further curtailed. Those who more forcefully articulated grievances, so-called troublemakers like Tokio Yamane, were tortured.

Some understandably went "back" to Japan. Although many immigrant elders gave up on the United States and repatriated, more common were the English-speaking twenty- to forty-year-olds who expatriated, who sailed away to Japan and took a chance on a place they'd never been. In a long American tradition of pathologizing dissent, such people have been labeled unstable, even certifiably insane; government collaborators have accused them of nothing less than murder in their skirmishes with Japanese American superpatriots. As historian Mae M. Ngai so aptly puts it, the scholarly "literature expresses incredulity that any American would renounce citizenship unless he or she was in an abnormal state of mind." But this book attempts to amplify the voices of those dispossessed former Americans.[26]

As detailed in chapter 9, from 1943 authorities pushed many inmates out of the camps. Not back to their homes in California, Oregon, Washington, and Hawaii, but into "normal" American communities in the Northeast, the Midwest, and elsewhere. Before the war, West Coast urban enclaves and farming villages had been important sources of mutual aid, shared customs, and safety. They were no more secretive and insular than they were supportive and inclusive. In many respects, they were the product of classic American residential segregation, the last resort of outcasts from neighborhoods zoned as lily-white. Now, at their most vulnerable, Japanese Americans were encouraged to confront that bigotry head-on and try to blend into predominantly white communities. Thus, so-called resettlement was in fact dispersal. Washington administrators and East Coast editorialists explicitly set out to destroy Little Tokyos. And while some Japanese Americans objected and asked to remain in the camps—offering dazzling proposals of agrarian utopianism—many defiantly returned to the West Coast and attempted, yet again, to rebuild their communities.

To chart incarceration's dubious legacy, we must look beyond the war years. Afterward Mary Tsukamoto taught until her retirement in the once-segregated schools of her native Florin, California, hailed as a local and national hero. Virginia Tidball likewise continued teaching but in relative obscurity. John Rankin's subsequent congressional career grew ever more farcical, the subject of national derision, whereas Earl Finch's humanitarian career—further detailed in the concluding chapter—grew ever more fantastical: he moved to Honolulu to live with his war buddies, he traveled to occupied Japan to dispense charity, he lobbied Congress to recognize his adoptions, he helped move Hawaii toward statehood, and throughout the Pacific, he actively promoted American culture—from rock 'n' roll to penny candy. Violet Matsuda moved to Japan, where many of her family members had been tragically affected by the atomic blast over Hiroshima. And Mary Nakahara—the superpatriot who authored inspiring editorials on American liberty and wrote letters of support to American servicemen overseas—declared herself a dupe. Though she remained in the United States, she increasingly challenged her government and became an activist in many African American and Puerto Rican freedom movements, thereby linking the struggle of Japanese Americans to those of a variety of cultural outgroups. Renamed as Yuri Kochiyama, she envisioned her crusade as less about American civil rights specifically and more about human rights broadly.

Two related impulses suffuse the conventional scripts about wartime incarceration. First, just as the WRA sought to "rehabilitate" a group wrongly imprisoned in the first place, historians have attempted to recuperate Japanese Americans as loyal citizen-subjects who overcame their doubts and rose above the injustice, precursors of the mythic model minority. Second, by drawing a sharp distinction between ideals and actions—what David Harlan refers to as "the terrible dialectic of national promise and self-betrayal"—histories of incarceration can become more than sad tales of flawed American practices and, in the end, can function as happy fables of lofty American principles, fully and finally realized by the admirable, upwardly striving minority group. By emphasizing that inmates were mostly birthright citizens—referring to two-thirds, 70 percent, or three-quarters—books help secure the Americanness of a group that was, in fact, made up of multiple affiliations, legal or otherwise. Thus, the focus, the cause for concern—indignation, even—is the abrogation of *United States* citizenship rights, not basic human rights. The former, for many, may seem a cut above, more worthy of development than the latter. Certainly present-day U.S. policies—the repeated refusal to accept the jurisdiction or scrutiny of global entities such as the World Court or the United Nations, the International Criminal Court or international conventions on the environment—suggest that this nation accepts no laws, no rights, other than its own, those it finds amenable.[27]

Only the most amnesiac neo-con legal theorist could today insist upon following the "original intent" of the "founding fathers"—who, after all, intended blacks to be enslaved and white women to be subjugated. Slaveholder Thomas Jefferson once proposed further, as a *liberal* measure, that men who had sex with men should not be executed but castrated. Even so, in our callous contemporary climate, so-called liberal intellectuals can reference "enduring" American values of "fairness and equality," as if their meanings are clear-cut, as if they are fixed, timeless, and unchanging, as if their contours are universally agreed upon and their tenets usually acted upon. Under such reasoning, in what has become a heavily subscribed national parable, the agents of inequality—bigoted white officials who, in truth, have held the greatest power as cultural standard-bearers—are portrayed as perverting American ideals; those with lesser power, the victims of bias, wave after wave of immigrants to the multicultural experiment, are cast as visionaries, those who see the *promise*—not of humanity, but of *America*.[28]

I have no investment in shoring up Americanness or any individual's or group's Japanese *American*ness. Though I may seem, at first glance, to most closely identify with one of this book's major figures, Earl Finch, as a queer white southerner who went a-wandering, far from home, seemingly beyond local ideologies, I also find myself curiously attuned to the troubles and dilemmas faced by many of the Japanese American women, described herein, who decided against America. As an expatriate of a sort, a dual national now living in London, I, too, experience allegiances as torn, conflicted: if not dual then multiple. Importantly, many brave souls in this book tend to minimize the significance of the nation. They suggest that national affiliations are often superseded by ties of other kinds, ties to other people, other hopes, other ideals.

As one of the targets of what has been called "the last acceptable prejudice" in America, I find it difficult to believe that once homophobia has been dealt with, bigotry then will begin to fade away. This is the falsehood of inevitable historical progress—one injustice after another, patiently, ploddingly, overcome. Instead, history suggests to me that Americans, all human beings, have an infinite capacity to *create* difference. When, if ever, human differences can be dispassionately noted, honored, and not capitalized upon for the purposes of dominance, remains to be seen.

1 | Expansion and Restriction

THE PRAYER had been said. The songs had been sung, extolling the virtues of America the beautiful, God's favored land, a land filled with his grace. Hands over hearts, the assembled had pledged allegiance, eyes set on the flag: red and white stripes, and white stars—the blue background a deepening night sky, revealing ever more stars, a growing constellation, a universe expanding. The lyrics, the melodies, the pastor's voice, his supplications. They intertwined. God country faith growth. A poetry of patriotism.

Violet prepared to be honored. She readied herself, in her seat among the others, sharing their anticipation. But she shared little else with them. Her life was markedly different, her achievement consequently all the greater. Each student walked across the stage, first one then the next, taking something from the top of the stack, an engraved certificate identical to all—except for the name of the recipient. Many looked up into the audience, into the beaming faces of proud parents. The parents clapped and waved. Near the end of the line, one of the few Japanese Americans in the group of white teenagers, Violet instead looked up at Mr. and Mrs. Stuart.

From sea to shining sea, young Americans were graduating, venturing out into a world of opportunity. Diminished opportunity it seemed in the spring of 1934, even here in California. Displaced persons, known by their state of origin, continued to roll into town in dilapidated cars and trucks, Okies, Arkies, and others. Like Violet, some had arrived by ship, over the waters of the second of the shining seas, from what was called the Far East to the American West. These movements—people in search of work, in search of a decent livelihood—were reflected in the very names in the graduation program. Near the end of the list was the name Yamane.

At age seventeen, after years of intensive study and after a fidgety wait this afternoon—the M's and S's especially long—Violet Yamane, the Hawaiian-born daughter of Japanese immigrants, stepped carefully toward the principal, shook his hand, and accepted her diploma. Second perhaps only to her birth certificate, which had declared her F, a female, and U.S., a citizen, this piece of paper marked her. A person with promise, in a land of promise. Enhanced prospects. Possibilities. With purpose, Violet strode off the stage, past the podium, past that potent symbol of nationalism, the star-spangled banner. She made her way around the crowd and, with the Stuarts, walked across the broad green expanse. For the last time, Violet walked off the grounds of Fresno's Theodore Roosevelt High School.

Commencement—a beginning.[1]

The little girl who loved nature—a collector of flowers, a writer of poems—was now an adult. Unpinning her colorful corsage, Violet Yamane pondered her future direction. The people around her wanted her to succeed. Today suggested that she already had, at least thus far in life. As she had proven, she was determined, motivated: the stuff of high school speeches. She had goals, aims, aspirations: the bywords of graduation exercises. But how should someone properly measure success? How to evaluate its forms? It was a careful calculus. At what point did ambition—a healthy desire to improve oneself, one's circumstances—give way to greed? When did the pursuit of dreams, the inclination to better the world around, yield to a crass striv[illegible]er what conditions would bonds of family and friendship be sac[illegible] would one's supporters, the cheerleaders of success, be left behi[illegible]ing *up* have to mean moving *away*? How should a young person l[illegible]ond her *self* in order to account for the needs of *others*? In exploring these questions, what beliefs, what value systems, should be consulted?

These same questions could be applied to a maturing American nation and its youthful empire overseas, the lands on which its flag would be planted afresh. Did expansionism, the movement into new territories, the incorporation of new realms, represent the crux of collective betterment? Or was it the epitome of excess acquisitiveness? Did it reveal a raw craving for power? Did faith in the Almighty—and the sense of a divine calling to minister abroad—spring from higher-level, spiritual imperatives? Or was it a convenient rationalization for a ruthless earthly avarice, as with the seizing of the sugary-sweet Hawaiian Islands for American business interests? From the cane fields of Hawaii to the strawberry fields of California, across the varied populations subsumed within the American empire, who would be excluded, restricted from this expanding universe?

Violet Yamane's experience suggests that the United States exerts contradictory influences on its chosen members. Its economic order supposedly rewards get-up-and-go. But that forward march of progress is predicated upon a number of leave-takings, the severing of ties to those things most optimistically associated with the best of America: family, faith, community. Literally and metaphorically, ancestral forebears such as Violet's own parents, the Yamanes—oddly absent on the big day—are given up for adoptive kith and kin, as with the Stuarts. Old ways are shed with the taking up of a new faith, a new people. Hard work is intended to move you out of one group and into another. It is meant to lift you up from the masses and into "the classes," into an elite. And yet ideas of America simultaneously seem to cherish a broad middle class, an equally situated, contented citizenry.

As Fresno High School's namesake, Theodore Roosevelt, once declared, "Everything is un-American that tends either to government by a plutocracy, or government by a mob." Fearing mobs—fearing, in particular, empowered groups of discontented workers, at home and overseas, campaigning for better conditions—late nineteenth-century business and political leaders had branded *them* un-American. That popular turn-of-the-century critic Mark Twain, however, equated Roosevelt and his Republican Party with plutocracy, with sovereign rule by the wealthy, for the wealthy. And immigrant workers, too, began to insist that it was these sorts of rulers, this sort of rule, that was truly un-American. During the first few decades of the twentieth century, the so-called American century, expansive and competing visions of Americanness would emerge. Some, such as Teddy Roosevelt, would have a greater say than others, a greater role in restricting the options for others. Violet Yamane would have to make a life for herself and those she cared about within and occasionally without those limits.[2]

CHRISTIAN EMPIRE

There is a fundamental contradiction in the U.S. relationship to empire: Over the span of roughly one hundred years, a once-aggrieved colonial people came to embrace a massive program of imperial expansion and domination all their own. In the late eighteenth century, American colonists of European descent had rebelled against imperial rule, with slogans lofty—life, liberty, the pursuit of happiness—and somewhat more materialistic: no taxation without representation. Staving off competing "explorers" and settlers of Dutch, French, German, and Spanish origin, and participating in a genocide of Native American tribal people whose land they stole, the British invaders and their descendants had come to see North America as home and England as the oppressor. By the late nineteenth century, with mounting force, the United States vied with these selfsame European powers for control of other parts of the Americas and, farther west, the Asia-Pacific region—a staggering level of avarice and acquisitiveness matched only by the mother country. For British leaders had designs on the entire earth and the sun too, tracking its movements with scientific precision—from zero longitude and zero hour at Greenwich—across the newfangled time zones of its worldly possessions. The sun would never set, they hoped, on this empire.

In America Theodore Roosevelt often led the charge, but his presidential predecessor, William McKinley, played a less-noted but no-less-crucial role in expansionism. McKinley perfected a religious rhetoric of righteousness that would resonate in foreign policy for at least another century. McKinley believed in God. Indeed, he believed, as many American presidents have, that God spoke to him directly. Never mind a separation of church and state, McKinley needed advice on his latest imperial theft, a group of Pacific islands known as the Philippines, and he looked much higher than his cabinet. As he told a gathering of religious figures, he got down on his knees many a night and prayed for God to give him guidance in the matter. One night God answered, in astonishing detail. The Philippines could not be returned to the previous imperial overlords, Spain, for "that would be cowardly and dishonorable." They could not be turned over to "our commercial rivals" France or Germany, for "that would be bad business and discreditable." They certainly couldn't be left alone, for—as McKinley and many white supremacists saw it—Filipinos were "unfit for self-government" and would surely descend into "misrule" and "anarchy." Thus, "there was nothing left for us to do but to take them all and to educate the Filipinos, and uplift and civilize and Christianize them, and by God's grace do the very best we could by them, as our fellow men for whom Christ also died. And then I went to bed and went to sleep and slept soundly."[3]

With phrases such as "manifest destiny," "divine mission," and "holy purpose" in the air, white Americans might have found it easy to believe that

Christianization was more a key objective than an after-the-fact rationalization of conquest. While McKinley occasionally deigned to describe Filipinos as "fellow men," his policies suggested he viewed them as less than human. As respected historian Robert Wiebe puts it, "The government's officials, along with a great many Americans, shared [a] certain predilection [that] separated the world into two parts. Above lay the civilized powers, principally Europe and the United States; below fell the subjects of their imperialism in Asia, Africa, and Latin America." As Wiebe elaborates, "This segregation involved much more than an allocation of status. Basically it concerned intrinsic worth and inherent capacities and carried with it a clear moral differential, one that not only attributed meager sensibilities to the barbarian but also freed advanced nations to deal with him by a code they would never have dreamed of applying to each other." An American moral code—always in the works, never fully, finally agreed—was under hot debate, leaving many to question the nature of barbarism, as well as its principal perpetrator. With characteristic sarcasm, Mark Twain reflected upon the U.S. military's engagement with the proponents of Philippine independence, whom we might call freedom fighters: "We have pacified some thousands of the islanders and buried them; destroyed their fields; burned their villages, and turned their widows and orphans out-of-doors; furnished heartbreak by exile to some dozens of disagreeable patriots; subjugated the remaining tens of millions by Benevolent Assimilation, which is the pious new name of the musket." And so, Twain concluded with reference to the U.S. slaughter of half a million Filipinos, "by these Providences of God—and the phrase is the government's, not mine—we are a World Power."[4]

World powers such as Great Britain and the United States indeed divided the world into two parts. They did so in a number of ways, allowing religious thought and medical reasoning to bleed into one another. Of relatively recent cultural invention, the notion of race was elaborated such that whites were distinguished from black and brown people and, related to that, the civilized from the primitive. Clunky instruments for measuring bodily features—the width of one's nose, the breadth of one's forehead—and convoluted graphs for tabulating intellectual capabilities purportedly proved that the former were keyed to the latter, yielding what recent theorists have referred to as scientific racism. Another category of human difference, handedness—whether one was right- or left-handed—likewise was said by respected reformers to expose other human traits and deficiencies at the level of broad cultural groups. In a series of interlinking dualistic arguments, right-handedness was said to be linked to the more complex, functionally superior left hemisphere of the brain, which was somehow linked to the Northern Hemisphere of the earth; and those suspect lefties—associated since medieval times with the devil—were supposedly shown to predominate in the "less civilized" lands below the equator. Thus, it was only logical—in this realm of illogic—that the nations of the North, namely, the United States and Western Europe, should rule over those people and places that their scientists literally and figuratively had placed at the bottom of their maps.

In a world of flux and change, ambiguity and uncertainty, many found desperately needed comfort and stability by sectioning off their fellow human beings with easy dichotomies of us and them, right and wrong, good and evil. In ever more complicated modern societies, with ethical dilemmas and interpersonal conflicts painted in the subtlest shades of gray, some demanded absolutes—a simpler, more readily comprehensible, black-and-white world. It's no accident, suggests the historian of literacy Tamara Plakins Thornton, that around this very time, during the late nineteenth century, when the left-handed were severely punished and forced to comport to a right-handed (or occasionally ambidextrous) ideal, a new breed of sexologists began to classify the great bewildering array of human erotic desires, acts, and identities into a pat, tidy twosome: heterosexual versus homosexual.[5]

Fearful of effete men and strong women, Teddy Roosevelt came to power on the heels of his imperial military heroics and in the face of a growing political radicalism at home. He was catapulted into elective office amidst tales of his Rough Riders' exploits in Cuba—cowboy-and-Indian-style, shoot-'em-up narratives, updated for the island context. Roosevelt's own account, published in 1900, necessarily had to dismiss the importance of two black regiments of regulars in the San Juan heights, as Americans who had aided colonial aggression but ostensibly shared the inferior racial qualities of the colonized—all of them, in the parlance of the times, the "white man's burden." Meanwhile, African American activists along with Americans of European ancestry—northern and western, and increasingly southern and eastern—violently clashed over the rule of law and the ethics of political and financial governance.

For a time a much-maligned and much-misunderstood group commanded headlines, the bane of presidents and pundits. Far from advocating chaos or disorder, anarchists believed in voluntary cooperation and free association, especially at the local level, distrusting big government and big business. Many, like Emma Goldman, also promoted principles of free love and birth control as a counter to the inequities of marriage and the sexual double standard for women. The metaphorical black-and-white world, they suggested, also split humanity up into men versus women—the latter almost always losing out, shortchanged as a result. Indeed, related to all these dichotomies, these stark societal binaries, was the crucial economic distinction between the haves and the have-nots, the anarchists pointed out. Usually proponents of socialism, anarchists supported workers' ownership of the means of production, and they decried capitalist profiteering as greedy, malevolent, evil. Some brought a revolutionary fervor to the struggle, as when Goldman's lover Alexander Berkman shot and stabbed industrialist Henry Clay Frick—not as an act of individual retribution but as a larger blow for workers' rights and economic justice.[6]

"With each major confrontation," writes historian Cecilia Elizabeth O'Leary, "the 1877 railway strike, the 1886 Haymarket bombing, the 1894 Pullman strike—industrialists joined publishers in branding labor activism as communist, anarchist, and un-American. Graphics regularly pictured Uncle Sam guiding American workmen away from the influence of swarthy agitators. The term *un-American* first came into significant usage as a political epithet during this period when 'true Americans' used it against striking immigrant workers and later against any militant opponents of the economic order, immigrant or native-born." After another true believer, anarchist Leon Czolgosz, assassinated the zealous Methodist-Episcopalian William McKinley, the popular vice president Roosevelt moved into the White House.[7]

Like America's modern monarchs, the Adamses before him and the Bushes after, Theodore Roosevelt was part of a wealthy family dynasty whose financial stakes were tightly bound up with that of the nation. So it became psychologically soothing and politically expedient to envision imperial offensives less as moneymaking operations than as character-building endeavors—if only for a certain class of people. Roosevelt deduced from the work of turn-of-the-century historian Frederick Jackson Turner that after the so-called closing of the frontier in the West, the country needed new fields for growth, new means for cultivating a national character seemingly predicated upon pioneering experiences. For the conservative Roosevelt, known as a tireless campaigner for manliness and the strenuous life—a "little imitation cowboy," as Twain called him—the end of the frontier meant "not the lack of economic opportunity, but the loss of those conditions that allowed their class to acquire the virile character that entitles and enables them to rule giant corporations or a modern nation-state," according to scholar Richard Slotkin. "To renew their virility and to save their class from leisured inanition, they must take up the challenge of empire." White women had a role to play as well. "One of

Roosevelt's chief anxieties during this period was the decline in the birthrates of the white, Protestant middle and upper classes relative to those of immigrants and the underclass. He characterized this tendency as 'race suicide,' because it promised the ultimate extinction of his class/race in the Darwinian struggle, and he once likened women who refused to bear children to soldiers who dropped their weapons and fled the field of battle."[8]

Notions of battle circulated freely from secular to sacred realms. On Sundays missionary societies studied the heathen ways of foreign lands, and Protestant congregations sang hymns that likened proselytizing to waging war. "Onward, Christian soldiers," one favorite went, "marching as to war, with the cross of Jesus going on before." Eschewing earthly kings and queens, worshippers held up "Christ" as "the royal master" who would "lead against the foe." "Forward into battle," they intoned, "see his banners go." English clergyman Sabine Baring-Gould's lyrics, written in 1864, carried new resonances in the United States during its watershed year of empire, 1898. With the seizing of the Philippines, Guam, Hawaii, and other Pacific islands, along with Cuba and Puerto Rico in the Caribbean, the United States needed to imagine a foe, a truculent but redeemable enemy. Thus multitudes of brown heathens were depicted as laggards, falling behind in the march of Christian civilization, a direct threat to it. And in an explicit yoking of the plight of people of Asian and African origins, African American commentators noted after the turn of the century that white officials considered themselves, in the words of W. E. B. Du Bois, "the natural and *divine* guardian of all the other races."[9]

For the middle classes especially, the National Geographic Society, founded in 1888, helped cement broad-based support for imperialism. Its popular magazine, as well as the academic disciplines of geography and anthropology generally, were often dedicated "to the search for evidence of evolutionary backwardness of subaltern peoples, inventing a wide range of biological and sociocultural indices for the purpose," as Catherine Lutz and Jane Collins attest. "From craniometry to the cataloging of marriage principles, the study of difference was directed toward the creation of hierarchy." In this sense, science and religion happily coexisted. Sermons elaborated the dominion of *particular* men over God's creation. Evolutionary biology was used to "prove" the physical and mental inferiority of colonized people.[10]

America's overseas adventures sparked internal resistance, however. The Anti-Imperialist League, for example, grew from a small conservative group opposed to the 1898 annexation of the Philippines—on legal, economic, racial, and "moral" grounds—into an elite, liberal cadre of influential thinkers and reformers, such as Jane Addams, Clarence Darrow, and Julius Rosenthal, and on to a mass movement of over thirty thousand members, with branches from Boston to Chicago, Minneapolis to New York. In its pamphlets and publications, the league looked back to Lincoln, who said: "No man is good enough to govern another man without that other's consent. When the white man governs himself, that is self-government; but when he governs himself and also governs another man, . . . that is despotism." Still, ever on the lookout for wayward markets and wayward souls, for far-flung safe harbors and military outposts, American opportunists held supreme confidence in their right and ability to subdue the world's peoples. Despite the best efforts of the Anti-Imperialist League, politicians and citizens began to line up behind expansionism, convinced that "that other"—as Lincoln put it—needed not self-determination but Christian subjugation.[11]

In the rhetoric of empire, an objective reality—the nation's military might—was wedded to two key value judgments: the assumed superiority of both a particular belief system and a particular economic order. An inherently supremacist activity, missionary work took for granted the inferiority of local religious customs and practices. Well-developed systems of faith, hundreds or thousands of years old, were often rejected out of hand as superstition; conversion represented the only means of elevating these lowly and unenlightened peoples. With perhaps even lesser concern for indigenous economies, capitalists sought to enhance their own—and their own nation's—financial interests in an increasingly global, competitive marketplace. To the extent that the United States, a relative newcomer to empire, succeeded in vastly expanding its sphere of influence, it was a credit to its three-pronged approach, as the Yamane family and countless other colonial subjects would learn the hard way. American colonizers brandished the sword, the Bible, and—foremost—the almighty dollar.

SELF-SUFFICIENCY, SANDALWOOD, AND SUGAR

How did members of the Yamane family—many of whom had tilled modest plots of Japanese soil for generations—end up living thousands of miles from home, across five time zones, far to the south and east? How did Katsuichi Yamane, in the 1910s and 1920s, wind up teaching Japanese on the big island of Hawaii, of all places? How did his wife, Shika, come to be a seamstress there with him, north of Hilo, on a sprawling sugarcane plantation? To understand these questions requires us to understand the population flows, as well as the cultural dynamics and economic rationales, of empire. It requires a view not only from Washington and from its colonies, but also from the other places that supply labor and lives. It begs an analysis of the decisions of both policy makers and individual immigrants.

The principal purpose of imperialism is to reap financial rewards from one land for the benefit of another. Often geographically removed, in "exotic" locations otherwise unconnected to the invading powers, colonies are forced to undergo radical transformations in their economies. Human and natural resources are redeployed to the advantage of the metropole. They are exploited so as to maximize profits for business enterprises owned and headquartered elsewhere and so as to aggrandize governments whose capitals lie elsewhere—what the imperialists refer to as the motherland, the homeland, "back home." The colony is not just a market for the homeland's products; it is, more importantly, a source of raw materials. Typically, early stages of production—the cultivation of a crop, the extraction of a mineral—are undertaken in the colony; higher-stage processes of refining and manufacturing are reserved for the homeland, leaving better-paid, skilled jobs for nationals. Only secondarily, if at all, is imperialism designed to benefit locals—through a sometimes cynical, magnanimous uplift or Christianization, and through so-called improved standards or "advancement." Pliant local leaders, in league with the expansionists, may profit.

Hawaii may be the classic example. Around the same time that fifty-five colonists from New Hampshire to Georgia gathered to sign their names to a high-minded Declaration of Independence, the British explorer James Cook was surveying the islands of the Pacific Ocean in the name of the throne of a smallish island on the opposite side of the planet. Hawaiians resisted the incursion, killing the notorious Captain Cook. But his legacy remained. Whalers coveted a base in Honolulu; navalists sought safe harbor at Pearl Harbor. European and American traders followed in the wake and "introduced manufactured goods in exchange for natural resources such as sandalwood." A flowering, evergreen hardwood, growing in several varieties throughout the islands, sandalwood—sometimes used for carving—had been prized for its lasting scent ever since the days of the spice trade. Sandalwood oil was made over into perfume. It was a key ingredient in cosmetics and medicines, especially for skin ailments. And with the decline of the Indian forests, the Western demand for sandalwood began to bring native Hawaiians into complicated international networks of exchange. Profiteering through taxes in such interactions, "chiefs diverted labor away from subsistence agriculture to producing for a world market that determined the terms of the trade." It was a bitter American contradiction. Founders such as Thomas Jefferson had touted yeoman farming or subsistence agriculture—cultivating a highly varied, homegrown crop to satisfy the needs of an entire family—as the epitome of virtuous living, just as in Japan the Yamanes' ancestors had long grown most everything they needed for themselves. But American expansionists often imposed upon colonized people a single cash crop, such that Hawaiian welfare came to depend crucially upon the worldwide price of only one commodity: first sandalwood, then—after almost complete deforestation—sugar.[12]

Under the gospel of growth, a successful regional economy of contented, self-sufficient farmers with measured ambitions was no longer enough. Missionaries "shared with the Yankee traders values rooted in mercantile capitalism and the Protestant work ethic. They equated leisure with vice and subsistence with improvidence." Samuel N. Castle, both a missionary and cofounder of one of the controlling Big Five firms of sugar production, put it succinctly: "As it is true that indolence begets vice, so it is true that industry promotes virtue. All successful efforts taken to produce industry by proper means tend to promote virtue and must be beneficial to that people on whom they are bestowed." Revising Jeffersonian notions of virtue, the land, and the labor value of property, a new creed sacrificed diligent work in one's own soil to specialized toil within the fields of large-scale agribusiness. Thus, as Gary Okihiro concludes, "that economic creed, presented to Hawaiians from the pulpit and in the classroom, supplied the justification for the capitalist transformation of Hawaiian precapitalist social relations."[13]

Though tens of thousands of native Hawaiians signed a petition in protest against American annexation, estimated as high as 95 percent of those approached, the islands became a U.S. territory and a vector of Pacific economic exchange. If, among others, the Caribbean island of Cuba was taken by force in the war with Spain, catapulting the bloodthirsty mustachioed and bespectacled lieutenant-colonel Teddy Roosevelt into the national spotlight, the subjugation of Hawaii proceeded mostly through diplomatic and economic channels. The islands' elite, the sugar bosses and Christian missionaries, had paved the way for the American takeover; they had made the lush chain of islands irresistibly lucrative, by luring thousands of immigrants, especially Japanese, to work the fields and build the social and physical infrastructure. Since Commodore Matthew Perry had twice sailed his intimidating fleet into Tokyo Bay in the 1850s, Japanese leaders had been forced at gunpoint to open up, to engage in trade with the United States. By the 1870s and 1880s, missionaries were canvassing Japan, establishing schools, and—with a lower success rate—

converting the locals. By the 1880s and 1890s, labor recruiters scoured the southwestern prefectures, offering farmers passage to Hawaii as an advance on wages, to cut cane and service budding communities. The once-reluctant Japanese government began to grant passports under a highly supervised program of often fixed-term emigration. After the turn of the century, Katsuichi and Shika Yamane began to consider the big move.[14]

Pushed by the dire economic circumstances in Hiroshima Prefecture, pulled by the promise of a better way—truly, enticed by agents who assured them of greater earnings across the waters, by friends and relatives who had gone before—the Yamanes set sail as part of the exodus to the plantations of the Pacific. Entering that global market, they had skills that would serve them well in their adopted home. In the village of Ninole, part of the Hakalau Plantation, Shika's sewing and mending kept her busy. Like so many nineteenth-century women before her, she washed, cleaned, and sometimes made the clothing for herself, her husband, and what would soon be a growing family. "To earn money" from outside the home, sewing was deemed by many Japanese immigrants as "work appropriate to women," as "the job most recommended for women at home." Because other women were employed full-time in sugar production, they offered Shika tasks that they otherwise would have done themselves. They gave her cash—occasionally traded fruits and vegetables from their own little gardens—in exchange for her impressive work as a seamstress. The female field hands, Japanese and especially the Filipinas, Okinawans, and others at the bottom of the plantation hierarchy, had little money to spend on outside services. Shika profited most from the Portuguese and Spanish women—those from Europe's faded imperial powers—who existed near the top of the pyramid, as the wives of teamsters and overseers of the operation. She also sewed for white people, haoles such as Mrs. Stuart, wife of a plantation official.[15]

Katsuichi didn't work in the mill or the cane rows, where most Japanese men and women found their paid labor. Within the elaborate racial stratification of employment and domestic life, they had had to take up these so-called unskilled posts as contract workers: less settlers than sojourners, who expected and were expected to return to Japan. Instead, Katsuichi taught his fellow Japanese—fully 40 percent of the Hawaiian population at 1900—about the language, culture, and customs of "home." On both the West Coast of the United States and here in the U.S. colony of Hawaii, Japanese immigrants may have been forced together into residential ghettoes or segregated plantation encampments. But they also found support and strength in numbers—and in the study of Japan. Language schools were attended by as many as nine in ten children of immigrants, even those who spent most of their day in the public schools. Thus, American education was supplemented by training in Japanese ways. Katsuichi was a well-regarded instructor. As compared to field workers, he and Shika were people of middling incomes, but with aspirations circumspect in comparison to the white men who charted the fate of Hawaii.[16]

With capital always moving more freely across national boundaries than labor, indeed with capitalists largely dictating the terms of labor movements, these men developed distinctive ideas about the best means of exploiting international pools of workers. Planters began to abandon the paradigm of single male immigrants, viewing the family as a key tool of labor control. Under harsh working conditions—typically three-year periods of what amounted to indentured servitude—field hands had often deserted. So marriage was encouraged as a means of retention. Bachelors, with the help of parents and go-betweens, were urged to settle into an arranged marriage, often with a previously unseen "picture bride" from the same hometown or prefecture. As scholar Evelyn Nakano Glenn reports, wives in this period felt that "they had no choice but to marry, since there was no other role for women in Japanese society." Increasingly, planters and their agents recruited couples. In the cramped encampments, private rooms and eventually detached cottages were established for married wage earners and families. But homosexual couplings were forbidden. In the bunkhouses, "a separate bed [was] provided each male unmarried laborer." And as was published prominently in plantation rules, "no two shall be permitted to occupy the same bed." This was as much a provision of social organization as a protection against overcrowding.[17]

Would the Yamanes stay? After their arrival in the 1910s, they seemed ever more inclined to remain in Hawaii as the years passed. Though dependent upon the plantation economy, they were not as bound by its contracts and—as compared to most of the 200,000 Japanese who came to the islands from 1885 to 1924—they were relatively self-sustaining. As part of the burgeoning Japanese (American) middle class, Katsuichi and Shika were service providers, beholden more to pupils, parents, and customers than the haole planters. Still, they faced a central dilemma of the capitalist marketplace. Old ties had to be loosened; new ones forever to be created. When they left Japan to work overseas, they had also left behind parents, established jobs, a community, a nation. Though the sojourner system made clear that planters wanted immigrant labor more than immigrant lives, wanted laborers—their prime of life depleted—to go away again, the Yamanes were now capable of settling. A surprising 55 percent of fellow immigrants did. The longer they stayed, the more attached they became to this new place, these new communities. But in Hawaii, as with the departure from Japan, every step up the socioeconomic ladder was a step away from these "lower" classes. Thus, affective bonds—of family, class, region, and nation—were tested by the imperatives of success, ambition, movement. After Shika and Katsuichi began to build their own family, additional ties developed.

In 1917 Shika Yamane gave birth to their first child, a daughter. She was an energetic, curious girl, alive with the wonder of nature. She thrived in the lush tropical climate, awed at the palms, ferns, and flowers, captivated by the waterfalls and beaches. To Shika, it seemed a good place for youngsters to grow up. Though every bit as humid as southern Japan, Hawaii was preferable. Summers actually were hotter back there, and there was no cold at all in the winter here. Within five years, the Yamanes had two more children, sons.

Because they were born in Ninole, in Hawaii, a U.S. territory, the Yamanes' daughter and two sons were citizens of the United States, a crucial distinction. Unlike their first-generation immigrant parents, they were second-generation birthright Americans. Since the government of Japan nonetheless continued to recognize each child as one of its own, their national identifications would prove even more complex than those of Katsuichi and Shika, who were forbidden naturalization in the United States. A new mother, Shika grappled with the implications for her children. How and where should they be educated? What sort of living arrangements would best insure their continued good health and emotional well-being? What sacrifices would the couple have to make for the sake of the children? What sorts of jobs would the future hold for them? As the Yamane family grew—and grew slightly more prosperous—Shika and Katsuichi would be required again and again to weigh the options not only for themselves but for the young ones: dual nationals in the increasingly international marketplace.

WHITE CITIZENSHIP, RACIAL HIERARCHY

Would the rights as well as the responsibilities of citizenship be accorded to Americans of Japanese ancestry? At the beginning of the twentieth century, the answer was not terribly difficult to discern. Since the first federal naturalization statue of 1790, legislators had evinced a distinct preference—a prejudice—for European settlers, making whiteness a prerequisite of Americanness, after a period of residency. The Civil War had shaken these values to the core, and three Reconstruction-era amendments to the Constitution literally changed the complexion of citizenship. After war's end the Thirteenth Amendment abolished slavery. The Fourteenth Amendment of 1868 extended citizenship to all persons born in the United States, thus taking in most black Americans, as well as the children of immigrants of any nationality—and extending to them due process and equal protection of the laws. But a new act of Congress that same year expanded naturalization rights beyond whites only to include persons of African descent. With the overthrow of multiracial Reconstruction governments in the southern states, the return of racist white rule, and the introduction of disenfranchising devices such as the grandfather clause, poll tax, and literacy test, most African Americans' newfound rights were effectively suspended. Similar devices for disenfranchising native Hawaiians were lambasted by women's activists there as "Mississippi Laws," while Hawaiian-language schools were all shut down. Combined with the Chinese Exclusion Act of 1882, the first immigration law aimed at a specific nationality group, it became increasingly clear that people of color would find it difficult if not impossible to secure equality of opportunity, not to mention equality of station, in these United States.[18]

In multinational, multiracial America, and on the Hawaiian plantations in particular, a hierarchy of racial and cultural groups proved the principal mechanism of labor management and manipulation. "Planters cultivated nationalistic consciousness in order to stimulate competition," as Ronald Takaki has shown. Their "divide-and-control strategy promoted interethnic tensions" and tended to forestall a sense of shared grievances. Whites were given supervisory positions; Portuguese and Spaniards served as foremen, or *luna*, in the fields; and along with native Hawaiians, Asia-Pacific immigrants—from China, Japan, Korea, and the Philippines—were relegated to the onerous work of hoeing, chopping, and gathering. As in the pecking order of the cane fields, plantation housing camps were usually segregated, and in some cases included sectors for black workers, as well as hands from the new Caribbean imperial possession of Puerto Rico. Puunene Plantation on Maui, for example, set up "Alabama Camp" and two "Spanish Camps." In the early 1920s at Pepeekeo Plantation, adjacent to Hakalau where the Yamanes lived, half of the nearly 1,000-strong labor force was made up of Japanese, one-quarter by Filipinos, then in lesser numbers Chinese, Puerto Ricans, Koreans, and Hawaiians—evidence of the many different routes, the many different ships, that individuals and families had taken to participate in the Hawaiian, American, and international economies.[19]

Many Japanese workers were promoted into the mill, to press cane, cook molasses, and sometimes process sugar. As their wages inched upward, and as a number found employment off the plantation and became sole proprietors, white legislators and planters fretted over the "Japanese problem" and sought to "eliminate the class that is now holding places as tradesmen, storekeepers, mechanics, fishermen, [and] coffee planters." For their part, some Japanese business leaders urged assimilation through a "reform and enlightenment campaign," undergirded by notions of bodily propriety and economic uplift. They "urged Japanese women to avoid breastfeeding infants in public, exhorted the Japanese to wear Western-style clothing, and advised them to invest in Hawaii." Officials of the Japanese government, Buddhist priests, and Japanese-language instructors such as Katsuichi Yamane were, in many ways, caught in between. While devoted to serving the legal, religious, and cultural needs of a large portion of the islands' inhabitants, they were described in a 1918 U.S. Army report as forces of anti-Americanism. And, in a persistent trope of racist thinking, the document warned of "prolific" Japanese women and the dangers of overpopulation.[20]

If language schools and Buddhist temples necessarily fostered a distinctive ethnic identity and pride in Japanese traditions, some plantation practices applied to all field hands equally and thus implied a potential for worker solidarity. Because white overseers ostensibly found names difficult to pronounce, they gave numbered metal discs or *bangos* to all nonwhite laborers: dog tags to be worn around the neck. Thus caught up in a mechanized, modern capitalist enterprise, workers would be known in the fields—and accounts would be kept in the offices—not by their names but by their dehumanizing numbers. In the 1920s at Pepeekeo, for example, the monthly ledger of days worked listed upper-level managers and overseers by name, including a few Japanese. But field workers were grouped by national origin and listed only by number, from 1 to 940. Trapped in a cycle of indebtedness, their measly wages rarely covering provisions bought on credit at the plantation store, many field hands shared the experience of debt peonage—and shared it with the Deep South's black, white, and Chinese sharecroppers and tenant farmers. To leave or desert became a punishable offense. To remain, together, became a necessity for some. To speak across linguistic divides in Hawaii soon was enabled by the evolution of a common language, pidgin English. That, in turn, "helped to create a new island identity for them."[21]

Occasionally, this common language and—importantly—a common deprivation yielded a sense of common cause, as evidenced by differing labor strategies during two major strikes. In 1909, when they still greatly outnumbered all other ethnic groups, Japanese went on strike by the thousands, demanding an end to the wage differentials between Japanese and Portuguese workers, among others. Further, the Japanese workforce, banding together across the islands in an act of "blood unionism," reappropriated that rich concept previously employed by mainland bosses during the upheavals of the late nineteenth century: it was not labor activism, they said, but rather the appalling working environment on the plantations that was "un-American"—and "undemocratic." In a bid to diversify a rich-versus-poor Hawaiian society of "plutocrats and coolies," strike organizers insisted that their ultimate goal was to bring about "a thriving and contented middle class—the realization of the high ideal of Americanism." After four months, equal pay for equal work was instituted, at least for Japanese moving into midlevel plantation jobs. By contrast, during the strike of 1920, Japanese, Filipino, and Puerto Rican workers joined together across ethnic lines in a universal demand for better wages. As with the previous strike, planters employed select Hawaiians, Koreans, and others as scabs, in an attempt to crush the campaign. Worse, they evicted strikers and their families from plantation housing. As this period of homelessness came during a major influenza epidemic, thousands of people fell sick and 150 died. A result of their highest sacrifice, wages were eventually increased for all workers, and a valuable lesson in interethnic, working-class solidarity was learned. But in a great irony of modern capitalist economics, lower harvests during the 1920 strike meant a spike in the worldwide price of sugar, and many a plantation, such as Hakalau's neighbor Honomu, reaped the highest annual profit in its company's history.[22]

By the end of the cane workers' strike of 1920, the Yamanes' daughter Kazue was nearly four years old—talking, walking, and running such that their little company bungalow could hardly contain her. At Yamagata Camp, the last of eighteen established at Hakalau, duplex structures predominated. In the middle of a front porch—often draped with laundry put out to dry—doors to two separate units stood side by side, a single front window adjacent to each. Inside each unit was only one room, with a kitchen tacked onto the back—as small as 250 square feet in all. So even if they got along with their neighbors on the other side of the wall, growing families yearned for more space. Surely with a second child on the way and hopes for a third, the Yamanes could convince Hakalau officials to assign them to a detached, single-family dwelling.[23]

Meanwhile, it was necessary to get out of the house as often as possible. On a rare day off, the Yamanes could take their wide-eyed daughter to the beach; they could splash around in waterfalls and swim in the river, so long as it was upstream of the mill and its waste pipes. On a long walk of several miles, they could survey the whole plantation, and Kazue could learn her first lessons in difference and hierarchy. From their all-Japanese Yamagata Camp, at the far north end of Hakalau Plantation, they walked south along the windward coastline, taking in places with funny names and different sorts of people. In addition to the other Japanese encampments such as Honohina and Sugimoto, there were Kahuku and Chin Chuck camps, Nanue and Kamaee Korean, Ah Ling and Wailea. As they came upon the villages around the mill, Kazue couldn't help but notice important disparities. As compared to the well-proportioned Hakalau Christian Chapel, the multifaith Lower Chapel for working-class families, built in 1907, was small, its interior walls unfinished. The closer they got to the mill, the more varied types of buildings they encountered. There were work-related structures: a lime house, scale room, fertilizer hut, lumberyard shed, and a warehouse made of brick, much sturdier than the unpainted, weather-beaten, wooden shacks of workers. There was a blacksmith shop, along with a number of stables, for the horses that drew wagons loaded with cane from the fields to the processing plant. Next to it was a round, two-story-high molasses tank. Evidence of evolving technologies, there also was a new garage to service the tractors that increasingly furrowed the fields, the novel but noisy automobiles that forced strollers like the Yamanes' off the side of the road.[24]

But it was surely the white folks' houses that impressed young Kazue the most. What a difference between Lower Hakalau and Upper Hakalau Village, their very names suggesting a commonplace social and geographical distinction: the poor down in the soaking-wet gulches, the wealthy up in the fresher air of the better-drained hillsides. Contrasted with the tiny duplexes crammed next to each other in odd arrangements barely admitting a breeze, the managers' large whitewashed homes in Upper Hakalau were set well back from the road, amidst carefully manicured lawns. Graceful walkways welcomed select visitors to the front door; screens on the big windows kept annoying insects out. Unlike the women in the workers' camps, the mistress of a house here had servants to help her. If she tended a garden, it was typically to raise flowers, not fruits and vegetables.[25]

Now and then Kazue and her parents would catch a glimpse of Mrs. Stuart, wife of the plantation attorney, who sometimes paid Shika to make her a special dress. Kazue was enthralled by the lady in nice clothes, her refined ways and her French accent; Mrs. Stuart in turn took a shine to Kazue. She wanted to show the little girl around cultural venues such as the theater, as well as the social club of the Upper Village, making all the more clear who was situated uppermost in plantation hierarchies, who could afford such luxuries.[26]

Long walks like these took their toll on Katsuichi. Older than his wife, he was in aging, ill health in the 1920s. Shika sometimes must have felt ill in spirit. Though first son, Tatsuo, and then second son, Tokio, brought new excitement and joy into the household, they also made apparent its limits. There wasn't enough room. The brothers were strong and hearty, bursting with vigor. Though Tatsuo seemed already to take after his father, bookish and reserved, Tokio's first toddling steps were followed by sprints—all requiring Shika's constant attention. Whereas before she could sew and mend during Kazue's naps and even take an occasional part-time position at the plantation's dressmaking operation, she now had to give up all paid work. So as the family size increased, their income actually decreased. The strains at home carried over to the language school. A financial imperative, Katsuichi had to attract and retain yet more students.

Events in Washington began to cast a pall. At the U.S. Supreme Court in 1922, Hawaiian Takao Ozawa, born in Japan, brought an appeal for citizenship, after it had been denied to him by a district court in the islands. He was, by the most relevant measures of the day, fully assimilated: an English-speaking Christian with a high school degree and university training in California. But in a unanimous, landmark ruling, the Court reiterated that only whites and persons of African descent could be naturalized as citizens of the United States. Ozawa—any Asian American—was ineligible. Congress went a step further in 1924. Despite Japanese Americans' tangible contributions to the U.S. economy in the Pacific territory and on the West Coast, and despite their scant numbers on the mainland—never more than a fraction of 1 percent of the population—Japanese were henceforth completely excluded under the terms of the new Immigration Act. No more Japanese immigrants would be permitted. People in Japan were incredulous that Americans would snub them in this way. When the act took effect, "A National Day of Humiliation" was declared by various newspapers, political parties, and civic groups; rallies drew thousands; and movie operators stopped showing American films—all signaling, some thought, another step toward war. Events in Hawaii also took a turn. In the early 1920s, an aggressive Americanization campaign was launched. Previously inclined to support Buddhism as yet another force for community stability, the big sugar planters paid "the most visible, zealous, and outspoken Japanese Christian minister," Takie Okumura, "to Christianize the Issei and convince them and their children to remain on the plantations." Japanese schools—where children learned cultural virtues of courtesy, duty, and respect, in addition to the language—were targeted as "un-American."[27]

Weighing all these factors and more, Katsuichi and Shika Yamane decided with great reluctance to return to Japan with their daughter and sons in the mid-1920s. The views of court justices and legislators, they reasoned, reflected those of a vast number of white Americans, a stinging world of bigotry poisonous for growing children. Further, any previous financial advantages had been offset by the demands of three growing children. Whereas there were relatives to lend a hand in Ninole, there were more still back home. And ever since the great earthquake of 1923—an economic disaster for Japan, a personal tragedy for countless thousands—Shika and Katsuichi felt less a need to stay away and more an obligation to go back and help. Further, there was Katsuichi's own precarious physical condition to consider. As Shika secretly worried, he might not be long for this world.[28]

With Katsuichi safely returned to his hometown, his earthly sojourn waning, Shika was now left to parent four children—as another daughter had come. Kazue had started her first hopeful days of schooling and was at Danbara Elementary for much of the day, but still burdens were heavy. Attempting to balance child care with the nursing of her ailing husband, Shika came near to the breaking point. A few years on, an interesting proposal arrived in the mail from Theodore Stuart, the prominent official of Hakalau Plantation and a captain of empire, as legal adviser to the Bank of Italy and the Santa Fe Railway Company, with a new permanent residence in Fresno. Why not let Mr. and Mrs. Stuart raise the young Kazue in California? There she could develop her budding interest in poetry and play tennis to her heart's content. And, as a U.S. citizen, she could pursue her education in the American way. Surely the parents would concede that her best opportunities lay on the mainland? In distress, Shika reluctantly agreed and sent her firstborn daughter away to America.[29]

She was picking flowers, when Mrs. Stuart, looking down on her from the window above, decided to rename her Violet. It was easier to pronounce than Kazue. The mistress of the house, the cook, and the gardener all were French nationals, uneasy with English not to mention Japanese. Violet pleased them, with her academic achievements, with her successes outside the classroom, with her willingness to adapt. After she graduated high school, marriage was just around the corner. Soon she would be wed. Chisa Taira would act as go-between, but the Stuart's Catholic priest, Father Bryson, would officiate. Violet's last name would become Matsuda.[30]

Shigeru Matsuda catered to the needs of a highly literate Japanese American public in and around Fresno. Along the sidewalk of Kern Street, under the awnings of the Matsuda Book Shop, his racks swelled with a variety of magazines and comics in English: baseball news, detective stories, hunting and fishing advice, popular science. Behind the plate-glass windows, he stocked Japanese fans, clothing, and accessories. He sold books in English but also in Japanese, everything from Buddhist scriptures to novels and poetry, as well as newspapers and women's magazines in Japanese. He was, in some sense, a literary go-between. He was a charter member of the Valley Ginsha Haiku Kai, a thriving club of local poets, professional and amateur, male and female, which Violet had enthusiastically joined—a new affiliation. But once again, for Violet, it was time for another leave-taking. After moving away with her family from her native Hawaii, after then leaving her family behind in Hiroshima, after quitting the Stuart's Fresno home as well—where she had been treated "as their own daughter"—Violet looked back on a range of models, at the marrying age of eighteen, for her own new household in California.[31]

The joining of Shigeru and Violet as husband and wife crystallized any number of combinations, odd and ordinary, resulting from movements in and out of the American empire. With parents from Hiroshima Prefecture, Shigeru might have seemed a logical match for Violet. The couple were well-read, fluent in both English and Japanese, part of a growing "network of haiku societies." They were experienced in life in both California and southwest Japan. But Violet spoke pidgin and some French, too, and had memories of Hawaii. There were other important differences. Shigeru participated in oratorical contests, staged dramatic productions, and corresponded for Japanese American newspapers across the state, mostly in Japanese. Indeed, like Violet's father, he taught at the Japanese-language schools. He was a fixture at the Fresno Buddhist Church. A graduate of Theodore Roosevelt High School, Violet was ever more at ease speaking in English and was drawn to Catholic religious practice. Crucially, Violet was a birthright citizen of the United States. Because Shigeru was born in Japan—and given the tightened restrictions on naturalization—neither he nor his immigrant parents would ever be fully welcomed into their adopted homeland. It was, in many respects, a mixed marriage.[32]

Their household and extended family soon encompassed even more complex sets of identifications and affiliations. Violet's brother Tatsuo came, Americanizing his name as Richard and answering to the nickname Dick. He joined the U.S. Army. Little brother Tokio eventually joined them too, actually moving into the Matsuda home on C Street, after attending a military school in Hiroshima. This set him apart further from his Nisei sister Violet and Issei brother-in-law Shigeru. Educated primarily in Japan, yet with the Nisei credentials of American citizenship, he was one of the many known as Kibei and assumed somehow to be less "loyal" to the United States, averse to assimilation, possibly even un-American. (After all, he had chosen not to change his name.) He would finish his schooling not at Roosevelt, but at the more racially mixed industrial/technical institute Edison High, where with three black friends, he starred on the track relay team, taking numerous trophies—little statues of success.[33]

Hardly an inevitability, the nuclear, patriarchal family is often held up as a "natural" model for national identity and social formation. It is used by capitalists, as we have seen, as a device for manipulating laborers, whether through the building of family cottages or the eviction of families from them. Ironically, in the convulsions of imperial expansion and citizenship restriction, households are displaced and broken up; familial ties are stretched until they snap. Under the demands of national allegiance and capitalist empire-building, individuals are made to reconsider their family, as well as their religion, language, and place. Indeed, with varying degrees of autonomy, highly dependent upon gender, one may alter his very name or be *compelled* to alter her name, for the sake of membership, livelihood, belonging. Thereby, origins are altered; they are, in some sense, remade, reimagined. Socially and physically, where we come from is made to fit with where we are going.

2 | Subversion

ON 15 APRIL 1937, U.S. Representative John Rankin rose to speak on the floor of the House. Members of every political persuasion took note. For Rankin was a consummate entertainer. Agree with him or not, the elected officials could always rely on him for an oratorical sideshow, marked by hyperbole, overstatement, excess. A seasoned veteran of Congress, the short and wiry, loudmouthed attorney from the First District of Mississippi had well-earned the sarcastic nickname "Silent John." On the topic of the "So-Called Anti-Lynching Bill," Rankin could not "remain silent," he said, for fear his "silence might be misunderstood." What the framers viewed as an act to stop white vigilantism and the extralegal execution of blacks, Rankin described instead as "a bill to encourage rape." If passed, this piece of "legislative stupidity" would incite "the more vicious element of the Negro race to attack white women." Warming to his audience, Rankin joked that the measure had been concocted by Irish American politicians in New York to appease their African American constituencies. It was, he said, "a bill to make Harlem safe for Tammany"—the city's political establishment. Laughter erupted from the chamber.[1]

A southern "boll weevil" Democrat, Rankin ingratiated himself to right-wingers in Congress. Reaching across sectional lines and party lines, he praised "the distinguished gentleman from New York," Representative James W. Wadsworth, who repeatedly opposed this type of legislation. Wadsworth, Rankin insisted, was the most "outstanding member of the Republican Party in public life today." He was "by far the ablest member of the Republican Party in the House"—"honest, courageous, and patriotic."[2]

Indeed, resisting racial equality amounted to an exercise in American patriotism and national preservation. The stakes were high; civilization hung in the balance. According to Rankin, "This is just the beginning of a series of drives to destroy the color line and try to force race amalgamation on the American people"—the worst of fates. "If they should succeed, America would sink into the mire of mongrelism, and instead of the proud Nation, the proud civilization we now enjoy, this country would go down to future generations inhabited by a mongrel race. God forbid that such a tragedy should ever befall my native land!" Rankin recited a familiar set of arguments, which he would use again and again, as he helped defeat the measure year after year.[3]

First, white southerners had bravely shouldered the burden of African American uplift. "Slavery," he declared, was "the greatest blessing the Negro had ever known up to that time. It elevated him from the position of savage to that of servant, and for the first time showed him the light of a Christian civilization." Second, that uplift was betrayed in the "horrors of Reconstruction," the post–Civil War experiment in biracial governance. Unfit for public life, no longer under direct white paternalism, African American men, third, had degenerated into a class of recalcitrant beasts, sexual superstuds bent on defiling white womanhood, as most vividly portrayed in D. W. Griffith's landmark 1915 motion picture, *The Birth of a Nation.* Lynching, thus, was only the logical response of white communities enraged by cross-racial sexual assault. This most salacious of justifications for lynching, usually fabricated, ignited rumors of rape that Rankin recapitulated in Washington and on the stump back in Mississippi. With relish, he referenced numerous "bestial outrages," even as decorum purportedly forbade description of "the worst ones." Rankin titillated colleagues with the tale of a black man who killed a white man, then "outraged his wife for two or three days, in a manner too horrible to relate." Still, Rankin felt impelled to relate case after case, as he participated in this uniquely southern practice, what Jacquelyn Dowd Hall has referred to as its "folk pornography."[4]

A favorite Rankin story went like this: "In Mississippi a little woman was standing before the mirror dressing to go to a W.C.T.U. [Women's Christian Temperance Union] meeting"—thereby characterizing her as the most innocent of victims, a white church lady, a reformer who campaigned against the evils of alcohol. "A Negro brute approached the house, eased up onto the veranda, and crawled through a window. She saw him, reached in the bureau drawer and picked up her husband's pistol and pointed it at him. He saw from her terror-stricken face and trembling hand that she was unable to pull the trigger. He walked up, took the pistol from her hand, stuck it in his pocket, choked her into insensibility, raped her several times, then took her husband's razor . . . and cut her throat from ear to ear and left her weltering in her own blood in the parlor of her own home." Such a story was usually followed by a direct question to liberal congressmen from the North: "I wonder what would have happened if that had been your sister, or your wife, or your daughter? Probably the next one will be."

These northerners—"an irresponsible element of so-called Democrats"—were pandering to their black voters, Rankin reiterated. In the process, he threatened, they were endangering their political clout. "You are . . . deeply offending Members from the South upon whose good will you must depend, not only for your committee assignments in the House, but for the success of any legislation you may sponsor." Rankin demanded that they stop "playing the roll of Judas Iscariot toward the southern Democrats," who by virtue of their perpetual reelection and seniority of service controlled much of the congressional machinery.

Importantly, Rankin went on to summon up a related case of racial unrest from the not-too-distant past, as he attempted to shore up cross-sectional alliances with other members of Congress. "Let me say to our friends from the Pacific coast who are supporting this measure, that less than thirty years ago"—around the time of Teddy Roosevelt's "Gentlemen's Agreement" with Japan to limit immigration—"you people were in a frenzy of excitement and fear over the danger of the 'yellow peril.' You called aloud for help, and the white people of the South responded to a man. It was the call of the race, the call of a white civilization. One Congressman from the Pacific coast told me that he never knew a southern Democrat to falter." "The white people of the South," Rankin continued, were "the best friends you had in the hour of your own danger." In other words, white nativists in the West had common cause with white supremacists from the South.

Rankin linked racial protest to national subversion, claiming that the proposed anti-lynching legislation originated with "communistic agitators" and "a few Negro politicians who are in league with the Communists"—promoters of costly "free education" and opponents of the discriminatory poll tax. While he belittled demonstrators for their "silly, asinine, stupid performance[s]," he nonetheless characterized the struggle as the biggest of American conflicts, requiring rigid adherence to a single course of action. "There are only four possible solutions of the race question," he deduced, summing up his speech: "amalgamation, extermination, deportation, and segregation." Attempting a judicious tone, Rankin ruled out amalgamation as "too horrible to even consider; deportation seems to be out of the question; extermination is too cruel for contemplation," though contemplate them all he clearly had. With a crescendo, he recited his forceful directive. "The only possible feasible solution is to follow the course mapped out and pursued by the people of the South for more than three hundred years—a complete segregation of the two races." He returned to his seat amid hearty rounds of applause.

Though considered by many, especially later in his career, as a marginal figure of the extreme right, John Rankin in the late 1930s and early 1940s often captured the spirit of mainstream American political discourse. Forging alliances with members of Congress from the North and the West, he helped shape legislation both on the floor and behind the scenes at a distinctive juncture in the nation's history, when nationalist and imperialist expansion became ever more tightly intertwined with racism, xenophobia, and anti-communism. Linking proponents of racial equality to sexual perversion and national subversion, Rankin implicitly supported the deeds of deadly white lynch mobs as a legitimate means of racial control. He thwarted federal anti-lynching legislation; he promoted the first major congressional anti-communist initiative, the House Un-American Activities Committee; and he applied the South's Jim Crow principles, targeting African Americans, to the new territory of Hawaii, championing the segregation of white and all nonwhite races on a global scale. Perhaps unsurprisingly, he proved an influential adversary of Hawaiian statehood, and he went on to argue early and often for Japanese American incarceration during World War II. Near the midpoint of the American century, he was a barometer of American racial, national, and sexual values.

PERVERSE SEXUALITY

Lynching commanded the nation's attention from the late nineteenth through the early twentieth century. In the South especially, African Americans suffered brutal deaths at the hands of whites, by hanging, shooting, and increasingly by burning. From ordinary bonfires to newfangled blowtorches, many white southerners adopted horrific techniques and took a morbid delight in so-called "Negro barbecues." With grisly overkill, groups tortured and mutilated black bodies, and individuals took home mementos of the event—body parts such as fingers, toes, and ears. The exact numbers of deaths will never be known, since night riders and other perpetrators frequently covered their tracks and local law enforcement ignored or condoned their efforts. But it's clear that thousands lost their lives. In Rankin's home state alone, at least six hundred were murdered from the 1880s through the 1940s. "Standing in the statistical and geographical center of the national lynching belt," according to historian Neil McMillen, Mississippi "ranked first in virtually every category—the most total lynchings, the most multiple lynchings, the most per capita, the most female victims, the most victims taken from police custody, the most lynchings without arrest or conviction of mob leaders." Nearly equal numbers of killings occurred in Georgia and Texas, and by conservative estimates, the national total over the period exceeded four thousand.[5]

Though lynching most commonly was justified as retribution for an alleged murder, nothing excited more murderous rage in southern lynch mobs than fantasies of rape. As Joel Williamson has meticulously documented, whites after the Civil War, in a twisted misreading of Darwinism, began to imagine black men and women as sliding backward on the evolutionary scale. Without the civilizing effects of servitude under slavery, as Rankin referenced it, African Americans were degenerating into a subhuman class of beings marked by uncontrollable animal urges and sexual excess. Notions of lascivious Jezebels, amoral females incapable of chastity, helped to excuse white men's repeated assaults of black women. In a toxic potion of fear, desire, and envy, white men depicted black males as incorrigible lechers, "black beast-rapists" obsessed with white women. These representations circulated in the hallowed halls of Washington, in popular media, and in countless conversations in the white communities of the South. Thus, the nation's new black citizens were degraded through related narratives of racial inferiority and perverse sexuality. Further, in the lynching belt, black male bodies were physically and symbolically sheared of their offending appendage—another sick souvenir—as victims endured, often before their death, castration. In this most perverse homoerotic of lynching, as Robyn Wiegman notes, we see "the image of white men embracing—with hate, fear, and a chilling form of empowered delight—the same penis they were so over-determinedly driven to destroy."[6]

Beyond the psychosexual dynamics of lynching, the extralegal execution of black southerners served to thwart their economic and political advancement. Historians have convincingly shown that white vigilantism sprung broadly from postbellum economic anxieties and often arose specifically in response to black attempts to get out from under a modified plantation system of tenant farming, sharecropping, and debt peonage. It was a tool for maintaining and exploiting a compliant labor force. Night riders punished blacks who ran out on inflated debts or stood up to whites in local land disputes. They also terrorized individuals who tried to vote or otherwise participate in the political process. Most of all, lynching created a pervasive environment of fear and intimidation extending over the whole of the South and beyond, encompassing all racial outcasts, whether they directly witnessed, read about, or were told about a lynching. White social, political, and economic dominance was demonstrated and sustained though the repeated lynching of black southerners. Though journalists such as Ida B. Wells and organizations like the NAACP campaigned for federal legislation to stop lynching, its failure signaled to African Americans that their citizenship rights remained precarious at best. They would not be safeguarded by national authorities.[7]

Just as lurid accusations of rape overshadowed the more numerous allegations of murder, local disputes or private lynchings—the killing of a black man by a white individual or small group—were eclipsed by the less frequent but more riotous spectacle lynchings. Arguing forcefully against the notion of lynching as an outmoded, premodern, precapitalist form of crime control, Grace Hale highlights the modern technological components of these large-scale phenomena. After a trademark jail raid or chase and after confirmation of the identity of a black perpetrator by an alleged victim or victim's relatives, announcements went out in that most modern of mediums, the daily or weekly press, setting a time and place for the execution. Reporters anticipated and covered the events, relying on telephone and telegraph communications. Hundreds, sometimes thousands, turned up, arriving by car, truck, and bus. After the fact, photographs circulated far and wide. And, with the help of antilynching activists, these images of the victims of lynch mobs began to rouse international sympathy and condemnation.[8]

Such was the case in Depression-era Alabama. When nine young men and boys were falsely accused of raping two white women on a train, a multiple lynching seemed inevitable. Extensive press coverage, however, insured that the so-called Scottsboro boys at least would receive a trial—an all-white jury trial, that is. The well-publicized pleadings by famed defense attorney Clarence Darrow and subsequent appeals launched by the communist International Labor Defense helped to spare their lives: death sentences gave way to lengthy jail terms. Therefore many white southerners pointed to the case as evidence of the failings of courtroom proceedings, insisting that the crimes warranted quick capital punishment and nothing less. Hatching conspiracy theories of a legal profession riddled with subversives, with leftist racial egalitarians, many southern politicians continued to view vigilantism as the most efficient method for meting out local justice.[9]

Lynching was not uncommon in Hawaii. In 1889 former contract laborer turned shopkeeper Katsu Gota was hanged from a telephone pole by men in the hire of his white business rivals. In the late 1920s, a Japanese worker from Puunene Plantation was doused in gasoline, set afire, and burned to death by a white mechanic, later acquitted; and a Japanese taxi driver was viciously killed by an influential white man charged only with second-degree murder—all signaling, for the *Hawaii Hochi,* second-class status, a double standard of justice. Roger Bell asserts that "in remote Hawaii, whites could commit acts of violence, even murder, with apparent impunity—provided the victims of such attacks were not Caucasians." Though referring more to private violence than spectator lynching, Bell implies that it was Hawaii's geographical isolation that imperiled nonwhite people and gave free rein to white perpetrators. Such discourses of remoteness were used by many whites in the North to describe lynching in the South, as well as the West. Seeming racial progressives, white nationalists thereby attempted to distance racism and racial violence from the American national project, literally making it remote from—instead of acknowledging its centrality to—United States nation-building and empire-building.[10]

A case from Hawaii in 1931, involving a false accusation of rape and the murder of the accused by the accuser's relatives, initially had all the hallmarks of a classic private lynching. Reportage on the islands and in the continental United States soon made it a media spectacle, resonant with many of the southern incidents. In September of that year, Thalia Massie claimed that she was abducted and gang-raped by five men of Chinese, native Hawaiian, and Japanese descent in Honolulu. After a racially mixed jury failed to reach a verdict in the case, and as prosecutors looked for ways to re-indict, Massie's husband and mother and two sailors kidnapped one of the men, Joseph Kahahawai, tortured him in an attempt to exact a confession, and then shot him to death. *Their* defense was coordinated by none other than Clarence Darrow. Once hailed for representing Tennessee high school biology teacher John Scopes, who taught theories of evolution contrary to state law, the radical lawyer Darrow had just withdrawn as counsel for the Scottsboro boys after communists—among America's most consistent white advocates of racial equality—got involved. Though Massie's husband and mother admitted the murder of Kahahawai, Darrow won them a reduced sentence of manslaughter. Territorial Governor Lawrence Judd then commuted their ten-year prison term, and the two were set free. Governor Judd's own investigation, after the fact, proved categorically that none of the five men could have been at the scene of the alleged assault on Thalia Massie. Still, "contemporary media reports," according to scholar Lillian Robinson, "combine[d] the worst elements of the Mainland Black-white paradigm with the colonial rhetoric about savage 'natives.'"[11]

Truly, across large swaths of the American empire, one category of human difference—race—was wedded to another—sexuality—in order to establish and maintain the dominance of whites. Amid outlandish acts of violence and sensational media coverage of them, racial outcasts were marked as doubly suspect through assertions of their seemingly perverse sexuality. As Roger Bell notes of the Massie-Kahahawai episode, "This cause celebre revealed a [white colonial] community subject to racial preoccupations sometimes very similar to those which shaped relations between blacks and whites in mainland states during the 1920s and 1930s. . . . [M]ost commentators expressed alarm that the American territory was unsafe for white Americans." John Rankin thus offered a bill in Congress allowing the president to appoint nonresidents of Hawaii as governor and as judges in the territory, in hopes "this might ensure a pattern of race relations more in keeping with mainland practices." In a startling reversal of most white southern arguments about Reconstruction—which blamed invading, opportunistic northerners for their post–Civil War problems—this bill to install "carpetbag government" in Hawaii was skillfully pushed through the House by Rankin. It failed to pass the Senate. Still, its sympathetic consideration and its crafty provisions signaled a continuing ambivalence around nonwhite self-governance or multiracial legislative coalition within the American national project.[12]

As Joane Nagel has summarized, America "was and is defined as much by what we *are not* as it is by what we *are.* Colonialism provided Americans and Europeans with a set of symbolic and actual places and peoples on which to stage their national dramas of self-discovery and self-invention. The invention of America was set against enslaved, indigenous, and immigrant Others. Part of our national self-construction process was the attribution of moral and sexual characteristics to them and us, the designation of their rights and our rights, the evaluation of their moral and sexual worth in comparison to ours." Such constructions included the attribution not only of an excess or hypersexuality to blacks and other nonwhite races, as with the *San Francisco Chronicle* headline "JAPANESE A MENACE TO AMERICAN WOMEN." As we have seen in the introduction, ethnic minority members also could be maligned—under a no-win scenario—for a deficient sexuality, as with depictions of effeminized Japanese American men: men who consequently performed their discredited masculinity with adamant disavowals of homosexuality. In yet a further move to stigmatize and ostracize, ideological conservatives linked racial exclusion and sexual perversion to national subversion—to the specter of socialism and communism, always ill-defined but reviled. Again, John Rankin would play a role.[13]

HOUSE UN-AMERICAN ACTIVITIES

As with so much political rhetoric against un-American activities, John Rankin's vitriol was ideologically inconsistent. His upbringing certainly did not foreordain a right-wing allegiance. Though Mississippi had a larger proportion of African Americans—the descendants of slaves—than any other state, Rankin was born and raised not in the plantation belt where most lynchings occurred but in the northeastern hills of mostly white, small farm holders. The region had harbored considerable resistance to the establishment of the Confederacy, driven as it was by large-scale planter interests, the interests of slaveholders. Still, in his biographies drafted for congressional directories, Rankin trumpeted the service of his wife's father and one of his own grandfathers in the Confederate army. Rankin's father was a schoolteacher; his father's father a pioneer Methodist preacher who moved to Mississippi from South Carolina. After setting up a law practice in Tupelo around 1910, John Rankin served a brief stint as a newspaper editor and a short tour of duty during the First World War. He was elected to Congress in 1920 and would be reelected for a total tenure of almost thirty-two years.[14]

Among the raft of bills he introduced in his first six months, Rankin proposed a federal anti-miscegenation statute akin to those in force in the southern states. It would have prohibited the "intermarriage" of whites with blacks or with "Mongolians." Rankin became known as a staunch defender of veterans' benefits. On other economic matters, he gave the impression of a progressive. With Nebraska Senator George Norris, he introduced the bill establishing the Tennessee Valley Authority (TVA) in 1933, and he helped secure authorization three years later of the Rural Electrification Administration (REA). "Cheap Juice John" thwarted private utility monopolies—"The Power Trust," as he called them—and he thus helped nationalize public services for the benefit of his far-flung rural constituents. The nation's taxpayers—mostly living in towns and cities of 2,500 or more as of the 1920 census—in effect subsidized lengthy power lines to outlying residences, on the assumption that electricity and, soon, telephone service were vital resources, the right of all. As TVA dams generated power for farmhouses, TVA waterways connected them to national and international markets, transporting their produce into larger rivers of commerce. Further, in the face of an agricultural recession that predated the Great Depression by several years, Rankin advocated a Federal Farm Board and urged Washington's continuing intervention in agricultural trade.[15]

In addition to a canal connecting the Tennessee and Tombigbee rivers and running right through his district, Rankin promoted other measures in a nationalized transport system, downplaying socialist rationales for what sometimes seemed cynical pork-barrel projects. He argued forcefully on the floor of the House for the creation of National Park Service highways, precursors of the 1950s interstate highway system. He championed the Blue Ridge Parkway and, especially, the Natchez Trace, connecting Nashville to southwest Mississippi and, again, running right through his district. Colleagues joined in, extolling not just the roads' "scenic and historic" virtues but also their importance to national security and armed-forces mobilization. Rankin looked back into the nation's military history, claiming that the original Trace was the "road over which Andrew Jackson marched to New Orleans [and] won the great victory of the War of 1812." Now, on the eve of U.S. entry into World War II, Rankin asserted that national "highways in Europe and the inland waterways have had more effect on this war than almost any other two elements you can mention." For the motorized movement of equipment and for troop transport, Germany in particular had benefited from its integrated system of roadways and waterways, colleagues insisted.[16]

Was John Rankin a lefty? In 1934 he welcomed President Franklin Roosevelt to Tupelo to symbolically throw the switch on hydroelectric power there. Among his enduring legislative triumphs, Rankin added the REA and TVA to FDR's alphabet soup of New Deal organizations. Decried as "make-work" by some critics, three-letter Depression-era outfits like the CCC, or Civilian Conservation Corps, were designed to reduce unemployment and expand federal jurisdiction, even as they sent budget deficits soaring to all-time highs. For his support of these and other initiatives, the *New Republic* in 1937 christened Rankin a liberal, a "friend of the common voter"—a voter, of course, understood to be white. Rankin was understood by some on the "lunatic right" to be a "Roosevelt red," a socialist. But in his anti-communist witch-hunting, race-baiting, and union-busting, there could no mistaking: Rankin was ultraconservative. A proposed Fair Employment Practices Commission, in his view, was "the most dangerous and brazen attempt to fasten upon the white people of America the worst system of control by alien or minority racial groups that has been known since the Crucifixion"—a product of the "deadly doctrines of

Karl Marx . . . based upon hatred for Christianity." With the help of Rankin, a "godless" communism became almost synonymous with the term un-American, and the House Un-American Activities Committee (HUAC) was founded.[17]

Since 1917 predecessor committees of HUAC had scrutinized groups at the margins of the American political left *and* right. The American Civil Liberties Union (ACLU) was branded communist in 1931, but investigators also focused on Nazi activity in the United States. Set up as a standing committee in 1938 under the chairmanship of conservative southern Democrat Martin Dies of Orange, Texas, HUAC likewise probed the far right, at least in its earliest days. It targeted Nazi and fascist organizations, and its investigations of William Dudley Pelley's Silver Shirts in North Carolina were followed by its dissolution—although critics of the committee claimed Dies was actually in cahoots with Pelley. HUAC quickly turned its attentions to the left. "Exposing communists" in the New Deal's Federal Theatre Project and Federal Writers' Project led to the demise of those agencies. Also in its first year, HUAC spotlighted "communist infiltration" of civil rights organizations, which suggests that resistance to racial egalitarianism was at the origins of un-American investigative culture, as much as resistance to subversion.[18]

A stalwart defender of HUAC and, improbably, a self-proclaimed expert on free-speech issues, Willmoore Kendall defined subversion not solely as "the overturning or overthrowing of existing governments or institutions. Another and more prevalent meaning is the undermining of a people's allegiance or faith in its institutions, which is often the precondition for the overthrow of these institutions." In this shrewd rhetorical maneuver, Kendall first disregarded the founding imperative, enshrined in the Declaration of Independence, for citizens to "throw off" unjust systems of governance. Second, and more importantly, with his capacious corollary on the definition of subversion, he advocated the suppression of any speech that would point up those injustices. And third, he implicitly gave sanction to government bodies to aggressively interrogate and harass organizations promoting such political views, whether or not with motive to "overthrow." Meanwhile, Kendall vilified the rhetorical strategies of the Communist Party, especially as regards race. Rather than genuinely promoting racial equality, their intent, he said, was to "foster internal dissent by exaggerating the misery of the Southern Negroes, or inducing a state of tension between white and Negro."[19]

Though invested in maintaining the color line, HUAC could not be characterized as a group of rabid southern Democratic racists. Though an impassioned and influential supporter, Rankin did not actually become a member until 1945, when in a cunning parliamentary move, he succeeded in giving the periodically appropriated standing committee permanent status. Among early members of HUAC was Republican Hamilton Fish of New York, who proposed to alleviate the nation's crushing unemployment problem by deporting "every single alien Communist." Republicans Kit Clardy of Michigan and Donald Jackson of California demanded probes into the activities of "professional Negroes" and later joined the racist, xenophobic John Birch Society. Not all members, however, viewed racial protest as a form of subversion. From the very outset and throughout the committee's history, the meaning of un-American activities was always contested, always up for grabs.[20]

Ironically, right-wing commentator William F. Buckley Jr. wanted to limit the scope of HUAC, siding "with those who believe that HUAC's designation is too broad. The Committee should not, in my judgment, consider itself free to explore 'un-American activities,' because when a semi-autonomous Congressional Committee has a running license to investigate any and all un-American activities, it is given, without the reassuring processes of public and Congressional debate, standing and plenipotentiary powers to *fix* the meaning of un-Americanism." A skilled debater in the Ivy League mold, Buckley used a revealing argument to support his point. "Racism, . . . if by that is meant white supremacism and its accompanying mystique, is not un-American in the historical sense," he wrote. "It is despicable—but there we go, and there the Committee might go: that which is despicable is un-American—so let's investigate?" Indeed, as we have seen, that is where the committee did go, from its beginnings. However, much more commonly than racists and Aryans, the committee condemned supporters of racial egalitarianism. While Buckley stated that racism was despicable, he implied that the investigation of racist groups was even more so. He didn't want Congress to label racism as un-American and thus go on the attack against it. Instead, he wanted it to relabel the group, more narrowly, as the House Committee on Communist Activities.[21]

As of the early 1940s, however, the remit remained expansive, and HUAC explored enemies real and imagined of various stripes. Before the war, its members went in search of sinister Japanese and Japanese Americans—the two rarely distinguished. After the war, supporters such as Willmoore Kendall, as well as Robert Stripling, author of *The Red Plot against America*, would claim that the committee had known of Japanese fifth-column activities in Hawaii and on the West Coast and had planned to release a report, but irresponsible bureaucrats in the Justice Department had quashed it. In truth, the findings of the president's own prewar investigation were suppressed. This

Munson report—which yielded no evidence of Japanese American espionage and which might have forestalled the rush to indiscriminate incarceration—was concealed from large segments of the executive branch. While the Roberts Commission report, on the heels of the Pearl Harbor attack, falsely hinted at Japanese American involvement, it was distorted by the press to imply their active role in sabotage. Meanwhile, Dies and HUAC had prepared another bogus report—and released it. It claimed that 17,000 defense workers had questionable national loyalties and would support an impending Axis invasion of the United States, necessitating Japanese American expulsion from the West Coast. An overzealous pursuer of phantom foes, intent on publicizing its efforts, HUAC thereby helped create the ideological environment so conducive to the wartime incarceration of 120,000 American citizens and longtime residents of Japanese descent.[22]

SEGREGATION VERSUS EXTERMINATION

Hawaii's uncertain status—as territory but not state, as home to large numbers of "aliens" but also their birthright citizen children—seemed to keep it at the margins of U.S. political life. But the looming war magnified its importance. In addition to the growing American business interests there, its strategic military position in the Pacific demanded attention. Still, how could Washington reckon with a nonwhite majority population? "Jingo John" Rankin's four alternatives of racial policy—amalgamation, deportation, extermination, or segregation—in fact had all been viable options in the American national project, as the history of race and the case of Hawaiian statehood help demonstrate.

I will not argue that Hawaii was or is the most multiracial of American jurisdictions, as some have. Similar descriptions of the United States as more multicultural than other nations imply a finite set of fixed categories of human difference, which can be quantitatively measured, whereby America somehow wins out in today's era that celebrates diversity, whereby Hawaii becomes a shining model. As race is invented, so too, simultaneously, is racial hierarchy invented—one of the many means of social categorization used to divide and subdivide humanity. Lines are drawn, if not in wholly arbitrary fashion, then with sometimes unpredictable and illogical results. Remembering that in the nineteenth-century Midwest the union of a Swedish American and a Norwegian American would be called a mixed marriage, we should look instead at the infinite capacity of human beings to invent differences and subcultures, to segregate, whatever the location.

Still, undeniably during the first half of the twentieth century, under then-prevalent theories of race, most white politicians viewed the territory of Hawaii as different from the mainland, different especially in its mix of races and in its purported racial accord. "To an extent," write historians Beth Bailey and David Farber, the white "haole elite really believed their Hawaii to be a paradigm of racial harmony. That they had economically excluded Asian and Pacific Americans for decades, that they had done their best to keep them out of real political power, that they spoke of them in prejudicial terms, and refused to mingle socially with Asian Americans; all this was omitted from their view of Hawaii as the land of racial and ethnic *Aloha.* To many of the islands' peoples, such a view seemed ridiculous, a malicious cover-up." Even so, Bailey and Farber conclude, "much more than the rest of the country, Hawaii did represent . . . the possibility of a rainbow society."[23]

Unsurprisingly for a racist inclined to class nonwhites as subhuman, as lower on an ill-understood evolutionary scale, John Rankin used a term borrowed from animal husbandry, mongrelization, to describe one possible outcome in Hawaii and—more worryingly for him—on the mainland. Melting-pot ideologies at the time could be radically interpreted to promote interracial coupling and child-rearing, and this kind of amalgamation truly was the order of the day on the islands, where almost one-quarter of marriages were "between people of different racial stock" as of 1939 and would rise to one-third by war's end. Nonetheless, many forms of segregation were practiced. If Rankin seemed to think in terms of a biracial white/nonwhite world, such binary thinking could be equated with other current dualisms of the period, as we have seen: Christian/heathen, civilized/barbaric. That bogeyman of the southern lynching belt, the mythological black beast rapist, resonated with the native barbaric or heathen Oriental rapist fabricated in the American West and Pacific. The Massie-Kahahawai case—in which native Hawaiians and Asian Americans ostensibly got too near, too physically close to a white woman—seemed to provide all the evidence necessary for a spatial segregation of the races. The Supreme Court's 1896 *Plessy v. Ferguson* decision had given sanction to "separate but equal" social and cultural spaces; American business owners utilized segregated workforces as a fundamental method of labor control.[24]

The islands' multiracial, multinational assortment was the major stumbling block in early attempts at Hawaiian statehood. Back around 1890, when white rule began to be reestablished in the South and when the western frontier was symbolically closed, six new states had been added to the previous total of thirty-eight: North and South Dakota, Montana, Washington, Idaho, and Wyoming. Soon, incorporating a distinctive religious minority group, the Mormons, Utah was admitted in 1896; and large groups of Native Americans were at least geographically annexed with the addition of Oklahoma in 1907. For many white nativists, the year 1912 was the limit. New Mexico and Arizona brought new levels of racial and ethnic diversity to the United States. (Never mind that the United States had stolen these lands in an unprovoked war with Mexico, yielding that classic, rightly indignant phrase of Mexican American activism: "I didn't cross the border; the border crossed me!") Almost forty-eight years would pass before the flag's forty-eight stars would extend beyond the continental United States.

Hawaii's claims to statehood in the 1930s were convincing, as historian Roger Bell has noted. "Its area exceeded that of three of the existing states. . . . Moreover, Hawaii had an advanced and expanding economy capable of sustaining self-government. It paid more in taxes annually to the federal treasury than fifteen of the states. This sum was five times greater than the amount expended annually by the federal government in the territory for local purposes"—proving yet again that in a colonial economy, the colony's wealth would be drained off to benefit the mother country, not the inhabitants. A 1937 House and Senate joint committee on territories investigated this question of statehood, as now a "comfortable majority" of Hawaii's citizens—including haole elites—favored it. "Predictably, most of the arguments against statehood were based, explicitly or implicitly, on appeals to anti-Japanese sentiment. It was argued that Hawaii's population was of predominantly Oriental extraction and could not be classified 'as truly thoroughly, fundamentally and unequivocally American.'" Investigators believed "it would be wiser to wait until another generation of American citizens of Oriental ancestry . . . had an opportunity to absorb American ideals and training." Once more, there was a sense that so-called nonwhite immigrants and their progeny—as opposed to the late nineteenth- and early twentieth-century immigrant wave from southern and eastern Europe, increasingly classed as white—required more time to master American ways, were biologically ill-disposed to American public life, even as the Fourteenth Amendment long ago had officially made African Americans a part of the citizenry. While the joint committee proposed postponing Hawaiian statehood for a generation or so, Rankin went further and issued a minority report recommending that it be deferred indefinitely.[25]

Thus in the 1930s, Rankin and southern Democrats "assumed the leadership of attempts to frustrate Hawaii's statehood aspirations. Various representatives of the conservative, segregated, race-conscious Southern states willingly performed this function for the next twenty-five years." Their fears of a larger nonwhite populace excited fears of un-American changes in social and economic policy, made possible by potential shifts in Congress. "My God," said Rankin, "if we give them folks statehood we're likely to have a senator called Moto"—referencing the fictional Japanese secret agent and echoing the sentiments of some whites in Hawaii as well. According to rapid segregationist Senator James Eastland of Mississippi, two senators from Hawaii would mean "two votes for socialized medicine . . . two votes for Government ownership of industry, two votes against all racial segregation, and two votes against the South on all social matters." Thus again, in a dangerous world of wanton "mixing," democratic socialism—health care for all, public ownership of the means of production—was linked to racial intermingling, communism linked to racial egalitarianism. Though racist white southerners often led the resistance, they were not alone. As Roger Bell is quick to point out, these ostensibly extreme "Southern" viewpoints "reflected a substantial body of mainland opinion."[26]

Extermination, which John Rankin spoke of as "too horrible to consider," in fact had long been a feature of American racial discourse. Puritan ministers in early America described the massive deaths of Native Americans from smallpox, measles, and armed warfare as evidence that God was on our side. "The last of the race" was perpetually asserted—"a dying breed." Similar sorts of language were used in European and American Pacific territories like Hawaii, as invaders decimated native populations, and like the Philippines, where U.S. troops crushed the forces of independence. Widely circulated notions of racial inferiority—scientific and popular declarations of subhuman status—inevitably led to "humane" judgments that heathens and savages rightly should be put down. In the early twentieth century, genocide was no longer *explicitly* articulated as a legitimate means to the ends of white dominance. That dominance took other forms. Hawaii remained segregated from the privileges of American statehood; nonwhite Americans remained largely separated from the full rights and privileges of citizenship.

As we've seen, in the 1920s and 1930s white residents of the U.S. South and West began to imagine a sectional alliance and national communion predicated upon a shared hostility to nonwhite races. Racist discourses of a feared amalgamation took on similar properties across the two sections, even as the ostensible sources of anxieties differed so dramatically. African Americans in the South, the descendants of enslaved chattel laborers, and Asian American immigrants to the West and to Pacific territories, recruited agricultural workers, had varied access to birthright or naturalized citizenship status, in national law and in local practice. But political leaders in the South and West, notably California's Hiram Johnson, capitalized upon related rhetorics of sexual predation and miscegenation to question the access of either group to national belonging. As contemporaneous lynching debates and nativist sentiments demonstrate, race, sexuality, and nation were mutually constituting categories of exclusion. The South's mythical black beast-rapist resonated with the native Hawaiians and immigrant Chinese and Japanese falsely accused of assaulting Thalia Massie in Honolulu in 1931. These representations and others would figure prominently in continuing battles over anti-lynching and anti-immigrant legislation, statehood for Alaska and Hawaii, and America's broader cultural and political imperialism.

Japan's "unprovoked," "surprise" attack on the United States was neither. True, the air raid on Pearl Harbor was unannounced, startling in its impact, and thus militarily successful in its crippling of the American Pacific fleet. But officials in Washington had long predicted that hostilities with Japan—the competing Pacific empire—would result in war. As early as the first decade of the twentieth century, President Theodore Roosevelt had begun to anticipate it. By the 1910s, his kinsman Franklin Roosevelt, as assistant secretary of the navy, fully expected it. "FDR seized on the 'yellow peril' as a lever to call for increased naval preparedness," Greg Robinson notes, and he "continued over the succeeding years to consider war with Japan an imminent threat." By 1940 the time was ripe. By upsetting a careful equilibrium with its chief rival, by "applying economic sanctions against Japan in 1940 and intensif[ying] them in 1941," the United States "provoke[ed] the attack on Pearl Harbor," as Warren Cohen demonstrates. So, although nearly forty years in the making, the seventh of December 1941 would still be labeled by President Franklin Roosevelt—in an act of official propaganda that would be preserved as official history—as a day that would "live in infamy."[27]

Histories of Japanese American incarceration often begin with 7 December 1941. Against Their Will: The Japanese American Experience in WWII Arkansas—the principal exhibit among eight coordinated displays mounted in Little Rock in 2004—opens with panels devoted to "the surprise attack by the Empire of Japan on Pearl Harbor": the exhibition's first eleven words. Citing but not detailing a "long history of suspicion and prejudice," the introductory narrative states: "Americans assumed that a Japanese invasion of the western coast was inevitable and that Japanese Americans would cooperate with the invaders. . . . [R]esidents of California, Oregon, and Washington demanded protection from what they saw as a possible enemy force in their own backyards." Thus, in a display about "Japanese American experience," the first context-setting label copy is not an elaboration of what it felt like to be the victim of decades of suspicion. It is instead a recycling of the dominant rationales of the time, perpetuating them as central mechanisms for understanding the prejudicial treatment of Japanese Americans during the Second World War. *Some white* "Americans assumed" Japanese American sabotage; *some white* "residents of California, Oregon, and Washington," we're told, were reacting to Pearl Harbor. The Honolulu military port likewise figures in the first sentences of Michi Nishiura Weglyn's powerful history of incarceration, suitably titled *Years of Infamy.*[28]

The U.S. entry into World War II did not spark anti–Japanese American sentiment or set it off; it rekindled it and fanned it. With the help of elected officials from John Rankin to Franklin Roosevelt, during a time of worldwide conflict and stress, Japanese Americans were scapegoated for the failures of military preparedness. Incarceration resulted not solely from a flare-up in the ongoing antagonisms of American racism; it also proceeded from economic envy at Japanese American agricultural and business achievements and from sexualized anxiety over white citizenship and national belonging. As the Native Sons and Daughters of the Golden West claimed, "Jap-dollars" and the "high Japanese birthrate"—which even government reports declared "a myth"—threatened to overwhelm white "natives." California had become a "breeding ground" for "treacherous Japs," they said. So Secretary of War Henry Stimson, Secretary of the Navy Frank Knox, and Lt. General John DeWitt, the chief proponent of incarceration, demanded imprisonment for virtually all persons of Japanese ancestry, citizen or no. President Franklin Roosevelt agreed. He signed Executive Order 9066 on 19 February 1942. It was, in the words of the eminent historian Roger Daniels, "a day that *should* live in infamy."[29]

John Rankin's hysterics over amalgamation were echoed throughout the land. "THE ONLY WAY THE JAPS IN THIS COUNTRY COULD BE 'ASSIMILATED,'" screamed the *Denver Post*, "IS THRU [*sic*] INTERMARRIAGE WITH WHITE AMERICANS." "Jap-lovers," it seemed, wanted to "MIX YELLOW AND WHITE BLOOD." This neither the *Post* nor John Rankin could countenance. Indeed, Rankin policed blood stocks with fervor, again linking interracialism to subversion: "One of the most vicious movements that has been instituted by the crack pots, the Communists, and the parlor pinks of this country is trying to browbeat the Red Cross into taking the labels off the blood bank . . . so it will not show whether it is Negro blood or white blood. This is one of the schemes of these fellows to mongrelize the nation." (Rankin later expanded his indictment, railing against either "Jap or Negro blood [being] pumped into the veins of white Americans.") Like Rankin's, the rhetoric of Western nativists emphasized physiological as well as physical, residential segregation: "They are Orientals by blood; and that means they cannot be assimilated. Inter-marriage is out of the question." Linking an effective, partitioned multiculturalism to the supposedly natural human tendencies toward self-interest and economic competitiveness, Western white bigots held that "each race would naturally live by itself, but each would wish to do business with the others. The result would be that we would have voluntary segregation, with Negro districts, Chinese districts, Japanese districts and as many others as we have distinct and unassimilable races. As each would be selfishly interested in keeping the business of the others, each would be selfishly careful to respect the prejudices of the others. Then the race prejudice against which so much is said would actually become the guarantor of racial harmony."[30]

To separate whites and nonwhites, to distance the two, California's Republican Congressman Leland Ford insisted that the War Department have "all Japanese, whether citizen or not . . . placed in inland concentration camps." To prevent "overpopulating," Rankin insisted that the camps be sex-segregated. Moreover, Rankin pressed for another method in his four-pronged approach to racial outcasts. Never "out of the question," deportation begged his consideration. Rankin was for "deporting every Jap who claims, or has claimed, Japanese citizenship, or sympathizes with Japan in this war." A few black leaders saw the parallels. As George Schuyler of the *Pittsburgh Courier* put it, "Once the precedent is established with 70,000 Japanese-American citizens, it will be easy to denationalize millions of Afro-American citizens. . . . We must champion their cause as ours."[31]

Rankin's blanket denunciation of "Japs" seemed to cover Violet Matsuda and her two brothers. Though all three were born in Hawaii, and thus birthright citizens of the United States, they were born before 1925, a time when Japan claimed all children of its citizens, regardless of birthplace, as its citizens too. Given the feelings of Rankin and countless others, given the incarceration, could Violet choose allegiance to America? Could her brother Tokio Yamane? Schooled mostly in Japan, he was viewed with even greater distrust, as a Kibei. Would conflicted or compromised allegiances always be counted as subversion? Could service to the nation redeem the racial outcast? Brother

Dick Yamane had already joined the army and soon would be sent abroad. Would he—would any of the 120,000 mainland Japanese Americans—be able to earn by their deeds the rights of citizenship already promised on paper? Not if John Rankin could help it. The short vain man with the high-pitched, piercing voice—mocked by veterans groups for overstating his own military record—used American war-making and race-baiting as an occasion for rhetorical muscle-flexing. Known for his boisterous debate techniques, which sometimes led to blows, he fought various battles of his own in the halls of Congress, shadowboxing with a host of American enemies.

3 | Concentration and Cooperation

MARY TSUKAMOTO wanted to help. She had a sense of mission in life, driven by a deep religious conviction. Her "dream," she said, "was to serve mankind," to be "useful in a thousand ways." Tsukamoto was a Sunday school teacher at the segregated Methodist Church for Japanese Americans in Florin, California—a recognized leader. Now that two-thirds of the people of Florin were to be evicted from their homes and forcibly moved out of the area, she would have an even more prominent position. As the "hastily appointed" emergency executive secretary of the local chapter of the Japanese American Citizens League (JACL), she and other members "took charge of urgent tasks related to the impending evacuation," as it was called by government officials. "We worked frantically with the U.S. Army, the WCCA [Wartime Civil Control Administration, the WRA's predecessor organization], the Federal Reserve Bank, Farm Security Agency and social welfare workers to coordinate the needs of Florin evacuees."[1]

President Franklin Roosevelt's Executive Order 9066 meant that virtually all Americans and "aliens" of Japanese descent living in California, Oregon, and Washington would be locked up for the foreseeable future. Eviction came to the Sacramento Valley farming communities of Florin and Elk Grove in May, just at harvesttime. Strawberries rotted in the fields, grapevines soon withered, as families hurried either to find guardians for their property or to sell it at a fraction of its value. These distress sales were commonplace, flooding the market with land, with used cars, farm equipment, and household goods, so that supply vastly outweighed demand. Prices plummeted, and unscrupulous buyers—capitalizing upon their neighbors' hardship—snatched it all up for a song. Did Mary Tsukamoto and her family "ever consider not obeying" the expulsion orders? "Never. We never questioned it at all. It was our duty."[2]

So on 29 May 1942, she and her husband, Al, their five-year-old daughter, Marielle, Al's sister Nami, and his parents left their fields to the care of their friend Bob Fletcher and reported to the railway station. They were allowed to bring only what they could carry, and "on each bag was the military number given to the Tsukamoto family—#22076." "Everyone was dressed in their Sunday best, men in suits and women in dresses and hats. . . . Children talked excitedly. Most had never been on a train before." But then, suddenly, Mary Tsukamoto "noticed the guns! The soldiers were carrying rifles with bayonets as if we were to be shot down if we tried to escape." Worst of all, as Tsukamoto struggled to assist in this massive removal, she discovered a stunning bit of bureaucratic incompetence. Japanese Americans on the West Coast were to be immediately shipped off to sixteen holding pens, so-called "assembly centers," several thousand per camp. But somehow, the "2500 men, women and children in the Florin–Elk Grove area designated for evacuation" were to be split up over four camps in California: Manzanar, Tule Lake, Walerga, and Fresno. Not only would the two sister communities be destroyed, but the bonds of friendship and neighborliness that held each of those communities together would be severed. Even extended families were separated. Yet according to Mary Tsukamoto, "there was no way to avoid splitting up families."[3]

In addition to her own kin, Tsukamoto has declared that "all Japanese American families" cooperated in the expulsion. "Amazingly, we lifted no voices in protest. As good citizens, we felt it was our duty to cooperate in this hour of need. Our President himself had signed the order; we had no choice other than to obey. None of us considered doing anything less." But Tsukamoto spoke of a consensus that, in fact, did not exist. Many were outspoken in their criticism of the government policy. They questioned the JACL's collusion in the eviction and removal process. And in Florin, community members wondered why the families of local leaders somehow were not broken up and sent to different camps. "As JACL Executive Secretary, I unexpectedly found myself the victim of vicious accusations," Tsukamoto stated. "I was accused of plotting to take all my relatives with me to Fresno." Tsukamoto felt that she was unfairly "singled out as a target of people's frustrations." "Mary took care of her family," they said. The Tsukamotos, as well as her own family of origin, the Dakuzakus, indeed "were not separated." With all the "anger and bitterness" in the air, Tsukamoto was falsely blamed, she says, of "wrong-doing."[4]

Though before the expulsion Mary Tsukamoto had endured numerous experiences of bias based on race and gender, she sometimes chose to downplay their effects on her. Her parents, Taro and Kame Dakuzaku, had come to America from Okinawa, one of the Ryukyu Islands. This Japanese territorial dependency was geographically situated well south of Tokyo and the main islands and—not unlike Hawaii's relationship to the United States—it was often politically relegated to the margins of national life. Many Japanese regarded Okinawans as racially different—that is, racially inferior. When writing about her family background, Mary Tsukamoto did not elaborate these racial hierarchies. She did, however, make clear the prized position of males within her family and community. Her immigrant parents had six children: all girls. That was not sufficient. Soon a seventh child was born and was declared special. "Finally I have a son," said Mary's mother. "At last I feel like a woman."[5]

Still, white locals considered her, considered them all, somehow less than, somehow sinister. In the early 1920s, Mary had her first memorable brush with American racism. Just one month before entering first grade, she was at home, outside with her father, when a car full of white boys passed "yelling ugly insults": "God damn you Japs." Mary saw her father's rage and felt her own budding anxieties. "Stark, cold fright enveloped me and froze my heart," she remembers. "Such fear would live with me forever." Around the same time, Issei writer Yuko Fujikawa, in a chilling tanka poem, described her similar encounter with racism, in a fleeting but psychologically enduring instance of transportation: "'JAP LADY . . .' / That whisper stopped me. / I became sad suddenly / At the very moment in the station." Florin school itself taught early hard lessons in bigotry, as the grammar school was formally segregated. "A new brick building was built at the west end of town [and] all the white children were paraded out of Florin School," as Tsukamoto recounts. "They carried American flags and marched down the muddy road" to superior facilities. The Japanese American children stayed behind at the renamed East School. "Our school was a segregated school, but the teachers were Caucasian." Two decades after, married with a child of their own, Mary and Al Tsukamoto and the local JACL would help the U.S. government organize the wholesale segregation of the town's populace.[6]

Historians from Roger Daniels to Michi Nishiura Weglyn have demonstrated incarceration's dire consequences. The upheaval caused catastrophic economic losses on the West Coast, destroying the financial stability of the vast majority of individuals and families affected. It wrecked many social and political institutions and permanently disrupted local communities. As the large-scale eviction was predicated upon racist hysteria, as well as economic exploitation, it fueled racist discourse, exposing Japanese Americans to harassment, danger, and violence. Perpetuating a centuries-long American tradition of discrimination and forced removal, it threw into stark relief the similarities to many totalitarian methods abroad—similarities spelled out by at least one U.S. legal consultant, who resigned rather than "collaborate in the defence of" government policies. For many Japanese Americans, incarceration caused deep psychological trauma, shame, anxiety, and hardship. Perhaps most importantly, imprisonment foreshortened or foreclosed the most basic human freedoms: speech, association, choice, mobility, and self-determination.[7]

During the war years, Japanese Americans made choices, but not in a world of their choosing. Within a tight set of limits to action, fissures erupted, alternative visions were offered, as people of a certain shared heritage developed different understandings of cooperation and Americanism. Some chose to join in, assisting officials in the pressing details of expulsion and eventually in the everyday necessities and routine tasks at the detention centers and the concentration camps. Others were less convinced of the imperative to aid their captors. Their dissatisfaction resulted in differentiation: authorities branded them as troublemakers. In fact, many who questioned the incarceration helped develop other forms of cooperation and collectivism within the camps. Hardly looking for trouble, they often simply turned their attention away from administrators and toward their own community members. They innovated new means of self-sufficiency and organization. Suspicion fell on them as un-American. But suspicion also fell on so-called collaborators such as Mary Tsukamoto, whom some referred to, even more derisively, as *inu*, or dogs. Across the political spectrum, all had difficult choices to make—to pursue the best of the limited options available, to build alliances. As artist Jenny Holzer has written, in one of her enigmatic Truisms, "You can watch people align themselves when trouble is in the air. Some prefer to be close to those at the top and others want to be close to those at the bottom. It's a question of who frightens them more and whom they want to be like."[8]

COLLECTIVE LIVING

Imagine you could create a small town from scratch. Imagine you needed to design, build, and then live in the town with 8,500 other people—people you knew, knew of, or had some prior connection to, people you mostly trusted. It would require lots of effort and tons of teamwork. Though some duties would be left to individual initiative, most would require collective involvement and planning. So let's imagine that *you* refers not to the second-person singular you, you-an-individual, but to the second-person plural you, you-the-group, everybody. Of course, you have to do it with finite resources; but you have infinite imagination. You have three kinds of resources at your disposal. You have labor, your own hands, backs, and minds to put to the task. You have some capital, which you could think of as previous work, stored-up labor, savings: surplus that has been set aside for later use. And you have some natural resources. Probably most important are clean air and water and good productive land. Imagine you have ten thousand acres of fertile ground, rich alluvial soils built up over millennia of river flooding. The air is fresh; the climate pretty good; there's water everywhere. Imagine that, although this town is in fact a prison, you're determined to make the most of it. You're determined that, to the extent possible, you'll make it your own.

People have done it before, so you have a variety of models to follow in building your town. In structuring the lives of the inhabitants, you have guiding principles, ideals, seemingly age-old but in fact of fairly recent historical vintage. They tend to come in a triad, a three-part chord. Call them life, liberty, and the pursuit of happiness. Or maybe *egalité*, *liberté*, and *fraternité*. The path, freedom, perfect peace. First, there is a shared sense that life is to be valued, the path deemed worthwhile. Second, there must be freedoms, particularly the freedom to choose your destiny, to take part and have a say. Finally, a higher-order need, there must be something more. So in addition to the material necessities and the means to choose among alternatives, there must be meaningfulness. As towns, the concentration camps at Jerome and Rohwer were largely successful in generating for their residents the material foundations of day-to-day life. Basic human needs were met, thanks to some combination of energies expended by Japanese American inmates and their European American keepers. As places of liberty and freedom, the camps were unmitigated failures, owing to the obstinacy of authorities and the unevenness with which they dispensed privileges. The camps originated in inequality, were conceived through domination, and maintained by force. To the extent that these towns nonetheless were homes, places of joy as well as sorrow, of harmony as well as harm, then Jerome and Rohwer were testaments to Japanese American strength and courage and to the human capacity to survive and thrive.

Of the basics—food, clothing, and shelter—housing in particular was centrally coordinated. It was designed to the specifications of federal bureaucrats and built, at least in the initial stages, by government contractors. Rife Construction Company of Dallas won the contract to build the Jerome camp, also known by the name of the local post office, Denson, after a pioneering preacher in the region. Rohwer camp construction was managed by Linebarger-Senne Company of Little Rock. Both firms relied on local workers, black and white, to plot the land and put up the principal buildings. Soon an advance contingent of Japanese American inmates joined them from the detention centers of California, including Violet Matsuda's husband, Shigeru, her brother Tokio Yamane, and Mary Tsukamoto's baby brother George, still a high schooler. As concentration camps, these facilities mirrored the designs of other large-scale prison facilities, training compounds, and detention centers. As towns, they can be contrasted with previous American designs for good living.[9]

Envisioning the biological family as the essential social unit and self-sufficient farming as the fundamental form of human labor, the Homestead Act of 1862 assigned tracts of 160 acres to yeoman farm families in the West, following Jeffersonian models. Within four years, the Freedman's Bureau had seemingly slashed that number by three-quarters, in the mythic promise to allot to newly emancipated black families 40 acres, plus a mule—never fully realized. Still, for a family of five or an extended family of eight, that would amount to five to eight acres of cropland for the feeding of each person. As years passed, and mechanized agriculture generated efficiencies in farm production, as with the introduction of the tractor, fewer fields were needed to feed more mouths. At Jerome and Rohwer each, there were 10,000 total acres to sustain 8,500 people, or just over an acre per person. But even more efficiencies would be gained through community organization. Individual families scattered across 40- to 160-acre tracts made transportation expensive, as well as the new utilities. As we've seen, members of Congress such as John Rankin campaigned feverishly for the Rural Electrification Administration and projects such as the Tennessee-Tombigbee Waterway, so that isolated farms could have all the modern conveniences and be connected to national and international markets. But these were costly undertakings. Some community planners envisioned farm and factory towns that could benefit from collectivization and centralization. In this sense, the WRA camps resembled many utopian schemes for modern, cost-effective, community organization.[10]

The WRA camps capitalized upon another Jeffersonian ideal, the grid. Instead of scattering families across a 10,000-acre site, to be connected by hundreds of miles of country roads meandering around swamps, over hills, and across other natural barriers, planners set aside a tight, flat 500 acres—roughly a square mile—for dense, orderly dwellings, platted on a checkerboard of streets and cross streets at ninety-degree angles. This also, obviously, made for a compact, fenced perimeter. So at Rohwer, for example, there were eleven gravel streets running north-south, numbered from First Street to Eleventh Street, and eleven cross streets running east-west and lettered from A Street to K Street. Thirty-six blocks contained Japanese American dwellings, and larger parcels of land, not subdivided, were set aside for schools, the hospital, administration offices, and other buildings. Though there were about twenty miles of streets, they were all within a one-square-mile area and thus much more easily maintained. The principal workplace—for many, the fields and woods—would lie just outside this small-town residential and service area, just beyond the barbed wire. The land would be farmed not by individual families in competition with each other, but as a collective serving the needs of the entire community.[11]

For those who worked within the town, walks of over a mile would be rare—unless they were unfortunate enough to reside at one corner of the compound and work at the other. As Haruko Hurt remembers of the winter, "I had not experienced such a cold climate. . . . We lived on the one end of the camp. My sister and I got a job as a hospital worker, and the hospital happened to be on the other end. So we had to walk. Of course, there was no transportation. We just walked everywhere. It was so bitterly cold. I remember that so well because our knees ached from the cold to walk to our jobs." Indeed, along with most administrative buildings, hospitals were typically located near the entrances of the ten concentration camps, sited for the convenience of the white staff, not Japanese American patients. A more central location would have meant that no one with a sick child on a wintry or wet night would have had to walk very far.[12]

There were other efficiencies to be gained in the ordering of the prison camp/settlement. As these decisions too were taken by government officials with little regard for the occupants, they were often unpopular. Conceived as a grid within the grid, the water and sewerage lines—sourced by two deep wells—were run to the center point only of each residential block. So while there were twelve residential buildings within each six-acre block—two orderly rows of six buildings—water was piped only to two other adjacent buildings between those two rows: the dining hall and washhouse. Meals would be taken collectively, and toilet, shower, and wash facilities would be centralized.

3. Nurse trainees at the Rohwer concentration camp, September 1944. 97.292.10C, MC, JANM.

Whereas residential buildings were not supplied with running water, each of the apartments within each residential building was provided with electricity—a single bulb strung from the center of the ceiling and, connected to it, a single wall socket. Though spartan, these living arrangements for Japanese Americans at Jerome and Rohwer, as with previous utopian designs for collective living, utilized government resources and planning to assure that everyone had roughly equivalent space, communally secured and provided, and allotted only according to household size, not status. This leveling of class hierarchies was liberating for some, distressing for others. Of course, new hierarchies emerged, since white authorities who controlled decision-making processes often played favorites, granting special privileges to Christians and English speakers. Still, as towns, Jerome and Rohwer began to evidence the attributes of vanguard socialist economies: with free education for all, free meals for all, free equivalent housing for all, free health care for all, free assisted living for the elderly, and water, electricity, roads, and public safety all collectively provided. Planners adopted another utopian ideal—municipal heat—but in its most rudimentary form. Though everyone agreed that each residence should have free heating, so that the poor wouldn't freeze in the winter, local administrators chose not the purchase of coal but the chopping of firewood—a decision that would have catastrophic results, as we will see in chapter 7.[13]

Though often denied input into community decision-making, and despite the traumas of eviction and concentration, Japanese Americans at the two Arkansas camps built new lives and living environments with extraordinary resilience. Within moments of their arrival in the fall of 1942, they set about transforming their tar-paper and plywood barracks apartments. All furniture, except for beds, they constructed themselves from scrap lumber, branches, and found objects. Many added overhangs, stoops, and small porches onto their front doors, personalizing their otherwise identical units; they planted gardens out front. According to Mary Tsukamoto, "we had quite attractive apartments in our tiny family spaces." Eventually, most men and women held jobs within the camps, working on a relatively flat, meager pay scale, about one-quarter of white women's wages in the South. "Unskilled" work such as cleaning, vegetable farming, and stock raising yielded $12 per month; clerical jobs in administrative offices and in the cooperative stores were paid $16; and at the top, professionals such as physicians, dentists, and legal aides received $19. Japanese Americans served alongside European Americans as teachers and postal clerks and retained all but the uppermost positions on the police and firefighting forces, at the newspaper and in the mess halls. Residents represented considerable diversity: Nisei and Issei, birthright citizens (almost 70 percent) and immigrants forbidden citizenship, English and Japanese speakers, entrepreneurs and farmers, urbanites and rural folk, Christians and (in greater numbers) Buddhists, and at Jerome, Hawaiians as well as Californians. Despite these differences, the camps became spaces of unique cultural solidarity. Though some older Issei such as Masako Nakayama, incarcerated at Rohwer, initially felt at a loss, she quickly adjusted herself to the life there. She described the settlement as one big family—if not happy, then at least at ease with one another. Whereas a very small group of administrators was firmly in control, Japanese Americans created a world of ethnic cohesion and mutual aid previously unparalleled, except perhaps in Los Angeles' Little Tokyo. Though surrounded by barbed wire, watchtowers, and armed guards, each camp began to take on the activities of a thriving small town.[14]

COOPERATIVE ENTERPRISES

Since no family farm—or community of 8,500—could ever be fully self-sufficient, some specialized products and services have to be acquired from elsewhere. How to acquire them becomes a linchpin of economic organization. Rather than inmates entering the wider marketplace individually, with their limited resources and limited mobility, New Deal officials decided early in the incarceration to promote consumer cooperatives as the most efficient means for fulfilling customer needs. Japanese American organizers seized the opportunity. Enormously successful undertakings, the cooperative stores not only allowed a unified, collective engagement with the world of production outside the camps. They also brought Japanese Americans together in common cause as consumers with shared needs and as workers and trainees in new vocations. Further, because there was to "be no private business," the cooperative stores and the cooperative movement of which it was a part allowed a critique, in theory and in practice, of profit-oriented American capitalism, the crass acquisitiveness and exploitation of hardship that had characterized expulsion. They demonstrated alternative ways of ordering economic life.[15]

Jerome Cooperative Enterprises began as a canteen and a mail-order department. From large outside corporations such as Sears, Roebuck and Montgomery Ward, Japanese American shoppers ordered those products unavailable within the camps, necessities not provided by the government. Whereas in the nineteenth century, a woman on a self-sufficient farm might be expected to spin yarn, weave cloth, and make clothing for the family, in the 1940s, the top mail-order requests from Jerome were for "ready-made" outerwear, underwear, and rainwear, comprising 32 percent of total sales; shoes made up an additional 10 percent. Sewing and dressmaking nonetheless remained popular, and orders for "yardage," fabric to be used in homemade clothes, accounted for 15 percent of sales. Other best-sellers were clearly linked to the shortcomings in camp construction. With no indoor plumbing in apartments, many chose to order buckets and chamber pots (5 percent), as opposed to making cold, late-night journeys to the communal toilets. To spruce up their homes, they ordered carpenter's tools (5 percent) and material for curtains (5 percent). At the Jerome dry goods store, "one of the busiest places in the center," winter sales featured wool blankets, sweaters, jackets, overcoats, and diapers. Clerks helped their mostly female customers also pick out infants' apparel and accessories as well as men's work and dress handkerchiefs.[16]

As the cooperative grew and new facilities were opened, sales at two general merchandise stores tended to reflect a desire for so-called luxuries, those items not essential to health and welfare—indeed, often counter to them—but a staple of life in industrialized nations during the mid-twentieth century. Two items long associated with imperial expansion, sugar and tobacco, were in high demand. Soft drinks and candy were the number-one and number-three best-sellers, respectively; cigarettes and other tobacco products number

4. Clerks Hannah Takeoka, *left*, and Namie Hamada assist customers at the fabric counter of the Jerome Cooperative dry goods store, Block 35, November 1943. Charles Lynn, photographer. NWDNS-210-G-B985, WRAR, SPB, NA.

five. Over-the-counter medications (#15) vied with cosmetics (#8), and soon a barbershop was opened, as well as a beauty salon, where manager Marie Uyama oversaw the work of five members of staff: Miyoko Fujisawa, Alice Kono, Virginia Nakaguchi, Kiyo Ohashi, and Toki Sakai. Potato chips were the number-two sales item at the stores, and toys likewise were in demand, such that Washington officials convinced operators in Arkansas to drop the minimum age for membership in the cooperative from eighteen to sixteen.[17]

With the WRA's blessing, consumer cooperatives in the concentration camps were run by Japanese Americans for Japanese Americans. Though initially funded by a start-up loan of $150 from a nearby bank, the Jerome Cooperative generated most of its capital from membership shares, and the debt was quickly paid off. An individual share sold for $5—raised by Washington from the $1 first proposed—and entitled the member to one vote. Unlike shares of stock in a corporation, however, additional shares in the cooperative did not give the shareholder additional votes, so power did not accrue to the wealthy.

In a capitalist economy, stockholders need not have any interest, other than financial, in the workings of a corporation. Their motivation was to garner profits, supporting policies to maximize income and minimize expenses in the short term. Shareholders in a cooperative were truly members and thus had different purposes. They purchased the goods on offer by the stores, getting to know the workers and supervisors there, developing a sensitivity to their welfare over the long term. They consumed the goods and thus were concerned foremost with quality and sourcing. The stores were not-for-profit entities. Any excess of income over expenditures was returned to members not as dividends but as a refund on sales. The more you bought, the larger your patronage refund—an additional incentive to get involved. As one official put it, "Every bit of money in the store[s would] accrue to the residents." Sales at each Arkansas camp surpassed $50,000 per month by the spring of 1943. At Rohwer the excess of revenue over expenses equaled 17.5 percent of gross sales, signaling cost-effective, well-managed operations, as at Jerome. Co-op membership at the ten concentration camps ranged from a low of one-third of the populace—itself impressive given the large numbers of children and youth ineligible—to a near-universal uptake of all eligible residents at Manzanar.[18]

Importantly, cooperative policy put collective good above individual gain. When wartime shortages resulted in a limited supply of soap and laundry detergent at Jerome, for example, store operators did not choose the capitalist answer. Laws of supply and demand dictated that prices would be jacked up, only the well-to-do would be able to buy, and the poor would have to do without. Instead, cooperative staff coached patrons in more frugal use of their soap, and they handed out coupons to insure that all patrons received at least some soap, in equal measure, until the camp's own soap factory was up and running. This form of small-scale, localized rationing mirrored the national rationing used to delimit wartime American consumption and to facilitate postwar European socialized medicine. Whereas the United States would opt for privatized health care, such that the wealthy would receive treatment and the uninsured poor would sometimes die on sidewalks outside emergency rooms, some Allied nations such as the United Kingdom chose to treat all patients with equal regard. If limitations arose, rationing would be based upon medical need, not ability to pay: cases would be prioritized on waiting lists such that less urgent treatments would be postponed. With careful assessment of customer needs and judicious reinvestment of net income—all audited by Washington—Jerome Cooperative Enterprises grew further, with sites across nine blocks, including a dry cleaning and laundry service, optical department, two shoe repair shops, newspaper and magazine subscription service, telegram facilities, photo processing, radio and electronics repair shop, carpentry service, and an almost nightly Hollywood movie screening. Facilitating wholesale purchases with quantity discounts from trustworthy, ethical suppliers, representatives from the concentration camps joined together to establish a central buying agency for all ten communities. Thereby, they achieved further efficiencies still.[19]

Especially as compared to the local WRA work-placement offices, Jerome and Rohwer cooperatives showed an extraordinary appreciation of the needs of their employees, who likewise were paid on the WRA scale. The co-ops highlighted the value of a safe, clean workplace, as well as training and continuing professional development, offering regular classes and opportunities for advancement. Though the block delegate congress and the board of directors were overwhelmingly male, employees were almost equally male and female, enabling new opportunities for women to earn wages in clerical, specialist, and supervisory positions, as well as to direct consumption for themselves and their households. With Ryuichi Murakami as general manager and Kay Kuwada as membership director, Jerome co-op policy emphasized preparation for employment in the world outside, designed to send laborers to ethical workplaces and, especially, other U.S. co-ops, which were characterized as "racially neutral." As children also patronized the stores, training began even with fourth graders, who launched a greeting-card sales program around Valentine's Day. As compared to America's Junior Achievement programs, which rewarded individual and small group profit-seeking, co-op initiatives for children promoted collective benefit and girls' equal participation.[20]

Broader educational efforts accompanied the setup of cooperative stores. Though New Deal advocates in the WRA's Washington headquarters tended to overlook Arkansas on their forays to the camps, the New York headquarters of the Cooperative League of the United States remained a constant source of support and information. Otherwise left to their own devices, the Jerome and Rohwer cooperatives spearheaded their own campaigns. At the forefront in Jerome were experienced labor and co-op organizer Mauritz Erkkila, a Minnesotan of Scandinavian descent, and inmate Kiyoshi Hamanaka, an "avid student of the cooperative system," formerly enrolled at Fresno State College. In addition to in-service training courses for employees, Hamanaka offered campwide classes in cooperative principles and the history of the cooperative movement. Along with their own publication *Co-op News*, Jerome Cooperative Enterprises received extensive coverage of their activities in the camp newspaper, and they further were given their own regular column, "Co-op Info." Here, the education campaign generated the most visibility.[21]

Hamanaka was unflinching. "The prevalent economic system of competition and profit," he wrote in the "Co-op Info" column of 13 August 1943, "has permeated [all] aspects of life. Even in these critical times, big business exacts enormous profits at the expense of unorganized and misinformed consumers." On the issue of grade labeling—grading eggs, for example, as A, AA, or AAA—he pointed up the tendency of corporations facing wartime price ceilings to "reduce quality" and cover it up. "The killing of grade labelling is an example of consumer exploitation under the guise of 'preventing fascistic standardization.'" As a complement to consumer cooperatives, Hamanaka promoted the credit-union model as "a cooperative saving and lending association organized and controlled democratically for the benefit of its members." The co-op office offered free pamphlets and furthermore reprinted their contents in the "Co-op Info" column. Resonating with many local concerns, national officer Harold V. Knight decried the "grosser vices of commercialized sport and amusement, the prostitution of press and radio for gain, . . . and the use of the church by the 'haves' to quiet the 'have nots.'" "So habituated are we to an acquisitively-minded economy," he concluded, "that we can hardly recognize how deeply it affects our thinking and acting."[22]

In the wake of the Great Depression and during wartime and postwar economic retrenchments, the larger cooperative movement reached its zenith, with organizations in over forty nations. Membership in the United States exceeded 12 million as of 1941, across commodity co-ops, such as consumer stores, petroleum co-ops, and farm suppliers; service co-ops, including medical, funeral, housing, and campus co-ops; and specialized consumer co-ops, such as rural electrification, telephone, insurance, and credit unions. An International Cooperative Alliance was consummated, and in New York a worldwide training organization, the International Cooperative Institute, was established in 1943 in anticipation of war's end. The movement's history—like all histories—was contested, but English-language publications usually pointed to the early nineteenth-century teachings of Welsh-born socialist Robert Owen and, especially, the founding of the Pioneer Society of Rochdale, England, in 1844, as the pivotal moments in the modern cooperative movement. These twenty-eight weavers who organized "the first permanently successful consumers' cooperative"—and their iconic shop on Toad Lane—were featured in numerous publications and films from the period, and Japanese American proponents took up the narrative as well. Indeed, the Jerome Cooperative Enterprises camp closing wrap-up publication explicitly celebrated a centennial of cooperation, from 1844 to 1944. There were specifically southern precursors too, though apparently unacknowledged in Arkansas, from utopian communities to utilitarian farmers' cooperatives.[23]

Kiyoshi Hamanaka was keen to demonstrate other antecedents as well. Of "purely Japanese origin," the Hotokusha was "the first Japanese credit society, if I may so term it." Established in 1843 by the disciples of philosopher Ninomiya Sontoku, it predated Rochdale, as well as the first German credit societies organized by Hermann Schulze-Delitzsch and Friedrich Wilhelm Raiffeisen, from the 1850s and 1860s. Unlike Raiffeisen, "who sought the principle of cooperation in the teachings of Christ," Sontoku's was a humanistic approach, rooted in work with the rural poor. With so many competing, sometimes nationalistic visions of cooperative history in circulation, *Co-op News* editors felt it necessary to address a key concern among inmates and administrators at Jerome, such that a front-page Q&A column in the 25 January 1944 edition directly queried, "Is the Co-operative an American Idea?" The reassuring reply insisted it's "as American as the Constitution. One person, one vote, regardless of the number of shares he holds, insures democratic operation of a consumer's cooperative. The last to join has just as much to say about the operation of the organization as the charter member." These two tenets would aid in the establishment of "economic democracy."[24]

However, in these two respects particularly, cooperatives appeared decidedly un-American. In the U.S. economic order, a greater share meant a greater say, in economic life especially. In political realms, as in labor relations, newcomers often were marginalized, if not completely disenfranchised, as Japanese Americans knew all too well. Indeed, unsurprisingly, Kiyoshi Hamanaka came under intense suspicion for his activities. A Kibei, he had twelve books from his personal Japanese-language library confiscated. A conscientious objector to war and a member of the American Civil Liberties Union, he was subjected to farcical WRA investigations into his background. His employers at Jerome wrote on his behalf, attesting to his loyalty and good citizenship. His political activism at Fresno State they held up not as evidence that he was a rabblerouser, but rather as proof that he was a "complete democrat and thoroughly Americanized." Still, Washington probed further. Eventually, Hamanaka was cleared to leave the Jerome camp, to resettle in Chicago. But Dillon Myer himself, the director of the WRA, wrote to insist that any further relocation on his part be reported immediately to Washington. In other words, Hamanaka's whereabouts would be monitored indefinitely. Hamanaka's experience, which soon would mirror that of so many others in the coming Cold War, demonstrated that in America, cooperation and, especially, socialism were highly suspect and under surveillance.[25]

COMPETITIVE SPORTS

The first big football game at Jerome was an unusual affair, about which language failed. In some respects, it seemed a classic American contest. Held on Thanksgiving Day, traditionally reserved for the fiercest rivalries, it attracted a massive crowd. One of every four residents attended. Like most American sports events of the day, the game was racially segregated—in this case, all Japanese American participants. A white observer served as referee, the WRA's William Love, placement officer at Jerome. But there were bizarre, almost inconceivable irregularities. Only one coach took to the field, Dick Kunishima, a former Whittier College standout. And because he "freely substituted players from one team to the other, no accurate score of the game could be kept." In other words, there could be no declared winners—nor losers. Indeed, the camp newspaper reporter struggled to name the two teams—were there opposing teams?—and had to settle on "the two elevens." In the end, only the three touchdowns could be described: Tak Abe's pass to Mas Nishibayashi, followed by Teizo Koda's rush for the extra point; Sus Ishikawa's pass to Jim Okura, plus Yosh Tsukamoto's drop-kick conversion; and Ishikawa's pass to Nishibayashi in the end zone, on the last play of the game. The confusing page-three sports headline read: "THREE GOALS FEATURE GRID TILT." Thus was reasserted individual point-scoring prowess in the face of an innovative, noncompetitive, community spectacle.[26]

Soon enough, however, organized competitive team sports of the conventional variety eclipsed all other forms of athletics at the camp, and American games overshadowed the matches and martial arts of Japan. As is common, teams took on the trappings of warfare, adopting place-names and mascots, colors and boosters, like soldiers trooping off to the battlefields. Budding sports journalists wrote of victories and defeats, groups trounced and beaten. "A result of racial discrimination," as scholar Rebecca Chiyoko King notes, Japanese American sports leagues before, during, and after incarceration allowed people "to come together, create community cohesion, and learn sportsmanship, which many thought would help Japanese Americans to be accepted as 'true Americans.'" But as we will see, team affiliations and affinities would also evidence the complexity of belonging in a World War II–era concentration camp. After repeated dislocations, loyalties to one particular place would not suffice. Japanese American sports in Arkansas proved symbolic not so much of fixed, severed, or divided loyalties but more of dual, multiple, even conflicted loyalties and affinities—some older, others newer. Also, team sports for Japanese Americans served purposes not envisioned by administrators and, in many cases, at odds with them. Baseball in particular became a weighty endeavor, rich with meaning, laden with controversy, anything but a "great American pastime."[27]

Though sports originating in Asia such as judo, kendo, and sumo were practiced throughout the incarceration years, administrators tended to treat them at best with fascination, at worst with suspicion—techniques of combat that could aid an insurrection. Overriding all was an ignorance of the philosophy, regulation, and practice of Japanese martial arts. When Senate investigator George Malone asked Jerome official Runo Arne if his Japanese American charges were "athletically inclined," the exchange served more to cloud than clarify:

ARNE: They have quite a bit of wrestling called judo.
MALONE: What does judo mean? What do they do?
ARNE: Wrestle. It is a very skillful performance.
MALONE: Is it rough?
ARNE: No. They throw each other some distance however. They wear white kimonos. It seems they take hold of the kimono rather than the flesh.
MALONE: Do they practice jujitsu?
ARNE: As far as we know, they do not. There is no organization sponsoring it.

At Camp Shelby, 442nd Private James Kamo organized a well-advertised judo exhibition, which he described as a "streamlined version of jiu-jitsu." Whereas jujitsu uses an opponent's strength and weight as leverage against him, to defeat him, judo is a mode of unarmed defense first used by Chinese monks, as Kamo explained. The House Un-American Activities Committee, under Martin Dies, was less inclined to accept such explanations, and unwarranted suspicions continued to swirl.[28]

Under Coach Masayoshi Fukute and his group of *yudanshas*, judo artists drew as many as two thousand spectators to camp tournaments at Jerome. Kendo matches between teams of five demonstrated the importance less of triumph in the one-to-one engagements than of the graceful, gentlemanly rapport of the two groups together, as a whole, in sometimes daylong performances. But in October 1943, Fukute and all other judo and kendo instructors were informed that, under orders from Washington, community activities divisions could no longer pay them WRA wages, after a damning HUAC report. Anyway, these sports already had been overtaken by baseball by spring 1943. As with American competitions generally, baseball allowed white administrators to get involved not only as spectators and umpires but as players and trainers. Also, many Nisei had grown up playing baseball.[29]

Baseball had been played in Japan since the nineteenth century, and the professional leagues that developed from 1935 amounted to "American baseball with Japanese characteristics, a group sport stressing harmony and discipline, with little room for individualism." Japanese Americans organized seventy-five softball and baseball teams at Jerome, requiring several leagues and four commissioners. Women and girls played softball; there were "Old Men's" teams. But young men's baseball dominated. "Two thousand sports fans jammed the Block 21 athletic field" on Sunday 9 May 1943 "to witness the official opening" of the season, as the camp paper reported. "Florin defeated Hanford, 3–1, in the inaugural contest." Likewise represented with top-rank, A-league teams were Bowles, Elk Grove, Fowler, Long Beach, Madera, and Hawaii. Teams were formed not only around allegiances to California hometowns, however, or the colonized Hawaiian Islands. At Rohwer football squads made up of former Santa Anita and Stockton detention center inmates competed under those names. (Jerome inmates came mostly from the Fresno and Santa Anita "assembly" centers.) At Jerome girls' softball teams often coalesced around the ubiquitous clubs, some of which literalized their dual loyalties, their bi-state attachments, as with the Cal-Arkettes. But many softball and baseball teams in the relegation or farm leagues either poked fun of their new surroundings, such as the Chiggers, or in straightforward fashion adopted the monikers of their latest homes and were known simply by their block numbers. Though alternative events surfaced—notably, the Buddhists' Track and Field Day at Rohwer—localized team sports reigned.[30]

In a carnival tradition, designed to temporarily ameliorate if not permanently upend tense social hierarchies, friendly games were organized across racial lines and other boundaries. In February 1943, high school girls at Jerome were outscored by their teachers, the "marms," in an exhibition basketball challenge. A year later at Rohwer, a gutsy group of softball all-stars took on the Military Police detachment ordinarily charged with guarding them at gunpoint. But there was a more phenomenal contest still: "Thousands of spectators cheering madly in the grandstand; rival bands playing to drown out each other; yell leaders exhorting their respective cheering sections to greater volumes; pulchritudinous beauties waving colorful pom-poms in front of the stands; banners waving, confetti flying, and megaphones tossed in the air." The 28 June 1943 "softball classic" did "not attract all of the foregoing" spectacle, as the organizers readily conceded. But it drew great interest and gave rise to innumerable camp conversations. After all, one of the teams, the staff of the camp newspaper, the *Denson Tribune*, was well placed to promote it—in its own pages.[31]

In a pregame spoof issue called the *Trifler*, editors, writers, and production crew launched a send-up of themselves and their "superiors" with stories about the upcoming match between "two of the Center's most highly ballyhooed outfits": the Tribune Depressers and the Personnel Bi-Tri-Focals. While the very team names referenced age and status differentials—and perhaps, with sly wit, administrative shortsightedness—Eddie Kurushima's hand-drawn caricatures gave both sides an equally good ribbing. Sweaty editor Paul Yokota was depicted "at the hot corner," slated to play third base. "Near Private" Dick Itanaga, an army inductee atop the mound, would "practice grenade pitching for the combat team." Harry Kuwada would be, in a timeless baseball joke, "left out." Of the opponents, Fire Chief Bill Brown, carrying a hose, was predicted to "put out the Tribune." "Irish Thrush" John McCormick, the employment officer known for his renditions of "Danny Boy," was pegged to "sing the press boys into submission." In a short article, the Depressers charged the Bi-Tri-Focals with spying on their training camp, by sending two interlopers: "a tall, lanky man in Hanes underwear," apparently a reference to registrar Bob "Glamour Legs" Allison, along with a "well-fed gent," likely camp director Paul Taylor's right-hand man, W. O. "Doc" Melton. Though filled with bad puns, corny turns-of-phrase, and harmless parody, such lampoons should not be read only as good clean fun. At a minimum, they functioned as a safety valve, a letting off of steam. A form of comic relief, they may have acted as an assertion of ill will that could not otherwise be articulated to higher-ups in everyday life. They may have masked harder truths still.[32]

A comparable, perhaps related, mock edition of the camp newspaper—filed in the same archival folder—suggests greater animosities. A scandal sheet of serious intent, the *Technique EXTRA* briefly referenced an upcoming tournament of some kind, but its portrayals of key camp administrators were so vitriolic and derogatory as to shift the focus of attention away from sports entirely. Inside jokes were so obscure as to make them almost indecipherable, to render interpretation very difficult indeed, especially sixty years on. Yet that may well have been the point. Perhaps circulating among a select, secretive few, whose words and actions might trigger harsh retribution, the mimeographed paper suggested that one former National Park Service official from the Ozarks was a dirty dope-smoker who should be dealt with by Hitler. Another midlevel administrator was depicted as an agitating arsonist, a "traitor" who offered bribes; yet another, a "snake-in-the-grass" propagandist who likewise attempted "two-bit" bribes. What is clear is that the anonymous author or authors envisioned Jerome personnel as falling into distinct, opposing camps or cliques. The "good people of the 'rebel' clique" included widely loved educators such as School Superintendent Amon G. Thompson and outspoken political liberals such as Co-op Superintendent Mauritz Erkkila. While two white ball-field buddies "were still very non-committal," with the paper warning, "there is no such thing as 'neutral' in time of war," the enemy camp clearly revolved around the "Taylor-Lynn clique." Jerome director Paul Taylor was embroiled at that very moment, November 1943, in the severest controversy of his administration, as we see in chapter 7. And, as detailed later in this chapter, the reports officer, former *Arkansas Gazette* journalist Charles Lynn—supervisor of the *Tribune* staff—was engaged in both covert and overt censorship of camp news. If typed up in the *Tribune* office, located in Administration Building No. 4, and reproduced on its mimeograph machine, the *Technique EXTRA* further evidenced its makers' daring and determination. Hardly a joke, the scandal sheet, no matter how occluded, suggested deep divisions and strife between some inmates and their keepers.[33]

And yet everyday life and leisure continued apace. Intercamp sports became a prominent feature of Japanese American athletics in the South, prompting both home and away games, as well as friends' and family reunions. Whether for "lasses' speedball," volleyball, or basketball, or boys' basketball, baseball, or football, the Denson High School gold-and-black regularly traveled up the road to take on the Rohwer red-and-black, or they played host to them back at Jerome. Also, since many Nisei had volunteered for the army before the war, high schoolers and young men from each concentration camp went up against the Japanese American team from the Camp Robinson military post, near Little Rock. Once the segregated regiment of Nisei soldiers was created, with thousands enlisting, Rohwer and Jerome all-star teams frequently played against the 442nd and its affiliated units.[34]

At Camp Shelby, Mississippi—the 70,000-person, multi-ethnic, multinational post where they trained—the 442nd Regiment fielded a first-class

5. Denson High School Principal Perry Carmichael inventories sports equipment, Jerome concentration camp, June 1944. Hikaru Iwasaki, photographer. NWDNS-210-G-1169, WRAR, SPB, NA.

baseball team that was not entered into the "colored" league. Reflecting more about the perceptions of white officials than the needs of black soldiers, "the comprehensive program on sports for colored troops" had been established to place "special emphasis on activities which tend to develop mental alertness, agility, initiative, and a competitive spirit." Given the extent to which African Americans—once allowed in—would come to dominate most collegiate and professional athletics in the United States, these policies proved absolutely ludicrous. Nonetheless, the colored league was segregated. More precisely, it was reserved exclusively for African Americans. Indicative of Japanese Americans' complex racial position in the World War II era, the main Shelby sports leagues opened a door to them—an opportunity for ethnic-minority pride, self-assertion, and achievement. Competing against white opponents, Japanese American athletes attained distinctions in bowling, boxing, and swimming, at Shelby and beyond. The barefoot Hawaiian golfer, Private Ted Murata, won the 72-hole Mississippi Junior Championship at three under par and was invited to play in numerous exhibition matches throughout the South. Similarly, both Rohwer and Jerome high school teams played against outside white opponents, occasioning reflection on the myth of racial superiority and the reality of racial divides. Victories could be particularly sweet in such scenarios, as evidenced by *Rohwer Outpost* sports coverage in October 1943 of other interracial competitions: "The Heart Mountain (Wyoming) Relocation Center high school football team has met and defeated two Caucasian high schools, Worland, 7–0, and Red Lodge, Montana, 25–0, so far this season." At Tule Lake, California, the baseball team twice beat their white semiprofessional opponents from Klamath Falls, Oregon, as was recounted with pride in both the camp paper and in official reports to Washington.[35]

With a growing national reputation, the army's Nisei baseball teams played all-white opponents from other military installations, as well as from semipro leagues in neighboring states. On the Shelby baseball diamond, the 442nd took the camp championship, in a game that, as the *Reveille* put it, "Horatio Alger would have liked." Ace pitcher Mitsuo "Lefty" Higuchi had given up only four hits, but the score was tied at 2–2 going into the bottom of the final inning against the 273rd Infantry. With one out and a man on first, rightfielder Goro Kashiwaeda stepped to the plate. The slim but powerful lefthander knocked a line drive over right field, "clear out of the lot," for a home run, two RBIs, and a title-winning 4–2 conquest. The 442nd's great booster, Earl Finch, had been on hand when the team won the nondivisional pennant a month earlier. He had hosted a victory banquet, featuring songs and dances by Private Harry Hamada and his Shelby Hawaiians, and he had presented individual gold baseball awards to each of the twenty members. So sure was he of their success in this campwide championship in October 1943 that he had purchased an imposing 27-inch trophy, had it engraved in advance of the game, and awarded it immediately after the heart-stopping homer.[36]

Inarguably, Japanese American athletes in the South excelled in their endeavors; their achievements warranted recognition. Earl Finch made splashy awards not only to the 442nd baseball players. He gave banquets for the 442nd "mermen" who nabbed individual honors as well as the team title at the Southern Amateur Athletic Union Swimming Championships in New Orleans. He also handed out trophies to the three league-winning basketball teams at Jerome, setting them apart from and above the members of the nine other Japanese American squads there. But many Japanese American coaches and observers held other views of sports and competition. In his editorial on "Equality" for the *Rohwer Outpost*, Barry Saiki cited sports as a potential mechanism for fostering equality, that ideal so denied Japanese Americans in the concentration camps. "Economic, social, and political barriers" within Japanese American communities had been torn down by the incarceration, putting everyone on a more equal footing. Through these circumstances, residents could "forget self-created individualism and try to promote a more fraternal spirit." Similarly, in a piece on "Laxity," he warned inmates against physical decline in the camps and urged organized play as the means to crucial *collective* objectives: "to strengthen ourselves," plural, "so that we might be able to adjust our lives" to postwar conditions and "fight for and maintain for ourselves," collectively, "the fullness of a real democracy and its fruitful assets." It was for all Japanese Americans, participants and spectators alike, Saiki wrote, "the ultimate morale builder." Though some viewed sports as an exercise in competitive, acquisitive individualism, amassing trophies and newspaper accolades, many incarcerated Japanese Americans—with ties to multiple people, places, and collectivities—summoned up alternative visions of athletics' rewards.[37]

Cultural theorists have noted the ways in which competitive team sports can solidify loyalties to place and, particularly, harden commitments to nation—fostering jingoism, racism, and xenophobia. Football disputes between national squads, for example, have sometimes led to open military conflict. A small but persistent group of Japanese American organizers during the war years offered different rationales for sports, even noncompetitive alternatives to team structure. Whereas many embraced the potentially Americanizing qualities of athletics—a widely critiqued but popular present-day children's book on incarceration is entitled, impossibly, *Baseball Saved Us*—some community leaders of a socialist bent insisted that the best way for Japanese Americans to save *themselves* was to abandon American competitiveness: to work and play in a spirit of cooperation and collective betterment.[38]

PARTICIPATORY DEMOCRACY

If electoral politics depends upon the broad participation of an informed electorate, then democracy within America's ten concentration camps largely failed. Up to a third of the populace was disenfranchised, and those who could vote did so with limited data. Issei could not run for most elective offices. Information networks were managed by Nisei, often in the service of the administration. The system of "self-governance" thus was a bad joke. Hardly a schism of high principles compromised by imperfect practice, it was a cynical, disingenuous process in which many participated but few fully believed. Politics in the camps were tightly interwoven with journalistic practice. Camp elections were first made known and publicized in the biweekly press; regulations and procedures for voting were listed there. Candidate slates were published in the newspaper pages; the results of these exercises were officially tabulated therein. Winners were declared, losers noted. In the same way that the war hastened a rise in the prominence of second-generation soldiers, as compared to their older and more experienced immigrant fathers, incarceration accelerated the ascendance of Nisei journalists in promulgating community norms, articulating Japanese American beliefs and values, and setting political agendas.

The political realm at Jerome, as with the camp itself, was in a constant state of flux. The camp was opened on 6 October 1942, five days after the WRA declared that inmates would selectively be allowed out, to be resettled in "normal" cities and towns off the West Coast exclusion zone. The Temporary Community Council (TCC) at Jerome thus was a far more apt name than first envisioned. Though a Permanent Community Council was elected a year after, it remained effectively temporary as well, since many prisoners, including councillors, started leaving the camp. The last camp to open, Jerome was also the first to close, in operation less than two years. In other respects, Jerome was atypical. Along with Rohwer, it was geographically isolated from the other camps. Its significant Hawaiian contingent—roughly 10 percent of the population—also set it apart. Hawaiians of Japanese descent had not been indiscriminately incarcerated, since they were an indispensable part of the island labor force. The over eight hundred slated for confinement at Jerome, mostly family members of men detained in Department of Justice internment camps, came with an understandable sense of embitterment, enraged at the abrogation of their rights. Owing in part to this Hawaiian presence, Jerome had an unusually high resistance to loyalty tests within the camps, as explained in chapter 8.[39]

Although eviction from the West Coast has been described as a triumph of military over civilian authority, the army actually implemented a program conceived and promoted by citizens' groups and politicians. Notable among the latter was California attorney general—and later Chief Justice of the U.S. Supreme Court—Earl Warren, seeking election as governor, in part, on an "anti-Jap" plank. The West Coast's small Japanese American minority thus had become victims of majoritarianism and the excesses of American democracy. Ironically, within months of expulsion from their homes and within weeks of transfer from California detention camps, Nisei in Arkansas were offered the chance to participate in the democratic process in the California election—by absentee balloting. Mostly decades-long residents of the United States, Issei had been forbidden citizenship and thus were not entitled to vote. But in elections at the assembly centers and at Jerome and Rohwer, many Issei voted for the first time. Though both Issei and Nisei over the age of twenty-one cast ballots, only U.S. citizens could stand for election.[40]

Levels of participation were extraordinary. At Jerome thirty residential blocks were charged with electing two candidates each as representatives to the council of sixty members. One hundred and sixty-nine nominees emerged. With each requiring a petition of ten names to assure their candidacy, around 1,700 signatures were collected from the camp's 5,080 eligible voters. On average, each block fielded nearly six candidates, ranging from only two in Block 44—subsequently elected by affirmation—to ten from Block 31. Scarcely two decades after American women earned the right to vote with passage of the Twentieth Amendment, nine female candidates threw their hats in the ring. Reflecting a communal spirit and, perhaps, a pessimism over the new elective body's powers, many candidates "campaigned vigorously for their opponents." On Election Day, 17 November 1942, turnout was high, with over 73 percent of the electorate marking ballots. This compared very favorably with American elections generally during the twentieth century, with peak turnouts of just over 60 percent for presidential elections and much less for congressional elections, which could drop as low as one-third of registered voters in nonpresidential years. Furthermore, at Jerome voters participated with urgency. By the noon hour on Election Day, 124 of Block 38's 150 voters, for example, had already handed over their ballots.[41]

The sixty councillors elected to the first Community Council at Jerome hailed from three counties in Hawaii and over twenty places in California—a geographical distribution roughly reflective of the camp population as a whole. From Los Angeles were eleven, from Fresno eight, Long Beach six, Florin four, Hanford four, two each from Bowles, Fowler, Sacramento, and Torrance, and one each from Alameda, Earlimart, Guadalupe, Kingsburg, Madera, Montebello, Monterey, Moneta, Morro Bay, Redondo Beach, San Diego, San Gabriel, San Pedro, and Selma. There were five Hawaiians. Physician Thomas Yatabe, the first national JACL president, was elected to the council. Ruth Yomagida of Block 7 and Kay Kawachi of Block 17 were the only women elected.

But the most interesting race was held in Block 6, where Asami Oyama, former women's editor at the *Santa Anita Pacemaker,* was up against a large field that included her husband, former *Pacemaker* city editor Joe Oyama. He outpolled her, 17 to 4, but Eddie Shimano won 44 votes, the most in the block.[42]

Shimano was well-known as the editor of the *Denson Communiqué* and the former editor of the *Pacemaker*. With nearly 19,000 residents, Santa Anita had been the largest of the sixteen detention camps by far. Shimano had cultivated a loyal readership in California with his pithy column, sharp editorials, and thorough distribution policy. "Rain or shine," he wrote on 24 April 1942, "residents of the Santa Anita Assembly Center will and do receive their copy of the *Pacemaker.* Despite the downpour last Tuesday, 14 delivery boys, working voluntarily, splashed through the mud to put a copy of the *Pacemaker* under each doorstep and if possible to the resident personally." Like the *Santa Anita Pacemaker*, the *Denson Communiqué* appeared twice a week, on Tuesdays and Fridays. Its staff included other veterans of the *Pacemaker*, notably art and production manager Roy Kawamoto, along with city editor Paul Yokota. Though Yokota would go on to become editor in chief of the renamed *Denson Tribune* after Shimano left Arkansas, on Election Day he received only one vote in his race for Community Council.[43]

Curiously, in his assessment of journalism at Jerome, scholar E. J. Friedlander asserts that the *Denson Tribune* was "one of the most editorially autonomous" of the ten concentration camp newspapers. It "apparently functioned with little WRA interference, both in terms of prior restraint and post-publication evaluation." This he tentatively attributes to "an enlightened camp administration" and reports officer Charles Lynn, "who came from a sound journalistic background." In U.S. Senate investigations at Jerome, however, Lynn was quick to describe his control over the paper. There was, he said, an "understanding about what is to be printed." Lynn had instructed Yokota "to show me anything that, in his opinion, I might wish to see because of WRA policy or outside relations. He complied fully with this request." Moreover, "everything" that went into the paper was "subject to approval of the project director," Paul Taylor. And in another hearing, officials confidently described the *Tribune* as "Pro-American as well as Pro-Administration." More curious still, in his analysis of the camp newspaper at Rohwer, Russell Bearden maintains that the *Rohwer Outpost* enjoyed "complete autonomy in return for unbiased and accurate reporting," even as he notes the administration's threat to fire an editor "unless the tone of the newspaper changed." "Anti-relocation" views presumably rendered the editor biased. A University of Southern California

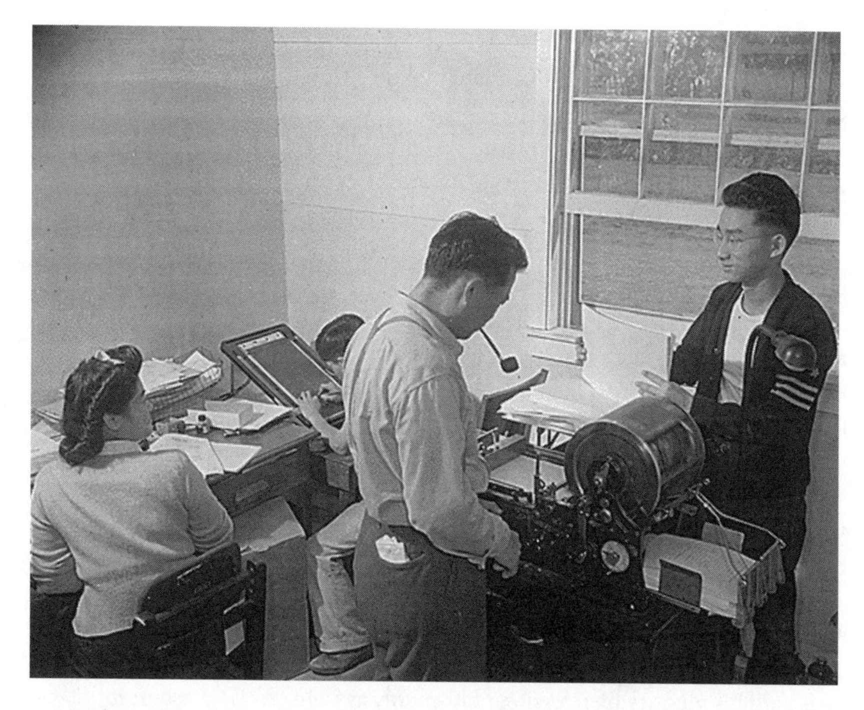

6. Members of the *Denson Communiqué* staff, *from left,* Eunice Yakota, stencil cutter; Kiyomi Nakamura, mimeoscope operator; Tsugio Makagama, mimeo chief; Roy Kawamoto, staff artist and mimeo chief. Jerome concentration camp, November 1942. Tom Parker, photographer. NWDNS-210-G-E263, WRAR, SPB, NA.

journalism graduate, Paul Yokota eventually would face similar difficulties at Jerome, as we will see in chapter 7.[44]

Of course, newspaper staffers often negotiated untenable positions, as *Rohwer Outpost* arts editors George Akimoto and Hiro Mizushima explained years later. "There were mixed emotions," Mizushima said, since writers "had to satisfy the people who were interned and also those who were in charge of the camp." Inevitably, some engaged in duplicity. "As a protest," Akimoto demonstrated, "about a half dozen of us got hold of a wire cutter, so we sneaked off into the outskirts to a wooded area of our camp. And we decided we were going to cut the barbed wire. One of the guys had glasses. We cut the wire, and the wire, you know because of the tension, sprang back and smacked him in the glasses. So we were groping around looking for the pieces of glass, because we didn't want the FBI to find them and identify them!" "Then we went back to the paper," Mizushima concluded, "and wrote that people shouldn't be doing things like that! I mean I can laugh about it now, but at the time, it was something serious."[45]

Other journalists aligned themselves more directly with the camp administration, participating in a secret network of confidential informants. Even after leaving the camp, Eddie Shimano and former city editor Dick Itanaga would be offered guest columns in the *Tribune*, in order to promote WRA policies and—in more sinister fashion—to engage in intelligence gathering. "Acting on a hunch or intuition or whatever you want to call it," Jerome director Paul Taylor launched a clandestine investigation of resident Toru Tim Abo, even though Abo's answers at a loyalty hearing "were all in order." Taylor sent a confidential letter to Itanaga at Camp Shelby, where he was newly training with the 442nd Regiment, to elicit his views. Private Itanaga dutifully responded with a lengthy letter placed in an envelope marked "Confidential," which in turn was placed inside another envelope addressed to Taylor but "not marked 'confidential,' with no return address." Among other things, Itanaga alleged that Abo "did his share of talking which was definitely anti-American and pro-Japanese," without specifying the precise content of remarks. For his part, Taylor promised to protect Itanaga's correspondence in the camp safe and safeguard his identity by referring to him only as "Mr. C." (Protestant minister George Aki of Jerome, later chaplain of the 442nd, was known as "Mr. A"; a Japanese American physician was "Mr. B"; and so on.) Itanaga apparently took to the work, encouraging camp residents in his *Tribune* guest column that very week to stay in touch and fill him in: "What's the latest 'fact' being so high pressuredly peddled by the block latrine oracles? . . . We invite anyone to go ahead and tell us what is the latest in Denson or cuss us out as some have. We want different views of the place. . . . We want to keep on learning so we may be better prepared to do our part."[46]

Though many historians of incarceration have demonstrated the role of white anthropologists, sociologists, and others in spying for the FBI, often as paid staff of a camp's community analysis section, comparatively little is known about the role of Nisei reporters in intelligence gathering, given the great secrecy at the time. Correspondence makes clear, however, that administrators considered them very valuable, especially as compared to social scientists, who were sure to be viewed by camp inmates with some level of mistrust. As Robert Leflar of Arkansas put it to the WRA's chief attorney in Washington: "An 'inquiring reporter' stopping 50 people on street corners might serve the immediate purpose as well or better."[47]

Camp newspapers provided important if partial coverage of daily life and events, notably downplaying conflict within the camps. Writers and editors were thrust into leadership positions, often by virtue of their cozy relationships with administrators. Indeed, some chose to actively collaborate in the suppression of dissent. Similarly, though Nisei elected officials had limited power, making rulings on relatively small matters of health, safety, and welfare—any of which could be vetoed by the camp director—they could use their wartime responsibilities to build a power base lasting beyond the war. Though Issei could stand for the position of block manager—formally involving maintenance of grounds and facilities, but often constituting other types of consultation—Nisei guided Japanese American community politics during the war years, often via the media. Mike Masaoka, public relations officer for the 442nd, became notorious in this regard, drafting accommodating articles, press releases, and speeches such that community fury would continue to be vented decades later, as through the poetry of David Mura. Pointing up Masaoka's self-satisfied assimilation, Mura notes: "At panel after panel, he *asks* the authorities / to isolate Issei (in private suggests they brand them); / *proposes* internment to prove our loyalty, / and proclaims in some senator's ear / how unfamiliar he is with Buddha, how Christ / and the flag have made his accent disappear."[48]

Though each camp newspaper contained a Japanese-language section, at Jerome and Rohwer these pages contained little more than abbreviated translations of articles first appearing in the larger, English-language sections, sometimes days afterward. Nisei editorial policy ruled the day. As David Yoo has written of the prewar Japanese American press, so too could be said of the camp newspapers: "Overall, the press promoted an ideology of racial responsibility that encouraged Nisei to respond to racism by embracing life in America as loyal, hardworking citizens who would 'prove' their worth. Many contributors conveyed an unwarranted optimism and, in essence, offered a sense of hope and agency within a difficult racial climate. . . . Although discussions of race could border on naïveté, more often than not, writers advocated a strategy for survival." Often too, however, they worked behind the scenes to make life harder for others. As Itanaga said of those he informed on, "I fully realize I may change the future of the individual in question."[49]

Through the years, Mary Tsukamoto has told a familiar story about the shock of incarceration. Not long after eviction from their prospering thirty-five-acre farm, after the claustrophobia of confinement in a barbed-wire enclosure, Tsukamoto's daughter Marielle expressed her bewilderment, as only a five-year-old could. She missed home, and she missed her dog. "I want my Uppie, Mommy," she said. "Let's go back home to Uppie. Let's go back to America."[50]

This narrative is a popular one, attributed to a variety of figures from the period and retold by any number of Americans today. A recurrent trope in Japanese American discourse, it scripts an innocent child in the role of truth-teller. A terrible misfortune has come. World-weary adults can't fully see it or articulate it plainly, but the uncorrupted mind of a child gives it clarity. To go back to America is to return to a place of justice; the totalitarian world of the camps is un-American. Older people hearing the story understand that an injustice indeed has taken place, reflecting a betrayal of seemingly well-established ideals. They know that, in fact, the camps are physically located in America; but their telling and retelling of the story relies on a perceived irony: this is not what one would expect from America.

In fact, incarceration was utterly characteristic of American racial policy, deny it though some may. "In facing the issue of race prejudice," David Yoo writes of a slightly earlier period, "many [Japanese American] commentators tended to portray racism in the United States as an anomaly, a misconception to be dispelled or the work of a few misguided agitators rather than a pervasive societal phenomenon." Such a view necessarily cast incarceration as unusual and un-American. It overlooked the reality that, on the one hand, the most un-American of practices within the camps, as further evidenced in the next chapter, were often the ones that made the camps most livable: anti-capitalist, collectivist, noncompetitive endeavors. On the other hand, some of the hallowed institutions of democracy—electoral politics, a free press—were among the most distorted and compromised of processes. One form of cooperation, a broad-based communal participation in ethical production, consumption, and community-building, proved satisfying to many; while another form, collaboration with administrators, proved tempting to a few—a path to greater power. Japanese Americans were left to wonder if success in America necessarily involved a self-serving, individualistic, cynical calculation of gain.[51]

4 | Camp Life

IN 1942 VIRGINIA TIDBALL found herself out of work. Born in rural northwest Arkansas in 1904, she had grown up on a farm, experienced firsthand the agricultural decline of the 1920s, and lived through the layoffs and Depression breadlines of the 1930s. Still, she had always managed to survive—and thrive. After high school, she was accepted into the freshman class at the University of Arkansas, in nearby Fayetteville. She had excelled in her classes in languages and literature, in part by taking the unconventional route. She had studiously avoided—or perhaps been snubbed by—the Greek-letter social sororities such as Chi Omega and Phi Mu, central to the development of many middle- and upper-class southern ladies. The daughter of a farmer and country preacher, she was active instead in the Young Women's Christian Association (YWCA), participating in Bible study groups, the outreach to disadvantaged children, and the Tuesday "tea days" for male students and faculty. By the time of her graduating year, 1926, Tidball was elected president of Skull and Torch, the academic honor society, a local equivalent of Phi Beta Kappa. On the strength of her undergraduate career, she went on to the University of California, where she earned a master's degree. Returning to Arkansas, she'd had no trouble landing teaching posts at high schools and beyond.[1]

At age thirty-eight, the unmarried Tidball was employed by El Dorado Junior College when it had to close its doors for lack of students—"a result of the war, of course, and having no endowment," as she explained it. Ever resourceful, facing an uncertain future, Tidball acted in her capacity as college treasurer to collect unpaid tuition and thereby meet unpaid salaries, including her own. As she wrote in a letter to a former student, "When you are ready to pay up, please send a draft or check payable to me personally and I will divide among the former teachers to whom it is due." Forced to return to her parents' home, she set about the task of finding a new position with equal determination. When she heard about the concentration camp schools to be opened at two sites in southeast Arkansas, she fired off letters to educator Amon G. Thompson of Jerome, who had attended a summer seminar with her in 1941, and to B. F. Albright, an acquaintance at the U.S. Employment Service in Little Rock. After a week had passed, with no response from either, she wrote again to Albright, expressing a fear that she might "not have addressed the [first] letter correctly." Thompson finally responded, encouragingly, insisting he would be back in touch soon. But within a couple more weeks, Tidball was "feeling a little bothered" at no follow-up correspondence from the superintendent-designate of Jerome schools. "Mr. Thompson said in his letter not to take any steps till I heard from him," she confessed to a friend who had intervened on her behalf. But unable to sit idly by, she pressed, "Do you think I should write him [again] or anyone else?"[2]

She wrote to Dillon Myer himself in Washington, outlining the range of her teaching abilities: English, French, Spanish, Latin, dramatics, and speech. She wrote yet again to Thompson, making reference to a minor point she had failed to mention in her previous letter. By late October 1942, Thompson sent Tidball an application form and suggested that he could find a place for her on the high school faculty. But then three more weeks passed without a word from Thompson. Tidball must have agonized over protocol in those long weeks, then months, of unemployment, eager to be hired, eager to leave the family farm. She didn't want to appear pushy. Yet she had learned that for women working outside the home, reticence rarely paid. By 18 November she could no longer resist, penning another note to Thompson: "Each day I have expected to hear from you that an effective date on my appointment has come." She assumed—wrongly—that classes had begun: "I should like to be there doing my part, too. I wish there were some way to expedite the decision." As with the first day of classes, amidst the disorder and delay of building two new elementary schools and two new high schools from the ground up, Virginia Tidball's appointment letter was very late in arriving. But arrive it finally did.[3]

So Virginia Tidball was faced with a new set of worries. How would she find enough money to travel down to southeast Arkansas? How would she get by until her first paycheck? After weighing all her options, the uppity English teacher sat back down at her desk and penned yet another letter—this time to farmer Hosea Fincher, on the other side of the county, a friend of hers and her brother Dabney. Perhaps Hosea held the answer to her financial woes. "The horse Dabney let you have to try out," she began, "is partly mine. And as I am expecting to leave home for a job soon, I should like to know if you want to buy Billy." Virginia and Dabney clearly were on the outs, perhaps over the horse, for Virginia closed her letter to Hosea with payment instructions that circumvented Dabney. "In case I should be gone when you come, you can do business with my [other] brother Albert."[4]

While thousands dreaded confinement in southeast Arkansas—with rumors of bloodthirsty mosquitoes, poisonous snakes, and inadequate food supplies—white women such as Virginia Tidball were clamoring to get in. At $2,000 per year, salaries for WRA teachers far exceeded those of teachers in the segregated white schools of the South, which in turn were as much as three times those of black teachers. Subsidized housing was available, and despite all the sensational journalism, the pupils were said to be well-behaved and bright. Educational staff eventually totaled around one hundred at Jerome, as at Rohwer. Of Jerome high school teachers, Arkansans made up three-quarters of the total. Though many were spouses of WRA officials, some like Tidball led a life with new degrees of autonomy and responsibility. Similarly, the camps enabled new clerical and professional openings for Japanese Americans—women, in particular. Though at a fraction of the pay, they took up positions alongside whites as elementary and high school teachers, assistant teachers, and librarians; as educational administrators and clerks; and as instructors at the preschool and adult school. Pursuing their own career development, they also served as highly visible role models to the children of the camps, suggesting that even under the worst of conditions, unparalleled opportunities might present themselves.[5]

As at Block 33, where Denson High School was located, and Block 23, home to the elementary school—with many classes designated for girls or boys only—many camp environments were starkly gendered spaces, reflecting dominant notions of appropriate rights and responsibilities for females and males. These notions were changing, and women both bore the brunt of policies designed to retain social stability and took the lead in exploring fresh new avenues for reorganizing everyday life to their benefit. As distinctive physical spaces—densely populated areas of generational stratification—camps promoted intimate interactions among unmarried heterosexuals, among lesbians, and among gay men, even as camp legal codes barred seduction, sodomy, and crimes against nature. Recognized as "unusual places," the camps could easily be put to use for activities counter to prevailing social norms. While miscegenation was similarly banned, mixed-race married couples were incorporated into the social structure, exposing segregation's inability to contain desires within racial and ethnic boundaries. The camp's organized programs of recreation, community leisure, and family life thus became vexed sites for experimenting with varied sexual and gender transformations. Much more was at stake than occupying spare time. Some of the central assumptions of the American social order were called into question.

GENDERED SPACES

As we've seen, a WRA camp ordinarily contained thirty-six blocks of residential dwellings for Japanese Americans. Each of these blocks included twelve barracks buildings, each of which in turn comprised six apartments (lettered from A to F). Thus, there were 2,592 residences. If averaging four persons per household, a camp could accommodate over 10,000 inmates. At either Jerome or Rohwer, the population never exceeded 8,500. Still, these were cramped conditions, an ordinary apartment measuring 400 square feet—the size of a studio apartment today. Some apartments were even smaller. Of the six apartments in each 20-by-120-feet building, two (A and F) measured 20 by 24 feet, two (C and D) measured 20 by 20, and two (B and E) were a measly 20 by 16. Whereas once people were known by the military's dehumanizing family number, now they were associated with a simple alphanumeric address. At the Fresno detention center, Henry Sugimoto had painted a portrait of his six-year-old daughter Sumile with a tag pinned to her dress, "NAME: Sugimoto, H., NO.: 24907." The Jerome high school art teacher now was known by a straightforward address, 28-2-D, stenciled by construction crews onto the outside of the home. The entrance to Block 28, building 2, apartment D, however, Sugimoto embellished with a palette-shaped wooden sign, identifying it as the residence of "Henry Sugimoto—Artist." Striking commentaries on the strength of family ties and vocational pursuits in the face of government oppression, the portrait and handcrafted house-marker also remind us that, in a patriarchal order, female identities are subsumed within relationships to men, first a father and then a husband. Sumile poses for and is painted by her father, who is allowed to pursue his artistic career in the camp. She is known not only by his surname, given at birth, but also the initial H for *his* forename, both written on the tag affixed to her clothing. Though a highly regarded teacher in her own right, instructing second-graders at Jerome, Susie Sugimoto (born Tagawa) is known primarily as Mrs. Henry Sugimoto. Her household is signposted only as that of her husband; Sumile's home is signposted only as that of her father.[6]

The Sugimotos, a small nuclear family of three, occupied a 20-by-16-feet apartment. Families with large numbers of children were allocated up to three adjacent rooms, as with the Asaki family, with eleven children, residing at 28-2-A, B, and C, and the Hurakami family, with thirteen children, living at 12-2-D, E, and F—still only 1,200 square feet of contiguous space. These families were exceptions, the biggest in the camp. The vast majority of inmates lived in two- to five-person households, sometimes including members of the extended family. But these peculiar living arrangements would bode significant transformations in gender roles for Japanese Americans incarcerated in the South. Even as the imprisonment had devastating effects, it likewise yielded many opportunities, especially for Issei and Nisei women, as Valerie Matsumoto has perceptively demonstrated. Authorities had not anticipated these benefits, nor did they necessarily view them as such. When the full consequences became known, they acted to shore up gender differences, reasserting women's subordinate position to men and reaffirming entrenched standards of heterosexual marriage, male privilege, patriarchal control, and female domesticity. At every step, they met with resistance.[7]

Incarceration partially reconfigured the gendered division of labor, often to the advantage of women. Generally, domestic responsibilities usually carried out by women were decreased in the camps. One-room apartments, though hideously cramped and uncomfortable, required less cleaning. Also, because they had no kitchens, meal preparation took new forms: it was collectivized, waged, and—on the whole—reduced. Dining halls were set up for each of the thirty-six residential blocks, with a single hall catering to all sixty households in the block. Thus, the camp capitalized upon economies of scale, diminishing the amount of labor required for meals. Whereas before the war, one individual, ordinarily a mother, might prepare meals for a family of five, a 250-person block did not require fifty part-time cooks and servers. Furthermore, unlike most household meal production, the cooks and servers were waged, on the ordinary WRA pay scale. Though a new gendered division of labor developed—men such as Taro Dakuzaku and Tokio Yamane had the professional status of cooks, with uniforms and chef's caps, and women usually served the meals and washed dishes—women nonetheless took home earnings over which they had substantial control.[8]

Another common domestic chore, laundering, was partially collectivized, if not waged. As noted, each block had a shared toilet, shower, and wash building, where individuals gathered daily, rightly with considerable resentment. But even if women were not paid for laundering their families' clothes, they now did so in the company of friends and neighbors—a rarity for rural Californians in particular. Even if they did not always pool loads, they shared several steps in the process, thereby reducing the amount of time and number of implements required for collecting and heating water, making soap—as at the Jerome soap factory run by Mr. and Mrs. Katsuji Oyama—hanging the laundry to dry, gathering, folding, and ironing. Perhaps most importantly, communal washing outside the private home drew public attention to the labor power needed to keep the community dressed. As the centermost buildings in the block, the wash house and dining hall made visible the most fundamental aspects of community life and the individuals whose work sustained it.[9]

Even child care benefited from economies of scale and collectivization, as with infant feeding regimens, well-baby clinics, and mothers' education programs. In dense living environments, growing children fell under many watchful eyes, including those of the internal security officers on the beat—the Japanese American patrolmen who often relied on the young for information and who, in accordance with their duty manual, would "make friends with the children in the center, care for their well being and instruct them on matters of safety and center regulations." With barbed wire and watchtowers encircling the camp, mothers further had some bleak insurance against children wandering astray. With equipment donated in part by Earl Finch, playgrounds became sites of collective recreation, overseen by community activities staff. Also, the school year was longer in the camps, to offset time lost in the eviction and in the detention centers. School attendance was mandatory, and children no longer needed to stay home to help on the family farm or in the family business. Increased education not only decreased mothers' child-care responsibilities. It also improved future prospects for girls, since sons' learning had sometimes taken precedence prior to the war.[10]

At the same time imprisonment decreased women's domestic duties, it also allowed them a greater number and range of employment opportunities outside the home. For women and men, an ethnically homogenous community with all the tasks of an ordinary town provided jobs without elaborate racial stratification and discrimination. At long last, the stereotype of the gardener or domestic with an advanced degree could be overturned. Though certainly other forms of discrimination existed—particularly officials' preference for

7. Soap factory operated by Mr. and Mrs. Katsuji Oyama. Also pictured are Mr. I. Telashita, *far left*, and Mrs. M. Nishikawa, *second from right*. Jerome concentration camp, March 1943. Tom Parker, photographer. NWDNS-210-G-E776, WRAR, SPB, NA.

younger, English-speaking citizens over older Japanese-speaking immigrants—Japanese Americans as never before could fill positions at or near the level of their highest capabilities. And women could participate in the labor force on the same WRA wage scale as men. Though inequities remained—men dominated certain professions and received slightly higher clothing allowances and "public assistance grants," a form of camp welfare payment—women and men employed in the same jobs received the same pay.[11]

As Evelyn Nakano Glenn notes in her excellent study of Japanese American women workers before and after the war, "Perhaps ironically, the camps had opened up new vistas for the nisei." For both Issei and Nisei, the need to recoup the losses in earnings and property during incarceration forced higher rates of participation in the postwar labor market; but it was also incarceration that made possible this participation, by giving women the experience of working in higher-level positions in the camps. Before the war, most "women continued to work under the authority of their husbands. They earned no independent income, so they had little control over economic resources. . . . Women were also prevented from meeting new people and forming relationships outside the family." With incarceration, all that changed.[12]

With meal preparation and consumption, in particular, placed outside the nuclear or extended family, many women were freed for clerical, administrative, and professional positions. With women, men, and children often dining in separate gendered and generational cohorts in the mess halls, husbands and fathers no longer sat as the patriarchal head of household at the dinner table. Nor did they have the control they once had over their wives' and daughters' whereabouts, work routines, and potential earnings. This sociologists and anthropologists of incarceration referred to, with great worry, as "family breakdown."[13]

Certainly, family life was changing, foremost as a result of government cruelty in emptying Japanese American homes and separating families into different camps—not only at the moment of expulsion, as with some Florin and Elk Grove families, but also later in the incarceration. Violet Matsuda's husband, Shigeru, for example, would be sent to a Department of Justice internment camp in Santa Fe, New Mexico. Thus, alarmists over family breakdown shifted attention away from these larger injustices and on to what they described as the flawed social organization of camp life and women's overreaching ambitions.

The stresses of eviction and imprisonment magnified tensions within patriarchal households, but such tensions also built upon and flowed from the inequalities of prewar American families. As Glenn cautions, "While issei marriages were extremely stable, one should not romanticize them or exaggerate the degree of harmony within the family. . . . [G]ender divisions generated serious conflicts: the discrepancy in power and privilege, the unequal division of household labor and childcare, and the separation of male and female social and emotional worlds made men's and women's interests fundamentally different." Men's drinking habits and profligate spending also came up for criticism. Though divorce rates were as low as 1.6 percent among Issei marriages, longevity did not equal equanimity. And while one historian of incarceration overzealously claims a lack of divorces in the Arkansas camps as a distinctive badge of honor for the prisoners, the camp legal offices in fact received constant queries about divorce. During 1943 attorneys at Jerome handled six cases of "domestic relations problems" per month, referring two of those on average to California and other attorneys for divorce proceedings. Thus, only jurisdictional issues prevented the securing of divorces *within* the Arkansas camps. Yes, incarceration opened up fault lines in marriages; but the fissures predated incarceration. Also, ironically, the camps offered new options to women envisioning life beyond marriage.[14]

Many single women lived apart from their families of origin in the camps. At least sixty-eight did at Jerome, though they generally were required to share apartments. While there were ten times as many single men—mostly older Issei bachelors, occupying entire blocks—Japanese American women's residences were conspicuous spatial innovations, since prior to the war a so-called "school girl," domestic, or other single worker typically had boarded in an employer's spare bedroom. Three unmarried women bore children at the Rohwer camp. Representing less than 1 percent of all deliveries there, these exceptional mothers and their financial inventiveness nonetheless were more noticeable in the densely populated camp community than they otherwise might have been. "Illegitimate" childbirth thus provoked actions at the highest levels of camp management. One Rohwer baby "born out of wedlock" was transferred to Jerome and put under the care of the Welfare Section until the mother had "more time to make a definite decision as to permanent plans" for the child. Clearly, camp authorities encouraged adoption, though the official record is conspicuously silent about the child's final placement.[15]

White WRA employees provided vivid examples of waged female independence, which some inmates found inspirational. While relatively few Japanese American women lived on their own in the camps as compared to white female teachers and administrators, they increasingly imagined and pursued a life on their own outside the camps. On a very "special night"—the night she "received [her] first pay envelope"—Haru Miyazaki wrote a letter before bedtime to her friend, Jerome teacher Virginia Tidball. Newly resettled in Denver, Miyazaki confided: "I doubt if I'll ever live with my folks" again. And she would gladly give up this first job stocking fruits and vegetables, even her baseball team, to train as an army nurse. The life of a single woman also had its erotic possibilities, as could be inferred from Miyazaki's closing lines to Tidball—who would remain unmarried for the rest of her life: "Good night, pleasant dreams. Take care of yourself. I think you have the most beautiful wavy hair and blue eyes I've ever seen. Haru."[16]

Note how this friendship complicates some of the central assumptions of an urbanist historiography of sexuality. Yes, women felt empowered by waged economic independence often associated with the city; likewise by separation from parental authority and oversight; by same-sex athletic competition (softball figures prominently in numerous herstories of lesbian community development); and by military service. Though many Japanese Americans in Arkansas felt enlistment an ideological impossibility, other women welcomed the assertive, take-charge roles and responsibilities and the same-sex environments of military mobilizations. Perhaps most notably, this intimate relationship was not a meeting of two race and class equals, protected by the perceived anonymity and autonomy of city life and bohemian enclaves. It was, rather, a coming together forged by war's inequitable dislocations and by the momentary opportunities afforded to two nonconforming women with markedly different degrees of social and physical mobility. Tidball enjoyed the mantle of spinster teacher, a suitable role for mobile, unmarried European American women since the nineteenth century. Her friend Haru Miyazaki represented a new generation of Japanese American women who would help define new limits for single workers and their public women's culture. In both cases, mobility resulted largely from new financial gains. Wages for women, white and Japanese American, enabled new ways of living and loving, without marriage.[17]

Rumors of gender nonconformity—so-called illegitimate births, divorce, and "family breakdown"—fueled editorials, feature stories, programs, and activities designed to bolster the family and reaffirm gender norms. In Arkansas women's economic gains stood in bold contrast to continuing political marginalization, as seen in the previous chapter. Only 9 of 162 candidates for the first Community Council at Jerome were women. Though women held posts at both Rohwer and Jerome newspapers, they never served as editor in chief. Such limitations often were inculcated at school. Young women at Jerome and Rohwer high schools served as class secretary or treasurer and newspaper features or style editor, but never as president or vice president, only once as editor in chief.[18]

While these ceilings mirrored the gendered dynamics of American schoolyards broadly, the camp schools carried added weight: whereas a decentralized educational system in the United States was administered locally by elected boards, these schools represented a rare federal government delivery of primary and secondary education and an enactment of official expectations for gender in everyday life. Many policies were handed down directly from Washington, and many more were vetted there. Washington's June 1943 "Community School Forum," for example, recommended a "core curriculum" for camp schools, with distinct tracks for males and females. "The core teacher has a responsibility to help her students choose the fields of service for which they are adapted," the bulletin read. Young women were *adapted*—if not as part of their innate essence, as implied, then certainly through their schooling—for domesticity. That included "provid[ing] valuable information to the homemaker" through the evening adult school, as well as to "*her* daughters" in day school. While "boys and girls both" should learn about nutrition, dehydration, and the scarcity of wartime food supplies, girls alone "should be learning cooking methods." Home economics for girls would "help them as consumers to conserve their clothing and their household fabrics, to make the household efficient, to fit budgets to the new fast changing conditions." Jerome school clubs also reflected a gender divide. Female instructors supervised clubs on etiquette, dramatics, music appreciation, and needlecraft; males led clubs on agriculture, stagecraft, debating, and mathematics. The adult school steered men toward courses in auto mechanics, watch repair, and elementary electricity; women toward shorthand and typing, pattern drafting and sewing, and flower making and arranging. Camp administrators thus continued to prepare both men and women for working-class occupations, even as women as well as men held ever more clerical and professional positions in the camps.[19]

In shoring up the most fundamental institution of gender subordination and complementarity, WRA authorities and Japanese American leaders in Arkansas used camp clubs and organizations, as well as the newspaper, to forward an agenda of social and sexual stability via marriage. As leader or adviser to various youth groups at Jerome, Mary Nakahara helped link premarital sexual restraint to cleanliness in her talks on "Sex and Hygiene." Camp social welfare officer J. Lloyd Webb lectured girls groups on "Boy-Girl Relations." And at Rohwer, Community Activities supervisor Nat Griswold pitched his "Forum on Our Families" to "all newley weds [*sic*], all nearly weds, all would be weds, all will be weds—in short, *all* younger persons." If young Japanese American men and women were able to envision a life without marriage, clearly Griswold could not. Still, his agenda for discussion did seem to acknowledge the potential dissatisfactions of kinship, asking his teenage audience how they might improve first "the life of your present family" and second "the family you eventually establish"—again speaking its inevitability. Nonetheless, in his third and final question of the forum, Griswold overlooked the unique burdens of women and implied that men foremost were disadvantaged by marriage: "When a man marries, does his troubles [*sic*] begin?"[20]

Contrary to this rhetorical question, camp officials clearly held out great hope in patriarchal marriage as the cure for incarceration's ills. And yet camp life offered the most visible critique of all. Among inmates, the collectivized preparation of food and clothing, the relatively undifferentiated housing, the employment of both women and men, the flat pay scale, and the nonprofit cooperative stores existed in stark contrast to the competitive patriarchal nature of a capitalist family-unit reliant on the father as sole breadwinner—and in contrast to a common prewar Japanese American family-unit economy in which all might work but the father exercised authority. While first and foremost a prison camp, with all the degradations and humiliations that entailed, it also—as testament to Japanese American resilience—was a community. Whereas many elite individuals bitterly complained about living next door to their class inferiors, in identical apartments, and many men deeply resented women's newfound status, the creation of this more egalitarian public culture marked a profound challenge. It exposed the otherwise unarticulated hierarchical political and economic assumptions of the dominant culture, just as it would expose the very constructedness of racial difference. How ironic that the United States government, in its self-appointed role as democracy's worldwide defender, dispensed with democratic values by imprisoning an entire ethnic minority population and placing them in a socialist world—that which soon enough would generate the greatest of American paranoias. This was the material context of "family breakdown," of the camps' perceived threat to the family. And from this sprang the need to promote courtship and marriage: not just to sustain gender distinction and inequity, but further to sustain the very foundations of the larger culture and economy.

With the aid of camp officials and government resources, Japanese American pastors and other leaders extolled the virtues of wedlock to the young. Along with a "blossoming Nisei dance culture," as scholars have surmised, there was "an epidemic of marriages that swept the centers." With astounding regularity, averaging almost four per month, Jerome celebrated marriage, ranging from simple to elaborate ceremonies, from Christian to Buddhist, from arranged marriage to—much more commonly—companionate or free marriage. Bucking tradition, most Japanese Americans contemplating matrimony during the war years shunned go-betweens. Instead, they chose their own partners, based on romance, physical attraction, shared interests, and companionship, as well as traditional economic considerations. While parents, friends, and white authorities encouraged them wholeheartedly, meticulous restrictions would be placed on the pool of potential partners, as we see in the next section and the next chapter.[21]

CAUCASIAN ENVIRONMENTS

Dramatic changes in domestic and family life, gender and sexuality, characterized eviction and incarceration for all Japanese Americans, no matter what their previous social status or circumstances. They were an inescapable part of imprisonment and were to govern experience for over 120,000 people for years. Seemingly mundane activities of everyday life, undertaken without thinking by white middle-class families in a wealthy capitalist nation, became fraught with difficulty and uncertainty. The very cycle from birth to death was imperiled, as Mrs. Morito Miyasaki of Fowler, California, learned to her great sorrow.

Whereas Violet Matsuda, suffering numerous "pre-natal complications," had given birth to her third child in the Fresno detention center—"sickly" five-pound daughter Kimi—Miyasaki was almost nine months pregnant when the second stage of the expulsion was ordered: from Fresno to the Jerome concentration camp. With only a hard wooden seat and no place to lie down during the four-day rail journey, Miyasaki was terrified. When she wasn't overcome with exhaustion, her mind raced. What would happen if she went into labor? Who would help her? What would she find at the new camp, this foreign, unfamiliar place, the subject of terrible rumors? Would the baby be safe? What about a hospital? A secure place to live? Would there be enough food for everyone? Most important, how would she raise her child behind barbed wire? To so many questions there seemed few if any answers, only the examples of the arduous making do and getting by of Fresno. Just days after arriving at Jerome, Miyasaki gave birth. This first new baby at the camp warranted front-page coverage in the newspaper. In a lighthearted story, Mr. and Mrs. Miyasaki and son Stanley were said to be "attended by Dr. Kikuo H. Taira, whose fish scale was used" to weigh him. However, Stanley died just three weeks later, on 14 November 1942, receiving comparatively little notice in the paper.[22]

White administrators and many Japanese American community leaders encouraged marriage and child-rearing within the camps, despite outside racist allegations of "overpopulating" so crucial in the decision to incarcerate. "Sly, treacherous, and hard-working," in the eyes of many white nativists in California, Japanese Americans were said to "thrive where a white man could starve. And breed!" Expressing similar sentiments, Idaho's Governor Clark declared,

"Japs live like rats, breed like rats, and act like rats!" Officials were highly cognizant of continuing scrutiny of Japanese American sexuality, and they set out to both police it and represent it in a favorable light to right-wing critics of WRA "coddling"—or what John Rankin called "pampering." That is, they hoped to situate it within acceptable white middle-class norms of respectability.[23]

In Washington, in the wake of early pitched resistance to incarceration at the Manzanar and Poston camps, WRA chief solicitor Philip Glick advised director Dillon Myer about policies and procedures in prosecuting the range of possible "offenses against the peace and security at the relocation centers"—from assault and carrying concealed weapons to "maintaining a place of prostitution" and "giving venereal disease to another." At Jerome Japanese American internal security officers were urged to engage in vice control and to stop prostitution. That is, men were again put in charge of policing women's sexuality. They investigated at least three unattached working women rumored to directly exchange sex for cash—two sisters and a widow. The sisters, aged seventeen and twenty-one, held clerical positions, one as a night typist. The sexually active young widow, aged thirty, had three children but took advantage of camp child-care facilities to work at the Co-op. Concluding their inquiries, officers reported that these were cases of "promiscuity, rather than definite evidence of prostitution."[24]

Responding to a "Sociological Investigation of Prostitution" initiated by Washington, Jerome director Paul Taylor insisted that "public opinion in the center seems to be so strong . . . that such activities would have to be carried on secretly." "It must be emphasized," he wrote to his superiors, that the evidence against the women "is hearsay." Similar to such contemporaneous accounts, historian Sandra Taylor insists that "social deviance," prostitution, and other forms of taboo sexuality at the Topaz concentration camp in Utah are "hard to document," founded upon untrustworthy rumors and partners' "male braggadocio." Even so, she somehow takes the measure of these deeds and concludes that "illicit sexual liaisons were uncommon in the camp"—evidence of Japanese Americans' "high moral values." Queer theorists such as Eve Kosofsky Sedgwick and Gavin Butt, however, insist that rumor and gossip have served as vital information networks for various cultural outgroups, enabling resistance and circulating their own forms of truth. They further help enrich and expand interpretive possibilities in the history of sexuality.[25]

Successful and satisfying to the extent that they remained secretive, sex work and other "sex offenses" surely were underreported. WRA statistics for 1944 record only one prosecution of the former, at Granada, and six cases of the latter. In addition to the three females above subjected to sexual scrutiny at Jerome in 1943, Paul Taylor had to concede "one instance brought to the attention of the staff here, in which there was proof of professional prostitution." Responding to the complaints of neighbors, officers interrogated a twenty-three-year-old unmarried block matron who "insisted on living alone" and "admitted prostitution." Magnifying her transgression, her desires were not contained within appropriate racial boundaries: "she was visited by [white] soldiers from the Military Police barracks." As a consequence, authorities of the WRA forced her to yet again relocate: she was "moved in with a family." So, as we see, women who dissented from sexual norms—in thought, word, or deed—were to be domesticated, if not expelled from the community. The block matron and other female transgressors further were urged to take long-term leave and move to the Midwest or East Coast.[26]

WRA officials then—and some historians afterward—were invested in minimizing charges of sexual deviance. Punishment frequently took the form of chastisement, reprimand, and familial sanction and reformation, as opposed to jail sentences. Had administrators chosen to, they could have tried any of these women and found them guilty, under stringent WRA regulations forbidding not only adultery but also fornication. Not to be left out in these proliferating and overlapping realms of sexual regulation, the Jerome Community Council as late as January 1944 adopted its own Ordinance No. 1, which forbade offenses against "public peace and order," "official authority and public property," "public safety," and "public decency and morals," never fully specified. Generally, enforcement of sexual provisions was lax, sometimes unnecessary. Because it was in the WRA's best interest to downplay such matters to critics, it was policed through informal mechanisms or overlooked. Medical conditions nonetheless were treated. Quietly. Though there would be at least two syphilis outbreaks at Jerome, with several cases noted in the fall of 1942 and ten cases documented in the fall of 1943, Dr. Joseph McSparran—when asked about the extent of camp venereal disease by a Senate investigator—insisted "we can almost disregard it completely."[27]

To authorities, marriage seemed the surest defense against unbridled lust and social instability in the camps. Japanese American newspaper reporters joined in, with the praiseworthy exchange of vows repeatedly capturing headlines. "SCHOOL HEAD'S LIVING ROOM BECOMES 'MARRIAGE PARLOR,'" the Jerome paper declared, after three of the first four weddings of camp inmates were held there, "at the edge of beautiful Lake Chicot" in Lake Village, Arkansas, "surrounded by natural scenery." "FIRST WEDDING IN CENTER"—that is, within the confines of the camp—was a Buddhist ceremony, uniting Genji Nakata of 45-5-B and neighbor Yoshiye Yamamoto of 45-6-F. Buddhist minister Reverend Gyodo Kono officiated, and 150 guests attended the reception. Especially laudable were women who married Japanese American soldiers, as is explained further in the next chapter. From late 1942, when "LOCAL GIRL WEDS ARMY CORPORAL" from Camp Crowder, Missouri, to late 1943, when "LOCAL GIRL WEDS SOLDIER" from Camp Robinson, Arkansas, the marital and sexual status of young women and—especially, enlisted—men was tracked, meriting newspaper headlines.[28]

8. Issei couple and Nisei couple at the Rohwer concentration camp, July 1944. 97.292.13L, MC, JANM.

The so-called epidemic of marriages was fully to be expected, given the demographics of Japanese immigration and the consequent age distribution of imprisoned Japanese Americans. At Jerome and Rohwer, as with the incarcerated population broadly, nearly 40 percent of inmates fell between the ages of fifteen and thirty. A numerical inevitability, marriages further were spurred by the wrenching separations and dislocations of incarceration. Early in the eviction process, Miyo Senzaki got married, in part, so that she could accompany her mate to the camps—first, Santa Anita detention center, then Rohwer. At the end of 1942, Yukiko Miyata of Jerome moved to Rohwer after marrying Mitsuo Miyamoto. These two cases and a multitude of additional examples demonstrate the way in which a woman was routinely expected to relocate and resettle—yet again—at her husband's place of residence, leaving behind her own family and friends. These patriarchal norms extended across most, if not all, racial and ethnic groups in the midcentury United States, though so-called "war brides"—especially those married to soldiers sent overseas—might legitimately remain in or return to their parental home.[29]

Young married couples faced an uncertain environment in which to raise their third-generation Sansei children. Balancing able doctors against the sometimes dubious hospital facilities and spartan camp conditions, Miyo Senzaki doubted the viability of family-building: "It's a crime to have children. We're not doing them any favors." Still, during the war years, there were nearly six thousand live births across the ten concentration camps. Contrary to detractors' wild claims about "excess leisure" giving way to "excess breeding," Japanese American birthrates in the camps—meticulously monitored by the WRA—were in fact lower than those of the U.S. population as a whole. In the early months of incarceration, they were well below national averages. Only during the last full year of imprisonment did they rise to meet them. Thus, Japanese American coupling and child-raising fell into line with broader American patterns.[30]

Defying cultural taboos against interracial marriage, some detainees presented a distinctive set of challenges to the military and the WRA administration. During expulsion and incarceration, what would happen to the non–Japanese American spouses of Japanese American detainees? How would their children be classed? Across the nine states in which assembly centers and concentration camps were built, what segregation and miscegenation statutes might apply? On the West Coast, eviction orders often could be deferred and mobility restrictions could be waived for Japanese Americans married to European Americans. Such was the case with Richard Hideo Naito, after officials certified that his wife, Helen Hansen Naito, was "Caucasian." Interestingly, as revealed by the investigation into her background, Mrs. Naito was likely of German origin, evidenced by the baptismal record from the German Lutheran Church of Leavenworth, Washington. Thus again was exposed the great irony of indiscriminately incarcerating one entire ethnic minority population—descended from a so-called enemy nation—and not another. Thus again was exposed the importance of race in wartime detention.[31]

Deferrals and waivers were granted almost exclusively to couples with children, demonstrating the centrality of the nuclear family to notions of normalcy. Couples without children could receive deferrals and waivers too, however, if one of the two served in the U.S. armed forces—another crucial means of incorporation into the national family.[32]

Of the two, was the mother or the father seen to have a more Americanizing influence within the nuclear family structure? As is implicit in the "Mixed Marriage Policy," a white mother was thought to hold greater sway than a white father. Thus, "mixed marriage families composed of a Japanese [American] husband, Caucasian [citizen] wife and mixed blood children" could be released from camps without further investigation. But families comprising a European American father, Japanese American wife, and their children would only be released if "the environment of the family" was proven to be "Caucasian." Similarly, those children, at adulthood, would only be released "if their environment has been Caucasian."[33]

With their frequent refusal to note non–European American/non–Japanese American mothers or fathers, WRA policies obviously could not account for the full range of human possibilities—or the flux of racial categorization. As with all attempts at drawing social distinctions, exceptions would always arise. At Rohwer several mothers of mixed-race children, as many as six or more, came from Mexican and/or Spanish backgrounds, as recorded at the highest levels of official correspondence. Interestingly, a mother of Spanish descent—presumably, thus, European American—would not be classed as "Caucasian." Her "race" was listed as "Spanish." A mother of Mexican descent could well have had Spanish origins as well; but it seems any ancestral intermarriage with native tribal populations resulted in her "race" being listed as "Mexican." Likewise at Jerome, among a number of *racial* types, mothers could be classed as Mexican *or* Spanish—seemingly *national* designations—*or* Caucasian. Regardless, by the middle of the period of incarceration, any family deemed racially mixed would now be subject only to the ordinary procedures of leave clearance. Neither "Caucasian" ancestry nor environment—nor any other—would alone suffice as reason for release.[34]

For Japanese Americans attempting to wed non–Japanese American partners, marriage licenses were difficult to obtain during the war years. When a man detained in Arkansas attempted to tie the knot with a white woman, Pulaski County authorities refused. State law forbade marriages between black and white partners, as was the case with all miscegenation statutes in the southern states. Usually, other races either were left out and perhaps exempt from miscegenation statutes or were expressly allowed to marry, all at the discretion of local officials. The Pulaski County Clerk declined to exercise his discretion. Despite intervention by the WRA, Judge Trimble upheld his decision. Meanwhile, in Alabama, where some Japanese American soldiers trained at Fort McClellan, state legislators attempted to revise their miscegenation law "to ban marriages between Caucasians and Japanese." This particular measure failed.[35]

From Washington to Arkansas, across the sixteen detention centers and ten concentration camps and beyond, major life decisions and family patterns were influenced, shaped, and even decreed by governmental authorities. Often at odds with one another—as between the federal and local levels—bureaucrats and administrators had the power not only to detain. They also investigated and intervened in the most intimate aspects of everyday life, revealing gender, family, and sexuality to be not private, domestic concerns, but public, national matters, symbolic of the largest modes of American belonging. They were, simply put, life-and-death issues. The stories of imprisoned individuals, couples, and families—such as the Miyasakis—are vital to the recuperation of a collective history of incarceration. Important in the recording of everyday experiences and concerns is to recount the ways in which relatively simple chores as well as momentous life processes became unmanageable tasks, often impossible to fulfill given the inadequacies of camp facilities and rigidities of bureaucratic structures. That they were increasingly undertaken with success, that a livable life was fashioned by most, is testament to the will and resourcefulness of Japanese Americans determined to master their environment.

UNUSUAL PLACES

How could lesbian, gay, bisexual, and transgender (LGBT) persons live satisfactory lives in concentration camps? In Nazi Germany, homosexuals were targeted for shipment to death camps along with Jews, Romany, disabled people, and others. Many thousands died. In the United States, LGBT Americans were expelled from the West Coast and moved to concentration camps only as part of the indiscriminate incarceration of *all* Japanese Americans. In many ways, the camps provided to them new means of interaction. At Jerome and Rohwer, companionship could build upon the advantages of both urban and rural forms of queer culture, as the case of Masao Asahara and Jack Yamashita demonstrates.[36]

Masao Asahara was born into a large farm family in Gardena, California, just south of Los Angeles, in January 1914. From the ages of twelve to twenty, he attended school in his parents' homeland in Japan. When he returned to the Los Angeles area, he worked in his father's fields near Long Beach. He began farming his own plots in 1937 but was forced to abandon them when the expulsion order came. Within Japanese American agricultural circles, the more reserved Asahara had met chatty Jack Yamashita. Also a Kibei, Yamashita had worked his way up in the world. Once the manager of a vegetable market in Long Beach, he launched his own small fruit and vegetable distribution company in 1932, trucking other farmers' produce, perhaps eventually the Asaharas'.[37]

Masao Asahara was sent with his parents and siblings to Santa Anita and then to Jerome, where Jack Yamashita had separated from his wife and their two children shortly after arrival. Though it's unclear whether or not Asahara and Yamashita were lovers in California, it's certain that they not only enjoyed each other's company but also each other's bodies in Arkansas. On a pleasant night in mid-September 1943, the two stayed up late, talking, drinking, and discussing Yamashita's plans to resettle. After midnight they ventured outdoors to be free of Yamashita's apartment mate. Unit 9-7-F was well located. At the end of a building, which was itself at the end of a row, it was as far away from other apartments as was possible, and with more grass outside for lying down. However it also was near the intersection of two streets. Asahara and Yamashita were partially undressed, apparently kissing, when a white security officer driving down C Street spotted them.[38]

Catching them in his headlights around 1:30 in the morning, associate chief C. R. Felker first assumed that "some boy was kissing his girl good night." When he pulled up alongside, he realized the two were males—and not so young. The pair of twenty-nine-year-olds "were supporting each other. Their clothing was disarranged, shirt tails out," and they "smelled strongly of alcohol." The fast-talking Yamashita capitalized upon this last point. While Asahara was reluctant to speak to Felker, Yamashita chatted "rather freely," explaining that they had been celebrating his imminent departure. He straightaway confessed to having split a pint of liquor with Asahara. He further admitted buying the contraband alcohol on the outside. At this point, the two seem to have warmed to a charade—an exaggerated performance, willingly taking on the consequences of public drunkenness. As with so many gay men caught with their pants down in midcentury America, Asahara and Yamashita appeared to own up to one illegal act in exchange for reprieve from another far more reprehensible crime. Asahara was "thick tongued," Yamashita "loud." And to Felker, both looked "bleary-eyed" and "unsteady on their feet." For his part, Felker did not pursue charges of indecency, though it was expressly forbidden in WRA policy. Instead, he arrested them for drunkenness and threw them in jail at Dermott for the night. The next day the two pleaded guilty and were sentenced to either ten more days in jail or a $10 fine each. Both chose to pay the fine.[39]

Internal security officers at Jerome had been instructed to "inspect periodically and irregularly the assigned district and . . . be observant of all persons seen in [the] district and especially of those out late hours or in unusual places," the very times and places pressed into the service of queer desire. As queer theorists and historians have demonstrated, illicit sexual activity finds outlet in forgotten pockets and corners, at odd hours and moments. WRA officials had fully expected the camps' close quarters to facilitate non-normative sexual activity, which it detailed at length, if not with precision. While the WRA prohibited rape in part I, paragraph 2, of its Uniform Classification of Offenses, as well as prostitution and commercialized vice in part II, paragraph 13, it attempted to criminalize all other sex offenses in paragraph 14: "Includes offenses against chastity, common decency and morals such as: abduction and compelling to marry; abortion; adultery and fornication; bastardy and concealing death of a bastard; bigamy and polygamy; buggery; incest and marriage within prohibited degree; indecent exposure; indecent liberties; intercourse or marriage with an insane, epileptic or venereally-diseased person; miscegenation; seduction; sodomy or crime against nature. Includes attempts."[40]

A careful spatial analysis of camp life suggests that it afforded unique opportunities to resourceful queer men. Like urban centers, concentration camps brought large numbers of people together into dense living environments. Meeting sexual dissidents was assured. For the majority who had lived in the rural farmlands of California and Hawaii before the war, it was now easier. Though the same level of urban anonymity could not be expected—parents and siblings often resided in the same or adjacent apartments or no more than a few blocks away—there were few if any of the racial boundaries that often foreclosed interactions in the cities' white-dominated gay enclaves. Even if among the small number of unemployed in camp, lacking the wage labor so crucial to independent urban living, single men were able to take up residences on

9. Block 1, known as Bachelor's Row, Jerome concentration camp, June 1944. Charles E. Mace, photographer. NWDNS-210-G-H432, WRAR, SPB, NA.

their own, apart from their family of origin. Further, camp life often hastened a break with parents, a break both agonizing and liberating. Asahara was estranged from his own. Several members of the family were tapped for transfer to Tule Lake, after registering as something less than "loyal" to the United States. Masao Asahara had changed his "no" answer on the loyalty questionnaire—detailed in chapter 8—to "yes," meaning he would be left to his own devices in Jerome.[41]

The entirety of Block 1 was set aside for over two hundred unmarried men, mostly older Issei who had little if any kin in America. Situated at the far northwest corner of the camp, at the bend in the three strands of barbed wire, "Bachelors Row" became a model community, known for its quiet tranquillity and its exquisitely manicured gardens. If we can apply Peter Boag's analysis of urban men's boardinghouses and rural workers' bunkhouses in the Pacific Northwest to this scenario, we should assume that men regularly developed close intimate relations that could involve the sharing of cots and beds—and bodies.[42]

Even as the concentration camps foreclosed countless freedoms, they opened up new possibilities for same-sex intimacy, as was clearly the case for

Jiro Onuma. In December 1923, just before the National Origins Act forbade all further Japanese immigration, Onuma had come to the United States from Iwate Prefecture. He found work and took up residence in San Francisco, where he would remain—with the exception of the war years—until his death. He never married nor had children. Onuma collected some of the early homoerotic photo-magazines, including those of New York physique culturist Earle E. Liederman from the mid-1920s. Just before the war, while in his late thirties, Onuma developed a close relationship with a younger man of Japanese descent. The two spent lots of time together. Once, they enlisted the services of a professional photographer to take portraits of themselves, each in dress suit, separately. Because they lived near one another, perhaps together, they were sent to the same detention center, Tanforan, and the same concentration camp, Topaz. There they met another young man, with glasses, who seemed to share their interests—a workmate of Onuma's on the kitchen crew at the Block 3 dining hall. In their all-male work environments and leisure pursuits, Onuma, his younger partner, and their young friend seemed comfortable in their intimacy. They even allowed someone to snap their picture, all together. Rich with connotations, the image shows the three seated on a dirt hillside, a guard tower and the barbed-wire fence in the background. The bespectacled man sits slightly off to the side. Described by associates as "quiet and honourable," "just a modest, good guy," Onuma is slightly above, his hand warmly, maybe proprietarily, rested on his partner's shoulder. The partner, at ease, smokes a cigarette.[43]

Rare among the thousands of black-and-white images of incarceration, this photograph—deposited with Onuma's papers at the Gay, Lesbian, Bisexual and Transgender Historical Society in San Francisco—provides a brief but suggestive glimpse into the lives of men with same-sex attachments under incarceration. Given the restrictions around photography in the camps, it hints that these relationships were important, worthy of recording, even at pain of potential punishment. It suggests that men had greater ease in finding friends and partners in the dense, often sex-segregated environments of the camps—both bachelor immigrants such as Onuma with no family in the United States and younger second-generation Japanese Americans whose ties to parents had been loosened in the camps.

Greater social liberties for young adults—boding "family breakdown" and "juvenile delinquency," alarmists feared—accompanied greater economic autonomy and permitted greater sexual exploration. Of the sixty-seven clubs at Rohwer, only twenty were for "mixed groups." The remainder were sex-segregated. There was a similar ratio of coed clubs to exclusively male or female clubs at Jerome. The community activities division's monthly report form, WRA-239, devised in Washington, demonstrated the gender, civic, and religious cast of national organizations that officials hoped to promote through local chapters. It listed the "Red Cross, Junior Red Cross, Boy Scouts, Girl Scouts, Camp Fire Girls, YWCA, YMCA, Hi-Y, Girl Reserves, PTA, AAUW, JACL, 4-H Clubs, USO." Historians of sexuality have well-documented the ways in which even Christian, sex-segregated, service organizations—while officially condemning homosexuality—could provide places of refuge for and spaces for experimentation between young men, between older men, and, in mentoring relationships, between younger and older. The YMCA has warranted its own history in this regard, John Donald Gustav-Wrathall's insightful *Take the Young Stranger by the Hand: Same-Sex Relations and the YMCA.* Research suggests that girls and women similarly have utilized same-sex environments to pursue same-sex eroticism. Depicting that potential, photos of the sophomore girls "weekly dance party" at Rohwer, female bodies pressed tightly together, mirror the images of and texts about the physicality and closeness of relationships at girls' schools and women's colleges, in women's workplaces, and in women's clubs and professional organizations. Certainly, the mentoring relationship can be particularly fraught and fruitful—particularly if they cross race or class lines as well as generational ones—as we've seen in Haru Miyazaki's affections for her former teacher, Virginia Tidball, and in various young men's fondness for Earl Finch.[44]

Similar to the GI drag that proliferated at army bases and camps throughout the war years, entertainment in the concentration camps included elaborately choreographed performances of cross-dressing—mostly of the humorous variety. In Arkansas one such masquerade served as comic relief in what otherwise might have been a terribly doleful presentation: "Parody of Leaving for Camp, Performed Outdoors." Put on by an all-male cast who first marched out in suits—tags with family numbers dangling from their lapels—the act was watched by countless spectators and recorded on film. Soon, a conspicuously tall man appeared cross-dressed in a skirt and top, with broad-brimmed hat, carrying a handbag. Referencing the overstated incarceration baby boom, he pushed a stroller along. He covered the stroller with one parasol, seemingly to protect a newborn from the sun, and with another, over his shoulder, he shaded himself. Hardly frail, however, the actor stumbled along in his high heels with a broad, manly gait. The transparency of this high-contrast, gender masquerade raised an important ideological point: that men had been, in the words of many observers at the time, "emasculated" by incarceration. Still, as Allan Bérubé and others have shown, male-to-female drag elicits multiple responses from multiple audiences. And while chauvinists might use it to ridicule women and attempt to strengthen their grip on male privilege, queer boys and men can find it empowering and inspiring in its gender transgression and homosexual eroticism. Within the tight physical confines of the camp, it could help in bringing together those who shared a desire to break out from narrow social norms.[45]

Some sexual outlaws were able to break free of the camp's physical restraints, traveling around a largely rural landscape nonetheless filled with sexual possibility. Masao Asahara's friend Jack Yamashita had a Packard automobile, and—one of the rare few—he was allowed to maintain it at the Jerome camp. He had, after all, declared that he was resettling, taking indefinite leave, as was permitted for some, as long as they kept outside the West Coast zone of exclusion. For six months Yamashita had declared he was resettling—and yet he remained, motoring around Arkansas. He was granted day passes with great frequency, once to talk with the gasoline rationing board in Lake Village. There, his plan to move well out of the state, to Denver, had secured more fuel for his journeys, difficult under wartime rationing. He also was cleared to take day trips to Rohwer and Little Rock. Did he have sex partners at Rohwer? Did he find the gay communities of the state capital? If so, did he circulate in black or white ones? His activities would have been highly secretive then, so with traditional historical methods they are difficult to ascertain *with precision* now. But it's clear that he made the most of every venture outside. Ordinarily cleared to be away from 9:00 a.m. to midnight, he was regularly signed out and back in within a narrow fifteen minutes of the appointed hour—perhaps suggesting a classic queer use of opportune times.[46]

Incarceration provided unique opportunities to sexual and gender nonconformists. In particular, as characteristic of most wartime mobilizations, dense homosocial spaces provided numerous homosexual possibilities. Women earned greater economic independence, beneficial to lesbians, bisexuals, and heterosexuals, and queer men took advantage of propitious camp environments, as well as neighboring regions, to enable not only congregation—as in urban gay enclaves and the camps' own bachelor blocks—but also circulation, as with Jack Yamashita's presumed interactions in the more sparsely populated but no less vital, rural queer networks of Arkansas: fueled by automotive transport and lubricated with alcohol. While the preservers of "tradition" lamented family breakdown and husbands' and fathers' emasculation under incarceration, sex and gender outcasts got busy forging new social arrangements that would help transform the postwar world.

Raised in a "Caucasian environment," a white middle-class neighborhood in San Pedro, California, Mary Nakahara was transformed by incarceration in ways markedly different from most Japanese Americans. Popular as a teenager, she had moved in white circles; at San Pedro High School and at Compton Junior College, she had dated only white guys. Then at the Santa Anita detention camp, over lunch one day, she "noticed that the boy across from me seemed a little different from most Japanese boys. (Perhaps it was that he seemed better-looking.)" The boy, it turned out, was named Vetter; he had a European American father. The two "talked for a little while. He was very polite; so well-mannered." The meeting led Nakahara to reflect in her diary that evening on the relative attractiveness of various racial types. "It seems there's quite a few mixtures," she wrote. Then, mulling over the unfamiliar terminology, she scratched out the word "mixtures." She started again. "It seems there's quite a few people who have mixed backgrounds through inter-marriage. They seem to be quite a bit better looking than the average Japanese."[47]

These views carried over to her new occupation, one coveted by many young women in the camps. "Although I never intended [to work] in a hospital, I'm certainly happy to have such a chance." There her sympathies were tugged by a very young patient, "a darling boy. He was completely Caucasian, with sort of an English accent. His last name, however, was Japanese." Nakahara worried about his future, and perhaps projected on to him her own worries for her own children—the ones she hoped to have one day. "I only hope that the outside world will be good to him when he grows older. It will probably be 'tough going' for him when it comes to jobs and marriages. But by that time perhaps people will be more broadminded on those issues." Inclined to intermarriage herself, Nakahara already fretted over the marital prospects for third-generation children of partial Japanese descent.[48]

Though she had worked at Woolworth's before the war, Mary Nakahara quickly took to her job as nurse's aide. She advanced rapidly, from "washing utensils and scrubbing floors" to assisting doctors on "housecalls" at the converted horse stalls that passed as homes: "several measles cases, a contusion on the foot, asthma, colds, nose-bleed, and stomach trouble." To her great fortune, a female physician, Dr. Sakaye Shigekawa, took her under her wing—a mentor in every best sense. Nakahara was amazed at her lack of pretense: "Her prestige as a doctor was of no importance to her. Her attention was on the comfort of her patient." Nakahara wanted to emulate her. "She's so kind and cheerful and warm." At Shigekawa's side, she witnessed an operation. She attended a death. And during her first night shift, marvelous to behold, she was present at a delivery. "I never dreamed I'd ever get the opportunity to watch a birth of a baby." She had feared she would "pass out"; in the end, she overcame her fear. Again anticipating her future, she wrote in her diary, "I realize now what a mother has to go through; the pains and anxiety that are part of bearing a child. . . . I *realize* it, but I can't quite *understand* or fully know. . . . Every woman has to experience that herself."[49]

What an education: "I feel I've learned more in this [one month] than I could have learned in three to five years if I had continued to live the kind of life I had been living." In addition to this professional development, so common for so many women in the camps, Nakahara was making enormous strides as a religious and community leader. Not long after her eager participation in the first Protestant services at Santa Anita, Nakahara helped organize the Sunday school and was tapped as one of its teachers. From her first class, with a small but "swell bunch" of fifteen- and sixteen-year-old girls, she aimed to "expand—not only within our Sunday School circle, but within the camp as a whole." Though she had to remind herself that "getting a lot of girls to come doesn't mean success," she tallied her gains, in part, by attendance figures. Four weeks on, there were twenty—"remarkable that we could have increased so much." Foretelling a Christian zeal that would become characteristic of incarceration, she prayed for more. "I hope it continues."[50]

From older Sunday school teachers, from Dr. Shigekawa, Nakahara learned: "Nobleness is only made real in *service*." The additional forms that service would take dawned on her gradually, over several months. Witness to wrenching upheavals, those of her family and the people she encountered at the hospital, Nakahara still rarely lost control of her emotions. Stoic, downright cheerful in the face of adversity—penning and singing welcome songs for new inmates, to the tune of "Yankee Doodle Dandy"—she swallowed her sorrows. Until the letters came. On Monday 6 April 1942, she received her first batch, greetings from friends back home in San Pedro. "Gosh! I was so happy. I was just overcome." And for the first time since being locked up, "tears just came to my eyes. Letters can really bring happiness. It makes you think how happy a soldier must become when he receives letters." "Words can bring such happiness," she wrote when receiving mail again a month later, "and what ties they can bind." Thus was born the Crusaders, a service organization providing, among other things, correspondence to Japanese American soldiers—a wartime pen-pal association generating hundreds and, then with the aid of mimeograph machines, thousands of letters per month. "I want to fight, shoulder to shoulder, with every Nisei, for the right to the same opportunities as Caucasians. . . . Even if it's just writing letters, I'll write then—as I've never written before; letters that might inspire and encourage. I'm sure I can do my portion—and by golly I will."[51]

A sense of belonging, or lack of belonging, nonetheless plagued Mary Nakahara in the camps, based in part on her class privilege and racial ambivalence. Each eventful day occasioned yet another epiphany: "I realize what an easy life I led; so easy it seems almost story-book-like to think my past could have been so childishly blissful, when the great majority of the Japanese had to *fight* their way for even limited happiness and work unceasingly toward better living conditions, with prejudice and race discrimination." Her dad had fought and worked hard, earning enough as a fish market owner to make possible her own life of relative comfort. "I wish I had shown appreciation," she wrote in her diary. "It's too late to say 'thanks' because he's gone now"—deceased. Without cause, the FBI had taken him away to prison on 7 December 1941, only one day after he'd had stomach surgery. They returned Seiichi Nakahara to his family, on 20 January 1942, to die. He did—twelve hours later.[52]

Mary Nakahara found solace in another father figure, a white policeman who stopped to chat with her at Santa Anita. A nice fellow, he was "just the remedy to get that awful home-sick feeling out of me." She jotted down an unusual sentence in her diary: "Somehow it made me feel so good talking to an American." She thought some more, scratched out the word "an," and inserted "a white." A white American. But then deciding that the two were one and the same, she scratched out "white." "A white American," after all, was tantamount to "an American." Such racial dilemmas duly considered, Nakahara recorded that she then "went home—and continued writing letters."[53]

Schooled in the values of a dominant white, middle-class culture, Mary Nakahara necessarily had imbibed its norms of beauty, standards of desirability, and modes of respectability. Her dating preferences seemingly beyond her control, she was attracted to white guys. Further, she developed a reverence for service. She admired men who chose to serve in the military, such as her twin brother, Pete, who volunteered; she looked up to women who served as civic, religious, and professional leaders. Now classed and confined with a Japanese American minority she previously "never gave much thought to," Nakahara tentatively critiqued her class privilege and questioned her racial positioning. Like so many other women under incarceration, she began to adopt new affiliations and associations, based in part on the economic opportunity and autonomy on offer. Whereas John Rankin claimed "this is a race war"—"the white man's civilization has come into conflict with Japanese barbarism [and] one of them must be destroyed"—Mary Nakahara soon saw the fallacy of simple dichotomies of white versus brown good looks, American versus Japanese traits, women's versus men's roles. Under incarceration, social categories would grow more complex still.[54]

5 | Race, War, Dances

TURNING EASTWARD into the morning sun, three busloads of women crossed the Mississippi River toll bridge at Greenville early Saturday, the first of May 1943. Within a few hours' drive through the flat Delta cotton fields, they arrived in Jackson. There they paid a courtesy call at the local YWCA, ate a late lunch, browsed through several downtown shops, then continued on their journey south. Before sundown, the ninety-five young women—mostly in their late teens and twenties—reached their destination, just outside Hattiesburg, Mississippi. After a "wild scramble" ironing dresses and a "much needed fresh-up," they were ready to meet their hosts.[1]

The dance was a momentous occasion at Camp Shelby, one of the U.S. Army's largest training grounds. In the ballroom of Service Club No. 5, uniformed soldiers greeted the women and their chaperones with great formality, offering corsages and programs. From the stage, an emcee guided the assembly through the elaborate festivities. Soon couples were swaying to the music of the Station Hospital Medical Detachment Orchestra. And during intermissions, new friendships were made while additional ensembles and soloists performed. Refreshments included punch and a mammoth 170-pound cake, cut with much fanfare. Lightbulbs flashed as public relations officers skirted around the crowd, photographing such highpoints. At the appointed moment, silence descended, and in a clear signal of the event's significance, Brigadier General G. M. O'Halloran, commander of the 70,000-person post, made brief welcoming remarks. Then the 442nd Regimental Combat Team's Colonel Charles Pence led his wife, his infantrymen, and their guests in the grand march. The evening's climax, as reported on the front page of the camp newspaper, *The Reveille*, "was the presentation of a lei to each girl by her dancing partner." The morning after, the women attended Sunday church services outdoors under the pines. They toured Camp Shelby, and in groups of four, they lunched with soldiers at two dozen mess halls. After more dancing that afternoon, they boarded their buses and began the long trip back home.[2]

Just as these guests were no ordinary partygoers—women on leave from the Rohwer concentration camp—the 442nd was no ordinary army outfit. Racially segregated, made up of Japanese Americans from both the territory of Hawaii and the mainland, it had been activated only weeks before by President Franklin Roosevelt. By the war's end, its ranks and that of its affiliated units would total over thirty thousand men. Congressman John Rankin had campaigned hard against the boot camp assignment in his home state, claiming Hawaiians had "aided in the fifth column work before the attack on Pearl Harbor," despite FBI director J. Edgar Hoover's congressional testimony to the contrary. "We in the South consider it an imposition that [they] are brought to such strategic defense zone states as Florida, Louisiana, and Mississippi for training. They are a serious menace to our Gulf Coast defense and steps should be taken to remove this threat." The military brass laughed off Rankin's charges. But they did weigh other threats.[3]

Concerned as ever with enlistees' off-duty activities, U.S. military officers took unprecedented steps to manage soldiers' lives outside working hours during the war. Though heterosexual prostitution, gambling, and other "vices" continued to enjoy tacit and sometimes explicit approval, officials increasingly crafted and publicized more wholesome entertainments. With the aid of quasi-public charitable organizations such as the YWCA and USO, they forged elaborate programs heralding a new era of regulated recreation, state-sanctioned courtship, and institutionalized heterosexuality. Growing numbers of nonwhite servicemen and the proliferation of segregated units—particularly African American squadrons and the 442nd—had aggravated white middle-class anxieties over interracial dating and miscegenation. And as historian Allan Bérubé has documented, the war's largely homosocial environments produced homosexual possibilities that commanders zealously attempted to thwart.[4]

Young women at the two southeast Arkansas concentration camps proved central in government and community schemes to promote intra-ethnic dating and matrimony. Enabled by their proximity to Mississippi, second-generation

Japanese American women participated in at least two well-structured programs. First, they joined in a series of army-sponsored dances with the 442nd at Camp Shelby, initiated with this May 1943 trip. Second, they regularly entertained visiting Nisei troops at USO facilities within the Jerome and Rohwer camps. This chapter examines and sets the broader context for these programs, as well as some Nisei women's resistance to them. Such resistance, I argue, reflected and shaped the workings of larger social hierarchies of nationality, race and ethnicity, gender and sexuality.

Of these, gender seemed dangerously unstable, as Japanese American women exacted surprising benefits from concentration camps and mounted subtle but effective challenges to patriarchal control, as we've seen. Racial positionings too were in flux, defying notions of a fixed continuum that seemingly would have located displaced Japanese Americans somewhere "between black and white" in the multicultural U.S. South. While black and white remained the heavily weighted extremities on racial scales for a host of human activities and ideologies, the experiences of Japanese Americans demonstrate that in a white supremacist world, it was not whiteness but rather blackness that represented the most inviolable of racial categories.[5]

In order to assess the multiple implications of these programs, this chapter elaborates two vital but often neglected aspects of Japanese American experience, which help to clarify the paradox of incarceration and war service, as well as the complex identifications and affiliations crafted by Nikkei—that is, all persons of Japanese descent—in wartime America. To probe the slippery gray area between resistance and accommodation, we first should consider the highly contingent, localized nature of racial categorization, especially given many Japanese Americans' ability to repeatedly pass in and out of the camps, into southern communities often ill-equipped to enforce anything other than a single, biracial, black/white color line. Second, we should further acknowledge and articulate the distinctive circumstances of incarceration for Japanese American women.[6]

COMPLICATING THE COLOR LINE

At 10,000 acres and a peak population of 8,500 each, Rohwer and Jerome developed into "the largest cities in southeast Arkansas south of Pine Bluff," as one official put it. They dwarfed their neighboring communities within rural Desha and Chicot counties, respectively. And they radically altered the racial composition. Of the approximately 27,000 people in each of the two counties as of 1940, African Americans had accounted for almost 60 percent, with most of the remainder European Americans. Thus, though seemingly confined to two discrete enclaves, Japanese Americans newly settled in the South would figure prominently in the renegotiation of racial boundaries and racial hierarchies. Such renegotiation would have regional as well as national ramifications, and it inevitably would involve the testing of gender norms.[7]

In Arkansas the boundaries of the WRA camps proved highly permeable. As historians of incarceration have noted, camp directors selectively granted inmates short-term leave to visit medical specialists, conduct business matters, and negotiate property transactions; seasonal leave to take temporary work contracts in agriculture and industry; and indefinite leave to attend college, accept permanent employment, and completely resettle in communities outside the West Coast evacuated area. Far more common, however, and not thoroughly examined by historians was the pass system that daily put Japanese Americans into contact with local people. Though the two southern sites and eight western sites were chosen in part for their geographical remoteness, detainees were not wholly cut off. They often walked or drove out of the gates, caught buses or trains, and maneuvered through countless interactions that ranged from friendly to frightening, mundane to murderous.[8]

Rohwer and Jerome residents regularly left the centers to shop in nearby towns and faraway cities. School outings and intercamp team sports meant numerous trips up and down the highway. Pastors and musicians were guests at congregations in town. Women and men, young and old, attended conferences from Little Rock to Jackson, sponsored by Girl Reserves, YWCA, YMCA, and other organizations. Though "shopping passes were issued to as many as seventy-five people in one day" at Jerome, as of June 1943 "one day trip passes" averaged sixteen per day, after "new more stringent rules" went into effect there. Even so, Rohwer Community Activities supervisor Nat Griswold wrote with alarm to his camp director a year later that "the pass system for groups has entirely broken down; also the requirement for an escort from the appointed personnel is inoperative at the gate." Again, fears centered on Japanese American martial arts. "The truck with the [judo] team left our [Rohwer] gate *without a pass*, went through the Jerome gate *without a pass*, returned through Jerome gate and our gate *without a pass.* There were on the truck persons who were on our stop list and others whose names were not on the pass. The truck left our gate and entered Jerome without an escort. . . . I reached the view that the responsibility rests somewhere between our Internal Security and the Military Police." Individuals and small groups left without passes too. Rohwer residents so frequently went shopping without approval that officials called it "French leave." Jerome residents used one back exit so often to go fishing that officials there dubbed it "the 'secret' route."[9]

In these movements, Japanese Americans encountered a southern racial order of extensive segregation, designed largely to accommodate two distinct if not always precise racial categories. Signaling not just difference but also dominance, these categories privileged one group over the other, in economic and social realms and—in much of Mississippi and eastern Arkansas—in a political structure of minority white rule. W. E. B. Du Bois's famous description of the problem of the twentieth century as "the problem of the color-line" implied a single, self-evident line. Marked as neither white nor black, however, Americans of Japanese descent visibly contested that line. As Japanese Americans exposed and were exposed to a multiplicity of racialized activities in the South, they disrupted racial practice. In undertaking these activities, they faced innumerable situations requiring various degrees of choice, acquiescence, complicity, and resistance.

Jim Crow segregation entailed careful spatial distinctions, and Japanese Americans in the South learned them, often for the first time, on the bus. Numerous contemporaneous reports and remembered accounts describe a revelatory moment on a commercial passenger bus line, which reserved the better seats for whites usually without any signage to that effect. One newly arrived Jerome resident, for example, took the bus into McGehee, Arkansas, and—"trained in Western courtesy"—he offered his seat to a "Negro woman" who got on at the next stop. Because the seat "happened to be toward the front of the bus," the driver physically removed the woman from the seat and "pushed [her] to the overcrowded back rows." In this "his first encounter with . . . such practices," the Japanese American passenger "looked on with amazement, . . . stunned [and] bewildered." Nonetheless, he was allowed to remain in the "white" section. Nisei soldiers on their way to and from Camp Shelby experienced similar conflicts, though they sometimes interceded on behalf of black southerners and joined them in the back of the bus. In one case, after the white driver "actually kicked a black GI off the bus with his feet," a Nisei soldier assaulted the driver. When another driver pushed an elderly black woman to the ground, a Nisei soldier and five others "kicked the hell out of him." According to one black local, Arvarh Strickland, "black Hattiesburg was rife with rumors" about the Nisei who "did not readily accept their classification as 'white.' . . . My community especially enjoyed the reports of conflicts between men of the 442nd Regiment and white bus drivers and policemen."[10]

Still, as George Mine recalls, when faced with explicitly marked "white" and "colored" ticket windows, water fountains, and theater sections, he and fellow Japanese American soldiers in the South were instructed by their white commanding officers to "put yourself in the white category." Indeed, the Hattiesburg City Council called a special meeting to address this quandary and ruled that Japanese Americans "would be permitted to use facilities reserved for whites." According to Mike Masaoka, "That meant using the white latrines, sitting in the front of streetcars and buses when we went to town, eating inside the restaurants instead of being handed our food out in the back. While we were uncomfortable with a double standard and sympathetic with the blacks, we as a matter of principle were not going to accept inferior status." Truly, ambivalence often was superseded by the attractions of higher status. As Thomas Taro Higa recalls, whereas an African American man suggested he should use a colored restroom in a small southern town, "a white gentleman came to my aid." Higa, with a sense of gratitude, used the white restroom. Ever since the formation of the segregated 442nd, some prisoners in Arkansas and elsewhere had expressed dismay about its potential use as "cannon fodder" and about the inevitable comparisons to African American platoons. "No American of Japanese ancestry wants to give his life for the preservation of Jap Crowism," as a *Heart Mountain Sentinel* editorial put it. Like African American troops at Camp Shelby, the 442nd and related Japanese American units were forced to sleep in segregated barracks and eat in segregated mess halls. But, as we've seen, whereas African Americans at Shelby had their own "colored" sports leagues, Japanese Americans successfully competed in "white" leagues.[11]

Of all Nisei soldiers, perhaps none took greater pride than Eddie Shimano in his ability to move in white circles, to make white friends, and to enjoy the privileges associated with white manhood. Previously incarcerated at Jerome, where he had been elected to the Community Council, he wrote back to the camp's magazine about his getting drunk with white enlisted men and, together, their making passes at female strangers. "To be out in the world again," he concluded, "after almost a year of the restricted subnormal and morbid life in centers makes me, to use a good old American phrase"—perhaps laced with sarcasm—"feel like a white man again." Aiding in this process, the WRA in 1943 increasingly encouraged Japanese Americans to leave the concentration camps for college, for war service, or to set up new homes in "normal American communities" off the West Coast—dispersed across dozens of predominantly white towns and cities so as to dilute numerical strength, as explained more fully in chapter 8. Though some aspired to whiteness, many negotiated an intermediate racial status, as they firmly disavowed blackness and downplayed the importance of Japanese American enclaves. As one "resettler" cheerfully reported from Denver, "Our immediate neighbors (just as in Los Angeles) are Jewish and Mexican Americans. No 'Boochies' live in this district." Though this statement obviously reflects the views of a single individual, its publication in the Jerome magazine's premiere issue—devoted primarily to resettlement—suggests that those views may have been shared, at least in part, by the editors, by some of the readers, and by camp director Paul Taylor, who penned the page-one introduction.[12]

Further, in reviewing leave clearance applications, Taylor and Rohwer director Ray Johnston readily approved long-term departures for prisoners who secured positions with white employers, especially Christian organizations. But WRA officials balked at extending leave to those with job offers from black institutions: "Japanese-American[s] in the Mid-South have been accepted as 'white people.' . . . If we approve Japanese-Americans to teach in colored schools, we may endanger the social standing of any evacuee relocating in the South." Even some Christian organizations went too far, as the WRA saw it, in their racial politics, as when Jimmie Woodward, of the Southwest Council of Student Christian Associations, proposed holding a multiracial conference at Rohwer. "We are constantly striving to keep the people in this region from treating the evacuees as they treat Negroes," as an official replied to her. "We are also suffering from political attacks which come from various angles. Having a mixed conference might be the very occasion which would suit those who want to find fault with the liberal policies of the WRA."[13]

The very imprisonment of Japanese Americans as a group suggests that they were not "accepted as white"—at either the regional or national level—as were, say, Italian Americans and German Americans. And the very language of acceptance, like the language of tolerance, signaled fundamental power differentials between (white) groups who determined acceptance and (nonwhite) groups who received it or were denied it. But even as federal prisoners, many Japanese Americans showed a significant ability to move in and across a number of spaces segregated as white.

Indeed, in the towns and cities of Arkansas and Mississippi, inmates with day passes and short-term leave almost exclusively patronized white stores, visited white churches, participated in white conferences, and stayed in white hotels. Camp officials brokered many of these contacts with outside white organizations. And yet Japanese Americans met subtle and overt resistance, such that Nat Griswold had to write multiple letters to conference organizers

10. Boy Scouts from Rohwer concentration camp host a five-day campout on the banks of the Mississippi River for scouts from Jerome, as well as Arkansas City, August 1943. Photographer unknown. NWDNS-210-G-G415, WRAR, SPB, NA.

and hoteliers, making certain that his traveling companions, whose names he spelled out and whose character he vouched for, would not be turned away. When 190 Rohwer and Jerome Boy Scouts prepared to go camping on the banks of the Mississippi, only one troop from the local white council agreed to go along. And when 125 Rohwer Girl Scouts volunteered to help out in the war effort, they were given the suspect and suspiciously symbolic activity of picking cotton on a private plantation.[14]

How appropriate, given that Asian—specifically, Chinese—laborers had been "introduce[d] . . . as substitutes for emancipated slaves in the South . . . after the Civil War," as Lucy M. Cohen has analyzed. Though their toil on the Delta's sugar and cotton plantations was relatively short-lived, many of their descendants remained in Arkansas, Louisiana, Mississippi, and Tennessee. Through the 1940s, Chinese Americans usually were schooled with and otherwise classed with *either* whites or blacks, depending on the local community. For example, Chinese Americans for a time were buried in the "Negro" section of the Memphis municipal cemetery. A notable exception were the

Chinese American groceries, which became "the only integrated milieux in the Delta," serving both blacks and working-class whites. Occasionally, three-tiered educational systems developed, as was briefly the case further south in Hattiesburg, after the children of Nisei soldiers were turned away from both public and private white schools and after parents refused to send them to black schools. But by the time of the Second World War, Chinese Americans in Dermott, just outside Jerome, attended white schools and churches. According to one white local, they were fully "accepted"—if not fully accepted as white or as American.[15]

In the 1940s race remained a principal marker of nationality; for many, including Mary Nakahara, Americanness was still equated with whiteness. For example, early in the three-year period of incarceration—amidst pervasive popular representations of shifty wartime "enemies within"—some white Arkansans demonstrated deadly hostility to Japanese Americans. On three occasions in November 1942, Nisei suffered gunshot wounds at the hands of irate locals. An incident at the beginning of that month was precipitated by ongoing tensions between camp building contractors slow in finishing their jobs and Japanese Americans keen to find wood for making furniture. A guard assigned to protect the contractors' supplies said he was "attacked" by boys throwing rocks. He responded by firing at the boys' legs with bird shot. WRA regional attorney Robert Leflar, based in Little Rock, insisted the boys "were not seriously injured[,] the boys admitted their fault and the matter was apparently closed up without any need for disciplinary action." Two further incidents likewise yielded no substantive disciplinary action against white perpetrators.[16]

Later that month twenty-two-year-old Private Louis Furushiro, on leave from Camp Robinson, Arkansas, stopped in a Dermott café en route to visit his sister at Jerome. Seventy-two-year-old W. M. Wood, eager to "shoot the next Jap he saw," produced a shotgun and fired from a distance of less than ten feet. Furushiro ducked and suffered only powder burns to his face, and somehow no one else in the café was injured. Wood was taken to jail but released on bond. Four days later three Rohwer residents and a white government employee were working in an unfenced wooded portion of the center when they happened upon tenant farmer M. C. Brown, age forty, returning from a deer hunt on horseback. Brown claimed he thought the men were escaping, and he fired on them with buckshot. As a result, one young man was injured in the hip and another in the calf. Though charged on a count of assault with intent to kill, Brown too was released on bond. WRA attorney Leflar assumed he could persuade district attorney Henry Smith, a fellow graduate of the University of Arkansas law school, to prosecute; however, it emerged that Smith was also a friend of Brown. They were deer-hunting buddies. Neither M. C. Brown nor W. M. Wood ever stood trial.[17]

Interestingly, though the WRA purported to give camp newspapers "full freedom of editorial expression," the Jerome paper's coverage of the Brown and Wood incidents suggests that pressure was applied. WRA officials in Arkansas wanted to minimize publicity about the shootings in order to calm their Japanese American wards and also, perhaps, to cover up the prosecution lapses. Thus, in the 17 November issue of the *Communiqué*—in which one front-page headline read: "PRE-SCHOOL MEET CALLED SUCCESS"—the first news of the shootings appeared on page four.[18]

The legal handling of the Brown and Wood assault cases differed sharply from that of Nebo Mack Person, a couple of weeks later. On 4 December 1942, the fifty-seven-year-old Person, a black employee of a Jerome construction contractor, propositioned two Japanese American women, one after the other, within earshot of other residents. In each case he offered $8. Person apparently "exposed his privates" and tore the coat of Asaye Waki, aged twenty-six. Sumiye Jitsumyo, twenty-one, ran away. Within four days Person was tried and convicted of indecent exposure and aggravated assault. He immediately began serving a two-year sentence without eligibility for parole. Afterward the prosecuting attorney promised to provide future Japanese American victims with similar "quick justice." Within weeks "Jerome Relocation Center [wa]s employing no Negro employees," as Paul Taylor assured Washington.[19]

If a white male Arkansan often proved immune to charges of attempted murder, especially of a nonwhite male, a black male Arkansan rarely escaped charges of attempted assault, especially against a nonblack female. Here, whites and Japanese Americans seemed to close ranks, as the Japanese American ascent toward whiteness was put into conversation with one of the key mythologies of southern racial control—what historians such as Jacquelyn Dowd Hall and Joel Williamson have referred to as the black beast-rapist. This figment of a paranoid white imagination, as we've seen in chapter 2, scripted hypersexualized black men as inveterate seducers and rapists of white women—and now, it seemed, other nonblack women as well. As American racial, national, and sexual meanings became even further intertwined through this particular case, women's roles in the discourse were circumscribed. The two victims did not give testimony in Chicot County Court. Rather, male community "leaders" were tapped to speak on their behalf.[20]

As all these interactions in the World War II South help demonstrate, Japanese Americans personified yet another American racial/ethnic category to be negotiated, even as they sometimes were used, or chose, to bolster a seemingly singular racial line or continuum. While problematizing any pat binary definitions of race, their experiences nonetheless simultaneously evidenced the primacy of the black/white distinction, propping up notions of black inferiority and white superiority. Thus, it was important for white "authorities," from bus drivers to army officers to concentration camp directors, to limit African American/Japanese American affiliation—that is, to maintain whiteness as the category worthy of emulation and aspiration (even as Japanese Americans could not *wholly* identify as white) and to maintain blackness as the inviolable category of abjection. Mirroring prevalent cultural assumptions about many nineteenth- and twentieth-century immigrants to the United States, Japanese Americans could be seen as at once white and nonwhite, but never as both black and nonblack. When faced with possible alliances by Japanese Americans with blacks, white officials encouraged a Japanese American/white identification. But when Japanese Americans and whites became adversaries in the criminal justice system—or, as we shall see, when they became potential partners in the intimacies of dancing, courtship, marriage, and thus interracial child-rearing—an undiluted white primacy and white privilege were reasserted.

Japanese American social and physical mobility in the South—the ability and willingness to move up some racial hierarchies and to move across many racially segregated spaces—is even more remarkable when considered against the homicidal rage of some white male Arkansans. Miraculously, no one was killed in these incidents. And though an aura of fear surely pervaded the camps, few seemed inclined to accept the limits of camp boundaries or the prejudices of local residents. By appearing in county courts, by testifying in print to such atrocities, and by shaking off these early altercations and continuing to travel around the South, Japanese Americans asserted their agency, even as they faced unparalleled limitations on their lives and livelihoods.

COURTING WITHIN THE COLOR LINES

Subtle intimations and explicit proscriptions characterized the ethnic partitioning of courtship under incarceration. Through spoken and unspoken sets of expectations, elders made clear to the young that dating had to follow precise racial formulas. For example, a Rohwer high school student who invited a white official's daughter to a dance had to "reneg[e]" once his parents voiced their strenuous "objections." These parents and other Issei generally frowned upon inter-ethnic dating by their children. But if romance strayed beyond racial/ethnic boundaries, then distinctive preferences were in evidence. As Paul Spickard has summarized, the "hierarchy of choice . . . , based roughly on skin color, prestige, and perceived cultural compatibility, . . . ran something like this: Caucasians; Chinese; Koreans; the outcast Japanese groups; Filipinos, Mexicans, and Puerto Ricans (in no particular order); and Blacks." Religious compatibility was important as well, and Buddhist temples in the Arkansas camps held numerous "couples-only" functions—not only to promote dating and matrimony within the faith, but also to reinforce that belief system against the onslaught of white Christian evangelists and missionaries invited into the camps for crusades and revivals, as described in the next chapter.[21]

Given these strictures, many teenagers had even greater difficulty finding a suitable mate after their parents resettled outside the camps in predominantly white communities. As Bob Kiino wrote from Kalamazoo, Michigan, to his English teacher, Virginia Tidball, back at Jerome, the upcoming Halloween hayride and Thanksgiving sleigh ride required that club members "bring our girls": "Boy, I'm in a jam. . . . I wish a Japanese girl was out here." A month later Kiino was able to reassure Tidball that at last he was "getting along swell in school and socially. Well as for the girl, I've found one and a Japanese at that and she's very cute too." Meanwhile, back at the camp, Jerome authorities worried that overtures by military police to female inmates—as with the previously mentioned case of prostitution—would provoke animosity in the local white community. Thus, WRA regional attorney Robert Leflar tried to squelch rumors that a guard had taken "an evacuee girl" to dinner in McGehee at the Greystone Hotel. Perhaps most importantly, despite—or because of—outside racist warnings about rampant sexual intercourse in the camps, Jerome and Rohwer authorities aggressively promoted dating and marriage *among* Japanese Americans.[22]

The most visible and most popular government intervention in courtship was the series of dances and other activities between female detainees and Nisei troops inaugurated on 1 May 1943. Despite the distance—ten hours by bus—the Camp Shelby dances became regular bimonthly events, requiring an intricate protocol of invitation, acceptance, registration, chaperoning, transportation, housing, dancing, entertainment, follow-up correspondence, and thank-yous. For many, however, these programs had a sinister edge. Though less publicized, some Japanese American women's initial enthusiasm gave way to grave doubts about the intentions and ideologies of would-be suitors and their higher-ups.

In her "Pot Pourri" column in the Jerome newspaper's 20 April 1943 edition, Ayako Noguchi expressed regret that the 442nd had extended their first dance invitation only to the women at Rohwer: "Say, what have the Rohwer girls got that we haven't got?" She raised her concerns with camp director Paul Taylor, who insisted Jerome likewise could send a delegation to Mississippi. Once the ninety-five Rohwer women returned from Shelby, however, and news of their affair began to circulate, Noguchi and others reconsidered. The men, it seems, had not been on their best behavior. Though carefully planned and staged, the event left many Rohwer residents feeling less like guests and more like harlots. The women were "handled roughly by the men." One enlisted man felt obligated to report the situation to Noguchi. Noguchi in turn felt obligated to share his thoughts with her readers: "Taking it from the standpoint of the girls, perhaps it was a good thing that your Center didn't come. The way the girls were mauled about on the dance floor was a pitiful sight." But describing a seemingly intrinsic masculine aggression, he excused the soldiers' actions, even as he warned women against them: "After all, what do you think would happen if a mere 100 girls were pitted against some 400 soldiers?"[23]

Perhaps sensing they had overstepped the bounds of propriety with their Rohwer guests, perhaps intuiting the increased disaffection with the government the soldiers represented, or perhaps responding to the suggestion from Paul Taylor, the 442nd next extended an invitation to young women at Jerome. Noguchi's column and heated camp discussion, however, had rendered the invitation a political letter bomb. Women at Jerome were put off by the overture of late May 1943, and by mid-June the response was lukewarm at best. Few wanted to go. Patriots at Jerome were ashamed; they urged women to accept the call "from the lonesome soldier boys . . . to drop in for a weekend visit." As John Naganimi put it, the response was "very poor because of the unfounded rumors about the boys' ruggedness." Yet in pushing women to attend, he acknowledged that very ruggedness, which could only be softened, he asserted, by the womanly type: "What those boys really need is a bit of that maternal touch. Though they may seem like a rough cut diamond outwardly, a little feminine polish . . . would bring out the priceless quality of these Nisei servicemen. How about you girls being a Pygmalion? It's a worthy cause." The *Tribune* city editor Richard Itanaga, himself a volunteer awaiting induction, concurred: "The importance of keeping a serviceman's morale high cannot be overly stressed. . . . If entertaining a group of soldiers, who on their own volition are preparing to stake their lives for the future security of all Americans with Japanese faces, at a carefully chaperoned social affair is 'cheapening,' we must change our definition of the word." Itanaga commended the Jerome women willing to participate for their "fine patriotic gesture." For making "the arduous and monotonous lives of the volunteers a little easier to bear, we say 'atta girls—you're women worth fighting for.'"[24]

The notion of warfare as an exercise in protecting womanhood was an enduring historical cliché. Many women at Jerome were having none of it. Though the camp's "pro-Administration" newspaper gave them little voice—indeed, Itanaga assumed their lack of interest could only be attributable to the "latrine magpies and jeering *male* bigots [who] swayed" them—women made up their own minds and voted with their feet. Whereas the 442nd invited a hundred women from Jerome for the second dance, held the weekend of 19 June, only forty-three had stepped forward by four days before the event. A front-page newspaper headline insisted: "MORE GIRLS NEEDED," and the "sign up date [was] extended." But even after the invitation was expanded—in a last-ditch effort—to include women from Rohwer as well, only a total of eighty-three from the two camps could be mustered. Throughout the two-year history of the dances, numbers would flag, even as Shelby officials learned to canvass both the Jerome and Rohwer camps simultaneously. For a May 1944 dance, not even half of the one hundred places would be filled. The August 1944 dance would attract only sixty-eight.[25]

The few women who went to the dances did so for many reasons. Some participants viewed the dances' skewed gender ratio as highly beneficial. As Emiko Lucy Kubo, a Jerome nursery school teacher, said of the dance in June 1943, she had "never felt so popular in all my life!" Mary Nakahara concluded that the second Shelby dance was such "a huge success [because] a girl can feel for once in her life just as popular as heck, there being so many boys to give her attention." In his thank-you note to guests, Colonel Pence likewise made clear the importance of sex appeal, commending the "girls" first and foremost for their "attractiveness," along with their "gentle demeanor and conduct." Brothers and other relatives were among the 442nd and its affiliated units, so many dances involved bittersweet reunions of family members separated by enlistment and incarceration, as with Nakahara and her twin brother, Pete. Moreover, many women surely relished an opportunity, of whatever kind, to leave the camps for an "all expenses paid" weekend, to visit the towns and cities along the way, to see a different part of the country.[26]

11. Dance hosted by the 442nd Regimental Combat Team for women from the Arkansas concentration camps. Camp Shelby, Mississippi, June 1943. Public Relations Officer photographer. LC-USZ62-89913, PPD, LC.

Still, many more women chose to avoid these occasions, with well-founded reasons of their own. Women's refusal of state-sanctioned intra-ethnic dating hinged upon much more than their objectification by military officials and the 442nd—for these were blanket invitations to "young ladies," not addressed to any specific individuals by name. At least initially, the supervisory structure for the dances added insult to the injury of incarceration. To accompany the first contingent from Rohwer, for example, officials called on "six chaperones from the Caucasian administrative personnel," as the *Rohwer Outpost* reported. Only when potential participants and their parents mounted a protest did authorities vary the policy and summon "six evacuee mothers" to join the caravan. Also, for young women accustomed to the relative autonomy of employment, leisure, and courtship in the camps, the permissions policy proved infantilizing, if not (re)feminizing. All those "applying" to attend the dances had to "have written notes of consent from their parents." While these "Letters of Consent" might have seemed logical for the youngest—since, in a further effort to boost numbers, the minimum age requirement was reduced from eighteen to sixteen years old—twenty- and thirty-something women resented the stricture, which intensified the intergenerational antagonisms within families during incarceration and resolidified norms of female dependency: parents could forbid their adult daughters from going. Also, in a slap at female immigrants widowed, divorced, or otherwise estranged from their husbands, only U.S. citizens were allowed to participate. Given the unique demographic characteristics of Japanese American immigration and the generationally distinct cohorts, the Americans-only policy represented the most blatant ageism, as well as jingoism. Camp officials wanted to insure that Japanese American soldiers dated and married women not only of the right ethnicity but also of the right nationality. Indeed, women who answered with anything other than an unambiguous "yes, yes" to the two highly ambiguous loyalty questions during the WRA's ill-conceived and incompetently administered registration program—discussed in chapter 8—found that they were excluded from the dances.[27]

Ironies abounded. Japanese American males were training to fight for a nation that had imprisoned Japanese Americans; Japanese American females went to socialize at those soldiers' training camp as prisoners of that nation. American military culture inculcated an aggressive masculinity and crude sexist behavior in some Japanese American men; American concentration camp culture stimulated feminist ideals of self-assertion and autonomy in some Japanese American women. These ironies were not lost on Japanese Americans, especially those incarcerated in Arkansas and thus most closely acquainted with U.S. war preparations at Camp Shelby. Given the disillusionment and despair of detainment and the compounded injustice of the loyalty questionnaire, Nikkei at Jerome refused to swear allegiance and were transferred to the "segregation" center at Tule Lake, California, at rates higher than any other concentration camp. Conversely, by April 1943 eligible male Nikkei at Jerome and Rohwer volunteered for armed service at rates lower than any other concentration camp (2.1 percent each). Concentration camp authorities urged women to enlist as well; but when Women's Army Corps officers came on a much-publicized recruiting mission to Jerome, young Japanese American women again voted with their feet. Community leader Mary Tsukamoto waited all day with the WACs, but not a single woman stopped by to even discuss military service. Soon Japanese American men, once urged to volunteer, were conscripted—drafted, often against their will—and "caskets started coming back." And, as is so common in wartime, officials tried to convince the populace of the necessity of the human sacrifice. To the Granada concentration camp in Colorado, "they sent a person from Washington," remembers Mo Nishida, "to give us a pep talk on how brave these guys were, giving their life for freedom and democracy and all that shit."[28]

AUTHORIZING GENDER ROLES

Within the Arkansas concentration camps, the politics of dancing were played out almost nightly, as Nisei soldiers from Camp Shelby, nearby Camp Robinson, and other military installations regularly turned up, expecting to be entertained. Such visitors, eventually numbering in the thousands, helped spark the establishment of a USO center both at Rohwer and at Jerome, where Mary Nakahara and Mary Tsukamoto took charge. Founded in early 1941 as a coalition of six nationwide religious associations—YMCA, YWCA, National Catholic Community Service, Salvation Army, Jewish Welfare Board, and National Travelers Aid Association—the United Service Organizations grew rapidly in tandem with expanding wartime mobilizations. However, the extent of civilian versus military, private versus public control of the USO provoked controversy from the outset. Though Roosevelt himself delineated lines of responsibility—instructing "these private organizations to handle the on leave recreation of the men in the armed forces [and] the government [to] put up the buildings"—ownership of and investment in the USO varied across locales, even as all facilities and activities enjoyed the imprimatur of Uncle Sam. While best known for its traveling stage shows, featuring the Andrews Sisters, Bing Crosby, Bob Hope, and others, the USO reached most military personnel through the hundreds of local clubs and activity centers, at which young women in particular provided hospitality. Three-quarters of United States servicemen visited USO clubs, and dancing topped the list of "activities enjoyed most."[29]

Federally supported, if not fully federally administered, the USO purported to open all its facilities to all enlisted personnel, regardless of race. But the seven clubs located in Hattiesburg, for example—each addressed to the needs of distinct target populations—demonstrated the racialized niche programming of the USO. And the extent of resources provided these clubs and the relative esteem in which each was held reflected pernicious racial hierarchies. Thus in Hattiesburg, which served the large and diverse Camp Shelby populations, the USO maintained seven clubs: four for a predominantly white clientele, a Jewish club, a Japanese American club known as "the Aloha center," and a "colored building," expressly constructed as such in 1942. The naturalization of this hierarchy is perhaps best evidenced by the local phone book. In 1944 the Hattiesburg telephone directory did not list the seven clubs in alphabetical order or by order of longevity. Rather, Southern Bell assumed it logical and indeed self-evident that under "USO," the clubs were listed—or, more to the point, ranked—in this white-to-black racial order. With the exception of the "Colored Club" at the bottom of the list, which apparently had to be spelled out, only the street addresses were given, leaving callers to sort out the ranking of the nonblack clubs.[30]

The ethnic partitioning of USO activities was not limited to the South. The *USO Bulletin*, sent out monthly from their Empire State Building headquarters, was filled with pictures from across the country and overseas, of servicemen and "hostesses" of all types. But these men and women rarely were depicted in cross-racial settings. Whereas the USO claimed "age, race, color, or creed made no difference," these were, quite the contrary, the critical vectors of difference-making and exclusion. The "interfaith altar" at the Los Angeles–area USO, for example, displayed only a cross and the Star of David; USO publications likewise illustrated reports of religious programming with only a cross and the Torah. Spiritual activities, however, accounted for a relatively small enrollment of 4.7 million in 1944, as compared to the dances, which annually attracted over 40 million participants. "When a contingent of Nisei troops stopped" at a predominantly white community in rural New York State, the USO "sent out [an] S.O.S." to New York City: "Wanted at Once: 100 Japanese-American Hostesses." "Within a few hours," a USO report happily concluded, "112 girls were on their way." For Chinese American soldiers stationed in rural Oregon, officials recruited and bused Chinese American women from Seattle, Washington, for dances. Thus, much was connoted when Mrs. Henry Ingraham, at an early meeting of the USO's national leaders in Washington, DC, declared from the dais of the Willard Hotel, "We shall . . . be serving men where they are and where their womenfolk are."[31]

Racist reportage of USO and related activities was not limited to the South either. In a piece for the *New York Herald Tribune* entitled "New York's Canteen for Japs," writer Richard Osk and photographer Charles Phelps Cushing chronicled the series of dances organized by the New York Church Committee for Japanese Americans and held in various Presbyterian recreation halls across the city. Largely sympathetic, the reporter nonetheless couldn't help describing the events in offensive language. The members of the 442nd who attended were referred to as "American-born Japs." Their hostesses were "almond-eyed sweater girls who come every week to chat, laugh, chew gum, flirt and jitterbug."[32]

Flirting was an activity of both national import and interpersonal diplomacy during wartime. Often gendered as female, it might just as well have been thought of as a male endeavor. The word's Old French etymology derived not only from the noun *fleur*—a flower—but also the verb *fleureter*—to touch lightly, as to move from flower to flower. A bee, so moving, often pollinates in the process. To flirt, then, in a sense, is to flower—or, perhaps in the parlance of the day, to deflower. *This* activity was firmly rejected by USO advisers. Given the skewed gender ratios of USO and other dances, women were expected to pay amorous attention to any number of soldiers but without serious intentions or emotional commitment—that is, to flirt. And yet one-to-one attachments, within racial/ethnic lines, were encouraged too. Both Mary Tsukamoto and Mary Nakahara gave talks about the protocol; and Dorothy Richardson herself, national director of the USO, came to Jerome to speak on "Do's and Don't's for USO Hostesses." Still, the contradictions seemed unresolvable.[33]

When not teaching Sunday school, directing the camp USO, or writing her *Denson Tribune* column "Nisei in Khaki," Mary Nakahara and her teenage girls group the Crusaders were busy sending letters to members of the 442nd Regimental Combat Team and its affiliated units throughout the world—as selected soldiers shipped out to the Pacific as translators and interpreters and many more were sent into battle in North Africa and Europe. One mimeographed letter, likely coauthored by several members, demonstrated the predicament for female patriots during the war years: to entertain the many while remaining chaste for that special one. Totaling over four typed pages, the Thanksgiving missive of 1944 combined poetry and prayer with cornball humor and combat cliché: "There are no atheists in foxholes." On the one hand, the young women promised to spend time with most any soldier: "You might not ever have a medal pinned on you BUT who knows—many a beautiful 'decoration' might come to rest on your manly chest." On the other hand, they promised to remain loyal and offer physical affection, once an exclusive commitment was established: "We don't kiss strange men. We wait until they get familiar." "Listen youse guys," they reiterated, "we're not the California Bungalow type—modern, no heart, and change owners every two weeks."[34]

To engage in the seductive banter of letter-writing and the flirtatious practices of dancing and, at the same time, to hope to refrain from sexual intercourse, it was important to maintain a "good reputation." That hallmark of the sexual double standard—women reviled for "giving" too much away, men admired for "getting" as much as they could—a reputation was established within the arena of social discourse: rumor, gossip, and the countless informal conversations of a community. At Jerome, as elsewhere, that also included the print media. And men participated as much as women, as when the *Tribune*'s male staffers scrutinized particular "girls" in their columns. "[I'll bet] Toki Tarimoto has the largest collection of army men's photos," wrote one journalist. Though only initials were used to identify her, fellow columnist Ayako Ellen Noguchi (AEN) was easily recognizable by anyone who read the paper—namely, almost any adult in the camp. She was said to "keep tabs of all visiting servicemen."[35]

In addition to male journalists, the Crusaders' correspondents rose to the challenge of sexualized wordplay, writing back to Mary Nakahara and others with equally suggestive language and corny innuendo. One soldier advised that at the next dance, the women would have to "hang on to your skirts." Several men requested photographs, but the women demurred: "It seemed you wanted a 'clothes up,' not a close up." Preferring to invert the ordinary gender imbalance, "another casually said he believed Mormonism should be practiced after the war." And "one offered to teach private hula lessons."[36]

Before its politicized revival in the 1970s as a prized form of indigenous cultural expression in Hawaii, modern hula was performed primarily by women, often for the gratification of male audiences, increasingly tourists. White men, in particular, were spectators of hula in the war years, so much so that it featured in a cartoon advertisement for Hart Schaffner & Marx. The men's clothier depicted its fictitious Private Jonathan Jeep and two of his fellow soldiers, in uniform, at an elegant nightclub, where white patrons watched two dark-skinned dancers onstage in short grass skirts, with only tropical flowers pasted over their breasts. Eyebrows prominently uplifted, the men's gaze fixed on the women's bodies, Jeep exclaimed, "Boy, the sergeant oughta see *this* flank movement." Ironically, on the same page of the *Camp Shelby Reveille* edition in which this ad appeared was a large photo of "Hamada the Hulaer." Ever since the first dance between the men of the 442nd and the women from the Arkansas concentration camps, Private Harry Hamada and his Shelby Hawaiians had performed with great success at Japanese American events and for wider audiences. As the combo played ukuleles and guitars, Hamada danced, typically in his uniform—and occasionally with another soldier. Another group, the Shelby Serenaders, managed by Earl Finch, went one step further. Their front man, Private Koichi "Kenneth" Okamoto, performed hula in a long grass skirt.[37]

Even as Earl Finch promoted heterosexual coupling—that is, intra-ethnic dating and matrimony—through support for USOs in Hattiesburg, Jerome, and Rohwer, he went on the road for ever more all-male homosocial interactions. Sanctioned as a legitimate activity of wartime boosterism, his visits to Japanese American servicemen wounded in action extended across the country, with journalists measuring his trips in the thousands and tens of thousands of miles traveled annually. A highly publicized tour of East Coast and southern military hospitals in 1944 featured performances in recovery wards by the Serenaders, who would go on to entertain an estimated twenty-five thousand hospitalized soldiers and veterans. Press features, likely authored by Mike Masaoka, summoned up the tensions and anxieties of male hula for male audiences: "For the men lying without a leg, or in casts, the high moment of the show came when Sgt. Koichi Okamoto, attired in a grass hula skirt, and wearing a beautifully sly grin on his elfish face, wriggled his hips." Though reports emphasized "rehearsals [in which] he dons hula skirt over khakis," photographs of performances show Okamoto with neither khaki pants nor shirt. Barefoot and bare-chested, except for colorful leis, he danced his "wicked hula" for male convalescents from New York to New Orleans, Staten Island to Tuscaloosa, Washington to Jackson. Unsurprisingly, however, a brief show and dinner with WACs from Fort Oglethorpe, Georgia, received disproportionate press coverage.[38]

Wounded soldiers returned primarily from Italy and France, where the 442nd achieved fame as "the most decorated unit in U.S. military history." On leave, men went to the south of France to find "wine, women and song"—Antibes, Cannes, and Nice, "even off-limits Monaco with its casino and gaming tables." Indeed, in Livorno, Italy, the spoils of victory included women's bodies, as a Japanese American soldier explained: "Our house of ill repute met the specifications as prescribed by the Colonel. It was run by a sergeant who relished the idea. They had a building with one madame and four girls, good-looking girls. We had four bedrooms. It was a two-story house. I was in the parlor and the sergeant was outside the door. He had a Tommy gun, I had a Tommy gun, and we had a cash box and the madame stationed on the first floor. . . . Since the sergeant could speak Italian, he selected the girls. The girls were happy to come into the city to serve that purpose." Happy or not, women seemed to have little choice—certainly not women labeled collaborators. While unenlisted male locals "got shot" for aiding the enemy, "female collaborators got a haircut"—or worse. As a chaplain explained, "One of the French collaborators had been raped and came to the medics." Her case would be repeated by the chaplain through the years as an amusing old war story, a joke. "The doctor took care of her but was too busy to take her home. 'Chaplain, will you take her home?' he asked. I said, 'Yes.' She was dressed in a flimsy nightgown and in no condition to walk. I carried her in my arms to her house. When we got there, I found a whole rifle company bivouacked in the house. The roof fell in [with the noise of laughter and ribbing]. Nobody listened to my explanation."[39]

Despite all efforts to the contrary, the U.S. Army and the USO helped inculcate European American norms of beauty and standards of desirability in its nonwhite troops. Though USO clubs back home were mostly racially segregated, USO shows in or near combat zones often played to mixed crowds. Indeed, the U.S. Army was not just multicultural; it was also multinational. In its ranks were citizens of various Asian and European nations, including Germans and Italians. Most were subsequently naturalized as citizens, just as Japanese immigrant veterans of World War I had been. Though obviously never wholly passive recipients of white entertainment culture—often preferring to attend segregated events, with highly self-conscious, even political motives—Japanese American soldiers in World War II nonetheless tapped "tennis and movie star" Jinx Falkenberg as a "favorite"; they mobbed her at USO functions. And, as we've seen, they took a shine to European women they encountered in combat and on leave. According to one account, at least nineteen men from the 442nd "married Italian and French girls [*sic*] overseas."[40]

Despite army-maintained houses of prostitution and sanctioned, interracial sexual intercourse—if not sexual violence—near the front lines, Japanese American soldiers ostensibly remained "clean." "We had no venereal disease all the time we were in Leghorn," according to the whorehouse parlor guard. Citing government condoms as the key factor, he explained that "the Pro[phylactic] Station was right next door." Again reflecting the perceived public relations value of good behavior and abstemiousness, the 442nd was reported to have "had fewer courts martial and venereal disease cases by far than any other comparable group in army history"—though no numbers or comparative cases were cited.[41]

Respectability—or the appearance of respectability—suffused the programs of regulated recreation back in Arkansas and Mississippi. To control the proliferating parties of girls and boys clubs, high school groups, and other organizations, the Rohwer Community Council codified dance etiquette into its statutes. Any dance event required a permit. It had to end by 11:00 p.m. The lights could not be dimmed. And to insure decent conduct, a dance had to be properly chaperoned. Signaling WRA support for the 442nd, however, the rules—especially the closing time—were sometimes waived for the USO and YWCA, who in response sent ingratiating letters to administrators. Y secretary Mary Tsukamoto dictated a letter to her secretary, to mail to Jerome director Paul Taylor, in appreciation of "the unfailing spirit of our Caucasian friends, teachers, and personnel in the administration [who go] out of their way to be human and kind [and] keep our courage high. Thank you again and again! It makes us strong in spirit to carry on jobs of feeding hungering minds and souls." Before these organized activities, she told him, the girls and women in the camp had been prone to "disinterest and despair," to "idleness and pathetic wasting of mind and spirit." Such middle-class rhetorics of reform rarely referenced the benefits—or busyness—of women's paid work outside the home and outside of service organizations.[42]

In Hattiesburg the city council, chamber of commerce, and USOs teamed up to direct soldiers' leisure toward appropriate amusements and to contain their sexuality within proper modes of intra-ethnic romance and courtship. Seen as a detriment to military preparedness, literally keeping soldiers out sick, venereal disease was a target in a new "vice crusade," as well as gambling and liquor consumption. But among the city's elected officials and community leaders, views were not unanimous. Gambling and drinking was tacitly endorsed by some; prostitution seemed an age-old inevitability. As an alternative, however, the council voted to vary blue laws—that is, Sabbath closing statutes—and open the movie houses "except during church and Sunday School hours." And officials looked to the USO to provide a range of activities to servicemen—dances, game nights, bingo, variety shows, movies, concerts, sing-alongs, and classes in magic, sketching, and photography. The USO further helped in securing scarce wartime housing for wives and children of enlisted men, typically with local clergy and lay leaders. They gave away Bibles. And, as repeatedly appeared in USO reports, they aggressively encouraged soldiers to attend worship services. A special "Go to Church" program was established to "help the Sunday loafers" by arranging carpools and designating representatives to greet them at the sanctuary.[43]

But this great range of activities could only be pulled off by the large white USO clubs. The Jewish American, Japanese American, and African American clubs in Hattiesburg received little support from their wealthier sibling organizations. When the Aloha center's director turned up at a meeting of Hattiesburg USO benefactors to describe its programming, he was relegated to the bottom of the agenda and given only a few minutes to speak—that is, to invite them to visit, which they clearly had not done. Aside from religious activities, nonwhite clubs spent their comparatively meager resources on entertainment and dances. Even so, there is little evidence of nonwhite alliances across the three clubs. Though the Aloha center had an open-door racial policy, few African Americans attended—except when Earl Finch brought in black musicians to play, after hours.[44]

Intra-ethnic dating and matrimony were the USO's undisputed success. At the main white club in Hattiesburg, organizers marveled at the frequency and rapidity of nuptials and cheered a spur-of-the-moment "triple wedding": "A couple came in planning to marry. While arrangements were being made a second couple, overhearing, joined forces. A third couple upon seeing the flowers, the photographer, and the minister, had the urge to join up!" At the Aloha center, marriages likewise sparked celebration. The events between the members of the 442nd and the prisoners from the Arkansas concentration camps proved most enabling. With the dances, "the single women in camp had a chance to meet some of the men. And there were a lot of marriages. The men would come in and meet the girls, and they would marry them. Some married even before they shipped out to Europe." And even Mary Nakahara—who once only dated whites—was smitten by a Japanese American soldier, former Topaz resident Bill Kochiyama.[45]

If Nisei servicemen in Mississippi required additional venues for ethnically homogenous entertainment, the Arkansas concentration camps struck U.S. military authorities as obvious solutions. Pro-American detainees supported these efforts, and women such as Mary Nakahara and Mary Tsukamoto—active members of Protestant churches and the YWCA—assumed visible leadership positions. But other Nisei women frowned upon the USO clubs at Jerome and Rohwer as critical links in the racial structuring of wartime American courtship. For some, the highly orchestrated, racially bounded heterosexual coupling broached the limits of decorum around sexuality. Criticism followed those Nisei women "seen talking to the boys in khaki": they were labeled "call girls," and the word "prostitutes" was scrawled across signs advertising the events. Also, to many women, the dances were part of a larger attempt to reassert male privilege and reinstate familial patriarchy just as women were beginning to take advantage of the concentration camps' unique social and economic character. Moreover, the selectivity of dance participants insidiously reaffirmed and bolstered hierarchies *within* Japanese American populations, privileging those who pledged undying allegiance to the very government that had imprisoned them and marginalizing others, especially the older immigrant generation, Buddhists, lesbians and gays, and various other skeptics—those whose racial, national, religious, and sexual affiliations were more ambivalently held or more openly oppositional. In their view, Japanese American supporters of the USO may have been protesting way too much when they insisted "there is nothing to hide in the doings of the local USO."[46]

Wartime American racial hierarchies relied on complex conceptions of race, made up of multiple components—color, physiognomy, language, national origin, religion, locality—each of which could be variously emphasized so as to create and justify inequality for particular groups. Instead of notions of a single racial continuum, progressive gradations of whiteness, or groups gradually becoming white, racial positionings in the World War II South functioned along a number of scales, each of which engaged a host of factors highly contingent and variable over the space and time of a few miles or a few hours. English-speaking Japanese Americans of Christian faith, especially those "loyal," heterosexual, second-generation citizens from California, could enjoy considerable physical and social mobility one moment, but could be confined to camp the next. And while Japanese Americans visibly problematized several binary black/white divides in the South, many accepted a dominant ideology that placed African Americans at the bottom of every racial scale. Of those privileged Japanese American prisoners allowed greater freedom of movement, association, and expression, men were at a distinct advantage. In addition to dominating elective political organizations such as the Community Council, they controlled key positions in camp cultural production, including the editorships of camp newspapers and high school yearbooks, film selection and projection responsibilities at the movie houses, and leadership roles in expressive culture, particularly poetry groups, photography, and painting.

Women nonetheless overcame the extraordinary burdens of incarceration to move up the socioeconomic ladder, working in a greater variety of jobs, in higher-level positions, on the same wage scale as men. A concentration camp's largely homogenous racial world meant increased opportunities for advancement outside the work environment as well, and the USO provided a distinctive culture for women's self-assertion and community-building efforts. But dances at Camp Shelby and at the Jerome and Rohwer USOs were implicated in federal initiatives promoting regulated recreation and state-sanctioned courtship for enlisted personnel. U.S., state, and local government policing of racial boundaries thus was not solely *proscriptive*—forbidding interracial coupling through miscegenation laws, barring interracial residential patterns via zoning ordinances and restrictive covenants, delimiting daily interracial interaction through varied Jim Crow strictures. It also was *prescriptive*—actively encouraging intra-ethnic dating and matrimony not only among whites but also among variously arrayed cultural outgroups such as Japanese Americans. To the extent that Nisei women discerned, critiqued, and occasionally defied the menacing implications of these initiatives, they made problematic and explicit what ordinarily functioned as commonsensical and implicit: the very real, palpable, and pervasive politics of dancing.

If some Nisei women's resistance to state-sanctioned courtship and institutionalized heterosexuality was motivated in part by a reluctance to participate in structured American ethnicity maintenance, many if not most Japanese Americans nonetheless seemed to share with most white Americans a belief in black racial inferiority—making African Americans the most unlikely of dance partners. This was made clear in late 1944, when Jerome became the first of the ten concentration camps to close. As incarcerated Japanese Americans prepared for transfer to Rohwer or elsewhere, they threw a series of campwide farewell parties and performances. At one, white camp officials and Japanese Americans shared the stage—and they even shared a dance. Inmates and keepers, prisoners and guards, together donned special makeup, blackface, to show themselves, to convince each other, what they collectively were not: black. There onstage in Arkansas, the last dance was an "All-American Minstrel Show."[47]

6 | Americanization and Christianization

FROM THE START, the concentration camps had been characterized by mismanagement, with few precedents from the recent past for bureaucrats to draw upon. The result for prisoners was a living environment that, at least initially, was soul-destroying, sickening—literally. As the Jerome camp director Paul Taylor conceded to his superiors in Washington, because a sulfite compound had been improperly used to seal pipes in the camp water system, "practically every person . . . suffers a 1 to 3 day case of acute dysentery, upon first arriving at the project." For Mary Tsukamoto, "it was a time of humiliation and despair."[1]

Even so, she pondered "how fortunate" they were. Invited to speak to the camp's Christian Youth Fellowship in late 1942, Tsukamoto acknowledged the "pain, disappointment and degradation" of incarceration, but insisted they could be "overcome with steadfast faith." Jesus Christ "could turn despair into triumphant joy," she told the teenagers. The burdens of this life would be more than compensated by the bliss of the afterlife. Indeed, combined, earthly and heavenly lives represented a single, everlasting continuum; thus it became imperative to live "eternity day by day"—a theology of resignation more than resistance.[2]

Even as more administrative blunders gave rise to a fuel crisis—and men and boys were sent into the adjacent forests to fell trees and women were enlisted to chop wood—Tsukamoto and other Japanese American leaders "began to celebrate Christmas." Holly and mistletoe also were dragged out of the woods, and several of the pine trees were reserved for decorating and display in the mess halls. Presents poured into the camp, "donated by sympathetic Caucasians from 30 states, gifts of friendship and gestures of the true Christmas spirit. Many were from Sunday Schools and churches." Further, officials orchestrated "a grand shopping trip" to the Arkansas capital of Little Rock. And they approved day passes for select Japanese Americans to go into the stores of neighboring towns and villages. Inmates "were requested to organize themselves into groups and authorize one or two persons to shop for the whole group," as Taylor reported to Washington. "In this way, approximately six hundred evacuees actually went outside the Center for shopping purposes, to supply the needs of the entire Center. All residents of the Center entered into Christmas activities with a great deal of zeal. . . . The effect was really wonderful."[3]

Ironically, nearly 70 percent of the camp's 8,000-plus "residents" were Buddhists. Ordinarily, attendance at ten different Protestant church services totaled 2,500 a week, whereas the Buddhist services drew 4,000. Though many Buddhists nonetheless would have observed Christmas rites—after all, the exchange of gifts was a bedrock Japanese social custom—to engage in Christian practices at this time and place was to become bound up in official strategies designed to pacify and Americanize the very ethnic minority population deemed so dangerous as to warrant wholesale confinement. As I hope to demonstrate, central to Americanization was Christianization. Of the myriad techniques used to sway Issei and Nisei to "American" ways of life, the WRA relied on religious organizing, revivals, and other modes of Protestant evangelism to shape the identity and conduct of their wards. Officials proposed a profound, linked pair of transformations: a nationalist reconciliation facilitated by a personal, spiritual redemption. Thus, Christmas particularly can be seen as a signal moment—for this religious observance was also a national ritual, exemplifying the intricate interconnections of sacred and secular endeavors, Christian and consumerist, in a country ostensibly honoring a separation of church and state.[4]

This chapter first examines the vital role of camp schools in Americanizing imprisoned Japanese American children and adults. Second, I look at a particular set of popular representations that traded on a long-standing American creation myth, the pioneer narrative, and that was taken up and partially transformed by Japanese Americans of an assimilationist bent. As set against the innumerable obstacles to Buddhist practice in the camps described in the third section, I finally probe the more explicitly religious components of Americanization and the leadership positions that Japanese American women took in those campaigns. Only by putting all these factors into conversation and by examining their gendered dimensions can we begin to understand the mutually constituting and mutually reinforcing quality of their relationships. For if members of cultural outgroups were to be certified as truly American, they had to perform any number of rituals and practices not always associated with the imperatives of the nation-state: a schooling in its protocols; a drawing out of its metaphors and structuring narratives; and a worshipping in its mission, seen as divinely ordained.

SCHOOLING IN THE NATION

Officials of the WRA viewed camp schools as unique opportunities to inculcate the tenets of nationalism in the impressionable minds of young and older captives. Within days of the opening of detention centers, "Americanism classes" were begun for Issei, and they would remain critical components of adult night school curriculum throughout the war. At the concentration camps, white teachers and select Japanese American aides and teacher trainees delivered an elementary and high school curriculum that would meet ordinary state guidelines for primary and secondary education, but further would foster a camp-specific program of patriotism and national allegiance. Proposed pedagogical techniques were circulated through the monthly *Community School Forum*, published in Washington and mailed to all educators in the camp school systems. "Here is an opportunity," wrote its editor, "to carry on a magnificent job of Americanization."[5]

The Arkansas camps made nurseries and kindergartens available to the youngest, at the discretion of their parents. But attendance at the elementary school and high school was mandatory, as Superintendent of Education Amon G. Thompson reassured a U.S. Senate Investigating Committee in March 1943. Each school day began and ended with carefully coordinated nationalist displays. As dictated by the Jerome schools handbook, "at 8:15, the sound of the bugle calls every student to attention while the flag is raised." At both schools, one particular grade, in daily rotation, would stand and salute as the "enormous" Old Glory was run up the mast. "The pledge of allegiance is then [recited] in every classroom. At the dismissal hour the students again stand at attention for the lowering of the flag." These flag ceremonies inspired sarcasm and resistance in at least some camp residents—for the high school flagpole was found toppled, perhaps as a result of anti-jingoist vandalism. Administrators again looked to the woods. "Stripped of its bark, the [new]

40-foot pole [was] about the sturdiest flagpole" Paul Yokota had ever seen. The camp newspaper editor, with wry humor, insisted that this mast, unlike the previous, "ought to stand for some time."[6]

Congressional investigators seemed disturbed to discover that only students—and not the entire 8,500 residents—were compelled to march out and salute the flag every day. Their confidence was restored, however, when Superintendent Thompson declared English to be the schools' official language. Aside from one or two other European-language classes offered by Virginia Tidball and colleagues, it was the only language of instruction. There were no classes, he categorically stated, in Japanese. Furthermore, as dictated from Washington, no Japanese holidays were officially observed in any of the camps—though residents nonetheless celebrated them.[7]

School periodicals—compiled by students but coordinated and copyedited by white teachers—likewise toed the patriotic line. The Jerome high school magazine, *The Condensor,* reprinted the lyrics of the state song of Arkansas, which ironically claimed that a "welcome awaits every stranger." This, at the very moment when the state legislature passed measures to prevent Japanese American resettlement and land ownership in Arkansas after the war. The 1943 high school yearbook was dedicated to Japanese American men serving in the segregated 442nd Regimental Combat Team: those "valiant defenders of the American way." And the annual graduation exercises provided the appropriate musical score. They were begun with renditions of "The Star-Spangled Banner" and "America the Beautiful." Audience members were reminded in the printed program that they were not dismissed until "after the lowering of the Flag." At these and any number of other occasions, even the youngest children were dressed in red, white, and blue and made to fall into formation and salute.[8]

Of course, such songs and displays would not be unusual at any number of American schools, especially during wartime. But curriculum proposals in particular demonstrated the added investment of the federal government in nationalist pedagogy within the concentration camps. Specific titles were offered as necessary for instilling high regard for America. Geography lessons should utilize the American Guide Series and "The Rivers of America," as well as Carl Carmer's "attractive companion songbook, 'American Sings.'" Literature instruction could make good use of works steeped in seemingly American values: Emerson's "Self-Reliance," Thoreau's *Walden*, and, tellingly, James Truslow Adams's *Our Business Civilization*, to name just a few. Indeed, the Washington manuals for teachers instructed them to concoct lesson plans that

12. For parents' visiting day, girls sport special hats and bouquets and boys salute. Nursery school, Jerome concentration camp, March 1943. Tom Parker, photographer. NWDNS-210-G-, WRAR, SPB, NA.

emphasized "competitive activities." And a "Check List for Teachers," circulated among instructors, reminded them to measure their teaching technique against this standard: "Was competition involved in the learning activity?" This seems to have been a direct response to the camps' enormously popular cooperative stores, run almost entirely by and for Japanese Americans on a not-for-profit basis. Scholar Jan Ziegler writes that assembly programs at Rohwer demonstrated "a rather zealous 'overkill' of Americanizing the students," and at least one school official at Jerome explicitly set about to "indoctrinate" the children.[9]

Perhaps unsurprisingly, history classes required the most careful selection of subject matter, as there was so much in the American past that mirrored the present injustice. Washington administrators suppressed such comparison cases by cagily forgetting them. They were simply unmentioned. Instead, "it can be shown that the history of America is one of continuous relocation. The story of the incessant movement of the American people from east to west, from north to south, from farm to city, has always been a thrilling tale of continuous readjustment to new environments. It has always been fraught with dangers and difficulties. It requires boldness and courage to made readjustments. These boys and girls must come to see this as a part of the American heritage. Through history and literature," the WRA insisted, "they can become imbued with this everlasting spirit of movement without which they cannot become a part of America. Americans have never settled down in one spot. Few of us live where we were born. Few of our fathers do either. Far greater dangers confronted the pioneers who were always moving westward than confront these people in relocating. The spirit of America is in such pioneering."[10]

Indeed the incessant forced removal of Native Americans from their lands, from east to west, from richer to poorer soils, rivers, and mineral deposits, might have proved the best analogy. But these movements—these trails of tears—would have disrupted the positivist mission of the schools. And they were otherwise routinely downplayed in American school curricula, inclined as they were to expose the violence and exploitation at the core of the American national project. Pioneering metaphors further obscured those additions to the immigrant nation who had arrived in California from Asia and continued moving from west to east.[11]

The WRA's Dillon Myer—after replacing Dwight Eisenhower's brother Milton as head of the agency in the early months of the war—underlined the concentration camps' nationalist agenda in his 1943 address to the American Legion, the powerful veterans group committed in its mission statement to "one hundred percent Americanism." "I realize that one of the primary aims of the American Legion is to foster Americanization," Myer said. "That has also been one of the major objectives of our program. . . . We have made every effort to create an Americanizing atmosphere in the relocation centers." On this much Myer and his HUAC critics agreed. A 1943 subcommittee report on the WRA concluded that the camps represented "an almost unparalleled opportunity to inaugurate a vigorous educational program for positive Americanism."[12]

The WRA relationship to the American Legion was a close if fraught one. Local Legion posts frequently disparaged the WRA for its so-called "coddling" of Japanese Americans. And they were invested in the spying and surveillance activities of the WRA, FBI, and HUAC during the war years. By the time that

J. Edgar Hoover determined the necessity of "a system of informant coverage" in the camps—with regional agents regularly called upon to carry out searches and seizures, as we see in the next chapter—the FBI had strengthened its ties with the Legion. "The FBI's American Legion Contact Program of 1940–1966," as scholar Kenneth O'Reilly reveals, initially "called for local Legion posts to investigate and report all indications of subversive activity to the Bureau." Slightly modified "to use Legionnaires as 'confidential sources,' . . . the Contact Program ultimately involved over 100,000 Legionnaires and their agents who collected information and submitted reports, with copies to the Bureau." Thus, it was crucial for Dillon Myer to assure Legionnaires of his own good stewardship of Americanization campaigns, in order to forestall too much American Legion snooping in and around the camps.[13]

In primary and secondary instruction as well as in adult education and "public discussion forums," Myer stressed, "we have established the curriculum for our schools with particularly heavy emphasis on the history of American traditions and American institutions." As with all histories, those taught in the camps would be partial, selective, and utterly political. Whose histories got told and how they were told—particular versions of the past—represented ideological interventions into both the present and the future.[14]

DRAWING OUT THE NATION

The pioneer myth was deployed repeatedly in camp discourse, well beyond the classrooms—and not only by camp administrators but also by Japanese American advocates of assimilation. Mary Tsukamoto, in her memoir of the war years, described her first views of the nation's heartland, when forced from California to Arkansas, as uplifting, as naturally inviting comparisons to pioneer forebears. She praised the "pioneering spirit" that propelled the summer school plan at Fresno detention center, where her experience as a Florin Methodist Sunday school teacher prompted her selection as a high school public speaking instructor. In many accounts of and from the war years, Japanese Americans likened their repeated dislocations to the experiences of the frontier.[15]

At the Rohwer, Arkansas, camp—thirty miles up the road from Jerome—residents regularly opened the pages of their morning newspaper to discover the latest antics of the sole cartoon strip's main character and namesake, Lil Dan'l, or Little Daniel. "Although he has kept his name a deep secret," his creator maintained, "we are led to believe that his full name is Lil Dan'l Boon [*sic*]." Unlike the rugged Kentucky legend, however, said to have faced innumerable life-threatening, indeed superhuman obstacles, the *Rohwer Outpost* mascot was shown tackling and recording "the little tragedies and minor comedies that we shall remember with a smile for future reference." The spry boy sported a trademark coonskin cap, rolled-up jeans, and boots, as well as round spectacles and prominent buck teeth, which would have marked him as Asian in mid-twentieth-century representational caricatures.[16]

Cartoonist George Akimoto's 1943 retrospective, *Lil Dan'l: One Year in a Relocation Center*, depicts the young hero in a variety of comic scenarios, neatly summing up the first year's experience at Rohwer. Indeed, Lil Dan'l was said directly to symbolize all "eight thousand and some odd evacuees of the Rohwer Center." Juxtaposition was the principle trope, as Akimoto simultaneously highlighted characteristics associated with America and Japan, the West and the South, young and old, male and female. But it was the construction of the main character himself—a youthful, energetic, male, and ambitiously American pioneer figure—that positioned the artist, the strip, and Japanese Americans broadly as pro-American. If visual juxtaposition usually suggested contradiction and ambivalence, the narrative components of the *Lil Dan'l* strips served to shore up nationalist sentiments.[17]

A native English speaker, Lil Dan'l was further adaptable to regional dialect, greeting locals with good-natured shouts of "How Y'all!" and "HOT, ain't it?" An aspiring assimilationist, he tried his would-be masculine hand not only at judo and sumo but also weightlifting and boxing. Still too young to know any better, he even mimicked the women in traditional kimonos who performed elaborate fan dances. However, artist Akimoto delineated and sequestered "Feminine Activities" on a single page, into which Dan'l did not tread. There women were shown knitting, weaving, arranging flowers, caring for children, and preparing to mop and wash—traditionally gendered tasks lately discarded for work outside the home. Though elsewhere Akimoto illustrated a woman chopping down a tree, yelling, "Timber!" the humorous effect seemed to rely in part if not en toto on an implied gender transgression. As we see in the next chapter, though women rarely felled trees, they frequently sawed logs and chopped wood.[18]

At the block bathhouse, Dan'l did respect the rigid gender binary. He gleefully joined the older boys and men in the crowded communal showers and instructed them to "Move over!" While *his* prepubescent innocence suggested a lack of familiarity with the homophobic anxieties accompanying such naked, all-male spheres, *their* anger and exasperation reinforced them. Compulsory heterosexuality no less than adult middle-class respectability had led to repeated calls for the installation of partitions and curtains in these camp bathhouses.[19]

If Lil Dan'l moved with increasing ease through a changing male world of sport and sociability, he proved exceptionally adept in the rugged outdoors environment, outmaneuvering turtles, serpents, rattlesnakes, and skunks. He learned to catch local crayfish, and he stole watermelons from the victory gardens so vital in liberal administrators' depictions of their Japanese American charges as skilled agrarians: a central component of Jeffersonian yeoman imagery. These farmers—raising corn, carrots, radishes, onions, and tomatoes, in tidy cultivated rows—were contrasted favorably against the "shadowy figures creeping through the woods," the "kobu fanatics and mushroom maniacs." As part of their forest activities, these older men—often bachelors—collected cypress tree knots and wild shrooms with, as Akimoto put it, "blood-curdling scream[s]," leading them ever "closer to the asylum." Age-old customs, their fastidious wood carvings and psychedelic mushroom tea thereby were portrayed as not only un-American but also unhealthy—truly, crazy-making.[20]

It's unsurprising, however, that men would look to the woods for intoxicants, given the WRA ban on alcohol. Like the misguided interwar American experiment with Prohibition, the WRA's puritanical restrictions only drove distribution and consumption underground, oddly enabling women's entrepreneurialism in the process. So while narcotics violations were exceedingly rare in the camps, liquor violations and arrests for public drunkenness—as with Masao Asahara and Jack Yamashita—were commonplace, often accompanied by gambling arrests. From neighboring communities of the concentration camps, the young as well as the old purchased beer and liquor, from legal as well as illegal operators. At Jerome officials seized a "Rube Goldberg" photo ID "gadget," used to doctor one-day passes, if not to produce cards for underage purchases by boys who couldn't live up to the wholesome Lil Dan'l ideal. Women as well as men were involved in the trade. And in Protestant evangelical Arkansas, punishments were severe, with violators doing time in Arkansas county jails. Jerome drinkers and others signed a petition and delivered it to the administration, insisting—as one official put it—that "Mrs. Kuriso, our lady [boot]legger, be released from the Bastille" at Monticello, Arkansas. The official's flip, indifferent attitude demonstrates that even older female prisoners would pay the price for their sins, whereas officials in dry southern states like Mississippi bent the rules so a soldier could have a drink and play the slots.[21]

Reflective perhaps of a cunning American acquisitiveness and a frontier lawlessness, Lil Dan'l once broke the law, stealing lumber from camp stocks.

Shown in a first scene with an effected angelic guilelessness, a halo above his head, Dan'l then glanced from side to side, nicked the scraps of wood, and ran for his life—leaving the cap and spectacles in his wake. A smoking gun referenced the previous incident at Jerome, where a white construction worker had fired buckshot at boys playing near the piles of plywood. This was a crafty critique of camp administrators' doublespeak. For on the one hand, they forbade use of project lumber stocks, threatening violators with jail terms. On the other hand, in photo shoots designed for the outside world, as noted in the introduction, Japanese American victims of incarceration such as Fred Hayarki were proudly staged as expert craftsmen, skilled woodworkers, and furniture makers in an American frontier tradition. In the image of his apartment interior taken by a white WRA photographer sent to Jerome from Washington, a potentially troubling, nonwhite Americanness was compensated by a bureau-top photo of a uniformed kinsman who served in the 442nd RCT, fighting in Europe for American "freedom."[22]

It was around this issue of patriotic duty and national loyalty that Lil Dan'l's true colors were revealed. Too young for military service himself, Dan'l nonetheless hung out at the camp induction center and occasionally helped out. In the physical exam, some reluctant recruits might fall a bit short—literally. If a Japanese American volunteer, short of stature, didn't quite measure up, Dan'l would hit him over the head with a mallet, thereby producing a knot that would reach just high enough to pass muster. "Yup," the sergeant would intone, yardstick in hand, "you just made it! You're in the Army now." Similarly, Dan'l confirmed his national fealty during the registration program, the most contested of WRA administrative fiats, elaborated in chapter 8. Indiscriminately incarcerated and confined to concentration camps, Japanese Americans were nonetheless required to fill out loyalty questionnaires, pledging allegiance to the very government that had unconstitutionally detained them. Questions 27 and 28 forever marked Japanese Americans and their progeny as yes-yes or no-no types. True to his buddies, Lil Dan'l shook hands and bid farewell to a friend boarding the train for the Tule Lake, California, concentration camp, which had been set aside as the "segregation center" for "disloyals." But significantly, Dan'l stayed behind, firmly in the administration's good graces, as a yes-yes.[23]

Indeed, as artist and illustrator for the Rohwer camp newspaper, George Akimoto would have been in the administrators' good graces himself, though we've seen in chapter 3 the fine line he had to tread. Still, he saw no choice but to cooperate, as he explained years later. "Some of the younger kids around town get angry at us because they say, 'Why didn't you protest?' like people do now. They don't know what they're talking about. In those days, you just didn't do things that way. Actually we just didn't have the time; it was a shock and you didn't have the time to sit down and think about it. You just do what you're told and try to make the best of it. I think we were forced into a situation and we weren't going to fight it. We just had to do the best we could in a bad situation."[24]

Similarly, Jerome's best known artist, painter Henry Sugimoto, cultivated a warm, friendly relationship with administrators, so much so that they helped sponsor an exhibition of his work at Hendrix College in Conway, Arkansas, and allowed him to travel there along with his wife, Susie, in 1944. As art historian Kristine Kim has perceptively noted, "The college carefully crafted its press release, describing Sugimoto and his family as 'loyal Americans and members of the Presbyterian [Church].' The artworks on view were said to 'contain no suggestion of bitterness' and to be 'marked by tenderness and occasional humor.'" Indeed, Sugimoto's paintings from the period—though open to multiple politically charged interpretations—were filled with classic American and Christian iconography: the flag, the cross, the Bible. Baptized in the 1920s, Sugimoto "sustained a deep faith for the rest of his life." But that faith and his growing patriotism overshadowed the great range of his work. Although he was born and raised in Japan, traveled widely, studied art in Paris and Mexico City, and was greatly influenced by the impressionists and muralists, his work would be described, with great consistency, as *American*—as if thus categorizing him and his work would help bolster the national affiliation of Japanese Americans broadly. A justly deserved retrospective of his work, organized by the Japanese American National Museum at the turn of the twenty-first century, was titled Henry Sugimoto: Painting an American Experience.[25]

After early works devoted to French and Mexican life and landscape, Henry Sugimoto painted any number of canvases detailing the sorrow of incarceration. *My Papa*, from 1943, depicted his father being taken away by an FBI agent. *Evacuation*, from 1942, showed an expensive family possession—a GE refrigerator—being sold off for a single, bright green dollar, a bold critique of American greed. *Thinking about Christ*, painted in 1943, compared his own suffering, and that of Japanese Americans, to the suffering of Christ. In this starkly symmetrical composition, the three crosses of Calvary were balanced by three camp structures. The heavy wooden cross over Jesus' shoulder was set against a weighty burden over the back of a man, apparently the artist. The man's head, in the very center of the painting, was bowed so as to almost touch the haloed head of Christ. In the foreground was an opened Bible, an implicit source of instruction to Japanese Americans about faith and steadfastness. It was left to Sugimoto's students to more directly engage the often bleak surroundings and terrible dread of life in camp. Eddie Kurushima's watercolors from 1943 included one entitled *Deep in the Heart of Arkansas—Mud* and another called *Kikanju ni Kyofu o Idaite* [Feeling scared of the machine guns].[26]

Like so many, George Akimoto and Henry Sugimoto harbored reservations, even resentments about the treatment of Japanese Americans during the war. But they cultivated the privileges and circulated the ideologies of the WRA leadership. By asserting their own national loyalty and that of their subjects, they positioned themselves uppermost in new social hierarchies that allowed some Japanese Americans greater liberties, particularly freedom of movement, the ability to pass in and out of the camp. Also, Akimoto, Sugimoto, and others helped the WRA characterize Japanese Americans broadly as loyal citizen-subjects. As custodians of an uprooted, displaced, and dispossessed people, the WRA paradoxically had to perpetuate the folly of their political subversion and to manufacture representations of their national reconciliation. It was in this latter area where WRA officials spent most of their time. In addition to public relations efforts, very real material steps were undertaken to assure the redemption of Japanese American captives. The task was to change the content not only of characterization but also of character.

SAFEGUARDING BUDDHISM

At ten o'clock each Sunday morning at Jerome, Buddhists converged on dining hall 23, which was temporarily transformed into a temple. There, the weekly service opened with meditation and the offering of flowers. A designated girl and boy placed incense upon the altar, then the congregation recited three homages and a pledge of loyalty and devotion to Buddha. After the first hymn, or *gatha*, another member of the community offered a story, a short symbolic narrative that prefigured the sermon's principal themes. Following the announcements, the leader and congregants recited the Golden Chain: "I am a link in Lord Buddha's golden chain of love that stretches around the world. I must keep my link bright and strong. I will try to be kind and gentle to every living thing, and protect all who are weaker than myself. . . ." After another *gatha* was sung, and the Creed repeated, the priest delivered a sermon. Reverend Tadao Kouchi, for example, preached that "life is like a journey in a dream." Stressing the oneness of all creation, discouraging excessive attachment to possessions, he said that "material things and our minds are as one. They should be thought of as one." "The value of a thing," he concluded, "is found in the way we make it live"—the extent to which individuals put objects to productive, peaceful ends. Over at Rohwer, Reverend Daitetsu Hayashima, in sharp contrast to southern fundamentalism's hellfire and brimstone, taught that "a life of sympathy and kindness by casting away your worldly greed and seeking earnestly to make life pleasant for others will eventuate in good fortune and happiness." Services ended with meditation. Friends and family members greeted one another and chatted, then they returned home before going off to their respective dining halls for Sunday lunch.[27]

As could be said of all ten concentration camps, the Sunday morning and evening services for Buddhists in Arkansas were extraordinary achievements in and of themselves. Though there were many more Buddhists than Christians in the camps, among both Issei and Nisei, Christians went to church more often, including the Wednesday evening Bible study groups conducted by George Aki and Hideo Hashimoto at Jerome and the Thursday night choir practices. Japanese American Christian congregations enjoyed distinct advantages under incarceration, whereas Buddhist temples faced sometimes insurmountable difficulties.[28]

These difficulties predated Executive Order 9066 but were exacerbated thereafter. Not unlike the small, so-called private lynchings of African Americans in the South, Japanese Americans in the West were subjected to depersonalized, dehumanizing violence and intimidation often aimed at religious institutions and intended to terrorize the entire community. White racist assaults in California were often dismissed in court, and many murders went unsolved, as when two Issei, twenty-six-year-old J. Kino and forty-three-year-old Frank Yoshioka, were killed one after the other, under similar circumstances, in Stockton in early 1941. A boardinghouse owner, Yoshioka was gunned down after answering his door just before dawn. As in the South with African American churches, whites in the West attacked Buddhist temples. The Fresno temple attended by Tokio Yamane, Shigeru Matsuda, and, less frequently, his wife, Violet, was the target of shotgun blasts in the war. The "potshots were particularly aimed at the ancient Buddhist symbol called the *manji*," says scholar Duncan Ryuken Williams, which "coincidentally—and unfortunately—resembles a German Nazi swastika (though reversed and predating the swastika by thousands of years)." At Jerome Buddhists felt obligated to articulate—and update—the explanation of the symbol to appease southern patriots: "The distinct difference between the Buddhist and the Nazi swastikas is the direction in which the four Ls rotate. In the Buddhist insignia the Ls revolve clock-wise while in the Nazi sign they turn counter clock-wise." The four L's of the age-old Buddhist symbol, originating in India, were said to represent—somehow, in English—Light, Love, Life, and Liberty.[29]

Before the war American Buddhist temples and shrines numbered nearly 300, with the great majority in California and Hawaii, and they were served by 250 priests, almost all Issei. But in camp Buddhist congregations lacked both leaders and literature. Priests in particular had been rounded up in the wake of December the seventh and sent off to special Department of Justice (DOJ) camps. Like Shigeru Matsuda, who sold books in Japanese as well as English, learned theologians feared that their libraries alone would subject them to scrutiny, and so had burned their books in advance of the sweeps. But before the war's outbreak, the FBI had already indiscriminately classed many Japanese American leaders as "known dangerous Group A suspects" solely by virtue of their profession: priests, martial arts instructors, Japanese-language schoolteachers—another strike against Matsuda—and fishermen. (Feared as naval saboteurs, this category apparently took in Mary Nakahara's father, the fish market operator, as well.) Further, "the wholesale categorization of all Buddhists as inherently suspect reflected the government's fear of social elements that seemed foreign and un-American [and] reflected the addition to racial discrimination of religious discrimination."[30]

Camp officials participated in book-burning. In detention centers, where evicted Japanese Americans were first sent, officials tried to allay concerns even as they continued to confiscate volumes written in Japanese. Hymnals and other religious books were generally okay, they now maintained—a little too late—but the edict was imprecise. "Japanese print of any kind, such as newspapers, books, pamphlets, periodicals or other literature, with the exception of approved Japanese religious books (Bibles and hymnals) and English-Japanese dictionaries, are not authorized." Were only *Christian* religious publications in Japanese permitted?[31]

Buddhist icons and relics also had been disposed of or seized. So the material culture of wartime Buddhism took on a folksy, homemade cast. For Buddha's birthday at the DOJ camp in Bismarck, North Dakota, for example, fruit wrapping tissue was transformed into imitation flowers, and a skilled carver devised "a splendid image of the Buddha" from a carrot. At Rohwer Kyuji Hozaki forged a tin can into a church centerpiece—an urn-shaped candlestick. With time, however, more elaborate, sculptural pieces were possible. One "hand-carved and hand-joined" Buddhist household shrine at Rohwer, for example, "was not constructed of waste materials . . . but of carefully selected woods. . . . Used in the carved designs [we]re lotus blossoms—Buddhist emblems of triumph over self—and flying doves; the border [wa]s of inlaid wood." New rosaries (*ojuzu*) were crafted first from dried peach pits and later with elegant beads and tassels. New religious books, published and partially authored in the camps, were covered in ornate cloth (*omyogo*).[32]

Indeed, Jerome became a center of American Buddhist publishing during the war, under the local leadership of the Young Buddhists' Association (YBA), which "in its collective membership," as scholar Tetsuden Kashima has noted, "was probably the largest Nisei organization" in the country. Organizers Roy Kawamoto and Ayako Noguchi, also employed as journalists on the *Denson Tribune* staff, helped issue a number of volumes. Drawing upon sermons, responsive readings, hymns, and lessons recalled by priests and donated by lay leaders scattered around the nation, the Denson YBA of necessity published nine hundred copies of a new *Gathas and Services* book, a collaborative effort that helped reexamine key tenets of the faith and the rituals of worship. Given the dearth of scripture, the Denson YBA donated copies to other camps, along with their new condensed version of *St. Shinran and His Religion of Pure Faith* and an illustrated Buddhist calendar, "probably the first ever to be made in this country." Letters of thanks poured in from as far away as Heart Mountain, Wyoming, where Buddhist groups immediately put the holy books to use.[33]

White administrators who perused the new literature couldn't help but notice the many parallels between Buddhist and Christian teachings. Remarkably similar to the eight beatitudes of Jesus' Sermon on the Mount, which it predated, Buddhism's Seven Jewels of the Law read, in part: "Blessed are they that reject evil, for they shall attain purity. Blessed are they that aspire to holiness, for they shall attain serenity. Blessed are they that pursue knowledge, for they shall attain comprehension. Blessed are they that promote peace, for they shall attain felicity. . . . Blessed are they that follow the Path, for they shall attain enlightenment." And while the Japanese American Christians found fortitude in frontier metaphors, so too did the YBA's Noguchi as she described the first Obon services, commemorating ancestors, acknowledging their gifts, and promoting a continual spirit of giving: "Here in the wilderness of Denson, Arkansas, away from the familiar surroundings of our churches, away from all the conveniences of the past, we observed our memorial service as a group of pioneers would have done under similar circumstances. And in this austerity we felt that there was even greater significance, for we were able to appreciate, perhaps for the first time, the tremendousness of our religion." Or, as Williams elaborates, "Especially for the Issei, the Buddhist barrack church became a meaningful gathering place not only for the inspirational aspects of religious practice, but also because it was a place where Japanese heritage was affirmed. For some Issei Buddhists, whose association with the Buddhist temple had been casual on the outside, camp became a place where such ties were strengthened, despite pressure from all sides to convert to Christianity as a means of demonstrating loyalty to America."[34]

The crucial difference between Buddhist and Christian organizing in the camps involved the levels of support from the WRA and from outside denominational bodies. While Buddhists were forced to make their own books and implements after the losses of expulsion, donations of "various Sunday School supplies" flowed into the camps from Protestants from Neodesha, Kansas, to Newtown, Pennsylvania; from Columbus, Ohio, to Minden, Louisiana; from Medina, New York, to Collinsville, Alabama. Whereas Buddhist priests were locked away in DOJ camps, sparking petitions to Washington for a reuniting with their families and congregations, an already disproportionate Christian ministerial staff of Japanese Americans in the concentration camps was supplemented by white Protestant preachers invited in for revivals and evangelism. Further, when officials in D.C. reluctantly concluded that "evacuee ministers shall not be compensated by [the WRA] for religious duties which they perform," Christian pastors continued to receive pay packets until authorities at the camps had successfully arranged for salaries to be taken over by the denominational headquarters. And, in a striking example of the WRA favoritism to Christian groups, although the Jerome Community Christian Church, USO, and YWCA repeatedly were granted special extended usage of camp buildings, the administration—with reasons all its own—decided to kick the Buddhist Church out of its house of worship in dining hall 23. Priests and congregants protested, but only after a petition of almost five hundred signatories reached director Paul Taylor's desk did he finally relent.[35]

Buddhists would be among the most vociferous opponents of the early closing of Jerome, using confrontational language impossible to find in the censored camp newspaper. Closure was "the subject of grave discussion," as the *Denson Buddhist Bulletin* called it, "a shocking blow . . . necessitating inevitable disbandment of the now active Bussei organization." "No sooner than a solid foundation for the YBA has been laid," said one anonymous editorialist, "preparations for dispersement must be made." Still, Jerome YBA's pathbreaking publishing arm had smoothed the way. Buddhists resettling outside the camps or serving in the military had needed a network to forge

13. Buddhist funeral at the Rohwer concentration camp, June 1944. 97.292.5A, MC, JANM.

connections to regional temples and local congregants. The National Council of Churches, various denominational bodies, and the USO had taken on this task for Japanese American Christians. Indeed, they organized many aspects of the WRA's resettlement program. According to Roy Kawamoto, due to the National YBA headquarters' "lack of initiative"—or perhaps more accurately, lack of resources—"Denson YBA formed the Buddhist Home Program . . . to take over this important responsibility." Chaired by Ayako Noguchi, the Home Program published and widely circulated a "Directory of Relocated Bussei" and a "Directory of Bussei Servicemen" and arranged countless introductions, referrals, and services. And although Ayako Noguchi had repeatedly expressed her own interest in the USO's programs for intra-ethnic matrimony with soldiers, she found her own husband on the staff of the camp newspaper and on the board of the Jerome YBA: Chairman Kiyoshi Nakamura.[36]

Against considerable odds, Buddhist worship thrived in the camps. It proved a wellspring of comfort and support for the majority of believers behind barbed wire. Even as a besieged national organization, stripped of its leadership, embarked upon a period of "organizational Americanization"—changing its name, for example, to the Buddhist Churches of America in 1944 at a Topaz confab—Buddhism during the war years "served as a source of moral and cultural resistance to the simplistic Americanization encouraged by the WRA," as Williams puts it. "The government's view of being American meant learning more English, converting to Christianity and joining organizations like the YMCA/YWCA." Resilient YBAs and temples offered an alternative path.[37]

WORSHIPPING OF THE NATION

The cheery yuletide consumerism of 1942—especially the gifts and donations sent by ordinary churchgoing Christians from around the country—had restored Mary Tsukamoto's faith in American traditions and the American people. But the Christmas shopping expeditions and subsequent excursions into neighboring Arkansas towns and villages had not been without problems. "The people of Dermott are increasingly friendly with the center's appointed personnel," Paul Taylor wrote in his monthly report to Washington, "but their attitude toward the evacuees has changed little. A few merchants still refuse to wait on evacuees." As one young female inmate reported, "A group of high school kids who went [to town] with their teacher yesterday were asked to leave almost every store and every restaurant they entered. It got so embarrassing that the teacher went into the stores first and asked if it would be all right if the kids came in. Then when they asked if they could eat at a place, they said okay; but before they were finished, they were asked to leave. It certainly is awful to be treated that way."[38]

Such encounters remind us that while the nation may frequently be constructed on a global stage—with presidents, generals, diplomats, and immigration officers policing the lines between one sovereign nation and another—national identity is often contested, mediated, and negotiated at the local level. For example, those self-selected agents of Americanism, the American Legion, attempted to regulate national belonging and allegiance on multiple levels: national, state, and local. The organization's national commander, Warren Atherton, a so-called "native" of Stockton, California—the prewar home of many Rohwer prisoners—declared that first-generation Japanese immigrants, most of whom had resided in the United States for decades without citizenship rights, were "unassimilable." Thus, to avoid "future problems," they should be repatriated to Japan. The Arkansas state meeting of the American Legion "passed a [similar] resolution; that after the war all Japanese be returned to Japan; that relocated evacuees be fingerprinted and required to report to Federal Court authorities every 60 days; [and] that they be prevented from buying food in nearby towns." As Paul Taylor informed Washington,

"A good part of this resolution is attributable to the Legionnaire at Dermott, Robert Gordon, who quite obviously is yelling about the Japanese [*sic*] in an effort to build back some political prestige lost recently in a state campaign. He has some personal animosity for some of the administrative staff" of the Jerome camp. Indeed, "relations with the town of Dermott, eight miles north of the center, remained unfavorable. . . . The Dermott and Lake Village American Legion Posts passed discriminatory resolutions against relocation," proposing that "the War Department take over" the running of the camps from the civilian Department of the Interior. In daily interactions, in town and in the camp, hierarchies of national identity were applied, resisted, and renegotiated.[39]

These local Legionnaires would have been among the leading local merchants and likewise would have been among the leading lay figures in local congregations. Thus, it was on the terrain of Christian charity, an appeal to a universalizing community of faith, that camp administrators and select Japanese American pastors and parishioners attempted to cultivate a common ground. At a "get-acquainted luncheon" in February 1943, "camp Protestant ministers met with ministers from Rohwer, McGehee, and neighboring communities." Soon Japanese American preachers, choir members, and other lay leaders were visitors to Sunday worship services at the segregated white churches of the mainline Protestant denominations: Baptist and Methodist, in particular. Also, the rapprochement worked in the opposite direction. Over a single week in March, for example, numerous Christian visitors, pastors, and officials came into the camp, whereas—as on most weeks—no Buddhist leaders were on the visitor rolls. This might be expected, given the overwhelming preponderance of evangelical Christians in the American South. But other factors were involved.[40]

Local and regional clergy set their sights on Jerome and Rohwer for what they called "missionary work." Often used to describe evangelizing efforts overseas, in this case it was applied to seeming foreigners nearer to home. Indeed, among many mainline Protestant denominations, "foreign missions" went hand in hand with "home missions" aimed at various nonwhite residents of the United States. "Here in our state," said Arkansas Southern Baptist President T. L. Harris, "we have had literally thrust upon us the greatest opportunity for winning to Christ those of pagan faith we have ever witnessed." The McGehee Ministerial Alliance urged local people to take an "American Christian" approach to their new neighbors and support religious activity in the camps. So many churches sent ministers to serve inside the camps that ten Protestant groups were represented in the Rohwer Federated Christian Church: Baptist, Congregational, Disciples of Christ, Episcopal, Free Methodist, Friends, Holiness, Methodist, Presbyterian, Salvation Army. However, the permanent eight-person ministers' council at Rohwer was made up entirely of ordained pastors of Japanese descent, who conducted services in both English and Japanese.[41]

WRA officials and Japanese American Christians also saw incarceration as an unprecedented occasion to evangelize on a grand scale. And in the gendered hierarchies of church leadership, just below the male clergy, women lay leaders in particular led the charge. Notable among them was Mary Nakahara. Like Mary Tsukamoto, Nakahara was a respected Sunday school teacher and youth group leader, as we've seen. She urged support for the Japanese American troops in her newspaper column, "Nisei in Khaki," and she also delivered that support through the service organization she founded, the Crusaders. Their creed: "Service to others is life's most satisfactory experience." In addition to letters to servicemen, the Crusaders "wrote and sent gifts to . . . the orphans at the Children's Village at Manzanar [concentration camp], and to the Japanese TB patients left in sanatoriums on the West Coast. . . . Because she wanted the teen-agers to rise above their own adversities, [Nakahara] rewrote the words to hymns and patriotic songs to fit the camp situation." "I was a super-patriotic American," Nakahara explained years later. "In other words, I was a naive, apolitical, provincial, idealistic do-gooder."[42]

As Paul Taylor proudly reported to Washington, "A group of twelve Christian church members presented a play at a young people's meeting of the Methodist Church in Little Rock. This play, 'The Exit We Search,' was written by Miss Mary Nakahara of this center, and depicted the people's feelings at being evacuated, the birth of the 442nd Combat Team, and the ultimate hope of most center residents to be relocated." As Taylor surmised, "The play created a favorable impression and the young people who participated were welcomed into the church members' homes and were taken on sight-seeing trips of the city. The play was repeated the following night before a still larger audience which filled the hall of the Pulaski Heights Christian Church, North Little Rock, and was just as enthusiastically received by them. Both [statewide newspapers] the *Democrat* and *Gazette* mentioned the latter meeting in their church news." Not content to preach to the converted, Nakahara and her troupe also presented the work to the Young Buddhist Brotherhood at Jerome. In a parallel effort aimed outside the camps, Charlotte Douglas Susu-Mago wrote a play that appeared in the April 1943 issue of the *Methodist Woman* called "Counting on You," which urged white Methodist families to assist in resettling Japanese Americans in their communities as "part of the church's missionary work."[43]

Indeed, more than exercises in public relations and Christian beneficence, church activity in and around the concentration camps included a zealous desire to convert non-Christians. With the help of Nakahara, Tsukamoto, and others, Jerome and Rohwer were chosen as the first camps for a six-day National Christian Mission—essentially a large-scale revival. In addition to camp ministers such as Hideo Hashimoto and Shin Kanow, recognized white leaders participated, including Albert Shirkey, pastor of the Travis Park Methodist Church in San Antonio, Texas; John B. Cobb, Methodist minister from Spokane, Washington; Jessie Trout, a Disciplines of Christ missionary to Japan, fluent in the language; and most famously, Dr. E. Stanley Jones, a longtime Methodist missionary to India and best-selling author known as Brother Stanley. At these daily and nightly meetings, countless congregants were "saved" and given the ritual baptism. As Jones commented to the press, with a typical, patronizing tone, "There is not a more lovable group of people in the world than the Christians in the relocation centers. . . . I don't believe any group in the world would have behaved better than, or even as well as the Christians of Japanese blood."[44]

Indeed, regulating behavior seemed all important. Among the week's morning and afternoon seminars, Mary Tsukamoto and George Aki chaired sessions on "Marriage and the Home." Unusually, given the marital expectations of much Christian domesticity, the unmarried "Miss Trout" spoke on "The Bible and Home." Evening worship was "conducted much like the regular Sunday morning services," according to an administration report, "except that after the sermon the speaker asked the people to come to the front to shake hands with the ministers as an expression of rededicating their lives to Christ. . . . About 300 persons dedicated their lives to Christian living and five persons were baptized. Later several adults and ten to fifteen high school girls expressed a desire to be baptized also. On the evening of Dr. Jones's talk, dedication cards were passed out to the congregation after those who were not interested were given an opportunity to leave." Though they downplayed the extent of proselytizing during the week, officials had to concede—no doubt with understatement—that "the young Kibei Buddhists who attended said they felt uncomfortable."[45]

Soon Mary Tsukamoto had developed a friendship with Jessie Trout. And with her husband, Al, she visited Indiana to accompany Trout on a statewide goodwill mission, vouching for the upstanding Christian character of prisoners who soon would be resettling in the area. Tsukamoto's efforts—and those of countless other members of United Methodist Women, Baptist women's organizations, circles, and missionary societies—insured that, in the South and Midwest, Japanese Americans were perceived to hold one of the most significant credentials of U.S. belongingness: Christian faith.[46]

Christian women such as Mary Tsukamoto enabled the post-camp urban and small-town pioneering of Japanese Americans, the often solitary movements of individuals and families into unknown territories, into white communities reluctant to welcome, incorporate, or integrate them. To officials, the prisoners who, like Tsukamoto, had become Americanized—and with that, Christianized—held out the best hope of adaptation to life in the postwar United States. Indeed, Tsukamoto could not have undertaken her goodwill mission and early resettlers would not have been allowed to leave the camps without authentication of their American ideals, without the certification of belonging. In this sense, patriotism and religiosity promised escape from confinement. So, although Christian religious services provided very real succor and comfort to Japanese Americans no less than Buddhist practice, the pressures to conform—the added benefits of Christian assimilation—were enormous.

Though Mary Tsukamoto compared aspects of her incarceration to an early American frontier experience—and though she would become a truly pioneering educator after the war—pioneers were still largely gendered as male, as the *Lil Dan'l* figure and the choice of his namesake, Daniel Boone, made clear. Unexpectedly, incarceration had altered traditional gender roles. As we've seen in chapter 4, domestic labor was collectivized and reduced in the camps, leaving women with more time for church and community service activities. Kitchen work was now waged, and women as never before took higher-level clerical and professional jobs in the camps, insuring that both during and after the war they had their own financial resources and, thus, greater independence from husbands and fathers. Yes, some women complained of "family breakdown," but men especially warned against their "emasculation," as new female employees and community organizers called traditional American gender roles into question. But if gender was in flux, patriotism and Christian evangelism could offset the dangerous, nonconformist implications. Women worked their way into leadership positions, but those positions were more readily sanctioned by the government if they furthered the aims of nationalism, evangelism, and consumerism.

Around Christmas 1943, during that eerie melding of religious, nationalist, and consumerist effusion, Paul Taylor was able to tell Washington about a significant improvement over the previous year's holiday season: "The center received no unfavorable reaction from the Christmas shopping of evacuees outside the center. The number was limited to 100 per day for the 8-day period prior to December 18. . . . One neighboring town sent a truck to the center for several days, supplying free transportation for the evacuees. An evacuee committee chartered a bus which made 2 trips to the second town." Thus the once-callous white merchants and humble Nikkei shoppers were joined together in Christian amity over the countertops and altars of southeast Arkansas. Truly, by imbibing national and religious mores as dictated at the local level, through rituals of consumption and worship, Japanese Americans earned the right to imagine themselves a part of the national community, even if from behind barbed wire.[47]

More than detainment, the World War II incarceration of 120,000 Americans of Japanese descent represented a highly coordinated if contested ideological campaign to Americanize a particular ethnic minority group, to "rehabilitate" the prisoners, as their keepers termed it. Labeling any number of complex syncretic attitudes and values, products and institutions, as straightforwardly Japanese or American, authorities designed a variety of programs to minimize the sway of the former and maximize the impact of the latter. They banned Japanese-language books, confiscated radios, urged English instruction at night schools for adults, and required it at day schools for children. Moreover, the federally mandated elementary and secondary curricula specified any number of nationalist lesson plans and rituals, including patriotic singing, Bible reading, and historical pageants. Camp newspapers toed the administration line; the largely ineffectual, male-dominated community councils served as exercises in "American" democracy; military recruiters promoted enlistment and eventually conscription; and the insidious resettlement program attempted to destroy urban ethnic enclaves and isolate small groups of Japanese Americans in predominantly white towns and cities. Central to these efforts, officials advocated conversion to Christianity and invited Protestant missionaries such as E. Stanley Jones and Jessie Trout for camp crusades to win over the majority Buddhist population.

An inherently supremacist activity, missionary work assumed the inferiority—indeed, the tragedy—of nonbelief versus belief in an unseen deity. Further, evangelism presupposed the superiority of one faith system over another: over *any* other. The ultimate arrogance, comparable to jingoism, it effectively held that one's own religion, as with one's own nation, was best—by virtue of the accident of one's own birth into it, as was the most common form of membership. All too often, to urge conformity, to press for conversion and assimilation, was to assert a superior faith, a superior culture.

Immigrant Japanese and second-generation Americans participated in these programs—and often led them. In the gendered hierarchies of educational and religious instruction, just below the principals and ministers, Nisei women especially directed study groups, conducted membership drives, led youth organizations, and supported the U.S. war effort. Not unlike the African American church structures analyzed by historians from Evelyn Brooks Higginbotham to Glenda Gilmore, Christian institutions thus provided women with vibrant platforms for self-assertion, community organizing, and political empowerment. But such endeavors met with resistance from many Japanese Americans who decried assimilationism as they highlighted persistent American racial and economic injustice. These conflicts also have occasioned radical reevaluation by successive generations of historians. In the vast scholarship on Japanese American "internment," with its ever more sophisticated attention to euphemism and doublespeak, the U.S. government's so-called relocation centers rightly have been characterized as concentration camps. This chapter asks, finally, if they further should be considered as indoctrination centers.[48]

7 | Strikes and Resistance

IN EARLY 1943 John Yoshida escaped from the American concentration camp at Jerome, Arkansas.

It was easy to get out; people did it all the time. With a day pass, you could catch a bus into town and go shopping. Even without a pass, many Japanese Americans sneaked out to go fishing or to take a walk in the woods. But unlike the shoppers and the hikers, John Yoshida had no intention of coming back.

Some time after noon on Sunday, 17 January, he slipped past the barbed-wire fence encircling the Jerome camp. Though U.S. military police were positioned atop guard towers and at the gates, outfitted with Springfield rifles, they either failed to notice Yoshida or failed to bother. On Monday afternoon, the father and stepmother of the twenty-three-year-old reported him missing to the authorities. A search of Jerome, as well as the neighboring camp at Rohwer, where his sister lived, thirty miles away, yielded nothing. Not a clue.

A full day after he'd gone AWOL, John Yoshida had gotten little farther than a mile. He eventually made his way to the railroad tracks, focusing on that potent symbol of Japanese American imprisonment. It was by train that Yoshida and his family had been shipped, shades drawn, to this sparsely populated southern flatland—a grueling four-day journey from the Pacific Coast to the banks of the Mississippi River. Shunted into the plywood and tar-paper barracks, they had already encountered a cold winter, a fuel shortage, and the countless indignities of confinement. Worse, the war now seemed protracted, the end far from sight. And in the dead of night, the trains—carrying troops, carrying weapons, carrying the stuff of a once ordinary life—rolled by, measuring the fitful sleep of the 17,000 at Jerome and Rohwer. The far-off *chunk-chunk* of wheels over tracks grew ever louder and closer, drowning out the crickets, then again faded away, the whistle crying out another hour of captivity.

Of the ten camps built for detaining 120,000 Americans of Japanese descent, these two in Arkansas were set up right alongside the vital supply line. So these trains had become an infuriating reminder of the injustice of incarceration. By day, boys pelted the locomotives and boxcars with rocks. By night, there was no fighting it—except in dreams and in thoughts of release. Now, in the dark morning of 19 January 1943, a train was about to pass. John Yoshida was ready.

Yoshida took off his overcoat and folded it neatly. He took off his hat. He double-checked the folded piece of paper, then stacked them all next to the tracks. He crouched down as the train approached.

The conductor didn't see him. The big machine passed, as usual, through the dewy Delta cotton fields' predawn haze, continuing on its course without stopping. Meanwhile, the fugitive had laid down on his stomach, perpendicular to the track, and placed his chin just over the first rail. When the train rolled over that stretch, just a mile and a half north of the Jerome, Arkansas, concentration camp, it severed John Yoshida's head from his body.[1]

Resistance to oppression comprises a range of behaviors, from the seemingly smallest acts of everyday dissent and insubordination to the most weighty deed of all, the taking of one's own life. If we humans make choices, but not in a world of our choosing, then this one option—taken under what for some were unendurable circumstances—can be interpreted as a final act of will. An important concept in social history, agency is generally conceived as the ability to think, to ascertain available courses of action, and to then act in one's best interest. When that interest runs counter to that of one's captors—who here wanted docile acceptance of incarceration—then the human agency of suicide can constitute struggle and can be equated with resistance. And, as we shall see, in the continuing, complex relationship between reportage and resistance in the camps, administrators and their most compliant Japanese American underlings utilized silence to minimize the ill effects, as they saw them, of resistance, to downplay the worst conceivable outcomes of incarceration. They often covered up or ignored acts of defiance. These silences, apparent absences in our historical sources, nonetheless must be assessed and deciphered. In looking back at this time, if we allow a gap in the record to stand in as an absence or a historical lack, then we will have lost the powerful stories of lives lived against the grain of official history, against the will of white oppressors.

DISPUTES OVER PAY AND CONDITIONS

Young men and boys repeatedly threw rocks and eggs at passing trains. On 27 August 1943, twenty-three were investigated after a Missouri Pacific Railway conductor left a note for the Jerome railway agent stating that roughly fifteen "Japs at Jap Camp are throwing rocks at caboose." All twenty-three were characterized by their foreman at the trackside warehouse as desiring repatriation or expatriation to Japan. Only two—Minoru Outa and Masaji Minamoto—confessed to tossing stones *near* the tracks. To a person, the remaining twenty-one, mostly in their late teens and early twenties, said they "did not see" or "could not see" anyone throwing rocks—demonstrating the utility of silence or dissembling for resisters as well. Though all were released with a warning, officials vowed to punish anyone caught in the act. A few months later, in February 1944, warehouse assistant George Hamada was sentenced to ten days in the Drew County Jail in Monticello after he admitted throwing eggs at a caboose. Everyday resistance in Arkansas took the form of both emotional gesture and psychological release, especially as trains had been the vehicle of expulsion and concentration.[2]

Symbolically superior in the pecking order of camp life and in the organizational charts of camp employment structures, white staff enjoyed superior housing and transport. Such property, therefore, was also the target of Japanese American indignation. "The most important trend inside the center, in my opinion," said one Jerome official, "is one which"—farcically—"I cannot explain. I refer to the increasing manifestation of contempt with which the lower class evacuees look upon the administration and appointed personnel." Though he couldn't put two and two together, the official nonetheless could explain material differences and emotional consequences: "I have seen resentment based on the fact that personnel apartments are more livable than barracks quarters." Since Japanese Americans as a rule could not have cars in the camps, bitterness over mobility and its means likewise crystallized the broader antipathy. "I saw two men spit on a staff member's automobile. I have heard other staff members relate similar incidents." The anger seeped down to children, crossing generational bounds. "I saw a young boy spit on a toy wagon belonging to the child of an appointed employee." Staff also received more expensive, if not more wholesome, meals. For the high-fat, less healthy "personnel menu," costs were fifty-two cents per person per day, compared to the "evacuee menu" at thirty-seven cents per person per day. These figures, reported to a U.S. Senate investigating committee by camp director Paul Taylor, overlooked labor costs—try as he might. Japanese American complaints about food, how it was produced and consumed, and their modest attacks on white perks, when coordinated in collective struggle, could yield marked improvements in standards of living and working.[3]

From the earliest days, labor disputes figured prominently at the Jerome concentration camp. As disagreements erupted over pay and working conditions, laborers developed techniques for airing grievances and managers adopted methods for containing dissent. While a ten-day general strike at Poston and riots at Manzanar momentarily focused public attention on Arizona and California, unrest in Arkansas involved a series of confrontations spanning over a year, beginning in November 1942. The WRA leadership in Washington feigned indifference. It seemed scarcely to take notice. The national press ignored the Arkansas events altogether. Still, against considerable odds, in the face of setback after deadly setback, Japanese American workers forced concessions from administrators. By the end of November 1943, they would achieve a major victory that reverberated all the way to Washington.[4]

Maltreatment emerged first from three related camp labor forces: food services, public works, and transportation and supply. Charged with building the camp's infrastructure, the public works crews toiled outdoors under exhausting circumstances. They constructed miles of roads within the camp and—in these remote marshy woodlands—miles of roads leading to and from the camp. To clear rights-of-way for drainage ditches and roads, men had to fell trees. Further, they had to cut the wood for transport and, along with women back in the camp, chop it up for use in each apartment's coal- and wood-burning stove. As winter set in, white supervisors pushed Japanese American workers to churn out ever more cords of wood with axes and handsaws. Despite repeated worker suggestions, weeks would pass before camp administrators, relenting, purchased chain saws and approved construction of a mechanized lumber mill for the efficient production of firewood, posts, and boards.

Work teams chafed at the meager wages they earned. Though the WRA pay scale was graded from $12 to $16 to $19 per month, generally for unskilled to semi-skilled to skilled and professional labor, everyone agreed that no woodcutter should receive less than fifty cents for a hard day's work. Indeed, in a stark reversal of capitalist economics, Japanese Americans floated "proposals that the highest wage should be paid for the most disagreeable work"—such that $19 would be given to fuel carriers and garbage collectors and "lower rates" would be paid to "the pleasanter and easier jobs, such as office work." In what Paul Taylor described as a "unified action," clearly "planned" and "not spontaneous," land-clearing crews mounted a half-day strike on 19 November 1942, demanding better pay and a better work environment. The camp's pro-administration newspaper reported it as a "sit-down" over "poor lunches," concluding happily that a special kitchen detail would be set up "for the sole purpose of preparing suitable lunches for the work crews."[5]

Inarguably, since work sites were located up to fifteen miles away from the camp—too far to return to the dining halls at midday—bag lunches prepared early in the morning had proven none too appetizing. Worse still, the diet was insufficient to meet the needs of strenuous manual labor. Hot tea breaks, condemned as an example of "coddling" the inmates in a sensational *Memphis Commercial-Appeal* story, only partially offset the cold, not to mention the hunger. And still, "DIES COMMITTEE SAYS INTERNED JAPANESE AMONG BEST-FED CIVILIANS IN THE WORLD," cried a popular headline from the period. WRA regional attorney Robert Leflar, on the other hand, surmised that Jerome woodcutters needed an extra midafternoon meal. Workers foremost wanted a decent wage. Taylor admitted that woodcutters "had plenty of backing for their argument." In addition to the hardship and dangers they faced, their labor, even if deemed manual, required keen attention and skill. Workers convinced Taylor to rescind the apprentice/training rate of $12 per month and institute a starting wage of $16, reserving the top WRA wage of $19 for raises and promotions. Similarly, after "a committee representing all waiters" lodged a formal complaint and met with the camp administration, food services staff negotiated a wage floor of $16 per month. Carpenters and hospital janitors were among several classes of employees who also protested over working conditions.[6]

In this way, Jerome employees achieved piecemeal—occupational class by occupational class—what could not be achieved wholesale across the ten camps in the WRA system: higher wages, at least at the bottom end of the scale. Though many administrators thought it unfair, the $19 ceiling lasted throughout the war, so that, for publicity's sake, a prisoner's pay never exceeded a U.S. soldier's base pay of $21 or more per month—not even pharmacists, dentists, or physicians. As soon became apparent in hospitals, offices, and workshops, white colleagues performing the same duties often received more than ten times the earnings of Japanese Americans, intensifying discontent. And in the case of Jerome, hard-fought pay concessions were tempered by unwarranted pay suspensions. At the very moment inmates sought to invest in heavier winter clothing and spend money on holiday gifts, food services personnel had to forego their pay envelopes. Administrative bungling of accounts had jeopardized the camp's cash flow, and November wages weren't distributed until 22 December due to a "shortage of cash."[7]

If Jerome workers had made significant advances in these crucial early struggles over employment rights, Paul Taylor—at age thirty-four, the youngest of the ten concentration camp directors—was determined to regain the upper hand, reassert his authority, and draw the line against strike action. Over December and January, he announced tough new policies regarding sick leave and terminations. Absence for illness would now require a certificate to be presented to the timekeeper: employees would need to obtain the supervisor's signature for up to two days' absence, a physician's signature for three days or more. Sick leave of more than fifteen days was forbidden. As was further dictated on the front page of the camp newspaper, failure to produce a certificate would result in "a penalty-loss of three days' wages." Ironically, on the same page, the newspaper reported "TAYLOR'S RETURN" to work "after a week's absence due to [an unspecified] illness." Instead of the camp hospital, he had received treatment in Lake Village.[8]

Taylor also announced through the newspaper revised procedures for terminations. Department heads were newly commanded to write extensive comments on employment separation forms, a ubiquitous feature of the camp labor market given the preponderance of short-term assignments. While the administration insisted that such written remarks would "reward the vast majority" of employees, they were designed to "work a definite hardship on indolence, un-cooperative attitude, and lack of ability." That is, the plan would help foreclose *future* job opportunities for anyone who "refused to accept work suggestions, showed no interest"—or, most revealing—"repeatedly stirred up unrest." Troublemakers, in other words, would be blacklisted. Early strike action in Arkansas had exposed the same inadequacies and injustices as had strikes at the Santa Anita detention center, where many Jerome residents were first held. Calling it "a shameful thing," doubting their motives, Mary Nakahara had outlined the four rationales for camouflage makers' work stoppage back in California: "They weren't receiving enough food, that their pay was too small, that this work was injurious to health, and that they were drafted to this project." Indeed, on this last point, Jerome workers soon would become expert, as administrators attempted both to force Japanese Americans to undertake the most unpleasant of jobs and to punish those who refused.[9]

THE WOODCUTTERS STRIKE AND THE DEATH OF SEIZO IMADA

Paul Taylor prepared to exercise his resolve as disputes with woodcutters continued. Though employment in concentration camps purportedly was voluntary and job opportunities extended across the range of goods and services essential to the functioning of any community of 8,000-plus residents, personnel offices manipulated applicants, pushing them toward unpopular areas of endeavor. Acknowledging inmates' aversion to land clearing, Taylor launched a "drive for additional wood crews, putting pressure on the workers in less essential jobs to either produce or transfer to the wood crews." For a time he succeeded in increasing the number of crewmen from 365 to 600. But for rookie cutters as well as veterans, the work was drudgery, incommensurate with the compensation. Still, Taylor goaded the workers.[10]

Senbinshi Takaoka was among the Rohwer inmates who answered the call to the forests. A portly man, getting on in years, he was much more comfortable at his desk. Takaoka's friends had long admired his enchanting calligraphy, his watercolor paintings of carp and fallen leaves, and they had tapped him to illustrate the monthly announcements and occasional collections of the Delta Ginsha poetry club back in Stockton, then at the Stockton detention center, and now at Rohwer. Takaoka had been writing freestyle haiku with the club for well over a decade—transferring his short, rich poems onto ornamented cards for presentation as gifts—and these *tanzaku* had earned the respect of his colleagues. More given to sketching trees than chopping them, Takaoka now joined the members of his block in the grueling work of securing fuel.[11]

Takaoka captured that first day on the job in a poem of extraordinary insight. Written in Japanese as a single line of elaborate *kanji* and *hiragana* characters running down the page, it reads in the roman alphabet as SHIMOASA NO ONO O WATASARE KYO KIKORI TO NARU. Translated into English, it is but ten words, a deceptive economy. For it reveals so much about Takaoka and the circumstances in Arkansas:

> Frosty morning
> handed a hatchet
> today I became a woodcutter[12]

Common in traditional haiku, the reference to seasonal change in the first two-word line here serves further purposes. It alludes to the wintry working conditions, men freezing outdoors in the early hours of the day, and it suggests the reason for the work: the cold weather seemingly necessitates the cutting of firewood to heat apartments. The word *handed* proves crucial, leaving ambiguous the issues of coercion and volunteerism around the job. As he words it, Takaoka hasn't so much taken up the hatchet as he has been given it. Who hands over the work implement? Implicitly, a supervisor—a person with authority and relative power—puts it in Takaoka's hand. Does he willingly grasp it? Or does he feel compelled, forced even, to take it? These last two questions likely coexisted and remained unresolved in the minds of many inmates at Jerome and Rohwer.

The last line speaks volumes. *Today* Takaoka faces a dual challenge. He must reconcile an identity as both a *woodcutter* and a poet. He must assent to the rough calloused *hands* associated with the former as well as, or in lieu of, the soft deft hands he already has cultivated as the latter. These differing traits, differing self-conceptions, compete. We can imagine Takaoka's trip back home from the forest and his hasty retreat to his desk. He has chopped wood by day, and he now writes verse—this selfsame poem—by night, all within the span of roughly twelve to sixteen hours. For the last line of the poem doesn't begin with the word *yesterday,* the phrase *last week.* His poem, like a diary entry, comments on his activities this very day. An acute observer of nature, he has hacked away at its beauty, marred it, so he uses the calligraphy brush to, in some sense, emotionally restore it—and to restore himself.

It's not a giant leap to read political connotations in Takaoka's suggestive last line, written as it is in the context of labor unrest, demands for greater occupational safety. It's a short step from the second to the third and final line, from being handed a hatchet, presumably for the first time, to becoming a woodcutter. Whether the role is thrust upon him, whether he embraces it, or some combination of the two, with irony and maybe sarcasm he asserts acceptance of or resignation to the duty, with the forthright usage of the first-person noun-subject, *I.* But it's a very short interval indeed in which to receive a tool and then, one moment to the next, be granted the title and the status: *I became a woodcutter.* Takaoka adopted a hazardous vocation, he ever so subtly suggests, with minimal training, the briefest of apprenticeships, perhaps none at all.

Despite his considerable poetic gifts, we can't know exactly how Senbinshi Takaoka felt about his new job. We do know, however, that after the camps, the immigrant repatriated to Japan. He died in Kyoto.[13]

In December 1942 four of the public works crews at Jerome banded together in a work stoppage. What Paul Taylor perceived initially as a "slow-up campaign" proved in fact to be a "sit-down strike." The woodcutters "reported to work," he wrote to the WRA in Washington, "but accomplished practically nothing. When supervisors attempted to talk with the evacuee foremen, in most instances the foremen would turn and walk off and would not discuss problems." Two crews in the transportation and supply division joined in the strike, bringing the total to seventy-five men. Their refusal to work left twenty railcars on the tracks unloaded, incurring demurrage charges for the administration.[14]

To appear in control, Taylor understated the severity of the problem. To remain in Taylor's good graces, journalists ignored the escalating crisis. And to hinder termination and blacklisting, striking workers surreptitiously coordinated their efforts and avoided being singled out by name. Thus, as is common in labor history, we now know the identity of few of these daring organizers. But it is certain that the entire camp was well aware of their struggles at the time and had a significant stake in the outcome. For the unloaded freight cars contained valuable cargo. They held not only supplies for various camp construction projects but also key components in a belated winterization scheme. Since the barracks apartments had been put up without interior walls and ceilings, gypsum board was ordered to insulate the units. And because woodcutting crews, regardless of strikes, couldn't possibly keep apace of the demand for firewood, coal was requisitioned for schools, hospitals, and workplaces. Strikers knew that their actions bore potential adverse consequences—and not solely for themselves. By slowing production of the camp's principal heating fuel, wood, they risked the health and comfort of their families and friends. That this latest strike lasted as long as it did—several days, perhaps a few weeks—suggests that many nonetheless supported it.

Why did Paul Taylor and Rohwer director Ray Johnston insist upon breakneck woodcutting operations, fraught with innumerable occupational hazards, when all the other concentration camps received outside supplies of coal and wood? In part, it was a simple environmental advantage: these southern camps were situated in the midst of harvestable timber. But why was Taylor so adamant that the deforested tracts then be rapidly converted into fields for cultivation? Even as he alienated woodcutters through unbearable working conditions—made worse over the harsh winter months of December, January, and February—he infuriated land-clearing crews by sending them mules in order to pull up stumps and dig rows for planting. Why would he allow labor relations to so thoroughly degenerate? Clearly, Taylor hoped to create a self-sufficient camp and thereby impress the powerbrokers in Arkansas and the higher-ups in Washington—notably fellow farm boy Dillon Myer, the WRA director, who "instead of becoming a Methodist minister" had fashioned himself as "an 'agricultural missionary' who preached the gospel of efficiency."[15]

Born in 1908 and raised in the village of Watson Chapel, near Pine Bluff, Arkansas, Paul Taylor had parlayed a University of Arkansas degree into a thriving career in agricultural management, not unlike Myer. From 1934 until taking up the post at Jerome in 1942, Taylor had served in various capacities for the U.S. Department of Agriculture, both in and outside Washington. Already a seasoned federal bureaucrat at thirty-four, he planned to demonstrate his prowess by generating all food and fuel for his concentration camp from adjacent acreage, even "helping out the war effort" with excess production. While the *Denson Communiqué* and its successor the *Denson Tribune* steered clear of strike reporting, they consistently quantified crop yields for readers, praising Japanese Americans for their skills as farmers and Paul Taylor for his expertise in agricultural economics. No sooner were stumps cleared than fields would sprout—in order of acres committed—corn, potatoes, carrots, pumpkins, soy beans, cabbage, beans, greens, lettuce, tomatoes, onions, peas, radishes, and other vegetables and fruits.[16]

Taylor would not allow his plans to be thwarted. The four public works crews and two transportation crews who went on strike to protest conditions "were terminated on the basis that they had refused to work." They were left without their old jobs and without hope of new ones. With plenty of free time on their hands, they now inaugurated a workers' education campaign and began to enlist others in a local labor movement. As in all such disputes, a war of words accompanied it. From their own perspective, the fired workers were legitimately engaged in explaining rationales for honoring the strike. Taylor, who could no longer write off the matter with Washington, characterized it much differently. The men, he said, had "started over the project in gangs attempting to intimidate other workers into leaving their jobs."[17]

Jerome woodcutters' complaints received tragic validation from Rohwer in January. As at Jerome, Rohwer logging was a complicated affair. Even after temperatures dropped below freezing, the forest floors were so soggy that trucks lost all traction. So once lumberjacks had cut the trees down and cut off the limbs, men outfitted in long rubber boots or "hip-waders" either had to drag the logs away with mules and ropes, no more than five or six at a time, or haul them out of the woods on makeshift "mudboats" or sleds. Only then could the logs be shifted onto trucks or mule-drawn wagons and taken away for sawing and chopping. Senbinshi Takaoko's friend Konan Ouchide, a fellow Issei previously employed in a camp dining hall, likened this to slave or convict labor. Ouchide's haiku on the subject references a whip but, tellingly, makes direct mention of neither mules nor men: "Crack of whip / lumber wagon begins / to creep out of mire." All told, it was "a type of work to which few of the evacuees [we]re accustomed," as Leflar conceded to Washington. On 19 January 1943, the men of Block 19 were among those pressed into the service of hauling wood. But they had been ordered to follow too closely on the heels of the lumberjacks. When a tree came crashing down around 2:00 p.m., it landed on sixty-year-old Seizo Imada.[18]

Assistant block manager Kazue Fukumoto said Imada may not have heard the first warning due to the wind. Imada's friend Tom Otani blamed the strong wind itself for an error in the felling: "It was difficult to judge where a tree would fall." And yet, in another sign of poor supervision, the cutting had continued. This tree made a dreadful "cracking sound" as it started to go down. The lumberjack cried "Timber!"—a second warning—but for Imada it was too late. His right leg was broken, his left ribs were fractured, and his hip and spine were badly damaged. By the time he was pulled out from under the tree and taken to the hospital on a tractor, Imada had gone into shock. The internal bleeding overtook him. At 3:00 p.m. Drs. Kobayashi, Uchida, and Sasaki pronounced the death of Seizo Imada of Block 19, barracks 2, apartment C, Rohwer concentration camp. He was survived by his wife, Koharu Imada, and their seven-year-old daughter, Kiyoko Betty Imada.[19]

What must the residents of Jerome and Rohwer have thought as they stacked cords of wood outside their barracks? As they stoked their stoves to warm themselves and their families? At what cost, this local source of fuel? How depressing, maddening, that the death of Seizo Imada of Rohwer came on the very same day as the suicide of John Yoshida near Jerome.

By June 1943 the Jerome newspaper could no longer ignore the crisis. In a crafty numbers game designed to again reshuffle workers from more desirable to less desirable jobs, Taylor announced limits on staffing in several divisions. The immediate goal, he made plain, was to bolster "the local agricultural program which is critically hampered by a shortage of manpower." The transportation division, beset by newer conflicts still, also required more workers. As a result, the *Tribune,* while still not mentioning the woodcutters strike, declared in an uncharacteristically bold headline, "SIX HUNDRED FACE TERMINATION." By the next issue, no doubt under fire from Taylor, the paper had recovered its Pollyanna sensibility. City editor Richard Itanaga acknowledged that Taylor's announcement had "caused quite a furore," but he attributed that to "misunderstandings" and "misinterpretations" on the part of Japanese Americans. "Gaps must be filled," he said, "if evacuees wish to eat decently." Protesting way too much, he concluded: "The move is born of necessity—not of a desire on the part of the administrative officials to punish the evacuees."[20]

THE MOTOR REPAIR STRIKE

Punitive, even vindictive, would accurately describe Taylor's response to yet more industrial action at Jerome. The camp owned or operated 112 vehicles, including 16 cars, 32 pickup trucks, 2 ambulances, a fire truck, and various other heavy trucks, mostly mid- to late 1930s models. In addition, the camp owned 22 new farm tractors, either Ferguson or International, 6 used Caterpillars, a secondhand Ford, and any number of smaller motorized farm implements. The motor repair shop, therefore, was a hub of activity, critical to the operations of the camp. On 22 April 1943 two Japanese American foremen, Frank Hirata and Hank Tashima, were fired without warning by their white supervisor, Fred McCain. As many as thirty of the thirty-four mechanics and shop assistants walked out in support. A new strike was on.[21]

Frequently away from his office, leaving operations manager W. O. Melton as acting director of the camp, Taylor went a month without discovering the nature of the workers' grievances. Instead, he and Melton set about recruiting strikebreakers or scabs. Taylor again castigated organizers and misrepresented their appeals for fellow workers to honor the strike. They were, he told Washington, attempting to "blackball" the superintendent of the motor repair shop. Meanwhile, Taylor took severe measures to punish the community as a whole and to blackmail workers into crossing the picket line. Even now not alluding to strikes, the *Denson Tribune* printed a front-page description of a draconian new policy, entitled "USE OF VEHICLES LIMITED":

> Because of the limited number of employees in the Repair section, Project Director Paul A. Taylor ordered the discontinuance of the following use of cars and trucks:
>
> (1) Trips to nearby towns to secure marriage licenses and to get married.
>
> (2) Trips to Rohwer to attend weddings, funerals, visit sick relatives, athletic events, etc.—all trips to Rohwer must be strictly WRA Business.

> Taylor expressed his hope that the existing emergency would only be temporary and a sufficient evacuee workforce could soon be obtained so the order could be rescinded.

More candidly, Taylor told several community leaders that, as far as he was concerned, residents could use wheelbarrows or wagons for their transportation needs.[22]

Of course, favored inmates with approved passes could still travel around the region by bus, as they always had. Without their knowing it, however, Greenville, Mississippi, just across the river, was put off-limits. At the same time that Japanese American mechanics were on strike in Jerome, Melton and other administrators met with white leaders in Greenville and discovered that African American tenant farmers and sharecroppers were on strike there. After a series of community meetings, black leaders had mounted a campaign to wrest concessions from wealthy planters, leaving the cotton in the fields untended. The Jerome and Greenville officials decided it was best to "not permit any shopping of any large groups [of Japanese Americans] in Greenville." Clearly, more than unseemly encounters in white-owned stores, administrators feared an interracial, nonwhite labor alliance. Understanding all too well the larger context for this concern, a Nisei high school student at Jerome noted: "Our teacher says that the Caucasians don't like it if the Japanese pal around or sympathize with the Negroes. They're afraid that two minority groups will get together and start a minor revolution. We're Californians and have been brought up with little, if any, discriminatory attitudes about the colored race. We can't help it if we're more democratic in that way than the Caucasian people down here."[23]

At length, on 22 May 1943, a fact-finding committee appointed by the Jerome Community Council reported the results of its motor repair shop investigation to a recalcitrant Paul Taylor. Whereas the shop superintendent had accused the foremen and workers of unauthorized use of motor pool vehicles, several workers attested that it was rather McCain, a former garage owner from Little Rock, who was the source of the conflict. He was verbally abusive to workers on the job and—like the overseers of Greenville—openly racist. According to one account, his obvious ill will toward Japanese Americans had been exacerbated, against all logic, when his son was killed in combat by Axis troops in North Africa. (Another account said it was his brother-in-law, killed in New Guinea.) Though Taylor insisted "dismissal of the shop superintendent was impossible," Melton acknowledged—months later—that McCain

14. Paul Taylor, director, Jerome concentration camp, November 1942. Tom Parker, photographer. NWDNS-210-G-E266, WRAR, SPB, NA.

was "a fanatic in many respects, highly temperamental, very inconsistent. . . . He irritated everyone he came in contact with."[24]

Taylor had conceded to Washington that such abuse was common among U.S. Army Corps of Engineers staff overseeing much of the public works projects at Jerome. Likewise, Robert Leflar flagged the persistence of "disagreements between some of the Caucasian supervisors and evacuee workmen," attributing it not explicitly to racial prejudice but to the "personalities involved." "None of us here," he divulged, "knew anything about the Japanese Americans at the beginning." Such ignorance, the hallmark of bigotry, had spawned the abuse. The abuse in turn had fueled the woodcutters strike, as it now fueled the motor repair strike. All the same, Taylor was not the person to ferret out racism. Though WRA director Dillon Myer and his staff officially shunned use of the epithet "Japs" to refer to Americans of Japanese ancestry, for example, Taylor was recorded using it at a camp directors conference in Little Rock as recently as February. He called the fact-finding committee's investigation into conflict in the motor repair shop "superficial."[25]

Community members begged to differ. Despite the privations, they supported the motor repair strike, no doubt enraged by Taylor's transparently cynical manipulations. As the administration had to confess, Japanese Americans at Jerome backed the workers "almost unanimously." They all held out through what otherwise would have been eventful summer months of cross-camp activity—with only four men crossing the picket line—until the Community Council prevailed upon Taylor to lift the transportation ban at the end of July. Adhering to his hard-line stance, however, he refused to let striking workers return to their posts, and short articles continued to appear in the *Tribune* announcing evening classes in auto mechanics. But a change in the motor repair shop was subtly noted, if not, per usual, straightforwardly reported. A drawing of the "Center Motor Pool" in the 3 August 1943 issue of the *Tribune* included an enlightening caption: "Maintaining a 24-hour service, the Center's motor pool is under the supervision of William Jenkins. . . . Charles Koyanagi is the chief dispatcher." There was no mention of Fred McCain. The administration referred to it obliquely as a "reorganization of appointed personnel."[26]

THE GENERAL STRIKE AND THE DEATH OF HARUJI EGO

Woodcutting remained Paul Taylor's fixation, if not obsession. By June he devised a two-part strategy to avert, in late 1943, a fuel crisis akin to that of late 1942. He would start earlier, and he would find more forest—enough to supply 8,000 to 10,000 cords. Of course, woodland abounded, but it wasn't always easy to reach. Taylor extended his control over his dominion in late July with the completion of Big Bayou Bridge. Hailed as "one of the biggest milestones" in the camp's one-year history, the oak-beam structure stretched 112 feet across the bayou, connecting the camp proper with an area known as Deep Elm, "tapping some 6000 acres of wooded area." The camp sawmill was already up and running there, so the bridge—which reduced journeys by five miles—promised to "be of tremendous aid in hauling fuel-wood this fall." As with so many camp projects, this one was hastily finished with local materials by Japanese American laborers. It was put up in eight weeks and made almost entirely from camp lumber and supplies, "everything but the nails."[27]

With roads and bridges in place and with the clearing of Deep Elm set to more than double the number of acres under cultivation, the public works division's industrial section began advertising for woodcutters in August. Men refused to step forward. Between school terms, administrators attempted to recruit boys as young as fourteen, and still the 150 volunteers could not be

15. Sawmill at the Jerome concentration camp, November 1942. Tom Parker, photographer. NWDNS-210-G-E232, WRAR, SPB, NA.

mustered. In early October, the administration declared a "WOODCUTTING EMERGENCY" in a *Tribune* front-page headline. All "non-essential" male workers were drafted into woodcutting on a block-by-block basis, such that everyone would be expected to put in one day each week. From community members friendly to the administration, Taylor marshaled a Japanese American "wood committee," with Al Tsukamoto's brother-in-law, Harold Ouchida, as chair. As at Rohwer, block managers also were enlisted in the campwide effort. Still, the measure was understood as yet another edict from on high—a product of Taylor's ego. A few resisters, such as hospital cook Takuza Matsumura of Block 40, openly refused to cut wood and warned others against it, both in the block and at work. Only "suckers" agreed to cut wood, Matsumura reportedly said. The block managers who went along with it were "stool pigeons"—"not interested in their own people as they should be." Unsurprisingly, white officers tried to discredit Matsumura and his family as agitators and thieves. His wife was fired from her job at the dining hall "because of her attitude."[28]

Relations deteriorated. Workers' rights became wedded to Japanese American civil rights broadly as a series of events in October brought Jerome to the edge of open conflict. First, sixty-eight-year-old woodcutter Keijiro Horino, a bachelor from Block 1, died of a heart attack, which many attributed directly to the strenuous labor. The key catalyst, however, was another appalling on-the-job accident. Though activists such as Kiyoshi Hamanaka for months had warned officials about occupational safety on the camp's numerous rush jobs, though they reminded supervisors of the ultimate sacrifice made by Seizo Imada, mishaps were frequent. The accident on 13 October 1943 proved the worst.[29]

As woodcutters were being taken out to the forest that morning, the truck driver towing their trailer passed into the left lane in order to get around two vehicles parked on the right shoulder. Although there was no oncoming traffic, the driver let the wheels of his truck slip off the left shoulder of the road into thick mud. He was able to slow the truck to a stop, but the trailer carrying the woodcutters was thrown off balance, and it turned over. Thirty-seven men were packed into the trailer, some sitting on wooden benches, others standing up. When the trailer tipped, they were thrown into one another, onto the floorboards, across the benches, and onto the ground. Eyeglasses were shattered, blood spilled out, and bones were snapped. Every single worker was injured. Twenty had to be rushed from the crash site, near Big Bayou Bridge, to the camp hospital. After initial treatment, six men remained in serious condition, including Reiichi Kayamoto, age forty-six, with a badly broken arm; Ken Koga, age forty-seven, with a dislocated shoulder; Masatoru Kubo, with a head wound; and Kazuma Nobuo with a skull fracture. At age sixty-two, with severe spinal injuries, Haruji Ego was taken by private ambulance to St. Vincent's Hospital in Little Rock. Word spread: he would probably never walk again.[30]

Disgusted, a group of labor organizers seized the moment. Over the course of the following week, they typed up a strike notice, commandeered a mimeograph machine, and cranked out dozens of copies. Under cover of night, they left stacks of the legal-size sheets in the one place that would be visited by virtually every Japanese American male and no white administrator: the men's communal toilets. When morning came on 21 October, men and boys all would be made aware of the clash—even those who didn't read English, for the message was translated into Japanese and mimeographed on the other side (see fig. 16).[31]

TO BE OR NOT TO BE — SUCKERS!!

HOW THE WRA EXPLOITS YOU IN THE WOOD SITUATION!!

"Chop, Chop," means "hurry up" in Chinese. For us evacuees it means chopping wood and doing that in a hurry before the cold spell hits us. But isn't it a laugh! We chop the wood while the appointed personnel sit on their fannies and use it up. Last year the schools, the appointed personnel quarters and the offices got coal. This year with about 1,000 able-bodied men resettled or at Tule Lake from this center, the WRA wants us to chop enough wood for the schools, offices, and appointed personnel quarters! AFTER we take care of these, we're supposed to be able to chop enough wood for ourselves! Who chops the wood? Most of the workers are old men in their fifties. They strain themselves and go to an early grave. For what? Sixteen dollars a month; fifty cents a day; less than seven cents an hour!

But chopping and hauling wood is half of it! We also clear the land. We clear the land so that Taylor and his yes-men—Melton, Arne, etc. can show the Arkansas big shots what a fine job THEY are doing in helping the state of Arkansas. And that state got the nerve to tell us that it doesn't want us; to get the hell out after the war! It's very simple: the more pressure the weather and the WRA puts on us to cut wood, the more we cut and the more land is cleared so that Taylor can brag about it to his pull-i-ticians! If this isn't exploitation, what is it? No matter how thin you slice it, it's still baloney!

Well, Evacuees, what are we going to do about it? Are we going to remain suckers? Or are we going to do something about it? What can WE do?? Let's do the same thing that was done in Poston. Let's have a GENERAL STRIKE until the WRA meets certain conditions. Here they are—

1. Have the WRA supply the schools, offices and appointed personnel quarters with coal. Except for Rohwer and Jerome, all the other centers get fuel supplied by the WRA. For that matter, the appointed personnel can buy their wood from their 200–400 dollar monthly salaries.
2. Have enough surplus coal on hand so that in the event that the evacuees cannot cut enough wood for themselves because of rain, they won't have to go out in the mud so that their families will have enough wood to keep warm.

3. Get more power equipment to cut wood; with less manpower, we must use power saws to do the work.
4. Give adequate compensations for injuries sustained while working. One evacuee carpenter got $12.50 for injuries from falling off the roof of an appointed personnel apartment. That amount for a couple of knocked-out teeth, several broken ribs and a broken arm.
5. Serve the evacuees better food. The present diet is unbalanced and lacks sufficient nourishment for hard work like woodchopping.
6. Raise the wage scale of the evacuees. At one time the WRA wage scale was to be the same as that in the armed services. At the present rate, most evacuees are losing their savings!
7. Get rid of Taylor, Arne and other incompetent administrators! Weed out the anti-evacuee elements among the appointed personnel.

We need a fair deal in this center. We are the loyal, but we are loyal to certain principles—justice, fair play, democracy. We must fight exploitation, race prejudice, and other fascistic tactics. We can do just that by conducting a GENERAL STRIKE beginning October 25. We cannot afford to be cowards; unless we stand for our rights, we will continue to be exploited. Are YOU man enough to ACT?

REMEMBER, THE GENERAL STRIKE — MONDAY, OCTOBER 25!

16. Replica of the general strike notice, Jerome concentration camp, October 1943. Part II, section 5, reel 138, JAERR, UCB.

The flyer called for a general strike, challenging fellow workers to face down the administration and resist all further coercive methods. Work assignments no longer were voluntary; working conditions amounted to nothing short of exploitation. This mistreatment, moreover, occurred within broader contexts. The marked improvements to southeast Arkansas infrastructure and agriculture had been met with legislative measures to forbid Japanese American land ownership after the war, to rid Japanese Americans from the state. Indeed, it all seemed a vast conspiracy between Taylor, his "yes-men," and bigoted "pull-i-ticians" to bully a servile workforce, to wring from captive laborers the maximum possible output of a few years detention. All were linked to the larger injustice of mass incarceration, the withdrawal of basic human freedoms from an entire ethnic minority group. Aligning themselves with the forces of democracy and fair play, the authors of the strike notice summoned the whole community into a battle against the forces of oppression. To WRA officials, the organizers issued a seven-point statement of demands, most all calm and reasonable, the last more strident. They sought better food, higher wages, better work implements, greater recompense for job-related injuries. They didn't even call for an end to woodcutting, only a backup supply of coal in case of shortfalls. Finally—surely without hope of success—they wanted to force Taylor and others out of the camp for good.[32]

From Thursday the twenty-first of October until Monday the twenty-fifth, everyone in the camp, perhaps Rohwer too, must have wondered if the general strike would take place, if Japanese American workers, en masse, would stay home from work and join in demonstrations. In the one-room apartments, Japanese American residents whispered their approval or cried out in heated debate. Administrators expressed confidence one moment and hatched contingency plans the next. There was yet more grist for the mill when, in a sharp break with tradition, *Tribune* editor in chief Paul Yokota spelled out his views on the matter. Subtle in spite of everything, he chose not an editorial but his occasional column, "At Random," to assert the unfairness of woodcutting operations. Japanese Americans cut down the trees, hauled the logs, and split the wood—but somehow they were behind in dividing it into little chunks for their own stoves. Even now, the second winter at Jerome, they were denied the proper power tools for this last, crucial step in the process. They weren't even issued two-man handsaws. Meanwhile, administrators had no worries about their homes and offices. As Yokota put it, laced with sarcasm, "We see that the appointed personnel have beaten most of the evacuee blocks in getting firewood cut into small pieces—by use of a power saw."[33]

The general strike never materialized. With gusto, apparent glee, camp attorney Ulys Lovell declared it "an absolute flop, so far as I am able to determine." Many residents may not have seen the flyer, as Japanese American members of the internal security force snatched up copies from the toilets and gave them to administrators, who forwarded them to the FBI. People at Jerome nonetheless would have heard about the strike. And still, very few workers were absent on Monday morning. The great majority who turned up—those who had tallied the pros and cons of open defiance and chosen the safe bet—must have recalled the blunt vindictiveness of Paul Taylor; they must have guessed the lengths to which WRA administrators would go to overpower the prisoners. Events bore them out. By Thursday Paul Yokota was gone, resettled in Cleveland with his wife, but without a job. The *Tribune* was left without an editor in chief for three issues. Investigators scoured the camp in pursuit of the organizers, securing "specimens from various typewriters in the Center" and identifying the paper as from co-op stocks. Having once searched every single apartment for a batch of stolen wood, they surely felt no compunction in storming into the homes of suspected labor organizers, now branded "wood dodgers." Paul Taylor further called on the FBI for help in "determining the type of . . . mimeograph machine, etc." used in this small, ill-fated campaign for justice.[34]

As if in sympathy with the would-be strikers, Haruji Ego gave up his own battle and passed away that Friday, 29 October 1943, far from Jerome, far from home, in the unfamiliar ward of a hospital in Little Rock, Arkansas. In remembrance of Seizo Imada's death, prophetic of Haruji Ego's, the fair-minded labor organizers had printed nothing more than the truth in their strike notice: WRA policies sent good men to early graves. In support of his family, there was a campwide funeral for Haruji Ego.[35]

Blameless bureaucrats to the end, administrators at Jerome painted a picture of order restored, calm returning, in their November missives to Washington. Stressing that "the project staff has been of a great deal of assistance to the Ego family during this time," Lovell reported that "the morale of the Center hasn't been materially effected by Mr. Ego's tragic accident and death." Japanese Americans, he claimed, were not unduly upset: "People realize that those things sometimes happen and the fact that he was injured and died ultimately was just one of those things which often happen and cannot be helped." He sent an almost identical message two weeks later, in a further attempt to convince superiors, perhaps in a vain attempt to convince himself: "It was, as I stated before, taken as just one of those things that couldn't be helped and doesn't appear to have adversely effected the morale of the evacuees." The acting director told Washington on 13 November that, as compared to before, the week had been "very quiet and peaceful." Paul Taylor had gone away for a period of rest and reflection. He had done some hunting and—"the biggest news" of the week—he had "killed his first deer, an eight pointer."[36]

Irony of ironies, Jerome's wily labor organizers, whose latrine leaflet had upended the camp for a time, succeeded in securing only one of their seven demands—the final, most incredible objective. Paul Taylor called it quits. He returned from his latest vacation and announced his resignation as director. He, his wife, and their two daughters would go back to the nation's capital. There the confirmed cost-cutter would take up the position of assistant to the director of the Bureau of Budget and Finance in the Department of Agriculture. The job at Jerome, he told his superiors, was "the toughest I have ever undertaken. I feel that the experience gained has been invaluable but I hope that I have the good judgment never to tackle another job just like it." Ever the networker, he promised to pay them a visit as soon as he arrived in Washington.[37]

On an early evening in the summer of 1944, when Paul Taylor was but a fading memory among camp residents, two boys shooting swallows with makeshift slingshots followed the birds into a barn where the mules were kept. There they saw, hanging from the rafters, the body of Sadao Nakao.

As preparations were made to dismantle the Jerome camp, the first to close, Nakao had been slated for transfer to the Granada concentration camp in Colorado—yet another unbearable, involuntary train journey across America. On the day, he was the only person absent at the railway siding. His apartment was searched, and his bags were found packed, tidy, ready to go. The boys happened upon him over a day later. Internal security officers then opened a suitcase and discovered the suicide note. The Drew County coroner therefore determined that an inquest was unnecessary. Camp attorney Ulys Lovell sent a teletype to Washington first thing the next morning. WRA head attorney Philip Glick thought that Dillon Myer and one other official should see it; after it circulated through their offices, Glick decided no further action was required, and he scrawled "no reply" across it. Lovell followed up later in the day with a full report sent by airmail. Though a copy of the suicide note was sent along too, it seems that neither it nor the original was retained. Sadao Nakao's body was cremated in Memphis.[38]

Sadao Nakao shared a number of traits with John Yoshida, who had taken his own life not long after the opening of the camp. Both were young adults: Nakao eighteen, Yoshida twenty-three. Both had previously lost a parent. And both spent more time indoors than outside. They apparently managed to escape the woodcutting details and likely were subjects of derision as a result. What were they called? Loafers? Wood dodgers? Sissies? Administrators claimed that each had an unhealthy relationship to his mother.

John Yoshida's suicide note, left by the railroad tracks, is an immeasurably powerful artifact, a sacred scrap of paper—like life, precious. It may or may not have survived these past decades. It seems not to have worked its way into safekeeping, into an archive. It may or may not still exist. But the words remain. Originally penned in Japanese, if faithfully translated and transcribed, they are a testament to one final act of will, a determination to, under the harshest of circumstances, retain the ability to choose, to chart one's own course of action. Appearing in the *Denson Communiqué*, the words reportedly said: "I am writing this before I die. If I cannot accomplish what I want, I am going to where my mother and grandmother are. Maybe I am doing a dishonorable thing but please disregard me. During my presence in this world, I have never done wrong to anyone so God will believe me. I have nothing to fear going to where I want." The article depicted Yoshida as pathologically devoted to his mother, who committed suicide, it said, when he was two years old. The pro-administration newspaper further characterized Yoshida, a devout Buddhist, as "an extreme introvert" who "spent practically all his time reading." If he was indeed "despondent," as seems only natural, the paper not once mentioned the indignities of expulsion, removal, and incarceration as contributing—if not principal—factors.[39]

What Robert Leflar dismissed as "rather incoherent reasons for suicide" strike me as utterly comprehensible, inspiring empathy, pathos. Newspaper editors were irresponsible in agreeing to a headline that misrepresented Yoshida's motives: "YOUTH WISHES TO JOIN MOTHER; COMMITS SUICIDE." As was unmistakable from the words they published, John Yoshida would go "to where my mother and grandmother are" *secondarily*, only if he failed in his primary objective: to "accomplish what I want." Who knows, whether to train formally as a monk, study literature at university, or pursue some other goal: whatever he wanted he could not achieve behind barbed wire. And as a Kibei, brought up in Japan, he could not expect to be released anytime soon.[40]

No doubt John Yoshida eschewed the he-man sensibilities and masculinist poses common in all-male work environments such as the Arkansas woodcutting crews. He perhaps dismissed administrators' importuning that hard work outdoors, in the fresh air, made for strong men. His religious beliefs called instead for a regimen of mental and physical cleanliness. Thankfully he felt he at least had achieved this much, leaving this world with a clean conscience, leaving a father, stepmother, brother, and sister to carry on. Yoshida didn't describe himself explicitly as a victim. He refused to admit to or account for any wrongs done. That responsibility, he implied, lay elsewhere.

If WRA administrators had incentive to downplay or cover up escapes from camp like Yoshida's and others', they had even more reason to disassociate the taking of one's own life from incarceration—and from American conduct in the wider world. Repeatedly, if not prominently, Japanese American camp newspapers and the JACL's *Pacific Citizen* would report suicides during the war years, only to leave open the question of motivation. The *Poston Chronicle* and subsequently the *Pacific Citizen* gave a brief account of the suicide of Jisaburo Aoki, sixty-seven, formerly of Buena Park, California, on 15 August 1945, scarcely days after Hiroshima and Nagasaki. "Motive for the suicide" they printed, "was not known."[41]

The WRA reported—perhaps underreported—the total number of suicides under incarceration as twenty-eight: arguably, a small number, a fraction of 1 percent of detainees over the three-year period. But as the records show, as many people attempted suicide as succeeded. Further, it seems likely that a number of suicides could have been willingly ignored and placed under the WRA designation "all other causes" of death, which totaled 164 cases out of a total of 1,862 deaths. Well over half of *reported* suicides—16 of 28—were by male Issei over the age of fifty-five. And yet when Henry Shuzo Fukuzawa, an Issei at Rohwer, was found dead in a pool of water northwest of the camp after "a two-day manhunt," officials only declared him "lost."[42]

The WRA obviously manipulated newspaper coverage; administrators further chose not to formally list in their reports the reasons individuals wished to take their own lives. As we see in the cases of John Yoshida and Sadao Nakao, officials were unwilling to accept responsibility for them. Nor did they cite incarceration as a rationale for the suicides that followed immediately upon release from the concentration camps. Neither did some Japanese American patriots, as we see in chapter 9.

Distressing to recall, exceedingly painful at the time, the deaths—as well as the lives—of Japanese American prisoners should be faithfully accounted for. They should be commemorated. Deaths resulting from accidents, from WRA negligence and incompetence, have to be acknowledged, as do deaths from suicide. After colossal efforts by the captors and psychological gymnastics by some peers to explain them away and to erase the suicides from collective memory, these deaths should be lamented but also honored, as the ultimate assertion of the right to self-determination. We should respect and uphold a decision so fraught, so sacrosanct. We should remember the dead: Sadao Nakao and Jisaburo Aoki, Seizo Imada and Haruji Ego. Finally, we should remember John Yoshida, last of Block 7, barrack 6, apartment C, Jerome concentration camp.

To borrow the words of playwright Arthur Miller: Attention must be paid.

8 | Segregation, Expatriation, Annihilation

IN CALIFORNIA IN 1945, poet and bookseller Violet Matsuda was engaged in pitched conflict. A mother of three, she battled her family's health problems. From the beginning, her youngest child had been "sickly," most recently with double pneumonia. Matsuda's mother-in-law was gravely ill with cancer. And Matsuda herself had overcome abdominal surgery for the removal of a tumor only three years earlier, just before eviction.

Matsuda also battled government bureaucracies on behalf of her family members. While one brother, Dick, fought in the Pacific Theater with the U.S. Army, the younger brother, Tokio, had been arrested, beaten, and locked away by U.S. officials. Authorities had taken her husband, Shigeru, away from her as well. So even as Matsuda treated her ailing children and cared for her elderly in-laws, even as she pleaded for reports of her brother's condition and petitioned for his and her husband's release, she was beset with yet another worry, one still more grave and ominous. Often her thoughts were elsewhere.

In Hiroshima, Japan, on 6 August 1945, Violet Matsuda's mother was going about her daily routines when the U.S. aircraft *Enola Gay* dropped the bomb. What was seen from above as a pristine, massive mushroom cloud was experienced on the ground as a horrific, earth-shattering force that destroyed the city center. Whereas countless thousands of civilians would "survive" the blast only to struggle through foreshortened lives of radiation poisoning,

140,000 people died within the first few hours and days. Among the injured was Shika Yamane.[1]

I begin this chapter on the consequences of Japanese American incarceration not, as so many do, with the bombing that began the war but rather with the bombing that ended the war. To me, Hiroshima as much as Pearl Harbor explains the U.S. government's indiscriminate imprisonment of 120,000 American citizens and residents of Japanese descent during the Second World War. Further, I find that the gendered experiences of incarceration helpfully illuminate the webs of familial, racial, and national affiliations that often structured the lives of detainees. Utilizing transcripts of hearings conducted within the concentration camps, I examine men's and especially women's responses to questions of allegiance posed by U.S. officials. Also, over the course of this chapter and the next, I use autobiographical accounts to contrast elements in the life story of Violet Matsuda with those of another Nisei mother from California, Mary Tsukamoto. I do so not to probe comparative states of "loyalty" to the nation, as the U.S. government attempted. Instead, I want to understand how women variously narrated feelings of ambivalence and uncertainty, while exercising agency and crafting complex subjectivities. With care, these women positioned themselves in relation to any number of given cultural and political categories, even as they exposed those categories as inexhaustive, insufficient, and unduly simplistic. These individuals rarely adopted postures of absolute affinity. More commonly they negotiated intricate, seemingly contradictory affiliations, highly contingent upon their shifting circumstances. Experiencing repeated displacements—geographical and ideological—they largely defied wartime American expectations of resoluteness and straightforward assimilation. They led lives that, though marked by purpose and commitment, demanded a capacity for open, irreconciled, unfixed modes of self-determination.

NEITHER A TRIAL NOR INQUISITION

Within the first year of the detention, U.S. government officials hatched plans to move some prisoners out of the concentration camps, to "resettle" them in "normal American communities." Japanese Americans would be dispersed across the East, South, Midwest, and even as far as the Rocky Mountain West, so as to dilute any numerical strength, to forestall ethnic enclaves, and to prevent the redevelopment of Little Tokyos. Simultaneously, as we've seen, the army inaugurated a segregated combat unit for the enlistment of Nisei soldiers. Thus, male prisoners of the United States were given the opportunity to fight in Europe for American "freedom and democracy." But before families could be forced out of the camps to live and work, to once again start anew in towns and cities unknown to them, before soldiers could be shipped off to kill and die on behalf of the very government that had incarcerated them, officials would have to ascertain their "allegiance" to the United States. Further, as both HUAC and Kentucky Senator A. B. Chandler's investigating committee insisted in screaming headlines, dangerous "disloyal" Japanese Americans had to be found out and isolated—or, in the words of an Arkansas official, "the sheep [had to] be separated from the goats." Thus was launched the ill-conceived and ill-administered "registration program" in early 1943.[2]

All adult prisoners in all ten concentration camps were required to fill out lengthy questionnaires to establish their identities, personal histories, and—most controversially—their national allegiances. According to Mary Tsukamoto, "Each questionnaire consisted of long pages that seemed to have been hastily put together by someone who had no understanding of the people who would be filling them out." Indeed, the questionnaire was based on a form the army had used in recruiting Nisei volunteers, which in turn was based on a form used in recruiting non-nationals of the United States. Questions 27 and 28 in particular fostered dissent and disagreement. "These two questions . . . caused the breakup of many families [and] tore the camps apart. Bloodshed and violence were their aftermath, all because of bureaucratic stupidity." Question 27 was meant to determine one's willingness to "serve in the armed forces." Question 28 was intended to gauge one's national affiliation: "Will you swear unqualified allegiance to the United States and faithfully defend the United States from any or all attack by foreign or domestic forces, and forswear any form of allegiance or obedience to the Japanese emperor, or any other foreign government, power or organization?" Those who answered with an unqualified "yes-yes" earned the right to day passes, short-term leave, and long-term leave for university education and other activities, as well as permanent leave for resettlement outside the West Coast zone of exclusion. Others found their "privileges" withdrawn, their movements restricted to camp; and many began to consider repatriation or expatriation to Japan.[3]

More than probing inalterable, fixed states of identity, these two questions ineluctably shaped identity, such that answers framed subjectivity for generations to come. To express doubts or reservations, to hint at ambiguity in the American national project, would so structure identity that an individual subsequently could become known, in the title of the 1957 John Okada novel, as a *No-No Boy*.[4]

But what about "no-no" women? And what about those prisoners whose responses were neither wholly affirmative nor negative? The very posing of the questions, the perceived need to ask not only decades-long residents but also birthright citizens about allegiance exposed nationality as an ambiguous identity, as Etienne Balibar and Immanuel Wallerstein have called it. And the very answering of the questions, in particular the elaborations required of those who qualified their responses, suggested that national affiliations were often ambivalently held and in flux. The great majority wrote a straightforward "yes-yes" to questions 27 and 28; a significant minority wrote "no-no." Either way, such a direct reply was, perhaps in many cases, a willed expunging of complexity, a mostly true pair of statements that went unembellished for simplicity's sake. But many professed a difficulty at the heart of the questions, a difficulty of language and of translation—not of Japanese into English, but of emotions into words.[5]

The War Relocation Authority's haphazard administration of registration forms in February and March and some prisoners' insistence upon well-refined answers meant that a series of hearings had to be held in July, August, and September 1943. Splashy HUAC interrogations may have served as a model, but camp questioning by contrast was undertaken in camera, a closed session patterned more after Department of Justice civilian review boards, set up to handle appeals of interned aliens. At the Rohwer, Arkansas, camp, the so-called Leave Investigation Committee (also known as the Leave Clearance Committee) summoned dozens of detainees, one by one. Composed of the camp attorney and one or more other officials—along with an interpreter of Japanese, if needed—the committee mostly called up prisoners who had placed caveats on a yes response to question 28. For example, asked whether he would swear allegiance to the United States, Isami Inouye wrote, "Yes, if my civil rights are restored to me." Masato Kamita wrote, "Yes, if they give us our constitutional rights." Hirofusa Okumura wrote, "Yes, provided I am treated as a full-fledged American citizen." And his sister Kuniko Okumura wrote, "Yes, if treated just like any other American citizen." These responses most likely referred to *white* American citizens, for many prisoners in Arkansas had witnessed firsthand African Americans' second-class status; indeed, many Japanese Americans had expressed doubts about the segregation of the all-Nisei combat team, because of the inevitable comparisons to segregated black platoons.[6]

Akira Oye had written, "Yes, if I am permitted to go back to Stockton, California *now*." Jimmy Kumamaru elaborated: "I am willing to defend America because America is my native land, if they let us go back to California, and resettle in . . . the same place and let us farm again like we used to before the war." These prisoners, all of them birthright citizens, demonstrated their knowledge not only of a citizen's responsibilities but also a citizen's rights. Theirs clearly had been violated, egregiously so. Thus a nation-state, a legal-political entity that had contracted with its members, should have expected challenges to its integrity, given its uneven application of the laws—that is, given its first breaking the social compact. But the reluctance of some to completely and categorically identify with the American nation went beyond the recognition of a broken contract. Immigrants and their second-generation citizen children had direct encounters with the institutional apparatuses—borders, customs, immigration procedures, birth certificates—that constructed nationality and the nation-state, and thus they often carried a well-developed sense of their constructedness. They understood through inevitable comparative analysis the varied ways in which two or more national communities might be imagined. Also, those who had experience living in two or more nations developed site-specific, place-bound affinities of myriad types. To attach oneself to one place did not foreclose attachments to other places. To value one place or nation did not mean to devalue another in inverse relationship. As I hope to show, the very real and multiple attachments that immigrants and diasporic peoples developed were so profound as to sometimes defy articulation.[7]

Often, when made to measure their attachments, Japanese Americans made clear that place and nation were bound up with people, particularly with familial relations. The explicit claiming of one nation was rarely the work of a single individual, acting alone, thinking only of her own allegiance or her own self-interest. Mary Shigetome wrote the word "undecided" next to question 27, about military service. "Where do your sympathies lie in the present war?" Rohwer chief attorney Jack Curtis queried. "With this country," she replied. Curtis persisted: "When you completed the registration form, you were undecided as to whether you might want to serve in the army nurses corps or the WAC's?" "I am still undecided," she replied, "because of my folks." An only child, Shigetome weighed her responsibility to the nation against the responsibility to her parents: "You see I am the only one they can depend on in case anything goes wrong."[8]

As thirty-year-old Maseto Takemoto explained to the Leave Clearance Committee at Rohwer, he first wrote the word "undecided" by question 28.

But five days later, after conferring with his wife, he changed his response to "yes," to comport to hers. In explaining his reasoning to attorney Curtis, Takemoto demonstrated the fallacy of a straightforward choice between Japan and the United States. Like so many, though he was a U.S. citizen and had never been to Japan, he had attended classes in Japanese culture and language in California, and he had relatives in Japan. What factors did he consider, what was his reasoning over those five days when he chose to change his response from "undecided" to "yes"?

CURTIS: What were the things you thought about?

TAKEMOTO: What's my right way. For instance, there is a road going one way and a road going another. Which is my right way to go.

CURTIS: When you speak of road, you mean whether you want to go with the United States or Japan?

TAKEMOTO: It was whether to be undecided or yes, not with Japan.[9]

If Takemoto could contemplate national affiliations that were multiple, open, incomplete, in the works, and thus unfixed and undecidable, Curtis understood allegiance to be singular, total, and essential. "Of course loyalty is a state of mind," he told another prisoner. "It is your feeling. It can't be partly one way and partly another. It isn't something to be changed at will for your own convenience." Similarly, a Jerome interrogator stated, "We consider loyalty or disloyalty [to be] like religion. Can't force it upon anyone." Ironically, WRA actions, as we've seen, had bordered on that: officials had encouraged Buddhists and nonbelievers to convert to Christianity with inducements and incentives for assimilating in this way. Likewise, now, there were immeasurable benefits in acceding to national association.[10]

Question 28, to Curtis, was an oath, which compelled a person to be "100 percent loyal to the United States and deny any loyalty to the Japanese emperor and the Japanese government or any other foreign government." "Loyalty," he said "cannot be divided." This epitomizes what theorist Lisa Lowe has described as the simple "'enemy/not enemy' logic of the state"—an "impossibly binary demand." But Curtis couldn't see such a demand as suasion; rather it was a search for an essential, hardwired state of being. Still, that search could result in opposite conclusions, as Curtis was forced to concede on occasion—as in the case of Yukiko Ota. After Ota's hearing, the Leave Clearance Committee reached a split decision, two to one. As a lone dissenter, Curtis found that even an essential national loyalty could be differently perceived. His colleagues felt Ota was "loyal." Curtis said, however, that even though she responded "yes" to question 28, Ota "was at the half-way point as to whether her sympathies lie with Japan or the United States in the present war." "It doesn't make any difference," she had said, who wins the war. Therefore, Curtis could not recommend "favorable consideration" of Ota's application for leave clearance to camp director Ray Johnston, who presumably exercised his veto power.[11]

Sachiko Tanaka expressed similar sentiments. And Curtis's interrogation of her led to an utter breakdown in communication, a linguistic disconnect that likely bespoke as much about the citizen's nuanced understandings of subjectivity as the questioner's belligerence. A twenty-year-old high school senior, Tanaka demonstrated extraordinary self-possession as she articulated a web of familial and national ties.

CURTIS: When you completed this form you answered question 28, "I don't know." What were the factors that caused you to say that? . . . You said you were loyal and wanted to say yes but you were undecided because of responsibility for your parents. . . .

TANAKA: Well, that was because I am the only child and I have to look after my parents. I thought if they sent all the Japanese to Japan, I have to stay with them. . . .

CURTIS: Does[n't] that question 28 mean loyal to America and denying loyalty to Japan?

TANAKA: No. But as long as I am an American citizen I am loyal to America, but I have to look after my parents—that is all.

CURTIS: Do you have any feeling of loyalty to Japan at all?

TANAKA: No, not as long as I am an American citizen. . . .

CURTIS: Do you know now whether your parents will be returned to Japan or not?

TANAKA: I guess they can stay here so I put yes.

CURTIS: Who do you want to win the war between the United States and Japan?

TANAKA: I don't think I could give you an answer.

CURTIS: What makes you undecided about that?

TANAKA: Well, I am not particular which side wins. I just want to have peace, that is all.

CURTIS: Just so the war is over, that is all? If Japan wins that is all right with you? Is that right?

TANAKA: I don't know what to say.

CURTIS: Just however you feel about it. All we want is an expression of your feelings, opinions, and attitudes. I understand you want peace; we all want peace, no doubt about that. Someone will have to dictate the terms of the peace. You have a right to your feeling and you should feel free to express your feeling whatever it may be.

TANAKA: I don't know how to voice it.[12]

Tanaka lacked not an ability to speak, but rather an available vocabulary for helping Curtis comprehend the limits of nationalist discourse, the complexities of her position. Did Curtis really believe she could "feel free" to answer fully his escalating badgering queries? Interestingly, in a disingenuous acknowledgment of the intersecting realms of legal, political, and national imperatives, Curtis described these hearings to those summoned as "not a trial nor inquisition," but rather a "discussion." Indeed, the due process connoted by a trial did not pertain; prisoners were rarely allowed legal counsel or—interestingly—a right to silence. And yet Tanaka here exercised silence, it seems, not as a defense against self-incrimination but as a polite refusal to thoroughly engage. Implicit therein was a denunciation of a dominant language and dominant cultural formation incapable of articulating the irresolute, irreconciled state of alterity. Asked to respond on Curtis's terms, Tanaka replied with extraordinary candor and insight: "I don't know how to voice it."[13]

Curtis as representative of the nation-state assumed as his object of scrutiny an autonomous citizen-subject, an individual detached from familial, racial, gendered subject positions, an individual of fixed national affiliation, whose allegiance could thus be investigated and found out. But of course such allegiance continued to be made, produced, through hearings such as this. This hearing or discussion or pseudo-juridical proceeding was yet another wielding of arbitrary, hierarchical state power that inevitably led the questioned, the prisoner, to again call that very state into question. In an Alice-in-Wonderland world, the state—embodied in officials such as Curtis—abrogated ever more rights of the citizen, all the while attempting to force not only that citizen's compliance but also allegiance. Within a concentration camp, within the disciplinary realm of a legal proceeding—the outcome of which determined yet further restrictions on freedom of movement and association—the nation expected the citizen-subject to voice unqualified affiliation.

As Lisa Lowe perceptively outlines it: "Once in the United States, the demands that Asians narrate themselves in liberal discourses of development, assimilation, and citizenship provide the grounds for antagonism to such demands. The imperatives that the subject identify—as a national, classed, and gendered subject—take place within the materially differentiated conditions of racialized workers of color that simultaneously produce *disidentification* out of which critical subjectivities may emerge." But as Lowe elaborates, "Disidentification does not entail merely the formation of oppositional identities against the call to identification with the national state. On the contrary, it allows for the exploration of alternative political and cultural subjectivities that emerge with the continuing effects of displacement." If, as Lowe suggests, the national imperatives bring with them subsidiary but formative structures of class and gender, it was in the realm of class and gender especially that alternative notions of allegiance and affiliation arose. In returning now to the stories of Violet Matsuda and resisters from Jerome, we may see how continuing displacements fostered ever more complex subjectivities.[14]

TULE LAKE

The chaotic, slapdash quality of both registration and the follow-up hearings in the camps was perhaps best evidenced at Jerome. In his 13 March 1943 report to Washington, Paul Taylor declared it "a historic week in the history of the Jerome Relocation Center. Registration has been completed. I believe that everyone is now registered—some of them twice." Later one official conceded that he was "not in the position to state definitely the number of hearings held by me or the total number held in the project"; another put the number at "some two thousand people." Procedures were inadequately spelled out even as the large-scale interrogations were hastily carried out. Further, the purpose of hearings differed from individual to individual, across five, sometimes overlapping areas of scrutiny, leaving administrators harried and befuddled. First, some hearings were conducted primarily to determine, with greater certainty, the prisoner's answers to questions 27 and 28. Second, most commonly, a ruling was made as to whether the inmate could be released on long-term leave as part of the resettlement program. Third, as the administrators urged of young men especially, potential leave-takers were asked about serving in the army's 442nd Regimental Combat Team and other units. Fourth, in the case of a qualified or "no" answer to questions 27 or 28 or in the case of nonresponse, a judgment could be made about isolation of the individual and non-adult family members at Tule Lake. One of the original ten concentration camps, Tule Lake was designated the segregation center in 1943, and in a WRA reshuffle, "segregants" from all nine other camps were sent there. To make room, some "loyal" Tule Lake residents had to be moved—yet again—to another camp. Finally, potentially bypassing Tule Lake, some individuals were questioned about deportation to Japan. Some Japanese nationals expressed a desire for repatriation; some Americans asked for expatriation. Indeed, after the injustices of incarceration, many prepared to renounce their U.S. citizenship.[15]

WRA headquarters statistics show that one in four adults at Jerome answered "no" to question 28 (1,089), qualified the answer (346), or didn't respond at all (28). When Tokio Yamane refused to reply, an official wrote "no" on the form himself. One-quarter of the entire center population (2,147), including children, was transferred to Tule Lake, the highest proportion of all camps. Near the other end of the scale, one in six Rohwer inmates was segregated. From both Arkansas camps, more citizens were sent away than longtime resident "aliens." As many women went as men. In total, 14,330 people transferred to Tule Lake from the ten camps; 6,249 original residents of Tule Lake remained, bringing the total to well over 20,000. As early as June 1943, the Matsuda family agreed to what the WRA called "voluntary" expatriation and repatriation. But they were not among the 38 Jerome residents onboard the steamship *Gripsholm* on 2 September 1943, taking the first group of 314 Japanese Americans to Japan. By 1946 a total of 4,724 WRA camp inmates had sailed to Japan. Many hundreds more would go directly from DOJ camps as well. In the end, the indiscriminate incarceration of 120,000 Japanese Americans during World War II would result in roughly 15 to 20 percent being labeled disloyal. Roughly 4 to 7 percent would give up on America and go to Japan.[16]

Registration and segregation encompassed not only tangled processes of bureaucratic analysis. They also amounted to corrosive forces, demoralizing an already despairing Japanese American population, causing further sorrow among leave-takers and those left behind. They also helped to turn individuals and groups against one another. In the daily conversations of camp, "no-no" women and men attempted to explain their rationales to "yes-yes" people. True to form, WRA officials branded this activity as pressure, coercion, intimidation. But "no-no" people—a distinct minority of outcasts—found it necessary to band together, to discuss the implications of their decisions, and to negotiate with the administration. At Jerome, Paul Taylor threatened anyone who refused to register with a ninety-day jail sentence, and a committee of six—including Buddhist priest Shizuo Kai, former internal security captain Mitsu Kimura, and George Kuratomi—came together to represent the concerns of over eight hundred of the potential segregants. The military police stepped up patrols and called in reinforcements from Rohwer.[17]

Meanwhile, Japanese American informants and collaborators—*inu*, or dogs, as they were known to many—became the subject of reproach, even violence. On 6 March 1943, as many as nine men assaulted JACL leader and Jerome Community Council member Dr. Thomas Yatabe at the hospital. They beat him about the face and kicked him when he fell to the floor. The same morning, three young men beat Protestant pastor John Yamazaki, who had translated the loyalty questionnaire into Japanese for administrators. Henry Sugimoto turned this event into a dramatic thirty-by-forty-inch painting, with Yamazaki, in clerical collar, in a striking crucifixion pose, blood all over his face and midsection. Also symbolic, his Bible, glasses, and hat were strewn on the ground with the blood. Yamazaki remembers it differently, as a more somber, oddly respectful encounter. "Reverend Yamazaki," one of them said, "we came here to beat you, so take off your glasses and hat and put them on this tree stump." Camp authorities reported that Yamazaki was uninjured, with only "his clothes badly muddied." Yatabe, Yamazaki, and their families were moved into the hospital and provided with guards for protection.[18]

With the FBI watching closely, the committee of six was finally enlisted by members of the administrative staff to assist in registering those individuals reluctant to answer "yes-yes." The committee, in effect, helped them complete the process by the 5:00 p.m. deadline on 10 March 1943. Paul Taylor resented it, but a WRA observer from the Little Rock office characterized it as a dignified procedure. "The committee . . . called on Mr. Taylor on March 11 and presented him with presents, expressed their appreciation of the consideration shown and requested him to respect their loyalty to Japan as they in turn expected to respect his loyalty to the United States. . . . This ceremony . . . was quite formal."[19]

Though the Jerome leadership took extraordinary measures to protect Yatabe and Yamazaki, they were less concerned about assaults on repatriates and expatriates. That summer the Japanese American judicial commission, an arm of the Community Council, in a rare prosecution, "tried one of the citizens here for beating a repatriate. The commission found him guilty." But they passed over to the camp's assistant director "the matter of assessing the punishment." In reports to Washington, Jerome officials discounted the findings of the commission. They delayed—as they downplayed any need for—sentencing. "The current rumor on the matter," wrote the camp attorney, "is that the [victim] had it coming to him." Meanwhile, a so-called disloyal, "a 19-year-old boy, a Hawaiian kibei who made threatening statements" to a white hospital staffer, received a sentence of thirty days in jail. Paul Taylor said he might "let him out after ten to twenty days if he shows a change of attitude."[20]

Violet Matsuda followed a difficult path. From apartment number 44-8-A at the Jerome camp, she and her husband and their three children, along with her in-laws, were sent to Tule Lake. Because Shigeru Matsuda and his parents were legal residents forbidden citizenship in the United States, responding "yes" to question 28 would entail forfeiting their Japanese citizenship and thus becoming stateless persons. So they had exercised the privilege of silence and left the question blank. "This was a dilemma" for Violet Matsuda. "I was an American-born citizen, as were my three children but, as was customary in those days, I had been trained as a mother and as a housewife"—the "good wife and wise mother" model prevalent among Issei women. Unlike the other Nisei women who took up paid employment in the camps, Matsuda had to work at home and act as nurse for this large extended family, since both she and her mother-in-law battled cancer and since young Kimi was repeatedly hospitalized. "I, too, in desperation finally decided to go to Japan with them in order to keep my family together." And yet her family was torn apart further. Matsuda's husband was taken from Tule Lake to the Sante Fe, New Mexico, camp for enemy aliens. His mother died of cancer at Tule Lake, but he was denied leave from Sante Fe to attend the funeral.[21]

Soon Violet Matsuda and Tokio Yamane were caught up in the bitter political struggles of inmates at the Tule Lake concentration camp, struggles between those who advocated reconciliation with authorities and those who had given up on the United States and thus promoted repatriation and expatriation to Japan. Though Matsuda at first steered clear of these debates and altercations, Yamane became a target of camp officials who assaulted him, arrested him, and confined him to the camp's stockade. Matsuda herself came under suspicion too. She was fingered as a "troublemaker" by Rosalie Hankey, one of the numerous anthropologists from the University of California, Berkeley, who "studied" the incarceration and who, as was ostensibly forbidden, spied for the WRA. As a result, Matsuda would be placed on a blacklist with lasting ramifications.[22]

Yamane's disillusionment with the WRA had already hardened by the time he reached Tule Lake. When the train arrived from Jerome, and he and others "saw the star-spangled banner flying," they refused to disembark, forcing officials to lower the flag. Expecting a fully segregated camp in which to wait out administrative processes with like-minded individuals, they were surprised to discover the great range of views held by fellow prisoners. As one said, "I was very disappointed to find those 'loyals' in Tule Lake, supposedly the camp for 'no-no' people." The WRA reserved the most dilapidated blocks for segregants, making their living environment unbearable: "In comparison, facilities here are much worse than those in Jerome, and the sanitary condition is very poor," as a new prisoner reported back to Arkansas. "Bathrooms are filthy and showers are dirty. Much worse than the stables at Santa Anita. Living quarters too are in shambles. No one would believe that people have lived here."[23]

Working conditions likewise were miserable, but forty-three striking coal workers forced some concessions from the administration, after it failed to recruit scabs from within the camp. And in another appalling on-the-job accident, bleakly reminiscent of Jerome, a truck carrying agricultural workers overturned, injuring twenty people, three critically. One died. Officials refused to allow a public funeral, sparking protests. More strikes for occupational safety followed, and the WRA brought in scabs from other camps. Food shortages developed, and people went hungry—except for the strikebreakers, it seemed. Residents accused officials and collaborators furthermore of selling camp rations on the black market to line their own pockets.[24]

Yamane worked as part of a negotiating committee, the Organization for the Betterment of Camp Conditions, but camp director Raymond Best was intransigent. By the time WRA national director Dillon Myer got there on 1 November 1943 for discussions, tensions were running high. On 4 November violence erupted. A cook in the camps, Yamane was attending a meeting that night when a report came of staffers stealing food stocks and loading them onto trucks, with protesters gathering in response. He and Koji Todoroki were sent to investigate. As they were "heading toward the warehouse area, several Caucasian WRA personnel suddenly appeared out of the darkness and attacked the two of us, without any provocation on our part, with pistols, rifles, and bats, and finally took us to the WRA office." There, internal security officer Kobayashi, who first witnessed the theft, was hauled in too. "During his interrogation Mr. Kobayashi was hit on the head with such force that blood gushed out and the baseball bat actually broke in two," as Yamane later affirmed in a deposition submitted to a government commission. "I was a witness to this brutal attack and remember it very vividly."[25]

The attacks on Yamane himself lasted until morning, with ten officials either watching or participating: "Nobody tried to stop it." "You goddamn Jap, you're an agitator," they screamed. "No," Yamane replied, "I am not." "Son of a bitch," they laughed out, "confess!" "The white people wouldn't listen. And whenever I said I wasn't an agitator, white people hit me again and kicked me again and clubbed me with rifle butts all over my body." At numerous points Yamane nearly passed out. "I thought I was dying. And the torture was a very long, hard time, and it is a miracle that I'm alive now."[26]

What HUAC referred to as the Tule Lake Riots was in fact a fierce army crackdown. Taking over policing of the camp, with tanks and tear gas, they had adopted a policy of beating up and locking up those leaders best prepared to negotiate with Myer. The next morning the three men—Kobayashi, Todoroki, and Yamane—were turned over to the military police. They were thrown into the "bull pen," a thirty-by-thirty-feet outdoor pen, surrounded by barbed wire. A khaki tent contained three wooden cots and only one blanket each for the cold winter nights in northern California. So it became a "life-and-death struggle for survival." There was "no toilet, no shower, no stove, no sink." MPs guarded the entrance, in rotation, twenty-four hours a day. The men took their meals in the military mess, with two MPs watching over. Only at mealtimes could they use the toilet.[27]

"If we three went outside" the tent, Yamane remembers, "we always felt danger, even in the daytime. So we lay in bed all day long. And in the night, we slept in rotation," so one could warn the other two of intruders, more beatings. "And I came to feel anger day by day. Because I hadn't done anything wrong at all, why did I have to accept this disservice, this torture? This feeling radically changed my direction in life." After a month the three were sent to the stockade, joining many others, for many more months. They were never charged, never allowed to see friends and family, never tried.[28]

At gunpoint, men from the stockade were made to stand "in the snow for three, four, five hours in our underwear," as Morgan Yamanaka remembers. They were beaten with rubber hoses. Ben Takeshita was enraged to learn that after the customary grilling of his oldest brother—two to three days of intense, abusive questioning—MPs staged a firing squad. They offered Takeshita first a cigarette then a blindfold, and they yelled, "Ready, aim, fire," only to click on empty chambers. In response to the psychological and physical abuse, Tokio Yamane and his friends initiated hunger strikes in the stockade, and word seeped out. Violet Matsuda was frantic. She canvassed for support, quickly developing her organizing skills. She wrote to various authorities in Washington: for news and, hopefully, intervention. Older girls and young women interceded with the Tule Lake administration, for fear that male negotiators

17. A Japanese-language school, Tule Lake concentration camp. 93.102.80, IC, JANM.

"might be detained as troublemakers." The WRA didn't budge. Meanwhile, Yaozo Hitomi, a WRA co-op manager accused of collaboration, was found murdered on 2 July 1944. Assumed to have aided officials in the taking of food, he was killed during the very period his so-called enemies were locked away. Still, unable to solve the crime, the WRA pointed fingers indiscriminately, at any perceived agitator. Matsuda "was grilled for hours on end," but she "knew absolutely nothing" about it. Finally, on 28 August 1944, with the additional deaths of captives looming, stockade prisoners—gravely weakened by hunger strikes—were released, nearly ten months after their first beatings. By now Tokio Yamane was fully radicalized.[29]

A "resurgence of ethnic religious belief" accompanied resistance at Tule Lake, as did instruction in the Japanese language, culture, and physical education, with schools and branches located "in all corners of the camp." The outrages at the stockade hardened discontent. Just as the Young Women's and Young Men's Associations for the Study of the Motherland evolved into the more strident Young Men's Association to Serve the Nation, Yamane and others who had once engaged in negotiation now advocated "resegregation"—a further segregation of the Tule Lake population, to separate loyalists and collaborators from those who planned to go to Japan. After the U.S. government, in an unprecedented legislative response to Tule Lake, began to permit

Americans to "denaturalize"—to give up citizenship in time of war—Yamane and others pursued the path of renunciation, forming a new Organization to Return Immediately to the Homeland to Serve. Combined with the Association to Serve, the joint group known popularly as the Hoshidan became a major force within the camp.[30]

The Hoshidan's key argument held that individuals might actually receive better treatment from the U.S. government as aliens—in accordance with the 1929 Geneva agreements regarding prisoners of war—than they had thus far received as citizens. Activists such as Tokio Yamane, Shigeru and Violet Matsuda, priest Shizuo Kai and his wife, and George Kuratomi, all formerly of Jerome, joined with others in advocating this lesser-of-two-evils approach. And, having searched their souls, they decided Japan held out better postwar hopes for them, even if defeated, than the United States. If this were indeed a race war, as John Rankin and others had asserted time and again, then perhaps the Japanese in the wake of war would more readily accept and incorporate members of their own "race." Among Hoshidan organizers, the former California high school track-and-field champion Tokio Yamane became head of physical training, leading hundreds in exercises and marches, chanting and bugling. In all, 5,461 American citizens at Tule Lake renounced their U.S. citizenship.[31]

In a compelling chapter on Tule Lake that she was especially proud of, Michi Nishiura Weglyn—an outspoken critic of Japanese American incarceration in her book *Years of Infamy*—nonetheless railed against resisters, referring to them as "ruffians" and "pressure boys": a "reactionary" "fanatic fringe." She described renunciation as a "fatal step." She spoke of a betrayal by Hoshidan leaders of their followers: "Bitterly resented by residents were the Hokuku-Hoshidan stalwarts, who, after talking dozens of others into realizing the 'honor'" of internment in Department of Justice camps, followed by repatriation or expatriation, "had decided against it for themselves." Indeed, though Shigeru Matsuda and Tokio Yamane were sent away to the Santa Fe DOJ camp in December 1944, in preparation for return to Japan—to be followed by Violet Matsuda and her children—other leaders like the Reverend and Mrs. Kai and Kuratomi had decided against renunciation by fall of 1945, after closure of the camps and suspension of the West Coast exclusion zone were announced. According to Violet Matsuda, the Kais resettled in the Pacific Northwest, Kuratomi on the East Coast, leaving in their wake considerable ill will—"continuing even to this day."[32]

In an important essay on Hoshidan activists and renunciants, scholar Teruko Imai Kumei admirably confesses that she "was biased against" her subjects when she first undertook the project. By its conclusion she had to concede that historians such as Weglyn and legal advocates such as the ACLU's Wayne Collins had overstated the suasion that activists exerted over other Tule Lake residents—those who since have attempted to remain in or return to the United States, recover their citizenship, and redeem the entire Japanese American minority as loyal. "It seems very doubtful to me that massive renunciation was caused by the militant threat or conspiracy of the pro-Japan organizations." Instead, "it seems more likely that those organizations were formed and won large memberships because of a prevailing embitterment among the 'segregees': embitterment which the 'segregees' had had since the days of forced removal from their homes on the west coast, and which had become aggravated since their arrival at the Tule Lake Center. Some . . . demanded immediate repatriation as a means of protest, while some others . . . did so to maintain ethnic pride. Still others claimed that the 'segregees' should not be drafted. All of these were taken as appropriate reasons for joining the group." Tokio Yamane first got involved because of Japanese Americans' collective suffering and shame under incarceration; he became a leader because of the torture he personally endured from U.S. authorities. Also, since his older brother, soldier Dick, would surely remain in the States, and his sister Violet had her own family to tend to, he decided to return to Japan to help look after his mother.[33]

HIROSHIMA

American bombs rained down on southwest Honshu in the summer of 1945, creating firestorms in several cities. Though sirens went on and off in Hiroshima on the evening of 5 August, keeping everyone awake all night, it was oddly spared. For weeks and months, there had been calm, as much of southern Japan burned around it. So locals speculated. "Hiroshima Prefecture had sent off more emigrants to America than had any other part of Japan. Their sons were manning the American battle lines in this war and performing well," the reasoning went. "So out of indebtedness to them the United States was not bombing Hiroshima." When the air raid alarm was lifted, just after seven o'clock in the morning on 6 August 1945, many people went back to bed, satisfied that at last sleep would come.[34]

For those near the central core of Hiroshima, like Shika Yamane, it seemed the end of the world had come. At 8:15 a.m. dreams of a "blue flash, like lightning at the bottom of the sea," gave way to the rudest of awakenings. The blue flash was real. People heard "a terrible sound, loud enough to shake the earth."

And "like a huge boulder tumbling down a mountain, the roof of the house came crashing down. . . . Everything came crashing down—windowpanes, exterior walls, *fusuma* dividing [one] room from the next . . . smashed to smithereens." The sun had faded behind clouds of dust. The living—among them Shika Yamane—tried to get up. They staggered around the rubble, dazed, looking back, looking ahead for signs, anything. "Inside the house there was nothing at all to be seen. But outside, as far as the eye could see—which was much farther than usual—there stretched ruined house after ruined house. The same was true even of those parts of town a long way off." Among the remains, bodies. All around, cities of corpses, as writer Yoko Ota witnessed it.[35]

In Hiroshima proper, tornadoes of fire. Some ran. But more common were dumbstruck stragglers, remembered by many as resembling zombies or mummies, clothing half burned off their bodies and half dripping off along with their flesh. It was "a procession of the naked, crying, walking in bunches," as poet Sankichi Toge described it, "trampling on brain matter: / charred clothes about waists, / skin hanging like rags, / from arms raised to breasts." "Some were vomiting as they walked," as the American-trained Methodist minister Kiyoshi Tanimoto recalled for writer John Hersey. As Hersey elaborated, "On some undressed bodies, the burns had made patterns—of undershirt straps and suspenders [on men] and, on the skin of some women (since white repelled the heat from the bomb and dark clothes absorbed it and conducted it to the skin), the shapes of flowers they had had on their kimonos."[36]

The sights were so fantastic, so inhuman, so unbearably horrific that many suppressed memories for decades. Most never would be allowed to forget. Beset with a host of related illnesses—keloid skin lesions, diarrhea, hair loss, perpetual fatigue, and much worse—they would form a new, unprecedented class of human beings, those forced to live through the bodily consequences of an atomic blast: *hibakusha*. They would have to be monitored for the remainder of their inevitably shortened lives. Such was the case for Shika Yamane. Others—a media-friendly group of young women who came to be known as the Hiroshima Maidens—were led by Pastor Tanimoto to the United States, of all places. There American surgeons would attempt to at least partially undo the horrendous damage done by the American military.[37]

The U.S. government protected its people from the horrors of Hiroshima. For years photos of the aftermath were censored. And Americans developed impossible—impossibly soothing—sci-fi visions of what it must have been like: a clean, instantaneous vaporizing of the city, as opposed to the excruciating pain of being crushed to death in a collapsing building or being burned alive. Even the prize-winning journalist Hersey claimed that "no one in Hiroshima recalls hearing any noise of the bomb." No. People heard. And saw. They felt the blast and smelled the carnage. They tasted the ashes. And those who survived were left traumatized for life. A month after the event, in a village on the outskirts, a group of schoolgirls, ten and eleven years old, walking home, looked into an unusually bright sky, the sun blazing. Trembling, attempting to shade her eyes, one cried, "I'm terrified! Punishment from Heaven! The atomic bomb." Likewise afraid, seeking comfort in company, the girls together sang an eerie chorus, "Punishment from Heaven! Punishment from Heaven!"[38]

Poet Sankichi Toge answers:

> Ah, that was no accident, no act of God.
> After precision planning, with insatiable ambition,
> humanity's first atomic bomb
> was dropped, a single flash,
> on the archipelago in the eastern sea, on the Japanese people. . . .[39]

It was dropped, of course, by a small group of Americans acting on the orders of superiors. Combined with the detonation over Nagasaki three days later, it was the first and remains the only act of nuclear warfare ever committed.[40]

Said to have justified the atomic bombs, which hastened the war's end, Americans are well-acquainted with atrocities committed by soldiers of Japan during its imperial expansion. Many come laden with sexualized associations. The Rape of Nanking. The plight of Korean comfort women—sex slaves whose misery is difficult to overstate. But American memories are selective. How many now remember that U.S. soldiers and seamen, in an almost cannibalistic ritual, boiled down the dead bodies of Japanese servicemen for their bones, and sent them "home as gifts and souvenirs" to family members and friends? Born of an "intense hatred," this is, observers concede, "a dimension of the war that seldom surfaces today." So "commonplace" was the practice at the time, however, so acceptable did it seem given the racist propaganda that fueled popular support for the Pacific War, that *Life* magazine included, as its full-page "Picture of the Week," the image of a navy lieutenant's girlfriend gazing with admiration at the "Jap skull" he had shipped to her—fulfillment of a promise he'd made before shipping out. Thus, over the grisly remains of Japanese bodies, did American romance proceed. And thus, amidst a swirling sea of representations likening the Japanese to a subhuman class of cockroaches, rats, and monkeys, did U.S. authorities garner backing for a merciless policy of annihilation.[41]

For many, many months after the bomb, Japanese Americans would visit surviving family members in Hiroshima only to find them still homeless. Violet Matsuda and Tokio Yamane—like their immigrant parents before them—had good reason to return to Japan, to try, somehow, to help out those caught up in this most hopeless of human conditions.[42]

No philosopher's meditation on free will could ever achieve the poignancy of Violet Matsuda's: "My refusal to answer the loyalty questionnaire was not the product of free will, but was forced upon me in an effort to survive, to keep my family from disintegrating, and by the unlawful detention and the humiliating and degrading conditions prevailing in the . . . camps." Still, her family disintegrated. From the Sante Fe camp, her husband repatriated to Japan in 1945 and remarried. In precise phrasing, revealing in its subtlety, Matsuda writes that she and her children "were expatriated" to Japan from the Tule Lake camp in 1946. Acknowledging the limits of free will, she states not that they "expatriated" but rather "were expatriated," in many ways were forced out by the U.S. government. Once in Japan, she tried to return to the United States. But because of the blacklist, she was forbidden entry to her homeland until 1957, after marrying an American citizen, an Italian American soldier who, like her brother and like herself, had to find postwar employment with the only viable game in town: the American and British occupation forces.[43]

"Unable to properly raise my children in war-devastated Japan," Matsuda writes, "and hoping that they might have improved opportunities in their native land, I made the heart-breaking decision in 1948 to send my son, aged twelve, back to America. U.S. consular officials refused to let me accompany him. . . . A few years later, in 1951, I again had to make the same distressing decision to send my daughter, age fourteen, back to the United States. . . ." Thus, Violet Matsuda twice made the same terrible determination that her own mother, Shika Yamane, had made in sending her away to California, to the land of opportunity. Matsuda's largely economic reasoning would have permanent emotional repercussions. "My children were unable to comprehend that my motive in returning them to America was solely to improve their future well-being. Nor could they perceive the political and legal convolutions of U.S.-Japan relations, which had been difficult from previous periods. They harbored resentment that I was rejecting them. To this day, they have repudiated me, refusing to see me or have anything to do with me."[44]

I conclude this chapter, as I began it, with another familial and national rupture, indeed a global rupture of the highest order. Hiroshima. Unspeakable in its horror. Indeed, I broach it here with considerable trepidation and misgiving, in light of these Japanese American women's reluctance in remembering it, their understandable need for a respectful silence around it.

But as I suggested, I believe Hiroshima helps explain Japanese American incarceration. Simply put, there is a racist and nationalist dehumanization at the heart of both. Long depicted as insects and vermin in wartime propaganda, Japanese people were slated for annihilation—with American scientific breakthroughs in chemical pest control morbidly applied to "advancements" in the technology of warfare. The great bulk of Japanese immigration to the United States in the nineteenth and early twentieth centuries had originated in southwest Honshu, much of that from Hiroshima Prefecture. Were military strategists uninformed of that? Indifferent to it? Even if hell-bent on creating—and, by virtue of creating, using—humankind's most terrible weapon of mass destruction, the world's first atomic bomb, why drop it on Hiroshima? Historians have tried to comprehend why a test detonation in the presence of Japanese officials wasn't used to force surrender. They further have attempted to understand why a second bomb was used on Nagasaki so quickly after the first, without sufficient time for Japanese authorities to accept defeat and accede to an armistice. Why Hiroshima? If we must use the reasoning of U.S. officials, who valued American lives over all others, why the one city—perhaps excepting Tokyo—with the greatest number of family members of American citizens, indeed with the greatest number of Americans? Why Hiroshima Prefecture, home to Tokio Yamane's parents, birthplace of Violet Matsuda's husband, birthplace of Al Tsukamoto's parents, and the ancestral origin of the greatest number of prisoners at Jerome? It seems they were simply—or negligently—unaware.[45]

The literature in English on Japanese American incarceration is vast. It constitutes, in part, a valuable recuperation of lives lost, livelihoods destroyed, life options foreclosed, by a racist government imperative. Often this literature further chronicles the resistance and resilience and the abiding hope of Japanese Americans. Historical studies helped secure the congressional restitution of 1988 for Japanese American victims and descendants. But even the most liberal to radical accounts of incarceration, while decrying this "dark chapter"—a seeming aberration—in United States history, participate in the consolidation of the nation through a process of reconciliation. Second-generation, mostly English-speaking Nisei patriots such as Mary Tsukamoto are depicted as more American than thou—admirably, tenaciously holding to "American" principles of equality and freedom even as their government betrayed those Americans and betrayed those principles. Those who repatriated or expatriated to Japan, who found the American dream too illusory, are described—with an astounding consistency of vocabulary, by a variety of scholars—as "confused." Indeed, very rarely does the literature articulate the postwar lives of those American residents and citizens who, at war's end, at incarceration's end, started anew in Japan. It's as if, once moved beyond U.S. territorial borders, they drop out of a "U.S." history. This despite the U.S.-led Allied occupation of Japan until 1952.

Violet Matsuda's ongoing ambivalent identification with the United States and her repeated physical displacements from and to its mainland and territories seem richer, fuller, more complex, and ultimately more instructive than many histories of incarceration can allow. Contingent upon hierarchies of race, class, and gender, a choice of national affiliation is never one of free will, but instead is laden with material and ideological limitations, overdeterminations. Matsuda's own agency was circumscribed, in thinking about where home might be found in 1946. In subsequently "choosing" a nation for her American-born children, Matsuda surveyed an uneven field. The odds were stacked in favor of the occupation forces, the rising global superpower, whose own land, industry, agriculture, and infrastructure had been largely unscathed by war. The superpower stood in stark contrast to the defeated nation, the landscape of nuclear holocaust.

A consistent trope in incarceration scholarship is the historian's tool—or, more accurately, the historian's creation—the chronology, or timeline. A chronology appears at the back of both Mary Tsukamoto's autobiography and Violet Matsuda's written indictment of the duplicitous anthropologist. In this sense, Tsukamoto's easily marketed assimilationist memoir and Matsuda's less-well-circulated affidavit, filed for posterity at the UC Berkeley archives, are similar. They further share a notable absence. Neither author includes in her chronology an entry for 6 August 1945.

9 | Resettlement and Dispersal

PERPETUAL LEAVE-TAKING. Perhaps more hurtful than all the intimidation and fear, bigotry and violence, corruption and confinement, Japanese American incarceration was characterized by constant separation—partings. An immigrant generation that had embarked upon the biggest of journeys, to a new continent, found they had many more journeys yet to make. Some, understandably, grew weary. In 1945, however, many Nisei—described as "pathetically eager" to be American—called upon the shopworn maxims of American mobility. A new frontier! Westward, ho! Go west, young man! Westward the course of empire makes its way! California or bust! California here I come! (Right back where we started from.)[1]

In Michigan a train set out for California with Taro and Kame Dakuzaku aboard. The two had already been all over creation. Around the beginning of the century, Taro had left Okinawa to go to Hawaii, then San Francisco, and on to numerous towns and crossroad communities in the Central Valley. He had worked on plantations and railroads, and in laundries, before finally settling, he thought, in Florin on a small farm. From Florin he and his wife, Kame—a former servant in the Okinawan royal palace, mother to six daughters and, at last, one son, now a soldier—were forced to move to Fresno, and then to a place called Jerome, in Arkansas. With rumors of Jerome's closing, they'd been set "free" to relocate to Chicago. From there, they decided to join three of their daughters in Michigan. A place called Kalamazoo. But the government's so-called resettlement program—which move in this series of involuntary displacements would, in truth, ever constitute *settlement*?—had not worked for them. So in June they decided to follow the lead of their Nisei children: to set off for, to go back to, Florin. A setback?[2]

Back in Arkansas, when Jerome closed, some of the fortunate ones were sent just up the road thirty miles to Rohwer. But with 5,700 to be transferred, there wasn't enough room. So some of the less fortunate ones were yet again compelled—yet again forced against their will—to go to other places, such as Heart Mountain, Wyoming, near the border with Montana. Back across the continent. "The reaction of the Jerome residents to the announcement was one of natural disappointment," an official conceded with dry understatement, "and of some bitterness that their cooperation in making it a clean and liveable center had gone for naught." Another administrator, Rachel Reese Sady, spoke in detail, with a bit more candor. "Complaints included accusations of splitting families," like the early days of eviction, "ignoring the second choices, insufficient weight given the needs of various [camps] for ministers"—again disadvantaging Buddhists—"inadequate explanation of the medical classifications, obvious clerical errors, [an] atmosphere of confusion and mystery in which the work was carried out, and dissatisfaction with the priority system set-up." The "priority system" was another WRA euphemism—code for what protestors rightly referred to as favoritism. Two groups were prioritized: those interested in working for major American corporations, as at the New Jersey vegetable farming and processing facility of Seabrook Farms—called "patriarchal and exploitative" by one scholar—and "soldiers' families, [who got their] preference regardless of choice or whereabouts of soldier." This "was considered by many to be uncalled-for 'flag-waving.' . . . Also, the interviews given by the Transfer Committee were severely criticized. Many got the feeling that they were only a formality, that individual cases actually had no chance at all, and that mistakes would not be corrected."[3]

Now that Rohwer too was closing and the Supreme Court's *Endo* case had reopened the West Coast to Japanese Americans, trains set out for California. Preparing to board on 30 May 1945 was *Rohwer Outpost* columnist and self-styled literary celebrity Bean Takeda. Trackside, Takeda shook hands, exchanged bows, and said his last good-byes. He felt "a small lump" in the back of his throat that made it "difficult to swallow." Reflecting on the conflicting emotions of that moment, on the difficulties of leaving this new home to return to a drastically transformed older home out West, Takeda described an experience that paralleled that of hundreds of other Rohwer residents: "When the time comes to leave the center, all sorts of things pass thru [*sic*] your mind. You think of the things you did and the things you didn't do. You think of the time wasted or the time well spent. . . . But mostly you think about the people you have met and the friends you have made. . . . You're going to miss these people. You're going to miss their companionship, their laughter, their encouragement, their intrinsic friendship. . . . For the moment, those friends and the fact that you're bidding them farewell are the most important things in the world." If Takeda articulated the sentiments of many Japanese Americans freed from concentration camps in seven states in 1945—the challenge to pick up stakes, sever old relationships, and start anew elsewhere—he also spoke to a pattern of events, a cycle of compulsory migrations, a perverse set of repetitions.[4]

The social and psychological effects of camp closing on over 75,000 Japanese Americans remaining in WRA detention in 1945 frequently have been overlooked by historians. While many have focused on the decisions and difficulties of expulsion or attempted to re-create life inside the barbed-wire compounds—as I have done in several chapters here—most writing about camp closing has probed economic hardships, tallying the intervening losses of income and private property, included only as an addendum to camp experiences. The story told usually has been of the ones that got away, the Nisei. A significant number left the camps for university or outside employment in 1943 and 1944, and thus didn't live through the process of shutting down the camps, the traumas it summoned. They experienced it vicariously, though the stories of friends and family members. Because many aged seventeen to thirty-five signed up for the well-publicized resettlement program, the camps, as historian Roger Daniels notes, "increasingly held a higher proportion of older adults and small children, of Issei rather than Nisei," over the course of the war. In the same way that the second generation populates most narratives about Japanese American incarceration during World War II, resilient self-starters tend to predominate in accounts of war's end too, as well as in upbeat histories of postwar Asian America, the march of the so-called "model minority," as coined in the 1960s. Issei and the relatively few Nisei still in camps in 1945 have been neglected. Further, some of the most destructive aspects of resettlement—in particular, the guiding principle of population dispersal—have been downplayed or implicitly validated.[5]

Bean Takeda and his Nisei colleagues at the office of the *Rohwer Outpost* promoted life after camp in narrow ways, as had their counterparts on the *Denson Tribune*. Their announcements, the WRA statements they reprinted, and the editorial comments they penned revealed a positivist, occasionally foolhardy optimism about postcamp and postwar possibilities. Starting over, for them, seemed much easier than many of their readers assumed—and for the first time, with original articles of a decidedly cynical cast, the Japanese-language section of the Rohwer paper, the *Jiho*, began to diverge sharply from the other pages of the *Outpost*, focusing repeatedly in 1945 on accounts of American prejudice on the outside. Issei mulled their options with great skepticism. Their misgivings circulated in stark contrast to Nisei trendsetters who followed and even helped formulate the federal government policy of resettlement and dispersal.[6]

Trains departed camps in 1945 with Nikkei who were uncertain about the options, unsure of their direction. In a beautiful Japanese ritual, pregnant with meaning, passengers at windows each held the end of a long, colored strip of crepe paper, and at the other end, a well-wisher clung tight. When wheels began to turn and the train pulled away, the streamers were pulled taut and slowly stretched, like so much elastic, supple and resilient, prolonging the connection, until at last they reached the breaking point. Individuals still in detention were left behind, standing at the tracks. People onboard were left to wonder about the way ahead. All were left holding the broken pieces.[7]

Of the songs that run through one's mind at such moments—the soundtrack to the movie of life—rousing tunes like "California Here I Come" surely gave way to more melancholy strains. "Ev'rytime we say goodbye, I die a little."

NORMAL AMERICAN COMMUNITIES

Orders came from the very top. President Franklin Roosevelt said that a key aim of the War Relocation Authority was to insure Japanese American "relocation into normal homes" after investigations and loyalty determinations. WRA director Dillon Myer dutifully reported the same to the House Un-American Activities Committee and the American Legion, emphasizing further a return "as quickly as possible to private employment." Both HUAC and the Legion feared release, overstating the dangers to national security—there were none—and ignoring the dangers for Japanese Americans. Roosevelt differed with his secretary of the interior, Harold Ickes, who advocated immediate, large-scale movements out of the camps in 1944, given the increasing realization of incarceration's unconstitutional basis and the utter lack of military necessity. Roosevelt insisted instead upon "a gradual release program designed to scatter the internees." Worried about his own political career leading up to the race for an unprecedented fourth term, Roosevelt proposed that only "one or two families" be sent to "each county" off the West Coast. "Dissemination and distribution," he said, "constitute a great method of avoiding public outcry." Thus, as historian Greg Robinson concludes, FDR's "exclusive focus on placating West Coast public opinion and his order that the internees be 'disseminated' betray[ed] a cavalier disregard for the concerns of Japanese Americans, whom the President saw only as a problem, and to their right to choose where they lived."[8]

Whereas the *American Legion Magazine* fretted over the potential longevity of the camps, hysterically predicting they would become powerful Little Tokyos sending representatives and senators to Congress, mainstream daily newspapers such as the *New York Times* espoused a widespread view that a necessary resettlement program must avoid the grouping of large numbers of Japanese Americans into new ethnic enclaves. Some Japanese American leaders and journalists echoed the call. *Pacific Citizen* editor Larry Tajiri "spoke of the breaking up of the [prewar] Little Tokyos as a positive aspect" of expulsion and incarceration. Writing for *Common Ground*, Eddie Shimano was determined that they not be re-created, referring to life in camps, in the article's title, as a "Blueprint for a Slum." As WRA official John Baker wrote in camp publications, "The War Relocation Authority is definitely committed to the task of helping people in the relocation centers to resume normal lives in normal communities where they can be contented and secure." Once again, such Americanization implied Christianization, for an accompanying illustration of a normal American community depicted a small town with only one house of worship—with a cross atop the steeple.[9]

Though Roosevelt's "one or two families per county" plan was unworkable in detail, the guiding principle of dispersing Japanese Americans remained a cornerstone of resettlement policy. Camp newspapers toed the line. A striking feature of the *Rohwer Outpost* in 1944, for example, was the prevalence of job offers and relocation announcements from a wide geographical area, particularly the Midwest. A single issue on 8 January listed "Outside Employment" opportunities for factory work in Cleveland, for domestic workers in St. Louis, a watchmaker in Omaha, and a short-order cook in South Haven, Michigan. A column on the same page told readers of successful relocations. George Yamauchi had gone to Davenport, Iowa; Alice Hatsumi Takahashi was now in Ann Arbor, Michigan; Eugen Toshio Yoshida had started a new life in Cincinnati; and three more people had moved to Chicago. Within the next week, it said on the opposite page, relocation officer Laverne Madigan would be visiting Rohwer from New York to outline further options. The *Outpost*'s

Bean Takeda was sent on a three-month tour of relocation destinations in the summer of 1944, reporting back regularly from Chicago, Cleveland, Atlantic City, Philadelphia, Washington, and Bridgeton, New Jersey, home of Seabrook Farms. His positive references to the employment and housing conditions demonstrated the utility of his writings to WRA policy makers. Takeda's column, along with a permanent feature of the *Outpost*, the "Relocation Calendar," served two functions. On the one hand, they told the camp community who was moving and where, thereby aiding individuals and families considering a departure. On the other hand, they constantly reminded inmates that people were on the move, leaving camp, starting new lives in new parts of the country. By implication, they asked: Shouldn't you be doing likewise?[10]

WRA headquarters insisted that resettlement campaigning was the duty of all camp administrators and didn't shirk from calling it "indoctrination." Teachers in particular were held to account. Adult schools inculcated skills foremost for "profitable relocation" during and after the war. As much as the traditional three R's, WRA high schools taught two others: "relocation of families and of individuals where they will find community acceptance and suitable work [and] re-assimilation of Japanese Americans into the normal social and economic order of the nation." Social studies teachers played a crucial role: "Upon large wall maps of the United States constructed by students, cities and states to which many center residents have gone out have been marked; others to which they will be welcomed have been indicated." Additionally, well-meaning supporters outside the camps, such as Earl Finch, wrote letters of introduction and letters of recommendation, helping connect prisoners with potential employers.[11]

At Jerome, Virginia Tidball required her high school English students to write compositions on resettlement, and, unsurprisingly, the majority seemed to favor it, repeating words read in newspapers or heard in lectures. Nisei should find new homes outside, Akiko Higake wrote, and once there, "should try to make a good impression [on] the public and not be conspicuous in any way." As Katsuto Nakano added, "We must avoid grouping together and practice assimilation. . . . The main part of gaining a favorable opinion is up to the evacuee." Hawaiians such as Clara Hasegawa felt differently. "I am just hoping that we will never be asked to leave this center until the war is over," she confided. "This relocating business is bound to separate us from all our friends." Hailing from Kauai, her father, a Buddhist minister interned in New Mexico, Michiko Odate worried about "racial discrimination," calling it "the worst problem that [a]ffects resettling." She also fretted that taking "employment near the eastern coast of this country" would leave people at war's end "quite far away from their former home." Teenagers understood the disadvantages for older inmates too. Higake noted that few Issei wanted to resettle. And "we can hardly blame them." After first coming "to this land with the dominant pioneering spirit of settling," why should they have to "face another [of] life's battles in the unknown regions"?[12]

As of mid-1944, the *Rohwer Outpost* prepared residents for the inevitable reopening of the West Coast while continuing to encourage resettlement elsewhere. Bean Takeda generally argued against thoughts of California. While acknowledging that a "certain number" should go back, he counseled caution, citing the vast movements of people into and around the state during the war, the subsequent housing shortage, and the likelihood that former friends there would be gone. Furthermore, news of vandalism and theft of property left behind on the West Coast, often in Buddhist temples, had circulated since the beginning of incarceration. Japanese Americans at Jerome and Rohwer feared that WRA "property officers may be consciously or unconsciously working with the Sons of the Golden West to make it possible that the former Japanese residents of California have no roots or ties to which to come back."[13]

With the lifting of the West Coast exclusion order, effective 2 January 1945, the *Rohwer Outpost* changed its tune. Bean Takeda began to consider a return to his native California himself. And he urged his readers to "discredit any rumors you might hear about unpleasantness in our California hometowns": "There seems to be an organized move along the Pacific Coast to bluff evacuees into not going back. If we believe these wild rumors and are frightened into not returning, we are going to be the losers, economically and otherwise." In March 1945 Takeda praised a San Francisco resident for refusing to be intimidated by telephone threats: "That's the spirit we need to lick those bluffers." In April he tried to buoy hopes further, even as he admitted the very real dangers to Japanese Americans. "Of course, you'll say that it's easy enough for me, here in the camp, to utter such words of bravado. But I'm returning to California soon, and when I do, I shall expect to be treated roughly at first and perhaps even shot at."[14]

There were, in fact, innumerable incidents of violence against released Japanese Americans on the West Coast, as well as in every other section of the United States. Those in so-called mixed marriages were particularly visible—and vulnerable. Herbert Sasaki, a 442nd soldier who had sung tenor solos at the USO dances for Japanese Americans, wedded white Mississippian Arnice Dyer, and after a brief period in the Midwest, the couple set up permanent residence back in Dyer's hometown of Purvis, Mississippi, running her parents' chicken farm. Given the difficulties of interracial marriage in a state with a miscegenation law, Sasaki consistently avoided talking about the ceremony in the interviews he granted through the years. But in its obituary on Sasaki in 2005, the *Los Angeles Times* noted that, as a result of the marriage, the Ku Klux Klan had burned a cross in their front yard.[15]

For many Nisei women, resettlement first meant a new life near Camp Shelby, Mississippi. Moving out of the concentration camps, wives of soldiers had to find accommodation and often raise their children in the heart of the segregated South. Kazu Iijima and her husband, Tak, rented a room from a Protestant pastor and his wife in the town of Petal, where they were viewed, at best, as a novelty. "People would be driving," she recalls, "and they would stop in the middle of the street to stare at us." The Iijimas "used to have big arguments" with Reverend O'Neil, "because he used to believe that the Negroes, as they called them, came from Adam's ribs so they were inferior people. And we used to play Paul Robeson records and Marian Anderson, . . . and he'd say that those were unusual people." Though white evangelicals might concoct any biblical excuse for African American subjugation, the Christian creation myth in fact held that women were formed from man's rib, and it served to justify *their* position of social inferiority. When the Iijimas moved out, Mrs. O'Neil sheepishly asked to borrow the Anderson and Robeson records to play for her women's group at the church.[16]

With severe housing shortages in Hattiesburg during the war years—such that some local opportunists rented out their chicken coops—Earl Finch stepped in to aid Japanese Americans in search of a home. Finch bought or rented area houses, which he then made available to couples such as the Taonos and Ishikawas. Given her college education, and given the reluctance of some white public schools to accept Japanese Americans, Kay Ishikawa was advised to home-school her children. But she insisted they needed the social interactions that only ordinary schooling could provide. So the Ishikawas then moved into another "Finch home" to be near a Catholic school that had accepted their son Robert. (The short-lived segregated public school for Japanese Americans in Hattiesburg apparently never enrolled more than five, and it closed after teacher Martha Suigi moved away.) Mary Nakahara lived in Finch homes in Hattiesburg, once she relocated there to help run the Aloha USO. Then, "Earl Finch sent me to Minnesota," she remembers, to manage an Aloha center near Camp Savage, home to the Military Intelligence Service. Nakahara assisted her mother and aunt in their move back to California from

Rohwer. Then, with her new husband, soldier Bill Kochiyama, she resettled—yet again—in New York. There she worked at a Chock Full o' Nuts coffee shop and, enlightened by her wartime experiences, she embarked upon a new lifelong commitment: to the struggles of working-class people of color.[17]

Whereas the USO dances at Shelby, Jerome, and Rohwer had marked an era of state-sanctioned courtship and intra-ethnic marriage—helping, in effect, to maintain racial segregation in the United States—the WRA resettlement program aimed to move Japanese American families into predominantly white "normal American communities" and thereby aid their social and racial ascent after the war. But these movements into segregated, often hostile white neighborhoods and workplaces came at a cost.

THE SUICIDE OF JULIA DAKUZAKU

Eddie Shimano, the former editor of the Jerome newspaper, was so convinced of resettlement's urgency that he overstated the dire conditions in the camps, which he had left at the earliest opportunity. Writing for the magazine *Common Ground*, he insisted that resettlement needed to be done and "done fast if potentially valuable individuals are to be salvaged for the nation and for themselves. It is an uphill fight to maintain a balance, a perspective, and a faith in the nightmare of demoralization and despair that is a relocation center." Indeed, the expulsion and incarceration had had nightmarish consequences, but the camps themselves proved habitable and supportive environments for many—at least as compared to the world of prejudice and bigotry waiting just beyond the barbed-wire fence. Still, Shimano advocated "dispersal resettlement" and "the integration of the Japanese into American life": "with surgical thoroughness and surgical disregard for sentiment."[18]

With leave clearance secured by their "yes-yes" status, Mary and Al Tsukamoto resettled in Kalamazoo, Michigan, with their only child, daughter Marielle, and other family members. There Mary's father, Taro Dakuzaku, sister, Julia Dakuzaku, and husband, Al, landed jobs at the Peter Pan Bakery. Gone were the mutual support and cultural cohesiveness of their California hometown—and of the concentration camp. "Our life there [in Michigan] was one of seclusion," says Mary Tsukamoto, "and those who worked at outside jobs did so at night when their Japanese faces were not so visible; the rest of us stayed indoors as much as we could." After nearly three years of companionship in what had effectively become an ethnic enclave at Jerome and Rohwer, how disturbing and off-putting it must have been for Taro and Kame

Dakuzaku—and for Issei from all the camps—to receive this sort of guidance from the JACL: "To avoid attracting attention, Issei are advised not to speak Japanese on the streets and in other public places. They should not bow to each other because this makes them conspicuous." Thus, a chief sacrifice in resettlement was the forfeiting of personal dignity—to make oneself small, indeed invisible, in the public sphere.[19]

The bakery was a dangerous, depressing place, largely devoid of pleasure or of safety measures. "There were many opportunities to make mistakes, but the employee who made them did not last long." By now an elderly man, Taro Dakuzaku "had the tip of his finger cut off one night while he was feeding dough into a cutting machine." But he and other Japanese American laborers were afforded few protections and little compensation. He received $500 for his on-the-job injury and nothing more.[20]

Julia Dakuzaku was even more of a worry to her family members, because she *really* "wanted to live a normal life like other twenty-year-olds." She was an avid painter and dancer. Wherever possible, she gave amateur singing performances with the Dakuzaku Sisters. She didn't like the night shift, the tiring routine of working in the dark, sleeping during the daylight hours. She asked for reassignment and was granted it, temporarily. "When the customers saw her Japanese face on the line however, they became alarmed and began to boycott the bakery." Though the personnel officer attended the same First Methodist Church as the Tsukamotos and was counted among Mary's "very special friend[s]," he insisted that Dakuzaku return to the night shift. When she refused, "they had to fire her," according to Mary Tsukamoto. Tsukamoto "worried about her [sister] and her attitude. She was stubborn but also vulnerable to depression and despair." Dejected, Dakuzaku was turned down by numerous other employers: "Advertised job openings were not for her. Even when caring church members walked the streets with her to find daytime employment, Julia could not get a job." Mary arranged "several counseling sessions" for her sister with the Methodist minister. "In desperation," Julia finally found work with the WACs.[21]

Whereas Japanese American men were once classified as 4-C, enemy aliens ineligible for service, the mobilization of the 442nd had been a highly coordinated and widely publicized effort to redeem Japanese Americans through voluntary military duty. Soon Nisei men were drafted, including the Dakuzakus' only son, George, who was sent to England. And as we have seen, young women were encouraged to join the WACs. Many men and women resisted. So not only Mary Tsukamoto, but also the national JACL newspaper, *Pacific*

Citizen, repeatedly described women's enlistment as the perfect means of reintegration into the body politic through service to the country. In her regular column, the pseudonymous Ann Nisei tried to overcome any misgivings on the part of potential inductees. Hardly Amazons, as some feared, Nisei WACs she encountered were "young, attractive and energetic," she wrote. They found army employment in a variety of occupations. They were not segregated from white women, and since "WAC requirements were specially lowered for Nisei women, you remember, to 100 lbs. and 59 inches in height," almost anyone could volunteer—provided they were citizens "of course." Newspapers gave significant coverage to Private Iris Watanabe, "the first Nisei evacuee to be inducted into the WACS." In what seemed a classic case of blaming the victim, however, Watanabe chided young women and men who, "by caging themselves [*sic*] in these relocation centers . . . don't give themselves a chance to succeed in life, just because of one rather unhappy and bitter experience." Nisei WACS also figured prominently in the broader campaign to "rehabilitate" the Japanese American minority and win over the white majority. Ayako Noguchi Nakamura, who resettled with her husband and over two thousand others at Seabrook Farms in New Jersey, went on a speaking tour as part of this campaign. She visited Christian aid organizations, social service agencies, and PTAs to trumpet the accomplishments of "Japanese Americans in the War Effort."[22]

Julia Dakuzaku had answered the waning wartime call of Uncle Sam and enlisted. But that too proved a crushing disappointment. The government, once again, proved it did not know what was best for her; it would not necessarily act in her best interests. She was stationed in a place called Pasco, Washington, far from friends, far from family. Shortly after Taro and Kame Dakuzaku returned by train to their farm in Florin, California, they received a telegram about their youngest, sixth-born daughter. Their hearts sank with the very first words, that hackneyed—utterly insufficient—expression of condolence: "We regret to inform you. . . ."[23]

The Tsukamotos too had returned to their hometown of Florin. Mary tried to act as simultaneous interpreter for her parents when a "tall, attractive, blonde lieutenant" arrived the next day with Julia's "flag draped pine box" and explained, for the first time, the cause of death: "She ended her life by her own choice." The suicide of Julia Dakuzaku would become a family secret. Some sisters weren't told "until many, many years later" how she died. And some had great difficulty comprehending why she did it. But Mary eventually would come to describe her sister Julia, quite rightly, as a "victim [of] incarceration and war." Julia Dakuzaku died on 9 September 1945, exactly one month after the bombing of Nagasaki.[24]

Like Mary's parents, the Tsukamotos returned to farming but finally had to give up and pull up their grape vines in 1949. That same year Tsukamoto used her experience as a teacher in the camps to help secure a position with the by-now-desegregated Florin School, her alma mater. She would teach there until her retirement. And her autobiography, coauthored with Elizabeth Pinkerton in the 1980s, would reflect what Pinkerton describes as Tsukamoto's "patriotic fervor that knows no rest." For Pinkerton, the Tsukamoto autobiography, entitled *We the People*, and the changes in the Florin schools before and after incarceration demonstrated, most forcefully, "why America is so great."[25]

PLANTATION VERSUS COOPERATIVE COLONY

It didn't have to end this way. Closing the camps was not a foregone conclusion—not for everyone. Though WRA officials again and again insisted that the concentration camps "by their very nature, can never be turned into normal communities," many people proposed just that. Through administrators' ruthless drives for efficient production and, more importantly, Japanese Americans' diligence in farming and service occupations that benefited their own, Jerome and Rohwer had been transformed into bustling towns that were, one after the other, difficult to abandon. Still, the WRA insisted that "life outside" was "infinitely preferable," and that as towns, the camps would "always have serious shortcomings." These shortcomings were taken as self-evident and were rarely articulated, as they bordered on falsehood: "As long as evacuees remain in relocation centers, their opportunities to lead a well-rounded and fully productive life will inevitably be more limited than in ordinary American towns and cities." In Rohwer in 1945, where almost five thousand people had chosen to remain in relative safety, within the heart of an ethnic support network, two alternative visions of the war's aftermath emerged. One represented a return to the old order; the other was a bold, more equitable plan. Naturally, the former, the American way, ruled the day. It could have been much different.[26]

By its own measures, the WRA's dispersal strategy succeeded. Of the 120,000 people who came into their custody—almost exclusively from California, Oregon, and Washington—nearly half left the camps to resettle in other sections of the country: a huge population redistribution. Though some of these, like the Dakuzakus and Tsukamotos, would again, shortly thereafter, relocate back to California, others by contrast found their old West Coast hometowns so changed as to necessitate the move east, as with Mary and Bill Kochiyama. With WRA regional offices in Denver, Little Rock, and San Francisco, with as many as fifty-eight special relocation offices from Salt Lake City to New York, and with publications such as *They're Friendly in New England*, administrators actively directed Japanese Americans toward particular jobs and communities. "The great social-engineering experiment of rounding up, penning, and strewing," as historian Richard Drinnon surmises, "had racist and totalitarian implications." "Through Myer's executive agency the Roosevelt administration told citizens where they might live, what to do there for a living, how to dress, how to behave, how to talk and with whom to associate." Of course, officials with the WRA held a range of views and performed their tasks with mixed motivations. There was considerable sympathy for the inmates, a faith in assimilation, and the desire to make release from the camps acceptable to a wider public. The great majority wanted to resolve racial and ethnic conflict, and as we've seen, some even resigned their government posts in response to army and WRA excesses. But Dillon Myer and others seemed to be of one mind about the closing of the camps.[27]

Even the JACL had to acknowledge that some Japanese Americans would necessarily, understandably resist yet another risky forced relocation to a dangerous new place. At an "all-center conference" held in Salt Lake City in 1945 to discuss camp closing and resettlement, Rohwer delegates Chester Fujino, Shintaro Ito, and Lloyd Shingu stood by helplessly as the WRA rejected out of hand a JACL proposal that the government agency "stay in business indefinitely and be prepared to accept back into custody those of the evacuated people who could not, for reasons of age, infirmity, or demoralization, make some kind of successful readjustment to life outside the camps." In addition to these disparaging characterizations, there were affirming rationales for maintaining the camps as ongoing concerns. First, however, activists at Rohwer had to point out the flaws in one of the WRA's most touted "relocation opportunities."[28]

Plantations evoked mixed emotions for Japanese Americans in Arkansas. For most Hawaiians, plantations had been the first site of employment and livelihood in the United States, a source of fond family memories and pernicious workplace inequalities. Some had managed to work their way up and out of the fields, forming the core of a local service economy. Similarly, smaller-scale, family farming had been a principal source of income on the West Coast, as it simultaneously gave rise to a host of related vocations and professions. During incarceration, large-scale collective agriculture, individual garden plots, and communal meal preparation demonstrated a continuing Japanese American affinity for food production. So WRA officials thought it only natural to promote outside employment on Wilson Plantation: "One of the Best!"[29]

Located in the far northeast corner of Arkansas, near the Mississippi River, Wilson Plantation was a massive operation spread over 63,000 acres—57,000 of which were under cultivation, mostly in corn, alfalfa, and soybeans. Across five towns, 10,000 people lived in 2,200 houses. In addition to farming, residents worked in 77 other trades, from lumber mills and granaries to an ice plant and box and crate factory, from a bank and medical clinic to filling stations and beauty parlors. Wilson officials marketed the plantation as a desirable postwar home for Japanese Americans. Carrying the WRA imprimatur, a January 1946 bulletin emphasized Arkansas's position as the leading strawberry producer in the United States, as well as the nation's number-three producer of rice. Also presumed relevant to Japanese Americans from California in particular, the plantation "is going to further diversify by entering into commercial truck crop farming." Ostensibly dedicated to truth in advertising—since readers of the bulletin could sign a form within and thereby enter into a binding contract—marketers cautioned that "there are no soft-cushion jobs. . . . Like all farming, no matter what section of the country, it is hard work. . . . But no one knows more about this than do Japanese American farmers."[30]

Of course, in the South plantation life carried all the connotations of exploitation and racial hierarchy that had made the section, as with the Pacific territories, immensely profitable for a small, avaricious planter elite. Further, it bore the specific legacy of slavery, a vicious economic system propped up by insidious social and cultural assertions of black inferiority. Despite occasional moments of alliance among people of color during World War II—as when Japanese Americans joined African Americans in the back of the bus or in confrontations with white bigots—Nisei and Issei throughout the war years fretted over modes of segregation and marginalization that cast them as similar to, as similarly positioned with, blacks on American racial scales. Wilson officials thus did not promise improved conditions for Japanese Americans along with African Americans; they vowed to effectively distinguish the former—indeed, segregate them—from the latter. That is, they agreed to let Japanese Americans participate in *some* white institutions and practices. "School buses are provided by The Plantation to carry all children to and from schools," the bulletin advised. "Your children will attend the white schools."[31]

Promotion threatened to degenerate into deception, with the hope that, if stated forcefully enough, any claim might be believed. "<u>EVACUEES HAVE</u>

NOTHING TO FEAR," said J. H. Crain, general manager. "There is a general feeling of tolerance and fellowship toward Japanese Americans in this entire section of the country and they can depend on the Wilson Plantation to defend their rights and privileges as citizens and loyal aliens." As an example of this tolerance, "at the beginning of the 1945 fall term of school, one of the Japanese [*sic*] boys, now relocated on the Wilson Plantation, was elected vice-president of the Junior H.S. Class at Wilson, Arkansas." Further, Japanese American students were free to play on the white school's "football fields, tennis and basketball courts and"—in a crucial test of segregation in the Jim Crow South, with its outlandish theories of disease transmission—"swim in its pool." Of the many perks of life in Wilson, the bulletin boasted "rural mail service daily, except Sunday"; in more measured tones, it promised "adequate hospital services . . . in case of injury or severe illness"; and, in a clear case of a liability recast as an asset, it noted that "favorite Japanese foods and other choice needs and desires will be stocked in Plantation stores for your convenience and pleasure."[32]

Plantation stores were the crux of the problem—for so-called evacuees indeed had everything to fear in the economic organization of Wilson. It was, simply put, a classic postbellum scheme of tenant farming and sharecropping. Whereas under the briefly described "Plan No. 2," land could be rented for $12 to $18 per acre, "providing you have your own farming equipment and finances to make your own crops"—out of reach for the great majority after incarceration—the elaborately detailed "Plan No. 1, for the family or bachelor with little or no money," was, in the end, the only option. Under it, the Wilson Plantation would "furnish as many acres of its rich alluvial soil to each family as its (the family's) workers can care for, advantageously"—that is, as judged by the overseers. "The Wilson Company will furnish all farming equipment," some to be logically shared with others, as well as "fertilizer, plants, seeds, housing and insecticides": "YOU will furnish only the labor." Proceeds from the harvest's sale would be split between sharecropper and owner, depending on the crop, at proportions from 50-50 up to 65-35. The critical paragraph 8 pointed out that "should you need financial assistance until proceeds of crops are in, the Wilson Plantation will advance you money. The same to be repaid at harvest time plus 6 percent interest per annum for the length of the loan." Thus did Wilson and all debt peonage schemes ensnare their laborers.[33]

Bragging that "no renter, sharecropper, or worker . . . was fired or lost his job on the Plantation during the depression period" was really beside the point. It was leaving the plantation that often became impossible. Located over forty miles from Memphis, residents were forced to buy basic consumer goods at a plantation store's inflated prices. In advance of harvest, they were forced to buy on credit, borrowing money at exorbitant rates. If the crop's yield—a "quick-cash" payment "at current market prices," dictated by the owners, the only game in town—did not cover expenses, as was all too common (and not just during agricultural depressions), then a cycle of debt resulted. The debts were compounded from one year to the next. Plantation housing—discretely sandwiched, in the contract, between potentially hazardous fertilizers and insecticides, all "furnished" by the owners—too often became jails. To leave would mean to run out on debts, an illegal act that would involve law enforcement officers, if not worse. To leave indebted, with nothing in the world but the clothes on your back, would mean to risk homelessness.[34]

As of early 1946, nearly one hundred Japanese Americans lived in Wilson. Others followed. Though the Arkansas legislature in 1943 had passed a racist, alien land law with astonishing majorities—only one dissenting vote each in the House and Senate—and though this law forbade sale or long-term lease of land to persons of Japanese descent, Wilson officials overlooked it. Though the measure, signed by Governor Homer Adkins, had sparked outraged editorials from as far away as Detroit and statements of protest from as nearby as Clarksville, the plantation adopted a liberal interpretation, suggesting the statute was unconstitutional: "Arkansas' constitutional law . . . permits Japanese Aliens to buy and own their own land." Thus did they further hold out the hope—perhaps a false one—that instead of a downward cycle of debt, Japanese Americans would enjoy an upward spiral of good weather and thrifty savings, leading in some distant unforeseeable future to private property of their own.[35]

There was an alternative. Imagine it. Instead of individuals and families working for their own narrowly defined self-interest—and that of an all-powerful overlord—competing ruthlessly for the best land, their gain another family's loss, they might come together and toil on a large tract for the collective good, to be shared equally by all Japanese Americans. Imagine not an urban Little Tokyo but a rural Little Prefecture. Notions like this had circulated since the earliest days of the camps, especially in Arkansas.

"Cooperative group farming" was under study at Jerome and Rohwer, as well as Tule Lake, as early as the summer of 1943. "A conference of the Councilmen and Block Managers of Rohwer Center" met on 28 October 1943 and subsequently sent their findings directly to camp director Ray Johnston and WRA director Dillon Myer in Washington. Instead of—or in addition to—"the WRA's dispersed resettlement aim," they asserted that "group relocation is the best solution, especially for prospective farmers." A group "need not be on a scale any larger than twenty to thirty families." But clustering was necessary, given that "the task of independent re-establishment of a large family amidst strangers and unknown territory is practically impossible to expect of these evacuees now." Though often remembered as a quiet camp with little if any outward signs of protest, Rohwer and its inmates' statement of dissent were taken very seriously, occasioning an eight-page response from Myer. While he circulated the proposal to all ten camp directors, conceding that it was "well thought up," he discouraged the leaders at Rohwer. "If by group relocation the Council means the purchase of a fairly large tract of land and the colonization of a considerable number of evacuees on this land, the WRA will have to answer that it actively discourages such plans." He argued that "fellow Americans"—presumably white—would mount "strong opposition." "Such special groups whether they are Japanese, Italian, Greek, Polish, or Turkish will meet with antagonism." One such special group had long lived in peace just up the road, in Stuttgart, Arkansas. So Rohwer organizers were not to be deterred. By the time rumors swirled of camp closing, a sweeping new proposal of utopian design was put forward.[36]

Authored by a three-person "citizens committee"—Saburo Muraoka, C. Sumida, and T. Takasugi—the elaborate proposition for a cooperative colony was hard to rebut, given the precedent of the camps' successful cooperative stores. A colony would be on the scale, roughly, of the Wilson Plantation: up to 100,000 acres supporting and supported by up to 13,000 people. They key difference, of course, would be in the ownership and distribution of earnings. As the land would be cooperatively owned by all, there would be no overlord to reap excessive profits nor an impoverished underclass to generate them. All would be sustained with livable, middling incomes. Three of the existing camps, including Rohwer, along with their neighboring unutilized farmland, might be converted in this manner, especially given the improvements already undertaken. Land in Arkansas, once valued at $6 per acre, had increased in value, with Japanese American industriousness, to ten times that amount, up to $60 per acre. It made no sense to now abandon it; it would be unjust for the government to take it back and give it away. The committee proposed instead to pay for the land with a government loan, to be repaid over ten to thirty years. The combined loan for three colonies would amount to little more than the WRA annual budget, and it could provide indefinitely for up to half of the Japanese Americans remaining in the camps.[37]

It was brash but otherwise wholly un-American. Health care for all. Elder care for all. Farmland for all. Income for all. Profits for none. All excess of income over expenses would remain with the cooperative, for the benefit of all. "Non-farming residents will work . . . in industrial enterprises." Hospitals, retail and service establishments, even an "Old Folks Home," would be "operated under the co-operative system." Like the camps, all the activities of an ordinary town would be carried out, but with everyone assigned to the jobs that best suited them, without coercion. A meticulous budget followed. Every angle seemed to be covered. It was a beautiful plan.[38]

18. High school students Shigeru Igarashi, *left*, and Tsuki Kawaguchi read the closing notice at one of the cooperative stores, Jerome concentration camp, June 1944. Hikaru Iwasaki, photographer. NWDNS-210-G-H476, WRAR, SPB, NA.

The WRA balked. In the end, the government did give it all away. For a song, the Surplus War Property Administration sold the land to local farmers, at public auction, a mere $5 to $10 per acre, a fraction of its value—as Japanese Americans were sent out into a hostile world, in small numbers, isolated, like the five families who followed Yokochi Nakagawa to a village east of Little Rock. Leaders of the cooperative movement exposed the government's rhetoric of pioneering as generational and ageist. Many of the Issei, they pointed out, were "well advanced in years and tired, [and] cannot be expected to have that dashing courage and undying pioneering spirit to open a new frontier alone. For them it must be security through unity." The cooperative colony, however, became one of history's forgotten alternatives.[39]

The extended period of incarceration and the growing familiarity and comfort with life in camp meant that, for most, the prospect of leaving was daunting. Roots had been laid down; bonds of friendship and community had been developed over nearly three years. The tar-paper barracks had been personalized and made as homey as possible. Victory gardens and flowering vines were established and lovingly tended. Despite innumerable curbs to freedom in Arkansas, decamping would be a wrenching act, a time of heightened emotion, especially for these older, world-weary Issei. Kikuha Okamoto—formerly of Stockton—perfectly captured the feelings of ambivalence and uncertainty in a haiku written near the end of her tenure at Rohwer.

> Pulled out
> morning glory vines
> as day of departure nears[40]

Here, vines are endowed with dual symbolism. They represent, in one sense, the roots established while at Rohwer, the countless supportive links and connections created with other Japanese Americans there. However, vines also suggest an ensnaring, suffocating, restrictive phenomenon, perhaps the barbed-wire fence itself—and its limits to freedom of movement. The poem evidences a widely held, contradictory feeling among long-term inmates toward the prospect of camp closure and resettlement: a sense of joy at breaking free from the shackles of incarceration, tempered by a deep-seated pain at being forced, through another relocation, to sever the ties of camaraderie that had sustained them throughout the war years.

As it happened, Okamoto did not have to endure the complex, conflicted experience of leaving camp. Leaving behind her fifty-seven-year-old husband,

Shiho, Kikuha Okamoto died of a heart attack in Arkansas on 27 March 1945, only months before the abandonment of Rohwer.[41]

Set in the year 2045, one century later, in Desha County, Arkansas, a short story from the *Rohwer Outpost* depicts a future for Japanese Americans in the state. Two figures emerge from a forest into a clearing where a row of broken-down shacks are visible. The two are "apparently human beings": one "a middle aged man, of Japanese descent," covered in hair, the other his fourteen-year-old son, who asks about the site. What, exactly, are they looking at? "That, my boy, is what remains of the Rohwer Relocation Center." His curiosity stirred, the boy asks more questions.

> "Where did all the people go, Pop?"
>
> "They scattered out, Son. Relocation they called it. Some went east, others went north to places like Chicago, and others returned to California."
>
> "Where is California, Pop?"
>
> "California, my son, is on the Pacific Coast. It used to be one of our great states, until it withdrew from the Union."
>
> "Why did it withdraw, Pop?"
>
> "Because they wanted to keep it a white man's country, my son. Some of the people there didn't believe in liberty, equality, and democracy." . . .
>
> "Where did we come from, Pop?"
>
> "My friend, we descended from the people who refused to leave the center here. They just stayed here, even after the center closed."
>
> "Why did they refuse to leave, Pop?"
>
> "For various reasons, Son. Some were afraid to leave, others liked it here, and still others refused to leave on general principles."
>
> "How many of us descendants are there here, Pop?"
>
> "About 300 of us, Son, scattered throughout the woods. There may be more on the other side of the river. But here, Son, let's be getting home. It's getting late, and mother probably has fried tree roots for us tonight."[42]

The author of this story, Rohwer journalist Bean Takeda, was something of an enigma. In his regular column for the *Outpost*, he vacillated between propagandizing for the War Relocation Authority and delivering blistering critiques of the American status quo—the circumstances that had led to the concentration camps. One week his column served as a vehicle for self-aggrandizement, the next it functioned as a thoughtful, sometimes poignant social commentary on camp life. Maybe he had made a frank trade-off with administrators, who closely monitored the paper: so many column inches of official policy in exchange for a few more individual musings. Such a trade-off would not have been uncommon for Japanese Americans under incarceration: the everyday substitutions, carefully modulated, of acquiescence to authority and resistance to injustice, the measuring of limits and opportunities, the necessary and the impossible.

Writing from the South, Takeda envisions a secession from the Union predicated upon race: that of a California given over completely to racial hatred and racial purity, with all nonwhites barred. The United States, it is implied, remains otherwise intact. And amazingly, by contrast with its former West Coast state, the United States remains associated—despite the historical traces in this very woodland clearing—with "liberty, equality, and democracy."

An inventive writer who well-articulates rationales for staying, Takeda nonetheless cannot imagine a suitable existence for Japanese Americans in Arkansas, other than a primitive, rustic separatism characterized by ignorance—a lack of awareness of what goes on just the other side of the river. Further, Takeda cannot imagine a world without gender inequality. Males, father and son, move about in the public sphere—even in this restricted rural one—debating its history, charting its future. Women remain at home, in the kitchen.

Some people in the camps could imagine much more. A world where both women and men could work in jobs outside the home. Jobs they enjoyed. A world where they earned the same income. A world in which racial categories no longer mattered. A world where all human needs were accounted for and—as best as was collectively possible—were met. A world where competitive individualism, self-centeredness, and greed were discarded in favor of cooperative endeavor and collaboration, with all benefits to be shared, equally. *That* kind of equality.

Imagine.

10 | Occupation and Statehood

A PAN AMERICAN CLIPPER glided into the waters alongside Honolulu Airport at a quarter past seven in the morning, on 5 March 1946, well ahead of schedule. So the initial reception was in fact modest for what would go on to be remembered as the largest welcome ever offered to any visiting dignitary in Hawaii's history.

As the plane ferried toward the terminal, committee members raced to the phones, calling and waking others across the island. Ground workers steadied the floating aircraft, and three people dashed into formation: Richard Chinen, Yoshinao Omiya, and Dorothy Hamada. All had ties to the deactivated 442nd Regimental Combat Team. The two men were decorated veterans, now out of uniform. But "Turtle" Omiya—as he was called, for his leisurely pace in running the bases on the ball field—bore the obvious signs of war wounds. Blinded in action, he wore dark glasses and was accompanied by a seeing-eye dog—purchased with the help of the distinguished guest. In a smart dress suit, Dorothy Hamada, sister of veteran Harry Hamada, carried the leis.

Neither a military hero nor sports figure, neither an elected official nor popular entertainer, Earl Finch emerged into the sunshine, stepped ashore, and first greeted his old friend Captain Bert Nishimura, who had scrambled into place: "Well, how are ya, fella?" A newspaper photographer snapped a picture, and one onlooker said that the special visitor in plain tan suit and red tie looked just like "a regular guy." By the time Finch's companions had fetched his bags and escorted him through the building, the committee had assembled a more fitting tribute: a hundred-car motorcade. Thousands of well-wishers soon lined the streets, as Finch was driven to ʻIolani Palace. There, Acting Governor Gerald Corbett extended the official aloha, then it was on to City Hall, where Mayor Lester Petrie presented the key to the city. At the base of the war memorial, in front of the Territorial Building, Finch laid a wreath in honor of the dead, many of whom he had counted as friends. Given to few words over the course of the day, he said simply, "If I didn't do anything else after traveling 2,400 miles to come here than place this wreath, my trip would be worthwhile."[1]

By the end of the afternoon, "pretty girls with leis and kisses flustered the broad-smiling Finch," as one reporter put it, and he was up to his ears in flowers. At nightfall, above its lead news headline, "CHURCHILL BLASTS REDS," the final edition of the *Honolulu Star-Bulletin* marked the grand occasion across the very top of the page: "HONOLULU HAILS FINCH, ONE MAN USO." The rest of the territory of Hawaii swung into action too, preparing a whole slew of events in his twenty-five-day itinerary.[2]

The next evening at the welcome luau, in his first formal address before 3,500 gathered at the Palama Auditorium, Earl Finch both expressed his gratitude and staked out his position on the key political issue in postwar Hawaii: "Hawaiian hospitality is wonderful," he declared. "I hope this isn't the last time I'll come here to enjoy it. And I hope the next time I come, I'll be visiting the 49th state." The veterans of the 442nd, whose new club would soon become a major force in island politics and business, received the words with enthusiasm. Later in the month, Finch was awarded an honorary lifetime membership of the Honolulu Chamber of Commerce.[3]

It was truly an extraordinary tour. Lavish banquets, whirlwind sightseeing, solemn visits to Gold Star Mothers and other relatives of the dead. Lanai, Kauai, Maui, Molokai. Beaches, craters, canyons, caves. Ball parks, ranches, teahouses. Rotary, Lions Club, American Legion. Schools, hospitals, barracks. Churches, temples, theaters. Hekka, hukilau, sukiyaki. Fishing, dancing, singing. Finch judged a beauty contest, sat for a portrait, planted a tree, viewed a sunrise, viewed a sunset, and reviewed a harbor filled with yachts. Singer Alice Johnson penned a song and performed it in his honor, "The Earl Finch Hula"; with Bill Lincoln's Hawaiians, she recorded it as a 78 for Bell Records. Even the Republican *Maui News* sang the Democrat's praises, calling Finch a "Samaritan from the South," "a true exemplification of Christian tolerance and generosity." "There was a forerunner for such democracy," the *Hawaii Herald* proclaimed, "far back in the ages. He was a carpenter in Nazareth. . . . Mr.

Finch," the editorial concluded, had "followed In His Steps." Full-page ads were run in the newspapers, massive hand-lettered signs adorned roadsides: "ALOHA FINCH." Many expressed a desire to get close to him, a wish just to see him. The motorcade around the Big Island of Hawaii came upon a placard near Honomu, begging, "MR. FINCH PLEASE STOP HERE A MINUTE."[4]

Like Maurice Zolotow in his wartime feature for the *Saturday Evening Post,* journalists in postwar Hawaii felt obliged to explain to readers Finch's celebrity, as well as his genuineness of purpose. The *Star-Bulletin* reporter Lawrence Nakatsuka described him as "a sincere, likeable man who has been doing good turns for thousands of Japanese American soldiers because he likes them, because he doesn't like to see a 'minority group' persecuted." Indeed, whereas Finch, it emerged, had entertained British, Canadian, Chinese, and French troops in New Orleans before the arrival of Nisei soldiers in Hattiesburg back in 1943, he made *their* cause a lifelong one because they were different, they were underdogs. Shigeo Soga, editor of the *Hawaii Times*, downplayed the hero's physical attributes: "Earl Finch is not a handsome man nor an impressive one." But "he possesses a radiant and beautiful sincerity. . . . There was no motive in what he did other than a desire to befriend and make happier many men who might not have been happy." Male happiness was also on the mind of *Honolulu Advertiser* columnist Ray Coll Jr., who was part of the Finch entourage around the islands. Since some observers had described Finch as "almost a nurse" to the 442nd, his facial features "almost feminine," Coll helped shore up Finch's masculinity, with a racy report of a visit to Senator Harold Rice's ranch. There they stopped to watch cowboys "roping and branding calves, de-horning them, and picking mountain oysters." Only referred to by this euphemism, the testicles were "harvested," then they were "baked right from the branding fire in the corral." According to Coll, "Finch seemed to be enjoying himself more than at any other time during his visit to the islands. Being an old ranch hand himself he felt right at home." Another column filed by Coll acknowledged that Finch had met with some skepticism, quoting him as saying, "Because I happened to be one Southerner who treated [Japanese Americans] like human beings and took them into my home, I have been accused of many things." Those things went unspecified, but Coll reassured his readers, with a bold title, that there was "NOTHING FISHY ABOUT FINCH." Though Finch would return to Mississippi with gifts of a Hawaiian quilt made especially for his "invalid mother" and some $12,500 in donations to continue his philanthropic activities stateside, "his friends in Hawaii have urged him to come to the Territory and make his home here."[5]

At midcentury the questions posed of Earl Finch seemed to be posed of Japanese Americans and of the territory of Hawaii as well. Where did they belong? Could they be incorporated? Were they certifiably American? Were they subversive of national institutions? Somehow perverse? Finch's relationships had already challenged numerous social categories and norms, and in the postwar era it would raise further questions still about humanitarianism. Why do we help others? What sparks generosity? Is a spirit of giving necessarily compromised if it is accompanied by an erotic charge? If we are attracted to others—in any number of ways—and are moved to assist them, is our kindness thereby tainted? As Finch's benevolence took new forms, as it took him to new places in an ever-smaller Cold War world of rotary and jet-propulsion air travel, yet more would be revealed about notions of the natural and unnatural—about American and un-American activities, at home and abroad.

ADOPTING THE AMERICAN WAY

As with long-standing service and veterans organizations such as the Rotarians, Lions, and Legionnaires, the new 442nd Club in Hawaii chose the beneficiaries of its philanthropy with care. In addition to assuring the worthiness of aid recipients, members demonstrated a concern for the symbolic power of giving. Wartime mobilizations had split up families, they noted; military training and preparedness, they were less inclined to point out, included tacit and explicit support for prostitution, often seen as a detriment to the nuclear family. Inarguably, battlefield deaths left innumerable children fatherless; the bombing of civilian populations left them motherless. So the 442nd chose charitable work of both geographical and ideological associations. Whereas once their dollars helped support an army whorehouse there, they now would sponsor an orphanage in Italy. As former chaplain Hiro Higuchi explained, it would be "a good will and peace project": "We are going to try to help the unfortunates of war we saw in devastated Italian areas."[6]

Earl Finch had a similar idea. After his permanent relocation to Hawaii in the late 1940s, he hatched plans to shift his philanthropic work to occupied Japan. In the mainland United States, the Japanese American resettlement program was complete. With the benefits of the GI Bill, former Nisei soldiers there and in Hawaii were securing university degrees and moving into successful careers. The wounded had organized into Disabled American Veterans groups, a powerful political lobby. And while Finch still supported such efforts, as through his service on the territorial governor's council on veterans' affairs, he looked further afield. His gaze naturally fell on Japan.

In early 1950 Earl Finch took the first of several highly publicized trips to Tokyo. Accompanied by three Honolulu veterans, he delivered twenty thousand lollipops to orphans and distributed blankets and roughly ten thousand comic books to other needy children, earning him the nickname "Santa-san." News of these activities circulated in the English-language dailies of Japan, including the *Nippon Times* and the U.S. military's *Stars and Stripes.* Of course, Finch also looked in on one hundred–odd Nisei servicemen still enlisted as part of General Douglas MacArthur's occupation administration, mostly as interpreters. Thanks to them, he was "sukiyaki'd to death." Finch met with Tokyo's Governor Seiichiro Yasui and with Japanese Prime Minister Shigeru Yoshida, who said that "in Communist east Asia," the answer to his country's security lay "in friendly relations with the United States." Despite these serious political discussions, as well as a few business inquiries on behalf of Nisei back in Hawaii, "Finch reported that the climax of his Japan visit was the massed singing of the 'Star-Spangled Banner' by 5,000 schoolchildren in his honor on the day before he departed."[7]

The choice of lollipops was no accident. In war-ravaged Japan, where cities such as Tokyo had been nearly flattened by Allied bombs, food shortages were still the order of the day. Frozen meats and vegetables might have made more appropriate contributions. But kids love sweets. And Earl Finch delivered—for additional logistical reasons. Selling off his bowling alley, furniture shop, and clothing store back in Hattiesburg, Finch nonetheless continued to fund his homespun humanitarianism with hometown entrepreneurialism. In Honolulu he was a partner in a restaurant for a time; he backed one or two other ventures. Finally he decided on a small operation of his own. With only the help of hula sensation Ken Okamoto—whose Serenaders he continued to manage on musical tours of the islands—Finch maintained a tiny office near the back of the Farmer's Market: a "crummy hole in the wall," as one friend called it. In another of the great ironies of global capitalism, involving that age-old staple of imperial mercantilism, the territory that from the late nineteenth century was built on the backs of exploited sugarcane workers now had to receive refined sugar products from elsewhere. Earl Finch's Asiatic Trading Company imported penny candy from the mainland United States for sale across Hawaii—as well as for donations to Japan. Cheap toys and small gadgets Finch imported from Japan.[8]

In roughly ten trips to Japan over five years, Finch both met with small-scale wholesalers—his import suppliers—and dispensed his humanitarian aid, increasingly in the form of used clothing. He also took free copies of Serenaders' recordings, and he arranged exchange shipments: thousands of letters sent back and forth between Japanese and Hawaiian children, a large scale pen-pal operation. He eventually branched out from the Wakakaryo Orphanage and twenty others in Tokyo to assist children from additional islands in America's Pacific sphere of influence: Guam, Okinawa, and the Philippines.[9]

Perhaps his most expensive undertaking, Earl Finch decided to establish a scholarship fund to enable Japanese students to come to the University of Hawaii (UH). Following the small, informal educational grants he had made to Nisei on the mainland during and after the war, his first full four-year scholarship for a Japanese national to attend UH "most likely" would go to "an orphan," he announced in December 1951. He set up a modest foundation for that purpose in April 1952 and took another trip to Japan that same month. But it seems he had already decided upon the recipient. For Seiji Naya landed in Honolulu on 28 May 1952, ready for classes and ready for adoption by Earl Finch.[10]

The *Honolulu Advertiser*'s Curtis Otani called it a "beautiful gesture of human kindness in this troubled world": "Seiji Naya, who never knew a happy, normal life, now looks forward to a bright future, because an American businessman has taken an interest in him." This language of uplift seemed to overstate Naya's deprivation and understate his considerable achievements to date. In comparison to most orphans in Japan—those whom Finch met in institutions or, say, those in Hiroshima and Nagasaki—Naya had fared well. After the death of his parents and other guardians, he was put under the care of an uncle. He lived in the back room of the uncle's small factory in Osaka, acting as a night guard. Though he had twice failed English proficiency exams—thus necessitating an additional foundation year in Hawaii, for a total of five—he had excelled in boxing, thereby enrolling on a scholarship at "a rich man's school" and then a university, near Osaka. "I still don't know how he happened to pick me out of the thousands of students in Japan," Naya told Otani upon his arrival, "and it's like a dream to me to be here in Hawaii." Finch said, "I am not expecting anything in return. I only hope Seiji will make good use of my aid, and become a good citizen."[11]

In fact, Finch had met the young Japanese national not in Japan but in Hawaii, when he came to the islands as part of the national amateur boxing team. That is, Finch had first encountered the featherweight standout the year before in Honolulu, at a party thrown by his friend, 442nd boxing coach Richard Chinen, a promoter of the tour. Finch had subsequently tapped Naya to act as translator and secretary during the April 1952 trip to Tokyo and Osaka. So the two were already well-acquainted.[12]

Otani's headline for the *Honolulu Advertiser* story suggested that Naya would only be symbolically "adopted" by Finch, with quotation marks around the word. But other press accounts reported that procedures were under way for formal, legal adoption through the State Department. Whereas Otani's Horatio Alger tale failed to mention Naya's age upon arrival, the *Star-Bulletin* reported it—incorrectly—as eighteen. Born on 20 December 1932, in Hyogo Prefecture, Naya was already well over nineteen, making the adoption much more difficult. Also an issue, as Naya remembers, was the fact that Finch was "a bachelor." The Immigration and Nationality Service (INS) checked into Finch's background, securing a copy of his FBI file in late 1953. Around that time, Finch and Naya flew to Washington in an effort to arrange the adoption in person. When they met with obstacles, Finch called upon elected officials he knew to sponsor a special bill in Congress. These apparently included Louisiana Senator Russell Long. Finch also consulted his friend Adlai Stevenson. But in Cold War America, not even these powerful figures could manage an unmarried man's adoption of another man, now nearing the age of twenty-one.[13]

Still, in Hawaii Naya was known—and well-known—as Finch's son. After a mandatory stint in the dorms of the Mid-Pacific Institute, where he brushed up on his English, Naya moved on to UH and moved into Finch's "orderly little home" at 2831 Numana Road, "way up" in Kalihi Valley, Richard Chinen's neighborhood. Naya helped out around the house, cleaning and cutting the grass. He occasionally cooked, though the two tended to eat out together. Naya also did his part for the Asiatic Trading Company, usually working on Saturdays, delivering candy and scales to retailers and collecting pennies from vending machines. Though Finch loathed boxing—insisting it resulted in brain damage—he let Naya join the UH squad, since his grades were strong. "He never wanted to see my fights," Naya remembers. "He just waited for me at home until I came home." Though the two initially shared Finch's station wagon, after Naya won the NCAA featherweight championship in 1954 and 1955 and was named the NCAA's overall outstanding boxer in 1955, Finch bought him a shiny new Cadillac convertible. "Earl Finch wanted me to be a scholar," Naya recalls. "After my B.B.A., I started taking some graduate courses, then I became a much more serious student." Indeed, in the late fifties, he was awarded a teaching assistantship on the mainland, and he prepared to leave Hawaii—and leave Earl Finch—to study at the University of Wisconsin.[14]

If Earl Finch's scholarship fund was his most expensive philanthropic endeavor, his "adopting" Seiji Naya was certainly his most daring. Yes, in 1952, at the same time that the occupation of Japan ended, the McCarran-Walter Act—"the first general revision of immigration law since 1924"—removed "all racial bars to immigration and naturalization." Yes, Finch was almost universally loved in Hawaii—as the former godfather of the 442nd and now as an honorary member of the 442nd Veterans Club. He was hailed in his new role as an "unofficial ambassador of goodwill to Japan." Still, writers couldn't help but hint at homosexual undertones in his activities, even as they heaped praise on him. At a time when the conventional understanding of the adjective *gay* was in flux, they made reference to Finch's wartime trips with "British and French seamen" to "the gay night clubs" of New Orleans. And in a campy photo caption with multiple, perhaps unintended meanings, a reporter asked—under a picture of seventeen Japanese American beauty contestants and one male, Earl Finch—"WHO'LL BE QUEEN OF THE 'GO FOR BROKE' CARNIVAL?"[15]

Known as a humble, good-natured, utterly ethical businessman, Finch fended off offers of political positions. His name was floated as a candidate for territorial high sheriff in 1951, but he only accepted the post of Hawaii Democratic Party treasurer. Later a proposed run for mayor was given up, for fear it might have resulted in "a smear campaign." Besides, his heart was in philanthropy. He began to receive awards for his charitable work with young male wards of the court and for the educational stipends granted to young *men*. (It seems no women were given scholarships.)[16]

After Seiji Naya, Saburo Nishida won a Finch scholarship, then Junji Matsui, in 1955. By that time, recipients needed neither to be orphans nor to demonstrate financial hardship. The attractive twenty-year-old Matsui—whose picture appeared in the *Honolulu Advertiser*—was identified as the "son of the president of Matsui Chemical Co. in Osaka." A former student at the university where Naya had studied, he was recommended by its president. Some appealed to Finch directly, perhaps intuiting a physical component in the selection process. In a personal letter written to Finch, for example, Shinichiro Tukumaru of Meiji University—learning about the scholarships in a *Reader's Digest* article—put his measurements front and center: "Let me introduce myself. I am a Japanese young man of about 24 years of age, 6 feet tall and 150 pounds."[17]

In the 1950s, when homosexuality and espionage, perversion and subversion, were increasingly intertwined in the popular imagination, Earl Finch won a service award from the World Brotherhood organization, which also named him chairman of Hawaii's 1952 World Brotherhood week; he further was honored as the American Way/Chamber of Commerce "American of the Week" in Honolulu—all, unsurprising. Indeed, as I've shown elsewhere, such awards in the 1950s could help to normalize and naturalize the philanthropic relationships between older unmarried men and younger impressionable men. They helped to explain—if not explain away—why some men in their thirties and forties chose to spend so much time with males in their teens and twenties.[18]

Earl Finch did not adopt Nishida or Matsui, as he had Naya. He did not, it seems, grant a scholarship to Tukumaru. And on occasion, he helped circulate stories to counter the gay rumors. For example, when he arrived in Japan for another visit in 1956, people there, as in Honolulu and the mainland United States, began to speculate about his marital status. "Kinnosuke Endo, prominent restauranteur," tried "to find a bride for the quiet-talking Mississippian who, Endo thought, must be lonesome, without a good housekeeper and better-half to comfort him. Finch politely refused to have a Japanese wife—or any wife," as the *Pacific Citizen*'s Tokyo correspondent described it. Tamotsu Murayama pressed Finch for an explanation, which he apparently concocted on the spot. "The story that was never [before] told is this. Earl had a 23-year-old fiancée, a beautiful hometown girl. She just turned him down and told him everything was over when he began to spend most of his time and much of his money befriending the Nisei. He determined thus to remain single to cherish his beautiful love. She still remains his idol and sweetheart." This tale not only reassured those who heard it in Japan; it also relieved many readers of the *Pacific Citizen* back in the United States. Though the Japanese American Citizens League, at this very time, sponsored charity drag shows and printed numerous pictures of participants in its newspaper, lifelong bachelors still generated anxiety. Earl Finch, well known in JACL circles, benefited from a belief in his mythical fiancée.[19]

Since a "beautiful hometown girl" rarely escapes the close scrutiny of a small town's people, it is unlikely that the FBI would have failed to find her, when it investigated Finch back in 1944 and 1945. Clearly, Finch was engaged in queer dissembling. A particularly pervasive strategy in his native South, as elsewhere, dissembling was second nature to queer men of the 1950s, many of whom married anyway. And as research into southern queer cultures has demonstrated, the most effective means to normalize a seemingly queer, intergenerational, male-male relationship, such as that between Finch and his associates, was to familialize it—to imagine it as a father-and-son, family relationship. Acceptance by others relied in part on a position of privilege on other social scales—for example, as a white man of middle-class respectability. Thus, Finch's strategy of adoption, even if unrecognized legally, could be seen as both a characteristically southern as well as an American method of potentially transgressing in one area of conduct by virtue of remaining reassuringly normal in others.[20]

QUEERING THE EMPIRE

At war's end liberal politicians had urged "the use of American soldiers of Japanese ancestry . . . in the occupation of Japan" to "show the Japanese," in the words of Utah Senator Elbert Thomas, "that this was not a racial war, and"—seemingly without a trace of irony—"that we are willing to give members of the Asiatic races equal opportunities with anyone else." Even renunciants of American citizenship such as Tokio Yamane and dissenters such as Violet Matsuda were offered work, reflective of the postwar marriage of Allied occupation forces under MacArthur and the defeated Japanese government of a chastened Emperor Hirohito, who escaped the war crimes trials and public hangings. Now head of a single-parent household, Matsuda welcomed the employment; Yamane felt he had no other choice.[21]

Earl Finch's high-profile role in occupied Japan was more open to scrutiny. Though he plied his trade, helping to bring Japan into America's Pacific commercial empire—such that millions of trinkets in the states would read "Made in Japan"—and though he further promoted American cultural imperialism, his philanthropy tested the limits of paternalism. How was Finch understood in postwar Hawaii and Japan? How can he be understood today? As a "rice queen"?

Whether as a label or social category, whether in European or Asian languages, "rice queen" is probably a term of relatively recent vintage, used to describe particular kinds of white men—consistently involved with Asian men—for less than a century, perhaps only a few decades. That is, it may have materialized along with the emergence of the modern homosexual, usually dating from around the end of the nineteenth century. And it may have reached its zenith recently, around the high point of the American empire. The phenomenon itself may be a product of empire: a unique type of cross-cultural relationship enabled by international travel and commerce.

Even within contemporary gay cultures, "rice queen" is typically a derogatory phrase. The exclusive attraction of some white men to men of Asian descent is maligned by many gay white males, for example, who practice white racial exclusivity in their own romantic and erotic pursuits—as when they refer to some racially mixed gay bars as "Chinese take-out," emphasizing the agency of takers more than the taken. Of course, the phrase is often reappropriated with a highly self-aware goodwill among rice queens and their partners. Many cultural critics rightly worry about the white racial fetishizing of nonwhite bodies, along with further social differences and power imbalances in certain same-sex interracial relationships. "The dominant Rice Queen dynamic so prevalent in the mainstream gay community," David Eng writes, "relies upon the racist coupling of passive gay Asian (American) men . . . with objectionable Rice Queens—white men attracted to gay Asian (American) men through their orientalized fantasies of submissive 'bottoms.'" "The pervasive stereotype of the white daddy and the Asian houseboy," which Eng says again is "endemic to mainstream gay culture," leaves the latter "in a relationship of economic dependence with a homely white man twice his age." Thus, in American racial hierarchies, the rice queen's partner is often the economic inferior, an underling given over to presumably unpaid domestic labor, a male housewife, in an enslaving debt peonage. Related to that, he is assumed to take the "feminine" receptive role in intercourse.[22]

These present-day understandings don't easily map onto mid-twentieth-century, interracial, intergenerational relationships formed in nonmetropolitan, colonial, or postcolonial settings—such as incarceration-era Arkansas or Mississippi, pre-statehood/early commercial-air-travel Hawaii, or occupied Japan. Such a mapping, however, can usefully complicate our models of place- and time-specific sexual identities. Such an anachronistic move can yield a better understanding of racialized desires, both then and now. It can better illuminate not only the relatively unrestricted movements of rice queens across global empires but also the complex motivations of so-called potato queens and snow queens, curiously underrepresented in the literature. Christopher Nealon advocates just such "an antiracist reading practice that historicizes rather than punishes the racialized sexual fantasies of modern subjects, white and non-white alike." Historicizing the rice queen enables a radical historicizing of desire. And yet, as is being recognized among a generation of social constructionist historians of sexuality, we can mark desiring and desirable historical figures as utterly, temporally other, while still yearning for affiliations, a sense of queer ancestry, queer forebears. As David Halperin usefully points out, "Attempting to rediscover the indigenous terms, concepts, logics, and practices of different societies . . . need not rule out identification, attention to continuities, or forms of queer multiplicity and solidarity."[23]

Does Earl Finch's apparent desire for nonwhite men in a period of white racial supremacy even more pronounced than our own make him a more enlightened racial progressive or a more culpable racial fetishist? If gay coupling, not to say cohabitation, was much less sanctionable then, does his interracial householding—in the form of guardianship—strike us as queer ingenuity or neo-colonial dominance? If interracial gay commercial spaces such as bars and clubs were far less available at that time, does Finch become a laudable ambassador of cross-cultural goodwill or an exotic tourist of the most odious type? Obviously, these distinctions are too sharply drawn. And perhaps most importantly, they are ethical anachronisms: applying dominant early twentieth-first-century, urban, moneyed, coupled, gay white male models of economic, social, and sexual equality and reciprocity to mid-twentieth-century gay or proto-gay, largely nonmetropolitan, colonial scenarios. But that's precisely the point.

To apply a present-day cultural category to historical actors can help to denaturalize our own time and to better speculate about theirs. This is an attempt not so much to document the most exotic of American locales and behaviors from the past, but rather to determine why particular places and particular sexualities have been exoticized in American thought and, as part of that, what has been normalized, and why. In other words, we should try to understand the implicit meanings produced when Americans rearticulate those age-old binaries of self and other, insider and outsider, normal and different, us and them, here and there. To examine the subjugated, we simultaneously must analyze the privileged. Further, I believe that *only* by assessing outcast classes can we *well*-understand those in power. Only through the study of twentieth-century ideologies deemed suspect can we best comprehend American doctrines made central.

ROCK 'N' ROLL AND REDEMPTION

In 1957 rock 'n' roll came to Hawaii, thanks in large measure to Earl Finch. Of course, teenagers on the islands had been rockin' around the clock for at least two years, with radio disc jockey Tom Moffatt of the NBC affiliate KGU. Replacing the old shellac 78s, Moffatt would spin vinyl plastic 45s at chaperoned ten-cent dances such as "The Pepsi Record Hop at Rainbow Rollerland," broadcast live: "No beer, wine, or liquor sold!" But it was Earl Finch, along with business partner and 442nd veteran Ralph Yempuku, who brought the stars to the masses, live onstage. Launching the "Show of Stars," the two introduced America's newest celebrities to the rising baby-boom generation, the teenagers.

And they helped incorporate Hawaii into a booming, postwar, mass-mediated, national culture. Given his prominent role—and given his cigars, cowboy hat, and southern accent—Earl Finch soon became known as the Colonel, after Tom Parker, the manager of fellow Mississippian Elvis Presley.[24]

After promoting the Shelby Serenaders and arranging entertainers for the 442nd Club's first major fund-raising carnival, featuring Martha Raye among others, Finch was well-situated to manage island rock. From his temporary mainland base in Los Angeles—the Nisei USO that he helped establish there—Finch would go on numerous talent-spotting expeditions. With the assistance of New York pal Ed Sullivan, he met sexy young rockers from coast to coast; he arranged for touring artists to stop over in Hawaii on their way to concerts in Australia and beyond; he convinced others to come take the sun at legendary Waikiki Beach—and to expand their audience. As airlines such as Pan American World Airways advertised ever-swifter service from L.A., San Francisco, and Seattle, Hawaii increasingly was within their reach. With the advent of large-scale mechanized agriculture, manual labor in the cane fields was in decline and, with it, the power of the Big Five planters and the(ir) Republican Party. Accompanying the growth of the Democratic Party and an increase in Japanese American political power was the rise of the service economy, driven by tourism. The same planes that shuttled mainland sightseers and sunbathers to Hawaii to experience island culture brought along the harbingers of a newly national—and nationalizing—popular culture. In addition to rock 'n' roll, Earl Finch promoted wrestling and roller derby.[25]

Mixing pop and politics, the Forty-ninth State Fair in the summer of 1957 was not, of course, the forty-ninth such occasion. It was, rather, a campaign to make the territory of Hawaii the forty-ninth state in the Union. "Hot news for teenagers," Finch and Yempuku's wildly successful rock show, one of many attractions at the Honolulu Stadium, compelled them to stage their own "Show of Stars" that November at the Civic Auditorium. With trendy Tom Moffatt as MC and the Five Satins and the Four Charms as headliners, Finch arranged a showstopping encore. Long before a four-piece combo from Liverpool covered it, black southerner Chuck Berry performed his top-ten best-seller "Rock and Roll Music" to thousands of screaming teenagers in Hawaii. A formula was established, and the Show of Stars would carry on with thirty-four original programs over the course of the late fifties and the sixties.[26]

With new rock stars often unleashed with little more than one or two three-minute studio recordings in their repertoire, early rock shows featured several acts on an evening's bill, with local backing musicians. In Hawaii these were multiracial performances right from the start, though bubble-gum white artists and respectably suited black crooners predominated. In the late fifties, the Show of Stars presented groups such as the Coasters, Buddy Holly and the Crickets, the Drifters, the Everly Brothers, Little Anthony and the Imperials, the Platters, and solo acts such as Paul Anka, Frankie Avalon, Eddie Cochran, Sam Cooke, Bobby Darin, Dion, Duane Eddy, Fabian, Connie Francis, Bobby Freeman, Jerry Lee Lewis, Frankie Lymon, Teddy Randazzo, Neil Sedaka, and Ritchie Valens—who died just two months later in the plane crash with Buddy Holly and the Big Bopper. Reflecting rock 'n' roll's hybrid origins in country-and-western and rhythm-and-blues, Earl Finch booked two influential Mississippians from two distinctive musical lineages on two different occasions. At the top of the bill for the fifth Show of Stars in March 1958 was Jimmie Rodgers. By the twenty-third program in June 1960, posters trumpeted "The Most Exciting Performer Ever to Appear on the Show of Stars." "Earl Finch has brought many Negro entertainers to Hawaii," the *Honolulu Advertiser* reported, "but Bo Diddley is the first one from Earl's former home state of Mississippi." Though Finch continued to support Hawaiian artists, such as fifteen-year-old Alec Ramos—renamed Ronnie Diamond—their tours of the states never achieved national stardom for any. And although Machiko Hanamura and "Japan's top singing idol," the guitar-slinging Masaaki Hirao, appeared in Honolulu, U.S. rockers ruled.[27]

In the sixties Finch and Yempuku signed up more women, black and white: LaVern Baker, "the blonde bombshell" Jo-Ann Campbell, Brenda Lee, the Shirelles, and Dodie Stevens. The all-male Four Preps once performed an encore in drag—in muumuus—and "the crowd went absolutely nuts," as Tom Moffatt unselfconsciously punned. Though a Stevenson Democrat—never a Dixiecrat—Finch gave his blessing to John Kennedy, after the Massachusetts politician foiled Adlai's third and final bid for the presidency. Again mixing pop and politics, Finch put together "the biggest band to ever back a show here, . . . thirty-two of the best island musicians," for a Frank Sinatra fundraising gig at the Waikiki Shell, 2 October 1960, in support of the Kennedy-Johnson ticket.[28]

The generous press coverage accorded to the Show of Stars contained repeated references to the newfangled technologies that made it all possible. With precision, reporters noted airport arrivals and departures; with fascination, photographers snapped stars next to Pan Am planes, now entirely airborne craft. Writers marveled at Finch's astronomical telephone bills, necessary to book acts from the mainland and to schedule tours around the islands.

And radio contestants and other prizewinners were awarded much sought-after transpacific "fone calls." Along with the twentieth century's most important musical innovation, Tom Moffatt was keen to break into the most significant new cultural medium. Earl Finch helped. After a late fifties meeting with Dick Clark, Finch became "convinced Hawaii should have a 'Bandstand' show because of their popularity across the pond." So for a short time he produced one. It aired—in words evocative of the novelty—"on a local teevee station with Tom Moffatt as host." Finch also formed a music publishing company affiliated with the trade's principal corporate outfit, Broadcast Music, Incorporated, known by industry insiders as BMI. Just as cash cropping and transpacific shipping had once brought an island sugar economy into wider international commodity and labor markets—making it dependent thereon—so, too, radio, telephone, TV, and air travel linked Hawaiian arts and entertainment into an increasingly hegemonic, global, Americanized mass culture that threatened to overwhelm and overtake local customs, to homogenize culture across U.S. imperial possessions and beyond.[29]

The international drug trade was a vital part of that sweeping new leisure culture. A teetotaler, Earl Finch never gave himself over to the rock 'n' roll lifestyle. Though the high-stakes, high-stress work of promotions sometimes had him "gulping tranquillizer pills as if they were lemon drops," the shy Finch shied away from the bottle. He frowned on visiting musicians who took drugs, got thrown in jail, and had to be bailed out. And he was particularly put out by artists who passed joints to the young. Finch, no doubt, was most concerned about his second adopted son.[30]

In December 1956, before the advent of the Show of Stars and before Seiji Naya's departure for grad school in Wisconsin, Hideo Sakamoto had arrived in Honolulu on a Finch scholarship and was soon put to work as chauffeur to the stars. In truth, he didn't much like rock 'n' roll. But he enjoyed the company of most rockers. The "ladies" were "so nice," Jo-Ann Campbell especially. Fabian was cool. And when stars like Masaaki Hirao came, Sakamoto could respond to their needs in Japanese, and he could corral their autograph-seekers: "Some wahine [local girls] would like me to get things signed, and I'd take care of them."[31]

Sakamoto wasn't an orphan. He'd simply left his father's house when they disagreed over the appropriate line of employment for him. Sakamoto ended up as a waiter in an *izakaya*, or snack and drinks bar, in the second district of Shinjuku, in Tokyo—an area well-known, then and now, for hourly rate hotels, girlie shows, and gay bars. Though Honolulu papers reported his age as eighteen, he was in fact twenty years old when the forty-one-year-old Earl Finch walked in, two or three weeks before Christmas 1956. Finch was accompanied, as was common on his evening excursions around Tokyo, by a group of young Japanese men, including Seiji Naya's friend Hiroyuki Kaji. As Finch "knew no Japanese," Kaji handled the money—"a stack of notes"—and did most of the talking. Though Kaji insists he "didn't know about such things" as homosexuality, their first encounter with Sakamoto surely bristled with homoerotic connotations. After all, the "boys" stayed late, nearly until closing time, "drinking and talking," and they asked Sakamoto to meet them, when he got off work, back at Finch's hotel, Frank Lloyd Wright's impressive Imperial.[32]

The revered Japanese novelist Yukio Mishima imagined a similar scenario in his novel *Forbidden Colors*, written around the same time, about the same place. We might imagine Hideo Sakamoto in a situation not unlike the main character Yuichi Minami:

> Yuichi had been called over to the table . . . by a water tank in which freshwater fish were swimming. It served as a screen. In the tank green lights had been placed that gleamed through the clumps of seaweed. Set off by the lights, the ripples threw patterns on the face of the bald-headed foreigner. . . . Th[is] older man spoke no Japanese and the [young male] secretary interpreted everything he said to Yuichi. . . . First the old foreigner poured Yuichi a beer; then he praised his beauty and his youth over and over. These flowery words and phrases made for a rare translation. . . . The gist of the conversation was becoming clear. The old foreigner was a trader. He was looking for a young, beautiful Japanese youth as a companion. It was the secretary's job to select that person. The secretary had recommended many young men to the employer, but they had not appealed to him. . . . This evening for the first time, however, he had discovered the ideal youth. If Yuichi wished, a purely platonic association would be satisfactory for the time being, but, the request went, would he enter into some kind of arrangement?[33]

Indeed, *some* kind of arrangement was made between Sakamoto and Finch. For the next day, Sakamoto landed a temporary job with Finch's Tokyo-based vendor, Akachi Shokai, and he proceeded to escort the American on a sightseeing tour of Japan, taking in the vaunted temples of Nikko and Kyoto, among other things. Though Sakamoto worried a bit that Finch "might be funny," he was nonetheless drawn to the man, warm and caring as he was. Finch's pull with government officials was even greater—for a passport and visa were arranged much more rapidly than assumed possible. Just in time for Christmas, Hideo Sakamoto landed at the Honolulu Airport, where the "old man was waiting."[34]

At their new home at 2839 Puuhonua Street, Manoa, Finch introduced Hideo Sakamoto to Seiji Naya. "Finch said, this is your brother. You and Seiji are brothers." Recalling his own experience as a newcomer to Hawaii, Naya took him under his wing. As Sakamoto remembers, "This guy was so nice to me. Everyplace I'd go, he said, 'This is my younger brother.' . . . And I met a lot of people. I met all the guys, his girlfriend. Everybody tried to help me. I thought, god damn I have a good brother. I was very happy at that time." But soon Naya left for Wisconsin and married his girlfriend, Jane.[35]

Sakamoto carried out many of the household tasks and small business chores that before had fallen to Naya. While Sakamoto distributed candy, restocked vending machines, and took deposits to the bank, Earl Finch's life became more sedentary. Mainland contacts firmly established, he traveled less. Prematurely bald, and increasingly it seemed prematurely aged, Earl Finch began to grow fat, no doubt nibbling on his own Kona Coffee Candy, as well as the sweets of American suppliers like Brach's. Sakamoto would "vacuum

19. Hideo Sakamoto, c. 1957. Courtesy of Hideo Sakamoto.

the house and do some outside yard work," cook occasionally, but they went to restaurants more often. There was the rare cross-cultural dispute: Sakamoto didn't like Finch wearing his shoes in the house, and Finch didn't like Sakamoto slurping his soup. Finch was sometimes exasperated by Sakamoto's habit of putting all the groceries in the freezer, including the shaving cream—a lighthearted story repeated again and again in the local press. But both men were easygoing on the whole, never sparring partners. In the morning Finch would ask, "'Hideo, what shall I wear today?' I had to tell him." Then, "every other day, I'd have to shave him. . . . He'd lie down, and I'd put on the lotion." At day's end they'd each return to the house—and to their respective corners, their respective sides of the bed. "I'd go there and take off the shirt and lie. He'd lie down and go to the other side and watch TV. The same thing. I used to copy him in that kind of stuff. . . . He was like a father, so I was happy."[36]

Not as successful in school as Naya, Sakamoto nonetheless graduated from McKinley High in 1960, a newsworthy item for the *Honolulu Advertiser*. Instead of university, he went on to a technical institute, in part to maintain the student visa. He remembers with candor the difficulties of immigration and the implications for family relations. After two years Sakamoto "graduated from technical school, [but] the old man wanted me to stay in Hawaii forever." So Sakamoto enrolled for yet "another two years," taking "a different trade." "Then, I met one girl; she had American citizenship. I got married." Sakamoto then quit school and started working in an auto body shop. As Naya went on to a successful career in academe, eventually returning to the University of Hawaii as professor of economics, Sakamoto's ambitions were more measured.[37]

Though Sakamoto "felt sorry" that he could not help satisfy Earl Finch's sexual needs, he took for granted that Finch found physical release when he traveled. There were "so many gay boys in Japan." But an assumed sexual nonconformity did not give countenance to gender nonconformity. Like former 442nd chaplain Hiro Higuchi of Hawaii, Earl Finch wanted his sons to be *men*. During the war Higuchi had written home to his wife about the proper way to raise their seven-year-old son, the delicate balancing of respectful virtue and masculine posturing: "I would like to have him grow up with pride in self and family. To be kind, and understanding of other people's problems and to learn to sympathize with those in trouble or need, . . . be a good Christian. . . . I should like to have him be courteous and simple in his ways," he summarized, "but not too feminine." Similarly, in what might today be referred to as a case of internalized homophobia, Finch grew angry at Sakamoto, "scolded" him, only once, when he stayed out all night with Masaaki Hirao. Finch thought

Hirao was "mahu." "Masaaki's not sissy," Sakamoto insisted. The two, in fact, had been out chasing women together. Earl Finch was, of course, jealous, imagining Hirao and Sakamoto engaged in activities he found desirable and dangerous. He wanted to protect his son from a world of menace, even as he had protected himself through the years, by virtue of lies—noble lies, those that shelter people from harm, from violence. Finch grew more possessive of Sakamoto, protective, until finally he gave his blessing to his marriage.[38]

Surveying the previous two decades, Earl Finch grew sad, dejected. In 1943 he'd met Nisei soldiers in Hattiesburg, and they had totally changed his life. They became "my boys," and he followed them to Hawaii. By 1953 they had changed their own lives. Those who survived the war had been buoyed up by the postwar economic boom and their own industriousness into new positions of political and economic authority. They had mostly married and settled down. (With husband Bill at her side, Finch's friend Mary Nakahara Kochiyama, speaking at the 442nd's tenth-anniversary gathering, claimed them all as "*my* boys.") Finch then had found new boys to help in Japan; he had brought a couple back to live with him in Hawaii. But by 1963 Seiji Naya and Hideo Sakamoto were married, fathering children of their own.[39]

America thrived. American families multiplied. Earl Finch began to sink in drink and despair.

Some called it a heart attack. Some called it a broken heart. Earl Finch died on 26 August 1965 at St. Francis Hospital in Honolulu, age forty-nine.

Newspapers disagreed over the number attending the funeral. The *Advertiser* reported three hundred; the *Hochi* called it four hundred. Whereas territorial Governor Gerald Corbett had officially welcomed him to paradise almost two decades before, Earl Finch received his final, formal sendoff from state Governor John Burns. For in the intervening years, statehood had came to Hawaii, thanks in large measure to Japanese Americans—who supported it at rates higher than Chinese, haoles, and native Hawaiians—and especially to Japanese American veterans, friends of Earl Finch who had led the charge and now held the highest elective offices. Senator Daniel Inouye's telegram from Washington was read at the ceremony. Representative Spark Matsunaga—later, senator—was honorary pallbearer.[40]

Burns's eulogy celebrated the man and his life: "He could not find it in himself to harbor animosity or enmity toward even those who failed to understand his feeling of brotherhood with his fellow man. He was truly a selfless man. In all his deeds he was most unassuming, seeking neither recognition nor reward." No doubt aware of the less flattering gossip about the dearly departed, Burns nonetheless concluded: "In mourning his passing the finest tribute we can pay to him is to model our attitudes toward our fellow man in the mold fashioned by Earl." The Honolulu Police Choral Group sang three hymns: "Holy, Holy, Holy," "Queen's Prayer," and—in both English and Hawaiian—"Savior, Like a Shepherd Lead Us." From Central Union Church, the casket was taken for burial to the Diamond Head Memorial Park, overlooking the Pacific.[41]

Earl Finch's legacy would remain. The Hawaii unit of the Military Order of the Purple Heart was christened the Earl Finch Memorial Chapter. Mary and Bill Kochiyama named their firstborn son William Earl Kochiyama. Apparently dozens did likewise. And as the saying now goes, if you're Japanese American and you're called Earl, you're no doubt named after Finch.[42]

In its glowing tribute to "The Man from Hattiesburg," the *Star-Bulletin* described Finch's acculturation in Honolulu, letting slip that persistent rumor: "Earl Finch became a part of Hawaii, continuing his good works, unselfishly, quietly, while building success as an importer and promoter of entertainment—a field more noted for its tub-thumpers than for its shrinking violets." In his column for the *Advertiser*, Eddie Sherman revealed about his friend, seemingly for the first time in print, the foremost "ugly rumor." Finch had told Sherman, apparently without explicitly denying it, "I was accused of being a homosexual." Business partner Ralph Yempuku heard the rumors too, but he chose not to believe them. Like tales of Finch's wealth, he thought they were overstated. "He was too good to be a good businessman. . . . He didn't take advantage. . . . That's why he never made it. Too scrupulous, too kind, too gentle, too moral. Always giving things away. Damn fool. But that's what he was." A failed capitalist—a new kind of hero who during America's most violent years of war and empire never took up arms against another, who instead modeled love for others—Earl Finch left final instructions to Seiji Naya and Hideo Sakamoto, joint heirs of his modest estate, to give a portion to *one other person.*[43]

Reporters had disagreed over the number of relatives who survived the deceased. Some made no reference to survivors. Traditionalists counted only one, his brother, Master Sergeant Roy "Brownie" Finch, of Cleveland, Ohio. Others tallied three, with reference to "two wards" or "two adopted sons": Seiji Naya and Hideo Sakamoto. The real news for many, since Finch had fallen out of the headlines of late, was the discovery—at the funeral—of a fourth survivor: "adopted son" Bernard Pahee. Little was known about Pahee except that he obviously was neither white nor Japanese, given his last name; he was native or part-Hawaiian. Early in life, he had been legally adopted by an Oahu family. Now Bernie was, in some sense, partnered with Finch.[44]

Sakamoto had met Pahee. And he spoke of Earl Finch's relationship to him with blunt sincerity: "He loved Bernie." Around the time of the funeral, Sakamoto happened upon Pahee at the Finch home: "He was alone by himself—and crying like a wahine." Crying like a girl. Sakamoto guessed he understood Earl Finch's attraction to Pahee. "Bernie was a nice-looking boy, . . . nice-looking bugger." But he looked less like a brother and "more like a sister."[45]

Though raised to go to church, Earl Finch didn't. At least not in the islands. Though often compared to Christ, he likely expected no paradise beyond Hawaii. The consummate entertainer, a promoter par excellence, Finch may have gone—I prefer to think—to that great big party in the sky. Yukio Mishima described its earthly counterpart, the closest we know of heaven, in the twelfth chapter of *Forbidden Colors*: "Gay Party." There, on the outskirts of Tokyo, beautiful young Japanese men and older white Western men mingled and flirted. Yuichi brought roses. "He was quite drunk, so he greeted everyone" in English, with a heavily accented "Merry Christmas!" "For a moment the boys felt as if they were abroad. In fact, many boys like them had been abroad, accompanied by their lovers. The stories that appear under the newspaper headline, 'Public Spirit Far from Home/Houseboy Studies Abroad,' generally have this meaning."[46]

Epilogue

A MECHANICAL BIRD dropped slowly from the sky. It hiccuped, sputtered, careening downward, ever larger. On the streets, on their way to lunch, people stopped and watched. Children between classes shielded their eyes as they gazed up beyond the sun. Clearly, the plane was in distress.

A person pointed, shouted, voice rising: It's coming this way. Peals of laughter, more frightened squeals, the sighs of the world-weary. Indeed, the plane was about to land. Steps quickened, hearts raced. The sound above grew louder, then died away altogether. It was strangely silent, as if time itself were suspended. The thing floated over the straight dirt road. Its wheels hovered a few feet above, now just inches. Everybody was now yelling, running. Get out of the way, get out of the way. A prolonged, heavy scratch, and the thing touched down, rolling, finally reaching a standstill. People ran back onto the street, the crowd clapped and cheered. And two white men in uniform climbed out, jumped down, and greeted their hosts: We ran out of gas.

From the motor pool, big cans were retrieved, and all were astounded that the ordinary fuel got the engine revved up again. Again, the way was cleared, the pilots raced down the street—this time shaking the windows in the apartments, sending vibrations throughout the camp—and took to the sky. Boys and girls waved, adults chatted a bit further. As the white strangers flew away, free as a bird, the prisoners at Jerome resumed their ordinary activities.

On to the dining hall, back to the books.[1]

DEMOCRACY IS FOR THE UNAFRAID

After war's end, in a bid to return the nation to calm and to a particular form of social order, Representative John Rankin insisted that "it's about time all those minorities stopped attacking the white majority in this country." He and some of his colleagues, he said, were doing their level best, "trying to keep the flag over a white government." Around the same time, black writer Chester Himes challenged this very notion. He anticipated, indeed welcomed the day when racial minorities, combined, would become the majority in America. "The eventual peace of the world and the continuation of progress depend upon the white man's ability to live in equality, integrity, and courage in a civilization where he is outnumbered by people of other races." (Of course, on a global scale, the "other races" were already the majority.) For the white man, Himes asserted, "*it is imperative that he be unafraid.*"[2]

"A race that is afraid bands in mobs to lynch, murder, intimidate, and destroy members of other races." In Mississippi in the 1950s, teenager Emmett Till was lynched in the Delta, Mack Charles Parker near the Gulf Coast. In June 1963, Fannie Lou Hamer was beaten nearly to death in the Winona jail, and Medgar Evers was gunned down in the driveway of his home in Jackson. In 1964 three civil rights activists were killed and buried in an earthen dam near Philadelphia. Though new trials would be called decades later in an attempt to reverse the rulings of earlier all-white juries—and Hollywood would rewrite these and related histories as tales of the heroism of liberal white attorneys and law officers, in films such as *A Time to Kill*, *Ghosts of Mississippi*, and *Mississippi Burning*—Rankin's home state both took on mythical otherworldly qualities and exhibited the grubby residues of America's very real racist roots.[3]

"People who are afraid are cruel, vicious, furtive, dangerous; they are dishonest, malicious, vindictive; they destroy the things of which they are afraid, or are destroyed by them." In 1945 Rankin started a fistfight on the floor of the House with Representative Frank Hook of Michigan. In 1946 he called Walter Winchell a "slime-mongering kike," and two weeks later he nearly came to blows with House majority leader John W. McCormack of Massachusetts in an argument over the House Un-American Activities Committee, which Rankin now controlled. Later that year Rankin attacked a photographer—scratching and clawing, shouting: "I'll kill you, I'll kill you!" The committee went on to investigate the so-called Jewish conspiracy in Hollywood, and it succeeded in blacklisting any number of actors, directors, and other employees of the film industry for their alleged communist affiliations. Following on their heels in the early 1950s, a lowly senator from Wisconsin named McCarthy took the red scare to new heights; emulators throughout the country harassed and interrogated suspected homosexuals in an equally rabid lavender scare, as historian David Johnson has described it.[4]

"The industrialist who is afraid sabotages public welfare; the politician who is afraid attacks leaders of weakly supported causes to hide his own compromises; the statesman who is afraid endeavors to isolate his nation; and the government head who is afraid fails in the execution of laws, both national and international." Rankin offered bills to "prohibit membership in, or participation in the activities of, the Anti-Defamation League" and to "terminate the participation of the United States in the United Nations." He said communists in Korea threatened "the life of this nation [and] the very life of civilization itself."[5]

"The other races of the world," Chester Himes concluded, "have reached the point where they will no longer be exploited or subdued."

CLICHÉS OF AMERICAN HAPPINESS

Stories of failed immigration are rarely told. Not here. Not in the land of opportunity. The failed immigrants have gone away, so they can't tell them. Perhaps they never learned the language in which stories circulate here, so they never had the means. Maybe they believed the hype—*anyone can make it*—and so they believed that the failure exposed inadequacies deep within themselves, not in their adopted land. Their stories, if told, would reflect poorly on them—would be *made* to reflect poorly on them. Mind you, troublemaker Tokio Yamane went on to become vice president of a major food manufacturer in Japan—"successful" in the American sense of the word. He lived a long, full life, outside Hiroshima.

We're left with the lucky ones, the ones who get to keep telling the tales. They appear in the history books. They appear on *Oprah.* Doesn't anyone notice that the once-destitute refugee from Ethiopia, the Harvard commencement speaker—no doubt as admirable in his tenacity as the black TV presenter suggests, with her winning smile—is also stunningly good-looking, incredibly telegenic? Likewise the Harvard-bound high school valedictorian, this "penniless" refugee from Cuba: handsome. Don't we all know how such factors *help* some get ahead? ("You are the maker of your own destiny," he insists. "You can dictate whether you want to succeed or not.") Haven't we all, by now, read the studies: the identical qualifications, the identical résumés, the different outcomes? Oprah is adamant, spellbound: "Their stories are some of the greatest you've *never* heard." Never? I seem to hear them all the time.[6]

The cheerleaders for America, the promoters of the American way, often fail to account for the failed, the exploited, the abject, those who—in fact—make it all possible, those whose deprivation enables the abundance. For some. Those stories are *depressing*. As poet Wesley McNair asks, "How does one respond to the maddening complaint of students that poetry which touches on sorrow is 'depressing,' when it is clear they speak for the American culture that made them?"[7]

As McNair explains, "I am told that a Russian does not, like the American, say 'Fine' when asked how he is. He uses the time-honored gesture of the hand that says 'So-so' or 'It could be worse.'" Similarly, in England the most common reply is "Not *too* bad." "The response suggests an awareness of life's difficulties, which we as human beings know well, wherever we live. It does not insist on happy endings or the need to provide them; it suggests that things do not always come out well, that life includes not only affirmation but tragedy. It is not mythic; it is realistic."

McNair continues, "Can anyone deny how dangerous our compulsion to affirm is to the affairs of the nation? Unable to address our complex social problems—the widening gap between rich and poor, the racial troubles, the murderous acceleration of American life—with a confident smile, we tend to deny them, insisting that 'we're number one' in the great country of happy outcomes, whether that country exists or not."

"The student who finds poetry that is grim or sorrowful 'depressing,'" McNair concludes, "must be shown the impoverishment of his American mythology . . . —developing early and late a tragic vision that might mature the nation." "Or," one last option, "show the student through his writing itself—how his truest work comes from dealing with the flawed world as he really knows it, beyond the clichés of American happiness."

Beyond the clichéd "lessons of history," scholar Gerda Lerner speaks of history's value, most broadly conceived, as a testament to our collective immortality. If nothing else, history shows that, as a group, the human race has endured, faithfully affirming life's worth. Despite the horrors we continue to visit upon one another, barring the most catastrophic of scenarios, there is hope that we will continue to endure. There is hope.[8]

Even so, within that bracing, lengthy timeline of humanity, I have often dwelled in this book on moments of mortality. Some might find my "touching on sorrow" very dismal indeed. The narration of countless deaths herein may

20. Cemetery, Rohwer concentration camp, November 2004. Photograph by the author.

seem morbid in the extreme. But how else should one document twentieth-century injustice—particularly World War II? How sorrowful, how pitiful, was humankind's capacity to rain down death upon itself. Unprecedented. The number of lives lost in a single incident at Hiroshima. The lives lost in the calculated program of genocide that was the Holocaust, history's single largest slaughter of Jews. And homosexuals. And disabled people. And other outcast groups.

The comparison between the unconstitutional incarceration of Americans of Japanese descent sixty-five years ago and the unconstitutional incarceration of so many Americans of Middle Eastern descent today has become so commonplace that it is now asserted on the most mainstream of U.S. television programs, not just *The Daily Show with Jon Stewart*, but also *The Practice* and *West Wing*. Still, some American officials insist such totalitarian measures are justified, necessary, a moral duty.

Any person, any group, any nation that dwells in moral superiority has the potential to take us all to the ultimate precipice.

A week later, in August 1943, another mechanical bird dropped from the sky. It crashed seven miles south of the Jerome camp, toppling pine trees and electricity poles. Every apartment, every club meeting, the night school, the hospital, went dark. Radios, sewing machines, the record players at the dances, all were quiet. An hour later, still nothing.[9]

Might as well go to bed.

Acknowledgments

BOOKS, LIKE PEOPLE, incur debts. Here, the amounts outstanding are so large that they could never be repaid. The creditors have been ringing, sending e-mail, but only with more offers of support. Otherwise, I'd have to call this chapter 11.

Mark Santoki contacted me about midway through the project. As a result, it was changed dramatically. He generously shared his knowledge and all of the primary materials he had collected for his own book on Earl Finch. A former editor of the *Hawaii Herald*, with an M.A. in American studies from the University of Hawaii, he well understood my particular concerns, and he respected my emphasis on a different set of questions, trusting as I did that it would only augment the legacy of his great-uncle. I'd also like to thank his aunt and uncle, Jane and Seiji Naya, for twice welcoming me to visit with them in Honolulu. Sumiye and Hideo Sakamoto also kindly invited me into their home, for what proved a most moving interview. Of other individuals who granted me interviews—all cited in the notes—I'm particularly grateful to Violet Matsuda de Cristoforo and Tokio Yamane for sharing not only their recollections but also items from their personal collections. Very sadly, the two have passed away.

Many of this book's debts are financial, involving considerable sums of money and valuable residencies. A grant from the Arts and Humanities Research Council enabled completion of the manuscript. On three occasions, the British Academy sponsored presentations of the work in the United States. The Fulbright Commission awarded me a semester in Tokyo. The Rockefeller Foundation granted one month in Bellagio, where I enjoyed the creative companionship of Jon Appleton, Kathy and Mark Berger, Laura Lio, and Diane and Wesley McNair. I benefited from visiting fellowships at Senshu University, Tokyo, and the Beatrice M. Bain Research Group on Gender at the University of California, Berkeley. There I profited on countless occasions from conversations with Ellen Fernandez-Sacco, Lynne Horiuchi—whose *Nuts and Bolts: A Guide to Researching Japanese American Internment in the Bancroft Library* is indispensable—and, of course, Patricia Penn Hilden and the reading group she organized. Thanks are also due to Evelyn Nakano Glenn and Gee Gee Lang.

Scholarly conversations often happen in highly structured but nonetheless enlightening contexts. I've been able to share portions of this work and benefit from feedback at conferences of the American Studies Association; Asia Pacific Studies Institute, with thanks to Sucheta Mazumdar; Association for Asian American Studies; Organization of American Historians; Nordic Association for American Studies, with thanks to Eric Guthey; and the Southern Historical Association; as well as the "Creating 'America'" symposium at Senshu University. Among a host of helpful formal commentaries offered at these events, I've been assisted most by those of Elena Tajima Creef, Yoko Shimada, and Susan Smith, as well as Roger Daniels, who furthermore lent a hand throughout the course of the project. Any historian of Japanese American incarceration knows his name; most all get to know his generosity as well. At conferences and by e-mail, Greg Robinson passed on suggestions and citations more often than I could count. The two, professors Daniels and Robinson, applied themselves wholeheartedly to reading the entire manuscript for the publisher. It was significantly improved as a result.

Colleagues at King's College London and, before that, the University of York shared not only their funds but also their insights and moral support. At King's, in the Department of American Studies, I'm particularly grateful to Kimberly Springer, along with Susan Castillo, Janet Floyd, Stephanie Green, Gail MacLeitch, Alan Marshall, Rosa Torrado, and Shamoon Zamir; in the Queer@King's Humanities Research Centre, Mark Turner, along with Simon Gaunt, Laura Gowing, Hector Kolias, and Robert Mills; and Lawrence Freedman, Keith Hoggart, Clare Lees, John Stokes, and Ann Thompson. At York, in the Department of History, I'd like to thank Peter Biller, Joanna de Groot, and—as always—Allen Warren; in the Centre for Women's Studies, Stevi Jackson and Ann Kaloski Naylor.

I enjoy ongoing relationships with three other British institutions of higher education where I have presented my work and otherwise, I hope, helped out. Thanks go to the Institute for Historical Research, its American History and Women's History seminars, and especially Marybeth Hamilton; to members of the American Studies faculty at the University of Reading, notably Jonathan Bell, David Brauner, and Emily West; and to the Department of American Studies at the University of Sussex, including Richard Follett, Maria Lauret, and Clive Webb.

I was enriched by a semester's affiliation with two Japanese universities during 2002. I appreciated the support at Tsuda College of Masako Iino, Misao Nishida, Takeshi Suzuki, Yuko Takahashi, and Kiyofumi Tsubaki; and at Kyoritsu Women's University of Hayumi Higuchi, Kazuo Ohta, and Hisako Yanaka. Of several graduate students at Tsuda, I greatly enjoyed conversations with Tomomi Iino, Junko Itaba, Mieko Kojima, and Kaori Yoshikawa, as well as Michiko Sakaguchi, whose friendship and insight carried over through her period of study in London. As interview interpreters and as translators, Hayumi Higuchi and Tomomi Iino proved invaluable. Sahori Watanabe translated Japanese sections from the Jerome and Rohwer camp newspapers; Junko Itaba translated portions of books on Japanese American incarceration available only in Japanese. And I received periodic translation services and other assistance from Takashi Ebina, Ryan Inouye, and Shotaro Yamamoto. Also, I'd like to thank Sachiko Takita-Ishii of Yokohama City University for sharing her work and that of her students. To all, *arigato gozaimasu!*

I was fortunate to be a member of the three-year study group, "Interrogating Race and National Consciousness in the Diaspora," under the auspices of the Japan Society for the Promotion of Science. Coordinated by Hayumi Higuchi, with colleagues from Japan, Mexico, the United Kingdom, and United States, this group greatly shaped my thinking about the project. In concert with their work, portions of chapter 6 first appeared in *Transforming Anthropology* 14 (Spring 2006): 187–95, and, with a skillful Japanese translation by Erika Sunada, in *American Histories: Narrating the Routes to Nationhood*, edited by Ken Chujo and Hayumi Higuchi (Tokyo: Sairyusha, 2006), 139–61. Portions of chapters 4 and 5 first appeared in *History Workshop Journal* 52 (Autumn 2001): 122–51.

Guest lecture invitations are commonly extended by scholars who have come to know one's work and not only endorse it but help to refine it. I'm grateful to Allison Wallace at the University of Central Arkansas and, during 2002, at the University of the Ryukyus; Charles McGraw at the University of Connecticut; Michael Coventry at Georgetown University; Marina Moskowitz and Simon Newman at the University of Glasgow; Ted Ownby at the University of Mississippi; Sandy Darrity and Steve Levine at the University of North Carolina; Yujin Yaguchi at the University of Tokyo; Leisa Meyer at the College of William and Mary; and Anne Enke and Nan Enstad at the University of Wisconsin.

To the extent that I remain at all current in the rapidly expanding literatures of my chosen fields, I'm indebted to my doctoral students, past and present, who repeatedly challenge me with smart questions: Zoe Colley, Deborah Lafferty, Althea Legal-Miller, Jason Narlock, Emma Robertson, Cara Rodway, and Brock Thompson. Along with other former University of York undergraduates cited in the notes, I would like to thank Peter Barker and Elliot Thomas for their insights into this project.

In addition to the University of California, Berkeley, I undertook considerable secondary research at the British Library and Library of Congress, as well as the libraries of Harvard University and the University of Cambridge, with thanks for college residencies there to Ross McKibbon and Michael O'Brien. Archives that enabled my primary research are outlined in this book's notes, and I thank the staff at those institutions. But I would especially like to acknowledge the assistance of Andrea Cantrell at the University of Arkansas. Thanks also to John Kirk for his suggestions about doing research in Arkansas. Also, in the Department of History at the University of Arkansas, Linda Coon and Jeannie Whayne were warmly welcoming.

Catherine Nickerson first sparked my interest in Japanese American incarceration when I was still a graduate student at Emory University. Friendships and intellectual companionships begun there in Atlanta continue to enrich my work, especially those with Cynthia Blakely, Steve Blakeslee, Nancy Koppelman, and Allen Tullos. I enjoy the continuing support and insights of Lynne Adrian, Beth Bailey, David Brody, Fitz Brundage, Dan Carter, Michael Cowan, Anna Davin, Martin Duberman, Lisa Duggan, Judith Halberstam, Chad Heap, Nancy Hewitt, Morris Kaplan, Richard King, Steven Lawson, Meredith Raimondo, David Serlin, Nayan Shah, Juliann Sivulka, and Brian Ward.

The University of Chicago Press backed the project early and often. Kudos to Tim McGovern for fail-safe tips, advice, and organizational know-how. Three cheers for Erin DeWitt, for her superb handling of the copyediting and page proofs. Through good times and bad, the latter unrelated to this work, Doug Mitchell has been an editor of unmatched grace and sensitivity—and a reliable friend. Years pass, but that remains a constant.

If much of my work is given over to questioning some of our fundamental assumptions about gender and sexuality, home and family, it is perhaps ironic—but, I feel, not contradictory—that my last heartfelt thanks must go to my own family of origin. My brother has never failed to ask, with genuine interest, “How’s the work going?” Financially, and in many other respects, my mother has supported it. My sister has been an unwavering source of love and encouragement; her companionship I treasure. Finally, this book’s principal moral frameworks—concern for the downtrodden, indignation in inequality, anger at injustice, the imperative of action—were first taught to me by my father, to whom this book is dedicated. He didn’t live long enough to see it, but I like to think he would have recognized his unmistakeable imprint upon it. We have to continue to struggle, don’t we, for generation after generation.

Notes

PRINCIPAL PRIMARY SOURCES AND ABBREVIATIONS USED

Archival and Manuscript Collections

GLBTHS	Gay, Lesbian, Bisexual and Transgender Historical Society, San Francisco, CA
OP	Jiro Onuma Papers
JANM	Japanese American National Museum, Los Angeles, CA
BCAA	Buddhist Churches of America Archive
HC	George Hoshida Collection
IC	Jack Iwata Collection
MC	Walter Wataru Muramoto Photographic Collection
ROHP	REgenerations Oral History Project
SC	Henry Sugimoto Collection
LC	Library of Congress, Washington, DC
PPD	Prints and Photographs Division
MDAH	Mississippi Department of Archives and History, Jackson, MS
JRP	John Rankin Papers
JRS	John Rankin Subject File
NA	National Archives and Records Administration, Washington, DC
RG 210	Record Group 210
SPB	Still Picture Branch, College Park, MD
WRAR	War Relocation Authority Records

UA	University of Arkansas Libraries Special Collections Division, Fayetteville, AR
CC	Arthur Brann Caldwell Collection
GC	Nathaniel R. Griswold Collection
JRCC	Jerome Relocation Center Collection
JRCL	Jerome Relocation Center Final Report, Legal Division
LC	Robert A. Leflar Collection
LUC	Ulys A. Lovell Collection
TC	Virginia Tidball Collection
USJRC	U.S. Jerome Relocation Center Records
USWRAJ	U.S. War Relocation Authority Jerome Relocation Center Records
UCB	University of California, Bancroft Library, Berkeley, CA
DP	Violet K. de Cristoforo Papers
JAERR	Japanese American Evacuation and Resettlement Records
USFBI	U.S. FBI War Relocation Authority Files
UH	University of Hawaii Library Special Collections, Manoa, HI
HCP	Hilo Coast Processing Company Records
HHP	Hiro Higuchi Papers
HSPA	Hawaiian Sugar Planters' Association Plantation Archives
VST	Veterans Student Themes
USM	University of Southern Mississippi, Archives, Hattiesburg, MS
CCR	Hattiesburg Area Chamber of Commerce Records
HUSO	Records of the Hattiesburg USO Club
UW	University of Washington Manuscripts, Special Collections, University Archives, Seattle, WA
MP	Minoru Masuda Papers
NS	Richard Hideo Naito Scrapbook

Periodicals

AG	*Arkansas Gazette*
CSR	*Camp Shelby Reveille*
DC	*Denson Communiqué*
DHSC	*Denson High School Condensor*
DHSV	*Denson High School Victoria*
DM	*Denson Magnet*
DT	*Denson Tribune*
FG	*Fresno Grapevine*
HA	*Honolulu Advertiser*
HH	*Hawaii Herald*
HSB	*Honolulu Star-Bulletin*
HT	*Hawaii Times*

JDN	*Jackson Daily News*
MCA	*Memphis Commercial Appeal*
PC	*Pacific Citizen*
RJHR	*Rohwer Junior High School Roar*
RO	*Rohwer Outpost*
RP	*The Rohwer Pen*
RSHH	*Rohwer Senior High School Hi-Lites*
SAP	*Santa Anita Pacemaker*
USOB	*The USO Bulletin*

INTERVIEWS

By Author

Violet Kazue de Cristoforo, Salinas, CA, 28 December 2000
Hiroyuki Kaji (Tomomi Iino, interpreter), Tokyo, Japan, 11 June 2004
Tom Moffatt, Honolulu, HI, 28 December 2005
Seiji Naya, Honolulu, HI, 11 January 2003, 21 December 2005
Hideo Sakamoto, Aiea, HI, 4 January 2006
Herbert Sasaki, Hattiesburg, MS, 22 September 1999
Virginia Tidball, Fayetteville, AR, 12 April 2000
Tokio Yamane (Hayumi Higuchi, interpreter), Fukuyama, Japan, 28 July 2002

By Mark Santoki

Kazu Iijima, n.p., February 2000
Yuri Kochiyama, Oakland, CA, 2 February 2000
Tom Moffatt, Honolulu, HI, n.d. (1999)
Seiji Naya, Honolulu, HI, n.d. (1999)
Dan Ogata, n.p., July 2000
Hideo Sakamoto, Aiea, HI, n.d. (1999)
Herbert Sasaki, n.p., n.d. (1999–2000)
Ralph Yempuku, Honolulu, HI, n.d. (1999)

By Mississippi Oral History Program

Herbert Sasaki, Hattiesburg, MS, 23 October 1998

NOTES TO INTRODUCTION

1. Mark Santoki, *The Earl Finch Story: One Man U.S.O.* (Honolulu: Seiji F. Naya, 2000). This volume—in English and in Japanese translation by Yoshitaka Yoshioka—is based on Santoki's four-part feature story published in the *Hawaii Herald*, 17 September; 1, 15 October; 5 November 1999. See also Audrie Girdner and Anne Loftis, *The Great Betrayal: The Evacuation of the Japanese-Americans during World War II* (London: Macmillan, 1969), 274,

330; Hawaii Nikkei History Editorial Board, *Japanese Eyes, American Heart: Personal Reflections of Hawaii's World War II Nisei Soldiers* (Honolulu: University of Hawaii Press, 1998), 59, 122; and Dillon S. Myer, *Uprooted Americans: The Japanese Americans and the War Relocation Authority during World War II* (Tucson: University of Arizona Press, 1971), xxi, 149.

2. *DT*, 24 December 1943, 11 April 1944; "War Relocation Authority, Monthly Report, for Month Ending April 30, 1944, Reports Office, Jerome Center," part II, section 5, reel 138, JAERR, UCB; Earl M. Finch, letter to E. B. Whitaker, 31 March 1944, RG 210, entry 48, box 206, folder 67.011, WRAR, NA; Wallace Tsuda, letter to Earl M. Finch, 17 April 1944, RG 210, entry 48, box 206, folder 67.011, WRAR, NA; Nat R. Griswold, letter to Mr. Finch, 10 April 1944, series 1, folder 5, GC, UA; Nat R. Griswold, letter to Earl M. Finch, 12 December 1944, series 1 folder 6, GC, UA; Earl M. Finch, three letters to Ray D. Johnston, 7 May 1945, series 1, folder 11, GC, UA.

3. Keiso Nakagawa, "Earl M. Finch," n.d. [1946], manuscript W24.01:7936d, VST, UH; *PC*, 3 July, 4 September, 27 November 1943, 19 August, 16 September, 4 November, 12, 16 December 1944, 3 March, 16 June, 17 November 1945. Mark Santoki says that of several Japanese American soldiers on the streets that day, Finch spoke to one in particular who stood in front of the drugstore, Richard Chinen of Hawaii, now deceased. *Earl Finch Story*, 9. Depending upon how it's told, the story of Finch's first meeting a soldier looking into a storefront can take on a decidedly queer cast, as idle window-shopping, with its reflective properties, has proven very significant in gay male cruising at least since the nineteenth century. Mark Turner, *Backward Glances: Cruising the Queer Streets of New York and London* (London: Reaktion, 2003).

4. *Saturday Evening Post*, 10 November 1945.

5. As will become apparent throughout the course of this book, of the rich literature in critical race studies, my analysis is particularly indebted to Michael Omi and Howard Winant, *Racial Formation in the United States: From the 1960s to the 1990s*, 2nd ed. (New York: Routledge, 1994).

6. Gina Marchetti, *Romance and the "Yellow Peril": Race, Sex, and Discursive Strategies in Hollywood Fiction* (Berkeley: University of California Press, 1993); Chester Tanaka, *Go for Broke: A Pictorial History of the Japanese American 100th Infantry Battalion and the 442nd Regimental Combat Team* (Novato, CA: Presidio Press, 1982), 79.

7. *Saturday Evening Post*, 10 November 1945. See also the photographic frontispiece to Santoki, *Earl Finch Story*, in which the author does identify Finch's five Nisei dinner companions: James Kamo, Kiyoshi Kuramoto, Robert Oda, Ken Otagaki, and Tamotsu Shimizu.

8. *Saturday Evening Post*, 10 November 1945; *HA*, 12 March 1946; George Aki, letter to Mark Santoki, 3 April 2000, in author's possession.

9. Subject: Earl Finch, File Number: 105-3749, Federal Bureau of Investigation, Washington, DC.

10. Ibid.; *Saturday Evening Post*, 10 November 1945.

11. Finch File, FBI; Allan Bérubé, *Coming Out Under Fire: The History of Gay Men and Women in World War II* (New York: Free Press, 1990); John Howard, *Men Like That: A Southern Queer History* (Chicago: University of Chicago Press, 1999).

12. *Saturday Evening Post,* 10 November 1945; *Hattiesburg American,* 16 September 1943; *Polk's Hattiesburg City Directory, 1939* (Birmingham, AL: R. L. Polk, 1939), 88.

13. On constructions of the rice queen stereotype, see David L. Eng, *Racial Castration: Managing Masculinity in Asian America* (Durham, NC: Duke University Press, 2001), 158–59, 220. See also my discussion in chapter 10.

14. Daniel K. Inouye, with Lawrence Elliott, *Journey to Washington* (Englewood Cliffs, NJ: Prentice-Hall, 1967), 96–98; Tanaka, *Go for Broke,* 79 (emphasis added).

15. Mike Masaoka, with Bill Hosokawa, *They Call Me Moses Masaoka: An American Saga* (New York: William Morrow, 1987), 142; Thelma Chang, *"I Can Never Forget": Men of the 100th/442nd* (Honolulu: Sigi Productions, 1991), 126; Santoki, *Earl Finch Story,* 49.

16. Rickie Solinger, *Beggars and Choosers: How the Politics of Choice Effects Adoption, Abortion, and Welfare in the United States* (New York: Hill and Wang, 2001), 24; William Petersen, *Japanese Americans: Oppression and Success* (New York: Random House, 1971), 190–95. See also Peter Hayes and Toshie Habu, *Adoption in Japan: Comparing Policies for Children in Need* (London: Routledge, 2006); Kirsten Lovelock, "Intercountry Adoption as a Migratory Practice: A Comparative Analysis of Intercountry Adoption and Immigration Policy and Practice in the United States, New Zealand, and Australia in the Post W.W. II Period," *International Migration Review* 34 (Autumn 2000): 907–49; and Ray A. Moore, "Adoption and Samurai Mobility in Tokugawa Japan," *Journal of Asian Studies* 29 (May 1970): 617–32.

17. Herbert Sasaki, interview with author, Hattiesburg, Mississippi, 22 September 1999.

18. Erica Harth, ed., *Last Witnesses: Reflections on the Wartime Internment of Japanese Americans* (New York: Palgrave, 2001), 1–2.

19. *DT,* 19 March 1943.

20. On describing the phenomenon as "incarceration" as opposed to the more popular "internment," see Roger Daniels, "Words Do Matter: A Note on Inappropriate Terminology and the Incarceration of the Japanese Americans," in *Nikkei in the Pacific Northwest: Japanese Americans and Japanese Canadians in the Twentieth Century,* ed. Louis Fiset and Gail Nomura (Seattle: University of Washington Press, 2005), 183–207.

Roger Daniels, *Concentration Camps North America: Japanese in the United States and Canada during World War II* (Malabar, FL: Robert E. Krieger, 1981); Michi Nishiura Weglyn, *Years of Infamy: The Untold Story of America's Concentration Camps,* updated ed. (Seattle: University of Washington Press, 1996); United States Commission on Wartime Relocation and Internment of Civilians, *Personal Justice Denied: Report of the Commission on Wartime Relocation and Internment of Civilians* (Seattle: University of Washington Press, 1997).

Richard Drinnon, *Keeper of Concentration Camps: Dillon S. Myer and American Racism* (Berkeley: University of California Press, 1987); Brian Masaru Hayashi, *Democratizing the Enemy: The Japanese American Internment* (Princeton, NJ: Princeton University Press, 2004); Peter Irons, *Justice at War: The Story of the Japanese American Internment Cases* (New York: Oxford University Press, 1983); Greg Robinson, *By Order of the President: FDR and the Internment of Japanese Americans* (Cambridge, MA: Harvard University Press, 2001); Page Smith, *Democracy on Trial: The Japanese American Evacuation and Relocation in World War II* (New York: Simon and Schuster, 1995). Bill Hosokawa, *Nisei: The Quiet Americans* (New York: William Morrow, 1969); Masaoka, *They Call Me Moses*; Myer, *Uprooted Americans.*

The historiography—and, often self-published, hagiography—of Nisei war service is extensive, particularly as regards the 442nd Regimental Combat Team. See Chang, *"I Can Never Forget"*; Lyn Crost, *Honor by Fire: Japanese Americans at War in Europe and the Pacific* (Novato, CA: Presidio Press, 1994); Masayo Umezawa Duus, *Unlikely Liberators: The Men of the 100th and 442nd* (Honolulu: University of Hawaii Press, 1987); Hawaii Nikkei History Editorial Board, *Japanese Eyes, American Heart*; Dorothy Matsuo, *Boyhood to War: History and Anecdotes of the 442nd RCT* (Honolulu: Mutual, 1992); Thomas D. Murphy, *Ambassadors in Arms* (Honolulu: University of Hawaii Press, 1955); Franklin Odo, *No Sword to Bury: Japanese Americans in Hawaiʻi during World War II* (Philadelphia: Temple University Press, 2004); Orville C. Shirley, *Americans: The Story of the 442d Combat Team* (Washington, DC: Infantry Journal Press, 1946); Tanaka, *Go for Broke*; and Jack K. Wakamatsu, *Silent Warriors: A Memoir of America's 442nd Regimental Combat Team* (Los Angeles: JKW Press, 1992). For a less flattering account, see Tamotsu Shibutani, *The Derelicts of Company K: A Sociological Study of Demoralization* (Berkeley: University of California Press, 1978).

21. Mine Okubo, *Citizen 13660* (New York: Columbia University Press, 1946); Monica Sone, *Nisei Daughter* (Boston: Little, Brown, 1953); Yoshiko Uchida, *Desert Exile: The Uprooting of a Japanese American Family* (Seattle: University of Washington Press, 1982).

Paul Bailey, *City in the Sun: The Japanese Concentration Camp at Poston, Arizona* (Los Angeles: Westernlore Press, 1971); John Modell, ed., *The Kikuchi Diary, Chronicle from an American Concentration Camp: The Tanforan Journals of Charles Kikuchi* (Urbana: University of Illinois Press, 1973); Douglas W. Nelson, *Heart Mountain: The History of an American Concentration Camp* (Madison: State Historical Society of Wisconsin, 1976); Sandra C. Taylor, *Jewel of the Desert: Japanese American Internment at Topaz* (Berkeley: University of California Press, 1993); Edward H. Spicer et al., *Impounded People: Japanese-Americans in the Relocation Centers* (Tucson: University of Arizona Press, 1969).

For an excellent evaluation of Adams's work, related volumes, the images of Dorothea Lange and Toyo Miyatake, and the visual iconography of incarceration broadly, see Elena Tajima Creef, *Imaging Japanese America: The Visual Construction of Citizenship, Nation, and the Body* (New York: New York University Press, 2004).

Leonard Broom and John I. Kitsuse, *The Managed Casualty: The Japanese-American Family in World War II,* reprint ed. (Berkeley: University of California Press, 1973). For a more subtle analysis of Japanese American families and the changes wrought by incarceration, see Harry H. L. Kitano, *Japanese Americans: The Evolution of a Subculture* (Englewood Cliffs, NJ: Prentice-Hall, 1969), 36–37, 60–78.

Arthur A. Hansen and David A. Hacker, "The Manzanar Riot: An Ethnic Perspective," *Amerasia Journal* 2 (Fall 1974): 112–57; Gary Y. Okihiro, "Japanese Resistance in America's Concentration Camps: A Re-evaluation," *Amerasia Journal* 2 (Fall 1973): 20–34, and "Religion and Resistance in America's Concentration Camps," *Phylon* 45 (1984): 220–33; Douglas W. Nelson, *Heart Mountain: The Story of an American Concentration Camp* (Madison, WI: State Historical Society, 1976).

22. Eric Muller, *Free to Die for Their Country: The Story of the Japanese American Draft Resisters in World War II* (Chicago: University of Chicago Press, 2001), 6–7, 198. The back cover of a recent book describes the incarceration as a "shamefully un-American event,"

and in his foreword to the book, John Kuo Wei Tchen writes: "Vigilante Americanism such as the scapegoating of Japanese Americans during World War II must be challenged and replaced with a truly patriotic ethic of Americanism." Karen L. Ishizuka, *Lost and Found: Reclaiming the Japanese American Incarceration* (Urbana: University of Illinois Press, 2006), xii. By contrast, Gary Okihiro's useful essay surveying the long history of Japanese American experience, including discrimination and incarceration, is entitled "An American Story," in *Impounded: Dorothea Lange and the Censored Images of Japanese American Internment*, ed. Linda Gordon and Gary Y. Okihiro (New York: W. W. Norton, 2006), 46–84.

Creef perceptively pinpoints a related popular and historiographical bent: "Silence has largely dominated Japanese American internment history for the last fifty years. What is new, however, are the current ways in which mainstream American culture has just recently chosen to break its own silence in remembering, even re-visioning, internment history itself as the truest test of Japanese American loyalty in a move that actually recoups minority history into an American success story. The internment narrative in this version details how the Japanese Americans may have suffered as a group (a long time ago), but have since managed to pull themselves up by the bootstraps and become successful model minority citizen subjects." She sees this as part of a larger "kind of multicultural representation appropriate for a 'New World Order' where reconciliation, assimilation, and celebration have replaced the real tensions inherent in an ethnically diverse culture." *Imaging Japanese America*, 168–69. I build on these ideas at the end of this introduction.

The problematic term "model minority," as applied to Japanese Americans, was coined by William Petersen in a 1966 article for the *New York Times Magazine*, eventually resulting in the publication cited above, *Japanese Americans: Oppression and Success* (New York: Random House, 1971).

23. Hayashi, *Democratizing the Enemy*, 5–6. Eiichiro Azuma, *Between Two Empires: Race, History and Transnationalism in Japanese America* (Oxford: Oxford University Press, 2005), 5. An examination of experiences elsewhere in the Americas might begin with Lane Ryo Hirabayashi, Akemi Kikumura-Yano, and James A. Hirabayashi, eds., *New Worlds, New Lives: Globalization and People of Japanese Descent in the Americas and from Latin America in Japan* (Stanford, CA: Stanford University Press, 2002); and Pamela Sugiman, "Memories of Internment: Narrating Japanese Canadian Women's Life Stories," *Canadian Journal of Sociology* 29 (2004): 359–88.

24. *Personal Justice Denied*, 107, 135, 138–39, 150, 157, 183, 209.

25. John Rankin, *Congressional Record*, 15 December 1941. Bilbo's reputation as a bigot extended even into popular culture. The 1948 Academy Award–winning film *Gentleman's Agreement* (dir. Elia Kazan, Twentieth Century-Fox), about anti-Semitism, mentioned him repeatedly by name. Thurmond's reputation reaches into our own day.

26. Mae M. Ngai, *Impossible Subjects: Illegal Aliens and the Making of Modern America* (Princeton, NJ: Princeton University Press, 2004), 198.

27. David Harlan, *The Degradation of American History* (Chicago: University of Chicago Press, 1997), xvi.

28. Jonathan Ned Katz, *Gay American History: Lesbians and Gay Men in the U.S.A.* (New York: Thomas Y. Crowell, 1976), 23–24.

NOTES TO CHAPTER ONE

1. Violet de Cristoforo, interview with author, Salinas, California, 28 December 2000; Violet Kazue de Cristoforo, ed., *May Sky, There Is Always Tomorrow: An Anthology of Japanese American Concentration Camp Kaiko Haiku* (Los Angeles: Sun and Moon Press, 1997), 15, 283; Violet Matsuda de Cristoforo, *Poetic Reflections of the Tule Lake Internment Camp, 1944* (Salinas, CA: Violet Matsuda de Cristoforo, 1987), 35.

Now deceased, Violet de Cristoforo (born Kazue Yamane) told me candidly in the year 2000 of her occasional lack of memory regarding aspects of her early days. Thus, some inconsequential details of her graduation ceremony are imagined here. Likewise below, I have attempted to creatively narrativize elements of her infancy and that of her brothers, with the help of primary sources on Hakalau Plantation. As regards her parents, there are a few contradictions and inconsistencies across de Cristoforo's published and unpublished works, her interview and correspondence with me, and my interview with her brother Tokio Yamane, cited below. I have attempted to remove such elements or, again, when inconsequential, to imagine and narrativize their details.

2. Robert D. Ward, "The Origins and Activities of the National Security League, 1914–1919," *Mississippi Valley Historical Review* 47 (June 1960): 65.

3. Howard Zinn, *A People's History of the United States, 1492–Present*, rev. updated ed. (New York: HarperPerennial, 1995), 305–6.

4. Ibid., 309; Robert H. Wiebe, *The Search for Order, 1877–1920* (New York: Hill and Wang, 1967), 225.

5. Tamara Plakins Thornton, "Deviance, Dominance, and the Construction of Handedness in Turn-of-the-Century Anglo-America," in *Moral Problems in American Life: New Perspectives on Cultural History*, ed. Karen Halttunen and Lewis Perry (Ithaca, NY: Cornell University Press, 1998), 80–100. See also Siobhan Somerville, *Queering the Color Line: Race and the Invention of Homosexuality in American Culture* (Durham, NC: Duke University Press, 2000).

6. For a compelling fictionalized account of these events, see Martin Duberman, *Haymarket: A Novel* (New York: Seven Stories, 2003).

7. Cecilia Elizabeth O'Leary, *To Die For: The Paradox of American Patriotism* (Princeton, NJ: Princeton University Press, 1999), 61.

8. Mark Twain, *Mark Twain in Eruption* (New York: Harper and Brothers, 1940), 30; Richard Slotkin, *Gunfighter Nation: The Myth of the Frontier in Twentieth-Century America* (New York: Atheneum, 1992), 51–52. On Twain, imperial masculinity, and sexuality in Hawaii, see Amy Kaplan, *The Anarchy of Empire in the Making of U.S. Culture* (Cambridge, MA: Harvard University Press, 2002). On Roosevelt, imperial masculinity, and sexuality, see Sarah Watts, *Rough Rider in the White House: Theodore Roosevelt and the Politics of Desire* (Chicago: University of Chicago Press, 2003).

9. Joan Jacobs Brumberg, "Zenanas and Girlless Villages: The Ethnology of American Evangelical Women, 1870–1910," *Journal of American History* (September 1982): 347–71; Olive Anderson, "The Growth of Christian Militarism in Mid-Victorian Britain," *English Historical Review* 86 (January 1971): 70; David J. Hellwig, "Afro-American Reactions to the

Japanese and the Anti-Japanese Movement, 1906–1924," *Phylon* 38 (March 1977): 94. See also Marc Gallicchio, *The African American Encounter with Japan and China: Black Internationalism in Asia, 1895–1945* (Chapel Hill: University of North Carolina Press, 2000).

10. Catherine A. Lutz and Jane L. Collins, *Reading National Geographic* (Chicago: University of Chicago Press, 1993), 18.

11. Anti-Imperialist League of New England, *La Política de Los Estados Unidos* (Boston: Foreign Language Press, 1903). See also Anti-Imperialist League Collected Records, 1899–1919, Swarthmore College Peace Collection, Swarthmore, Pennsylvania. Jim Zwick, ed., *Anti-Imperialism in the United States, 1898–1935*, http://www.boondocksnet.com/ai/ (30 March 2005).

12. Gary Okihiro, *Cane Fires: The Anti-Japanese Movement in Hawaii, 1865–1945* (Philadelphia: Temple University Press, 1991), 4.

13. Ibid., 4–5. On Jeffersonian thinking, see Henry Nash Smith, *Virgin Land: The American West as Symbol and Myth* (Cambridge, MA: Harvard University Press, 1950).

14. Noenoe K. Silva, *Aloha Betrayed: Native Hawaiian Resistance to American Colonialism* (Durham, NC: Duke University Press, 2004), 145–59; David J. O'Brien and Stephen S. Fugita, *The Japanese American Experience* (Bloomington: Indiana University Press, 1991), 3–13. See also John E. Van Sant, *Pacific Pioneers: Japanese Journeys to America and Hawaii, 1850–1880* (Urbana: University of Illinois Press, 2000). On Hawaiians recruited into the service of American imperialism, see Davianna Pomaika'i McGregor, "Engaging Hawaiians in the Expansion of the U.S. Empire," *Journal of Asian American Studies* 7 (October 2004): 209–22.

15. De Cristoforo, interview; Shiori Nomura, "Japanese Immigrant Women and the Idea of 'Home': Voices in *The Nichibei (Japanese American Daily)*, 1914–1924" (Ph.D. diss., University of Birmingham, 2006), 274; Ronald Takaki, *Pau Hana: Plantation Life and Labor in Hawaii, 1835–1920* (Honolulu: University of Hawaii Press, 1983), 77–80. On American women's domestic labor during the nineteenth century, see Susan Strasser, *Never Done: A History of American Housework* (New York: Pantheon, 1982).

16. Paul R. Spickard, *Japanese Americans: The Formation and Transformations of an Ethnic Group* (New York: Twayne, 1996), 73–75.

17. Ronald Takaki, *A Different Mirror: A History of Multicultural America* (Boston: Little, Brown, 1993), 246–51. See also his *Strangers from a Distant Shore: A History of Asian Americans* (Boston: Little, Brown, 1989) and *Pau Hana*. Evelyn Nakano Glenn, *Issei, Nisei, War Bride: Three Generations of Japanese American Women in Domestic Service* (Philadelphia: Temple University Press, 1986), 44; Edward D. Beechert, *Working in Hawaii: A Labor History* (Honolulu: University of Hawaii Press, 1985), 72. See also John Liu, "Race, Ethnicity, and the Sugar Plantation System: Asian Labor in Hawaii, 1850–1900," in *Labor Immigration under Capitalism: Asian Workers in the United States before World War II*, ed. Lucie Cheng and Edna Bonacich (Berkeley: University of California Press, 1984).

18. Eric Foner, *Reconstruction: America's Unfinished Revolution, 1863–1877* (New York: Harper and Row, 1988); Lacy K. Ford, ed., *A Companion to the Civil War and Reconstruction* (Oxford: Blackwell, 2005); Silva, *Aloha Betrayed*, 136, 144–45; Mae M. Ngai, *Impossible Subjects: Illegal Aliens and the Making of Modern America* (Princeton, NJ: Princeton University

Press, 2004), 27–50. See also Najia Aarim, *Chinese Immigrants, African Americans, and Racial Anxiety in the United States, 1848–82* (Urbana: University of Illinois Press, 2003).

19. Takaki, *A Different Mirror,* 253, 262; Time Book, 1921–1936, pv. 1, Pepeekeo Personnel and Payroll, HCP, HSPA, UH.

20. Okihiro, *Cane Fires,* 66, 83, 103–5.

21. Takaki, *Pau Hana,* 54, 73–75, 89–91, 117–19; Time Book, 1921–1936, pv. 1, Pepeekeo Personnel and Payroll, HCP, HSPA, UH; Pete Daniel, *The Shadow of Slavery: Peonage in the South, 1901–1969* (1972; repr., Urbana: University of Illinois Press, 1990).

22. Takaki, *A Different Mirror,* 257–61; Historical Chart, 1900–1941, box 2, folder 14, Honomu Miscellaneous Records, HCP, HSPA, UH.

23. Insurance Valuation, Dwelling #802, Camp 18, Waikaumalo-Yamagata, 1946, box 4, folder 5, Hakalau Building Valuations, HCP, HSPA, UH. This representative structure, photographed by insurers in 1946, was built in 1920. Others from this camp, where the Yamanes apparently lived, date from as early as 1911.

24. Photographs and valuations of all these structures can be found in box 4, folders 1–6, Hakalau Building Valuations, HCP, HSPA, UH.

25. Ibid., folders 1–3.

26. Ibid., folder 1.

27. Roger Daniels, *The Politics of Prejudice: The Anti-Japanese Movement in California and the Struggle for Japanese Exclusion,* 2nd ed. (Berkeley: University of California Press, 1977), 98–105; Desmond King, *Making Americans: Immigration, Race, and the Origins of the Diverse Democracy* (Cambridge, MA: Harvard University Press, 2000), 199–228; Tomiko Kakegawa, "The Press and Public Opinion in Japan, 1931–1941," in *Pearl Harbor as History: Japanese-American Relations, 1931–1941,* ed. Dorothy Borg and Shumpei Okamoto (New York: Columbia University Press, 1973), 534–35.

About the Americanization campaign in Hawaii, Eileen H. Tamura adds, "Both Americanizers and Japanese agreed that the Nisei should adopt American ways, but each group has its own interpretation of what that meant. . . . [They] agreed that the Nisei should be patriotic American citizens, obey laws, work diligently, and learn to read, write, and speak English. But while Americanizers believed that the Nisei should discard all vestiges of and pride in Japanese culture, become Christians, and stay in their 'place' as plantation laborers, Japanese thought the Nisei should fuse the best of Japanese and American cultures and move up the occupational and social ladders . . . aspiring to American middle-class life. Ironically the Nisei goal of economic advancement was more mainstream American than the Americanizers' goal for them, that they be good, docile plantation workers." *Americanization, Acculturation, and Ethnic Identity: The Nisei Generation in Hawaii* (Honolulu: University of Hawaii Press, 1994), xiv, 15, 152. See also Noriko Asato, *Teaching Mikadoism: The Attack on Japanese Language Schools in Hawaii, California, and Washington, 1919–1927* (Honolulu: University of Hawaii Press, 2006), 21–41.

28. Tokio Yamane, interview with author, Fukuyama, Japan, 28 July 2002. The best primary source on the earthquake remains *The Great Earthquake of 1923 in Japan* (Tokyo: Bureau of Social Affairs, 1926). On a Japanese Christian evangelist converted in the after-

math of it, see Shotaro Kogo, *Earthquake Evangelist: A Spiritual Odyssey* (London: Japanese Evangelistic Band, 1977).

29. De Cristoforo, interview with author; de Cristoforo, *May Sky*, 283; de Cristoforo, *Poetic Reflections*, 35.

30. De Cristoforo, interview with author.

31. Ibid. The bookshop description is taken from a 1938 photograph shown to me by Violet de Cristoforo, in the possession of her estate.

32. De Cristoforo, *May Sky*, 208–9; Nomura, "Japanese Immigrant Women," 166.

33. Yamane, interview with author.

NOTES TO CHAPTER TWO

1. *Congressional Record*, 75th Congress, 1st session, 1937, 142775: 13822. So proud was Rankin of his speech on the "So-Called Anti-Lynching Bill" that he had it published by the Government Printing Office as a broadside for distribution to constituents, hardly unusual for members of Congress. I cite the broadside, as found in JRS, MDAH.

2. *Congressional Record*, 76th Congress, 3rd session, 1940, 204192: 17798.

3. Rankin delivered virtually identical versions of the speech in the 1920s, 1930s, and 1940s, and a number of political emulators from the local to the national level took up and elaborated the discourse. The views were both widely circulated and widely held. The second of these two speeches, referenced immediately above, was made on 10 January 1940 and also was entitled "So-Called Anti-Lynching Bill." I have interwoven the two to give a sense of Rankin's distinctive turns of phrase, rhetorical strategies, and consistent thematic concerns.

4. Jacquelyn Dowd Hall, "'The Mind That Burns in Each Body': Women, Rape, and Racial Violence," in *Powers of Desire: The Politics of Sexuality*, ed. Ann Snitow et al. (New York: Monthly Review Press, 1983), 328–49.

5. Neil McMillen, *Dark Journey: Black Mississippians in the Age of Jim Crow* (Urbana: University of Illinois Press, 1989), 228–37.

6. Joel Williamson, *A Rage for Order: Black-White Relations in the American South since Emancipation* (New York: Oxford University Press, 1986); Deborah Gray White, *Ar'n't I a Woman?: Female Slaves in the Plantation South*, rev. ed. (New York: W. W. Norton, 1999); Robyn Wiegman, *American Anatomies: Theorizing Race and Gender* (Durham, NC: Duke University Press, 1995), 99.

7. W. Fitzhugh Brundage, *Lynching in the New South: Georgia and Virginia, 1880–1930* (Urbana: University of Illinois Press, 1993).

8. Grace Elizabeth Hale, *Making Whiteness: The Culture of Segregation in the South, 1890–1940* (New York: Pantheon, 1998), 199–239.

9. Dan T. Carter, *Scottsboro: A Tragedy of the American South*, rev. ed. (Baton Rouge: Louisiana State University Press, 1979).

10. Gaylord C. Kubota and Bob Dye, "The Lynching of Katsu Gota: The Tragic Fate of a Successful 'First Ship' Japanese Immigrant," in *Hawai'i Chronicles: Island History from the Pages of* Honolulu *Magazine*, ed. Bob Dye (Honolulu: University of Hawaii Press, 1996),

197–214; Dennis M. Ogawa, *Jan Ken Po: The World of Hawaii's Japanese Americans* (Honolulu: University of Hawaii Press, 1973), 141–42; Roger Bell, *Last among Equals: Hawaiian Statehood and American Politics* (Honolulu: University of Hawaii Press, 1984), 57. See also William D. Carrigan and Clive Webb, "The Lynching of Persons of Mexican Origin or Descent in the United States, 1848 to 1928," *Journal of Social History* 37 (Winter 2003): 411–38; William D. Carrigan, *The Making of a Lynching Culture: Violence and Vigilantism in Central Texas, 1836–1916* (Urbana: University of Illinois Press, 2004); and Michael J. Pfeifer, *Rough Justice: Lynching and American Society, 1874–1947* (Urbana: University of Illinois Press, 2004).

11. Carter, *Scottsboro*, 98–103; Lillian S. Robinson, "'There Are No Beaches in Hawai'i': Race, Rape, and Capital Punishment in the Massie Case" (paper presented to the American Studies Association Annual Conference, Atlanta, GA, 13 November 2004).

12. Bell, *Last among Equals*, 57–59.

13. Joane Nagel, *Race, Ethnicity, and Sexuality: Intimate Intersections, Forbidden Frontiers* (New York: Oxford University Press, 2003), 155; Paul R. Spickard, *Japanese Americans: The Formation and Transformations of an Ethnic Group* (New York: Twayne, 1996), 28.

14. Several draft biographies can be found in JRS, MDAH. See also JRP, MDAH. The great bulk of Rankin's papers are on deposit at the University of Mississippi Special Collections, where they remain sealed from researchers.

15. *Collier's*, 1 December 1945. On support for the TVA, see Rankin's speeches, "The Tennessee Valley Authority, Muscle Shoals—The 'Yardstick' for Light and Power Rates," *Congressional Record*, 73rd Congress, 2nd session, 1934, 40647: 9845; "Power Policies of the Roosevelt Administration—The TVA Yardstick Rates," *Congressional Record*, 73rd Congress, 2nd session, 1934, 67958: 10577; "How the Power Trust Is Robbing Mississippi," *Congressional Record*, 74th Congress, 1st session, 1935, 10302: 11772. See also *MCA*, 21 June 1939.

16. *Congressional Record—House*, 76th Congress, 2nd session, 1940, 10819–10822.

17. Thomas N. Boschert, "Rankin, John Elliott," *American National Biography Online*, February 2000, http://www.anb.org/articles/06/06/06-00542.html (accessed 10 July 2003); Richard Gid Powers, *Not without Honor: The History of American Anticommunism* (New York: Free Press, 1995), 131; *Collier's*, 1 December 1945.

18. William F. Rickenbacker, "A Short History of the Committee; and a Chronology, 1946–1960," in *The Committee and Its Critics: A Calm Review of the House Committee on Un-American Activities*, ed. William F. Buckley Jr. (New York: Putnam's, 1962), 100–101. See also Walter Goodman, *The Committee: The Extraordinary Career of the House Committee on Un-American Activities* (New York: Farrar Straus and Giroux, 1968).

19. Willmoore Kendall, "Subversion in the Twentieth Century," in *The Committee and Its Critics*, ed. Buckley, 67–68.

20. Kenneth O'Reilly, *Hoover and the Un-Americans: The FBI, HUAC, and the Red Menace* (Philadelphia: Temple University Press, 1983), 7–8, 15. On "Rankin's Coup," securing permanent committee status for HUAC, see Goodman, *The Committee*, 167–89.

21. William F. Buckley Jr., "The Committee and Its Critics," in *The Committee and Its Critics*, ed. Buckley, 24. Emphasis added.

22. Kendall, "Subversion," 102; Michi Nishiura Weglyn, *Years of Infamy: The Untold Story of America's Concentration Camps*, updated ed. (Seattle: University of Washington Press,

1996), 33–53; Greg Robinson, *By Order of the President: FDR and the Internment of Japanese Americans* (Cambridge, MA: Harvard University Press, 2001), 94–102.

23. Beth Bailey and David Farber, *The First Strange Place: Race and Sex in World War II Hawaii* (Baltimore: Johns Hopkins University Press, 1992), 140.

24. Ibid., 194.

25. Bell, *Last among Equals*, 64–65.

26. Ibid., 134; Roger Daniels, *Prisoners without Trial: Japanese Americans in World War II* (New York: Hill and Wang, 1993), 90.

27. Robinson, *By Order of the President*, 25; Warren I. Cohen, *The Asian American Century* (Cambridge, MA: Harvard University Press, 2002), 11.

28. Weglyn, *Years of Infamy*, 33. For a useful account of representations of 7 December 1941, see Emily S. Rosenberg, *A Date Which Will Live* (Durham, NC: Duke University Press, 2005).

29. Weglyn, *Years of Infamy*, 77; United States Commission on Wartime Relocation and Internment of Civilians, *Personal Justice Denied: Report of the Commission on Wartime Relocation and Internment of Civilians* (Seattle: University of Washington Press, 1997), 38, 68; Robinson, *By Order of the President*, 73–124; Roger Daniels, *Concentration Camps North America: Japanese in the United States and Canada during World War II* (Malabar, FL: Robert E. Krieger, 1981), 45–70. Emphasis added.

30. Weglyn, *Years of Infamy*, 14; *Collier's*, 1 December 1945; Daniels, *Prisoners without Trial*, 35; Daniels, *Concentration Camps North America*, 43; *The Forum of Stockton, California*, n.d. [1944].

31. *PC*, 1 July 1944; Jason Morgan Ward, "'No Jap Crow': Japanese Americans Encounter the World War II South," *Journal of Southern History* 73 (February 2007): 90; quoted in Caleb Foote, *Outcasts! The Story of America's Treatment of Her Japanese-American Minority* (New York: Fellowship of Reconciliation, 1943), 18.

NOTES TO CHAPTER THREE

1. Mary Tsukamoto and Elizabeth Pinkerton, *We the People: A Story of Internment in America* (Elk Grove, CA: Laguna, 1987), 7, 29. See also John Tateishi, *And Justice for All: An Oral History of the Japanese American Detention Camps* (New York: Random House, 1984), 3–15.

2. Tsukamoto and Pinkerton, *We the People*, 22. On Executive Order 9066, see Greg Robinson, *By Order of the President: FDR and the Internment of Japanese Americans* (Cambridge, MA: Harvard University Press, 2001).

3. Tsukamoto and Pinkerton, *We the People*, 7, 11, 23–24.

4. Ibid., 8, 10, 73.

5. Ibid., 30, 270. As Fumiko Nakamura has said, "We Okinawans have always been made to feel inferior by the Japanese" (53). For her oral history, ranging from the 1920s to the postwar occupation and beyond, see Ruth Ann Keyso, *Women of Okinawa: Nine Voices from a Garrison Island* (Ithaca, NY: Cornell University Press, 2000), 33–53. See also Furuki Toshiaki, "Considering Okinawa as a Frontier," and Yoko Sellek, "Migration and the Nation-State: Structural Explanations for Emigration from Okinawa," in *Japan and*

Okinawa: Structure and Subjectivity, ed. Glenn D. Hook and Richard Siddle (London: RoutledgeCurzon, 2003), 21–38, 74–92.

6. Tsukamoto and Pinkerton, *We the People*, 30–31, 40–41; Shiori Nomura, "Japanese Immigrant Women and the Idea of 'Home': Voices in *The Nichibei (Japanese American Daily)*, 1914–1924" (Ph.D. diss., University of Birmingham, 2006), 182–83. The poem, published in Japanese, was translated into English by Nomura.

7. Maurice Walk, letter to Philip M. Glick, 8 September 1943, series 1, folder 2, JRCC, UA. Of the numerous works on Japanese American incarceration, I have relied most heavily on Roger Daniels, *Concentration Camps North America: Japanese in the United States and Canada during World War II* (Malabar, FL: Robert E. Krieger, 1981); Edward H. Spicer et al., *Impounded People: Japanese-Americans in the Relocation Centers* (Tucson: University of Arizona Press, 1969); United States Commission on Wartime Relocation and Internment of Civilians, *Personal Justice Denied: Report of the Commission on Wartime Relocation and Internment of Civilians* (Seattle: University of Washington Press, 1997); and Michi Nishiura Weglyn, *Years of Infamy: The Untold Story of America's Concentration Camps*, updated ed. (Seattle: University of Washington Press, 1996). See also Tetsuden Kashima, *Judgment without Trial: Japanese American Imprisonment during World War II* (Seattle: University of Washington Press, 2003). To situate incarceration within the larger historical trajectory of Asian American immigration, settlement, oppression, and resistance, see Roger Daniels, *Asian America: Chinese and Japanese in the United States since 1850* (Seattle: University of Washington Press, 1988); Sucheta Mazumdar, "A Woman-Centered Perspective on Asian American History," in *Making Waves: An Anthology of Writings by and about Asian American Women*, ed. Asian American Women United of California (Boston: Beacon Press, 1989), 1–22; Gary Okihiro, *Margins and Mainstreams: Asians in American History and Culture* (Seattle: University of Washington Press, 1994); and Ronald Takaki, *Strangers from a Different Shore: A History of Asian Americans* (Boston: Little, Brown, 1989).

On the Arkansas camps in particular, I have consulted Russell E. Bearden, "The Internment of Japanese Americans in Arkansas, 1942–1945" (M.A. thesis, University of Arkansas, 1986); Guy E. Dorr, "*Issei, Nisei,* and Arkansas: A Geographic Study of the Wartime Relocation of Japanese-Americans in Southeast Arkansas (1942–1945)" (M.A. thesis, University of Arkansas, 1977); Holly Feltman Twyford, "Nisei in Arkansas: The Plight of Japanese American Youth in the Arkansas Internment Camps of World War II" (M.A. thesis, University of Arkansas, 1993); and Carole Katsuko Yumiba, "An Educational History of the War Relocation Centers at Jerome and Rohwer, Arkansas, 1942–1945" (Ph.D. diss., University of Southern California, 1979).

8. On the artist's series, see Jenny Holzer, *Abuse of Power Comes as No Surprise: Truisms and Essays* (New York: Barbara Gladstone Gallery, 1983).

9. *AG*, 8 October, 8 November 1942; Russell Bearden, "Life Inside Arkansas's Japanese-American Relocation Centers," *Arkansas Historical Quarterly* 48 (Summer 1989): 172; Violet Kazue de Cristoforo, "A Victim of the Japanese Evacuation and Resettlement Study," 30 June 1987, 9, DP, UCB; Tsukamoto and Pinkerton, *We the People*, 102.

10. Henry Nash Smith, *Virgin Land: The American West as Symbol and Myth* (Cambridge, MA: Harvard University Press, 1950), 165–73.

11. *National Historic Landmarks of Arkansas: Rohwer Relocation Center* (Little Rock: Arkansas Historic Preservation Program, 1999), 13–14. Of the many maps of the camps, see "Rohwer Relocation Center, Desha County, Arkansas, Layout Plan," RG 210, entry 16, box 292, folder 41.060, WRAR, NA; and "Jerome Relocation Center, Chicot & Drew Counties, Arkansas," series 2, folder 3, USWRAJ, UA. Also see Frank and Joanne Iritani, *Ten Visits: Brief Accounts of Our Visits to All Ten Japanese American Relocation Centers of World War II* (Bakersfield, CA: Blueprint Service Co., 1992).

12. Haruko (Sugi) Hurt, interview by James Gatewood, Gardena, CA, 28 February 1998, ROHP, JANM.

13. "War Relocation Authority, Jerome Relocation Center, Report on Meeting in Project Director's Office, March 14, 1943," series 2, folder 3, USWRAJ, UA. A particularly illustrative pencil drawing of an apartment interior is George Hoshida, *A Corner of Our Apartment, 39-9-F, Jerome R.C., June 14, 1944*, item 97.106.2DS, HC, JANM. On utopian housing schemes, see Dolores Hayden, *The Grand Domestic Revolution: A History of Feminist Designs for American Homes, Neighborhoods, and Cities* (Cambridge, MA: MIT Press, 1981).

14. Jibunryu Bunko, ed., *Nikkei America-jin 43nin Ima Hiraku Kokoro no Tobira* [43 Japanese Americans opening their hearts now] (Tokyo: Jibunryu Bunko, 1995), 156; Tsukamoto and Pinkerton, *We the People*, 115. I'm grateful to Junko Itaba for translating the former passage.

15. "Section V—Community Enterprises Trust and Corporation," 7–11, JRCL, UA; *FG*, 10 October 1942. Hawaiians at Jerome likely remembered the territory's own promoters of the cooperative movement, referred to as "a new frontier." See Franklin Odo, *No Sword to Bury: Japanese Americans in Hawai'i during World War II* (Philadelphia: Temple University Press, 2004), 76–78.

16. "War Relocation Authority, Jerome Relocation Center, Report on Meeting in Project Director's Office, March 14, 1943," Appendix No. 15: "Cooperative Association—Best Selling Items, Mail Order Sales, and Monthly Volume," series 2, folder 3, USWRAJ, UA; *DT*, 11 June 1943; *AG*, 8 November 1942; *Co-op News*, 18 January 1944, series 4, folder 3, TC, UA.

As one historian of women's work points out, "At one time, it fell upon American women—virtually all American women—to do the miles of stitching required to keep their families and, collectively, the nation in clothing." Moreover, "mending [of burned clothing] was frequently necessary for people who lived in [homes] heated by fireplaces and stoves," as was the case at the Arkansas camps. Susan Strasser, *Waste and Want: A Social History of Trash* (New York: Metropolitan, 1999), 38, 40. See also Susan Strasser, *Never Done: A History of American Housework* (New York: Pantheon, 1982).

17. *AG*, 8 November 1942; "War Relocation Authority, Jerome Relocation Center, Report on Meeting in Project Director's Office, March 14, 1943," Appendix No. 15: "Cooperative Association—Best Selling Items, Mail Order Sales, and Monthly Volume," series 2, folder 3, USWRAJ, UA; *DT*, 11 January 1944; Larry J. Collins, memorandum to Mr. Leflar, 5 March 1943, series 1, folder 1, JRCC, UA. Images of the Rohwer beauty parlor and photo studio are included in *National Historic Landmarks of Arkansas*.

18. "Section V—Community Enterprises Trust and Corporation," 7–11, JRCL, UA; "Souvenir Album, Jerome Cooperative Enterprises, Inc., May 1944," part II, section 5, reel 140, JAERR, UCB; *DT*, 10 November 1942, 4 June 1943; *RO*, 16 January, 6 March 1943.

19. *Co-op News*, 25 January, 15 February 1944, series 4, folder 3, TC, UA; "Jerome Cooperative Enterprises, Inc., Denson, Arkansas, Report of Audit, May 31, 1944," part II, section 5, reel 139, JAERR, UCB; "Souvenir Album, Jerome Cooperative Enterprises, Inc., May 1944," part II, section 5, reel 140, JAERR, UCB; *DT*, 18 June, 8 October 1943; Bearden, "Life Inside," 183.

20. "Souvenir Album, Jerome Cooperative Enterprises, Inc., May 1944," part II, section 5, reel 140, JAERR, UCB; *DT*, 21 May, 3 September, 26 October 1943; *Co-op News*, 25 January, 15 February 1944, series 4, folder 3, TC, UA.

21. Arthur A. Hansen, ed., *Japanese American World War II Evacuation Oral History Project, Part II: Administrators* (Westport, CT: Meckler, 1991), 187; "Souvenir Album, Jerome Cooperative Enterprises, Inc., May 1944," part II, section 5, reel 140, JAERR, UCB; *DM*, April 1943; *DT*, 4 December 1942.

22. *DT*, 18 May, 9, 30 July, 13 August 1943.

23. *DT*, 9 March, 20 April, 26 October 1943; "Souvenir Album, Jerome Cooperative Enterprises, Inc., May 1944," part II, section 5, reel 140, JAERR, UCB; W. Fitzhugh Brundage, *A Socialist Utopia in the New South: The Ruskin Colonies in Tennessee and Georgia, 1894–1901* (Urbana: University of Illinois Press, 1996). For movement histories, see Johnston Birchall, *The International Co-operative Movement* (Manchester: Manchester University Press, 1997). Of filmic representations, see *Towards Tomorrow: A Pageant of Co-operation*, dir. Frank Cox (London: London Co-operative Society, 1938) and *Song of the People*, dir. Maxwell Munden (London: Cooperative Wholesale Society, 1945). See also Allen Burton, *The British Consumer Co-operative Movement and Film, 1890s–1960s* (Manchester: Manchester University Press, 2005). Finally, see the website of the Co-operative College, www.co-op.ac.uk.

24. *Co-op News*, 25 January, 15 February 1944, series 4, folder 3, TC, UA.

25. Kiyoshi Hamanaka, letter to Dillon S. Myer, 26 May 1944; E. B. Whitaker, letter to Dillon S. Myer, 29 May 1944; D. S. Myer, letter to Kiyoshi Hamanaka, 7 June 1944, all in series 1, folder 1, USJRC, UA. Additional postal and teletype correspondence and hearing transcripts can be found in this archival folder.

26. *DC*, 1 December 1942.

27. Rebecca Chiyoko King, "'Eligible to Be Japanese American': Counting on Multiraciality in Basketball Leagues and Beauty Pageants," in *Contemporary Asian American Communities: Intersections and Divergences*, ed. Linda Trinh Vo and Rick Bonus (Philadelphia: Temple University Press, 2002), 128.

28. "War Relocation Authority, Jerome Relocation Center, Report on Meeting in Project Director's Office, March 14, 1943," series 2, folder 3, USWRAJ, UA; *CSR*, 26 May 1943. Right-wing Republican Malone would go on to serve two terms as senator from Nevada, 1947–59.

29. *DT*, 15 June, 12 October 1943; Takeo Kaneshiro, *Internees: War Relocation Center Memoirs and Diaries* (New York: Vantage Press, 1976), 52; House Special Committee on Un-American Activities, *Investigation of Un-American Propaganda Activities in the United States: Majority and Minority Report of the Subcommittee Investigation, War Relocation Authority* (Washington, DC: GPO, 1943). On kendo, see Jinichi Tokeshi, *Kendo: Elements, Rules and Philosophy* (Honolulu: University of Hawaii Press, 2003). For an interesting ac-

count of sumo from the period, see Marvin K. Opler, "A 'Sumo' Tournament at Tule Lake Center," *American Anthropologist* 47 (January 1945): 134–39.

30. Warren I. Cohen, *The Asian American Century* (Cambridge, MA: Harvard University Press, 2002), 50; Bill Brown, "Waging Baseball, Playing War: Games of American Imperialism," *Cultural Critique* 17 (Winter 1990): 51–78; Donald Roden, "Baseball and the Quest for National Dignity in Meiji Japan," *American Historical Review* 85 (June 1980): 511–34; "War Relocation Authority, Jerome Relocation Center, Report on Meeting in Project Director's Office, March 14, 1943," series 2, folder 3, USWRAJ, UA; *DT*, 19 March, 14, 28 May, 15 June, 10 September 1943; *RO*, 29 April 1944.

31. *DHSC*, 23 February 1943; "Community Activities Report for March 1944, Narrative Section," part II, section 5, reel 145, JAERR, UCB; *Denson Trifler*, 28 June 1943, series 4, folder 3, TC, UA.

32. *Denson Trifler*, 28 June 1943, series 4, folder 3, TC, UA.

33. *Technique EXTRA*, 17 November 1943, series 4, folder 3, TC, UA.

34. *DHSV*, 1943, 1944; *DT*, 12 February, 4 June, 6 July 1943.

35. *CSR*, 26 May, 30 June, 7, 21 July, 4, 25 August, 1, 8 September, 6 October, 30 December 1943, 30 March 1944; *RO*, 30 October 1943. Alison M. Wrynn, "The Recreation and Leisure Pursuits of Japanese Americans in World War II Internment Camps," in *Ethnicity and Sport in North American History and Culture*, ed. George Eisen and David K. Wiggins (Westport, CT: Greenwood, 1994), 128.

36. *CSR*, 27 October 1943; *RO*, 30 October 1943; *PC*, 23 October, 6 November 1943.

37. *PC*, 4 September 1943; "Community Activities, Jerome Center, Monthly Report, for Month Ending 5-1944," part II, section 5, reel 139, JAERR, UCB; *RO*, 24 October 1942, 16 January, 27 February 1943.

38. On the class and nationalist dimensions of sports in European and American contexts, see Pierre Bourdieu, "How Can One Be a Sports Fan?" in *The Cultural Studies Reader*, ed. Simon During (London: Routledge, 1993), 427–40; Gunther Barth, *City People: The Rise of Modern City Culture in Nineteenth-Century America* (New York: Oxford University Press, 1980), 148–91; Ryszard Kapuscinski, *The Soccer War* (London: Granta, 1990), 157–84. See also Ken Mochizuki, *Baseball Saved Us* (New York: Lee and Low, 1993).

39. In this section, I am indebted to the work of Mathew Weir, a former undergraduate at the University of York, and his research essay, based on archival materials I provided, autumn term, 1999.

40. United States Commission on Wartime Relocation and Internment of Civilians, *Personal Justice Denied*, 174; *DC*, 23 October, 3 November 1942.

41. *DC*, 13, 17, 20 November 1942.

42. Ibid.; Paul A. Taylor, memorandum to Division Chiefs, 24 December 1942, series 8, folder 1, LC, UA.

43. *DC*, 20 November 1942; *SAP*, 24 April 1942. On Santa Anita, see Anthony L. Lehman, *Birthright of Barbed Wire: The Santa Anita Assembly Center for the Japanese* (Los Angeles: Westernlore Press, 1970).

44. E. J. Friedlander, "Freedom of Press behind Barbed Wire: Paul Yokota and the Jerome Relocation Center Newspaper," *Arkansas Historical Quarterly* 44 (Winter 1985): 307,

313; "War Relocation Authority, Jerome Relocation Center, Report on Meeting in Project Director's Office, March 14, 1943," series 2, folder 3, USWRAJ, UA; Charles R. Lynn, letter to Gilbert F. Castleberry, series 1, folder 2, USJRC, UA; Leave Clearance Committee, memorandum to Project Director, 20 March 1944, series 1, folder 2, USJRC, UA; "The False Rumor of Tuesday: Arkansas's Internment of Japanese-Americans," *Arkansas Historical Quarterly* 41 (Winter 1982): 335–36.

For more careful evaluations of press censorship, see Lauren Kessler, "Fettered Freedoms: The Journalism of World War II Japanese Internment Camps," *Journalism History* 15 (Summer/Autumn 1988): 70–79. Also see Takeya Mizuno, "The Creation of the 'Free' Press in Japanese American Camps: The War Relocation Authority's Planning and Making of the Camp Newspaper Policy," *Journalism and Mass Communications Quarterly* 78 (Autumn 2001): 503–18; "Journalism under Military Guards and Searchlights: Newspaper Censorship in Japanese American Assembly Camps during World War II," *Journalism History* 29 (Fall 2003): 98–106; and "Self-Censorship by Coercion: The Federal Government and the California Japanese-Language Newspapers from Pearl Harbor to Internment," *American Journalism* 17 (Summer 2000): 31–57.

45. Quoted in Deborah Gesensway and Mindy Roseman, *Beyond Words: Images from America's Concentration Camps* (Ithaca, NY: Cornell University Press, 1987), 62, 95.

46. Paul A. Taylor, letter to Pvt. Richard Itanaga, 21 October 1943, series 1, folder 4, USJRC, UA; Pvt. Richard Itanaga, letter to Paul A. Taylor, 24 October 1943, series 1, folder 4, USJRC, UA; "Confidential, Toru Tim Abo, October 27, 1943," series 1, folder 4, USJRC, UA; *DT*, 22 October 1943.

47. Bob Leflar, confidential memorandum to Philip [Glick], 23 January 1943, series 2, folder 2, LC, UA.

48. United States Department of the Interior, *Community Government in War Relocation Centers* (Washington, DC: GPO, 1946), 47–49; David Mura, "Gardens We Have Left," in *The Open Boat: Poems from Asian America*, ed. Garrett Hongo (New York: Anchor, 1993), 219. See Patricia A. Curtin, "Press Coverage of the 442nd Regimental Combat Team (Separate—Nisei): A Case Study in Agenda Building," *American Journalism* 12 (Summer 1995): 225–41. Also on Masaoka and JACL "constructive cooperation," see Jere Takahashi, *Nisei/Sansei: Shifting Japanese American Identities and Politics* (Philadelphia: Temple University Press, 1997), 85–96.

49. A sample of translations from the Japanese-language sections of the two Arkansas newspapers were carefully prepared by research assistant Sahori Watanabe. David K. Yoo, *Growing Up Nisei: Race, Generation, and Culture among Japanese Americans of California, 1924–1949* (Urbana: University of Illinois Press, 2000), 74; Pvt. Richard Itanaga, letter to Paul A. Taylor, 24 October 1943, series 1, folder 4, USJRC, UA.

50. Tsukamoto and Pinkerton, *We the People*, 72.

51. Yoo, *Growing Up Nisei*, 75–76.

NOTES TO CHAPTER FOUR

1. Virginia Tidball, interview with author, Fayetteville, AR, 12 April 2000; *The Razorback*, 1926.

2. Virginia Tidball, letter to Mrs. J. B. Moody, 8 July 1942; Virginia Tidball, letter to Mrs. G. A. Curry, 29 October 1942; Virginia Tidball, letter to A. G. Thompson, 1 October 1942; Virginia Tidball, letters to B. F. Albright, 24 September, 2 October 1942; Virginia Tidball, letter to Edwin Stitt, 23 October 1942; all in series 3, folder 5, TC, UA.

3. Virginia Tidball, letter to D. S. Myer, 2 October 1942; Virginia Tidball, letters to A. G. Thompson, 26, 29 October, 18 November 1942; all in series 3, folder 5, TC, UA.

4. Virginia Tidball, letter to Hosea Fincher, 23 November 1942, TC, UA.

5. "Denson Schools Hand Book, Jerome Relocation Center," series 4, folder 1, TC, UA. See also Jan F. Ziegler, "Listening to 'Miss Jamison': Lessons from the Schoolhouse at a Japanese Internment Camp, Rohwer Relocation Center," *Arkansas Review* 33 (2002): 137–46. For a list of Rohwer High School teachers, including courses offered and—for white teachers only—degrees held, see *RSHH*, 1942–43.

6. For a floor plan, elevations, and sections of a Jerome barracks apartment building, see Jeffery F. Burton, Mary M. Farrell, Florence B. Lord, and Richard W. Lord, *Confinement and Ethnicity: An Overview of World War II Japanese American Relocation Sites* (Tucson, AZ: Western Archaeological and Conservation Center, 1999), 437. The portrait is cataloged as 92.97.68, SC, JANM. On housing assignments, see "Housing, Jerome Center, Monthly Report, for Month Ending Sept. 30, 1943," part II, section 5, reel 139, JAERR, UCB.

7. "Housing, Jerome Center, Monthly Report, for Month Ending Sept. 30, 1943," part II, section 5, reel 139, JAERR, UCB; *DC*, 22 December 1942, 2 February 1943; Valerie Matsumoto, "Japanese American Women during World War II," *Frontiers* 8 (1984): 6–14. See also Matsumoto's important study *Farming the Home Place: A Japanese American Community in California, 1919–1982* (Ithaca, NY: Cornell University Press, 1994); and Mei T. Nakano, *Japanese American Women: Three Generations, 1890–1990* (Berkeley, CA: Mina Press, 1990).

8. Photographs of the "Block 7 kitchen crew" at Jerome show six men in aprons, coats, and chef's caps. RG 210, series G, items E289 and E295, WRAR, SPB, NA. Film footage by Masayoshi Endo in Arkansas shows women serving meals and washing dishes. *Something Strong Within: Home Movies from America's Concentration Camps*, Robert A. Nakamura, dir. (Los Angeles: Japanese American National Museum, 1994).

9. For a floor plan of a lavatory/laundry building at Jerome, see Burton et al., *Confinement and Ethnicity*, 442. Oyama soap, both before and during the war, likely relied on nineteenth-century domestic manufacturing processes. The two principal ingredients, lye and grease, abounded in agricultural communities. Indeed, the wood ashes needed to produce lye could be found in every Arkansas barracks apartment, as we see in chapter 7. See Susan Strasser, *Waste and Want: A Social History of Trash* (New York: Metropolitan, 1999), 31–32.

Women at Jerome further were drawn together and overcame regional differences through the sharing of clothing. Though initially women from Hawaii "could not relate" to the women from the mainland, "to their surprise—even shock—they found the Mainlanders had collected sturdy shoes of many sizes, knitted gloves, heavy socks, woollen pants and shirts, scarves, baby blankets and booties[,] worn but warm body-hugging underwear [and] even some overcoats with warm lining"—all to be given to their underdressed neighbors, accustomed to warmer climes. Patsy Sumie Saiki, *Ganbare! An Example of Japanese Spirit* (Honolulu: Kisaku, 1982), 147.

10. Susan McKay, *The Courage Our Stories Tell: The Daily Lives and Maternal Child Health Care of Japanese American Women at Heart Mountain* (Powell, WY: Western History Publications, 2002); Internal Security Section, *Duty Manual* (Denson, AR: Jerome Relocation Center, 1942), 6; Earl M. Finch, five letters to Nat R. Griswold, 13, 22 April, 2, 10 May, 8 November 1944, series 1, folder 2, GC, UA; Nat R. Griswold, four letters to Earl M. Finch, 10, 25 April, 4 May, 15 July 1944, series 1, folder 5, GC, UA.

11. United States War Relocation Authority, *The Relocation Program: A Guidebook for the Residents of Relocation Centers* (Washington, DC: GPO, 1943), 11.

12. Evelyn Nakano Glenn, *Issei, Nisei, War Bride: Three Generations of Japanese American Women in Domestic Service* (Philadelphia: Temple University Press, 1986), 35, 207. Similar arguments were forwarded by the government at the time. See United States Department of the Interior, *People in Motion: The Postwar Adjustment of the Evacuated Japanese Americans* (Washington, DC: GPO, 1947), 198–200.

13. The trope of "family breakdown" appears again and again in the literature of incarceration. These include contemporaneous reports of official observers and Japanese American inmates, as in *DT*, 16 June 43. Likewise, recent studies of sociologists and historians. See Leonard Broom and John I. Kitsuse, *The Managed Casualty: The Japanese-American Family in World War II*, reprint ed. (Berkeley: University of California Press, 1973). As one historian described the Arkansas camps: "The mandatory communal style of living—community dining halls, toilets, and shower facilities—not only destroyed morale, but also led to a breakdown in the manners of children and the traditional strong unity of the Japanese family." C. Calvin Smith, *War and Wartime Changes: The Transformation of Arkansas, 1940–1945* (Fayetteville: University of Arkansas Press, 1986), 72.

14. Glenn, *Issei, Nisei, War Bride*, 49, 214–15; "Rohwer Quarterly Report, Apr. 1–June 30, 1943," series 4, folder 39, LC, UA; "Project Attorney, Month Ending Jan. 31, 1942, Jerome, Arkansas Project," and subsequent monthly reports through 30 September 1942, part II, section 5, reel 138, JAERR, UCB.

In his essay "Life Inside Arkansas's Japanese-American Relocation Centers," *Arkansas Historical Quarterly* 48 (Summer 1989): 191, Russell Bearden relies on WRA statistics to assert that "not one divorce ever took place *in* the Arkansas centers." Emphasis added. But as WRA correspondence makes clear, this was only technically true. That is, since detainees were not considered legal residents of Arkansas, they were advised against pursuing divorces through Arkansas courts. Pursue divorces they nonetheless did, with the aid of camp attorneys. United States War Relocation Authority, *The Evacuated People: A Quantitative Description* (Washington, DC: GPO, 1946), 135, 141; Robert A. Leflar, memorandum to E. B. Whitaker, 9 December 1942, series 2, folder 4, LC, UA; Robert A. Leflar, letter to Philip M. Glick, 17 December 1942, series 4, folder 29, LC, UA.

15. "Quarterly Report of Housing Unit, April 7, 1943," part II, section 5, reel 139, JAERR, UCB; "Summary of Monthly Listings and Certificates of Live Births, Rohwer Relocation Center, October–December 1942," and all subsequent annual summaries, part IV, section 2, reel 88, JAERR, UCB; Ray D. Johnston, letter to E. B. Whitaker, RG 210, entry 48, box 20, folder 61.520, WRAR, NA.

16. Haru Miyazaki, letter to Virginia Tidball, 10 June 1944, series 1, folder 1, TC, UA.

17. For a critique of the urban bias in American lesbian and gay history, see John Howard, *Men Like That: A Southern Queer History* (Chicago: University of Chicago Press, 1999). On lesbian baseball and softball, see, for example, Daneel Buring, "Softball and Alcohol: The Limits of Lesbian Community in Memphis from the 1940s to the 1960s," in *Carryin' On in the Lesbian and Gay South*, ed. John Howard (New York: New York University Press, 1997), 203–23; Susan K. Cahn, "From the 'Muscle Moll' to the 'Butch Ballplayer': Mannishness, Lesbianism, and Homophobia in U.S. Women's Sport," *Feminist Studies* 19 (Summer 1993): 343–68. On lesbian military service in World War II, see Allan Bérubé, *Coming Out Under Fire: The History of Gay Men and Women in World War Two* (New York: Free Press, 1990); and Leisa D. Meyer, *Creating GI Jane: Sexuality and Power in the Women's Army Corps during World War II* (New York: Columbia University Press, 1996).

18. *DHSC*, 1943; *DHSV* 1943, 1944; *RJHR*, 1943; *RSHH*, 1942–43.

19. *Community School Forum*, June 1943; "Denson Schools Hand Book, Jerome Relocation Center," series 4, folder 1, TC, UA. Emphasis added.

20. *DT*, 25 July, 5 November 1943; "Forum on Our Families," series 2, folder 6, GC, UA.

21. Paul R. Spickard, *Mixed Blood: Intermarriage and Ethnic Identity in Twentieth-Century America* (Madison: University of Wisconsin Press, 1989), 52–53; Robert O'Brien, *The College Nisei* (Palo Alto, CA: Pacific Books, 1949), 50; *DC*, 26 November 1942; *DT*, 19 May 1944.

22. Violet Kazue de Cristoforo, "A Victim of the Japanese Evacuation and Resettlement Study," 30 June 1987, DP, UCB; *DC*, 27 October 1942; *DT*, 16 May 1944. Here and in other parts of this section, I am indebted to the work of Helen Taylor, a former undergraduate at the University of York, and her research essay, based on archival materials I provided, autumn term, 1999.

23. Roger Daniels, "Why It Happened Here," in *The Lost Years, 1942–1946*, ed. Sue Kunitomi Embrey (Los Angeles: Moonlight Publications, 1972), 31; Caleb Foote, *Outcasts! The Story of America's Treatment of Her Japanese-American Minority* (New York: Fellowship of Reconciliation, 1943), 9.

24. Philip M. Glick, memorandum to the director, 7 January 1943, series 2, folder 3, LC, UA; Internal Security, *Duty Manual*, 4; Paul A. Taylor, confidential memorandum to John H. Provinse, 24 June 1943, RG 210, entry 48, box 207, folder 67.012, WRAR, NA.

25. Taylor, confidential memorandum to Provinse; Sandra C. Taylor, *Jewel of the Desert: Japanese American Internment at Topaz* (Berkeley: University of California Press, 1993), 162–63; Eve Kosofsky Sedgwick, *Epistemology of the Closet* (Berkeley: University of California Press, 1990), 23; Gavin Butt, *Between You and Me: Queer Disclosures in the New York Art World, 1948–1963* (Durham, NC: Duke University Press, 2005).

26. "Total 1944 Cases, Internal Security Section, War Relocation Authority," RG 210, entry 16, box 388, folder 65.100 #5, WRAR, NA. Taylor, confidential memorandum to Provinse.

27. *DT*, 21 January 1944; Taylor, confidential memorandum to Provinse; "Public Health, Jerome Center, Monthly Report, for Month Ending October 31, 1943," part II, section 5, reel 139, JAERR, UCB. JRCL, UA, 20; "War Relocation Authority, Jerome Relocation Center, Report on Meeting in Project Director's Office, March 14, 1943," series 2, folder 3, USWRAJ, UA.

28. *DC*, 27 October, 26 November, 29 December 1942, 19 January 1943; *DT*, 6 August 1943.

29. War Relocation Authority, *Evacuated People*, 100, 102, 103; John Tateishi, *And Justice for All: An Oral History of the Japanese American Detention Camps* (New York: Random House, 1984), 104; *DC*, 29 December 1942.

30. Tateishi, *And Justice for All*, 104; War Relocation Authority, *Evacuated People*, 138, 150; See also myth #14 in United States War Relocation Authority, *Myths and Facts about the Japanese Americans: Answering Common Misconceptions Regarding Americans of Japanese Ancestry* (Washington, DC: GPO, 1945).

31. Robert A. Leflar, memorandum to E. B. Whitaker, series 2, folder 3, 29 October 1942, LC, UA; "Temporary Deferment of Evacuation Order, Headquarters, Northwestern Sector, Fort Lewis, Washington, May 2, 1942," and "Puyallup Assembly Center, Evacuee Inter-Area Pass, 7/1 1942," NS, UW.

32. Lewis A. Sigler, "Solicitor's Memorandum No. 15," 3 August 1943, series 1, folder 2, JRCC, UA.

33. Ibid.

34. Ray D. Johnston, letter to Dillon S. Myer, 19 November 1943; Paul A. Taylor, letter to Dillon S. Myer, 24 November 1943; both in RG 210, entry 16, box 229, folder 31.007, WRAR, NA. The Nakashimas likely were the largest mixed-race family at Jerome, with seven children of Japanese and Spanish ancestry, ranging from sixteen to twenty-seven years of age. At least three—Angelina, Bessie, and George—had relocated to the Midwest. Albert was serving in the 442nd RCT.

These particular racial designations seem to have been necessitated by research into cross-racial, comparative dental patterns by Dr. Henry Klein, Senior Dental Officer, of the United States Public Health Service. Such research also was undertaken by 442nd regimental dental surgeon Captain Wayland F. Hogan. "The records of approximately 3,800 men in each of three other regiments were put alongside those of the same number of Japanese Americans"; and, as proclaimed in the Camp Shelby newspaper story headline, "442 MEN WIN HANDS DOWN WHEN IT COMES TO MOLAR BUSINESS." Without falling back on essentialist racial thinking, Hogan pointed to environmental factors: "correct oral hygiene in elementary schools," especially in Hawaii, "diet during formative years, climatic conditions and efficient corrective measures." *CSR*, 28 July 1943.

35. Ulys A. Lovell, letter to Philip M. Glick, 13 July 1944, series 1, folder 1, LUC, UA; Philip M. Glick, memorandum to the director, 11 November 1943, series 8, folder 3, LC, UA.

36. Heinz Heger, *The Men with the Pink Triangle*, trans. David Fernbach (London: Gay Men's Press, 1980); Richard Plant, *The Pink Triangle: The Nazi War against Homosexuals* (New York: Henry Holt, 1986); Bérubé, *Coming Out Under Fire*.

37. "Internal Security Case Report, Jerome Project," 13 September 1943, RG 210, entry 51, box 8, project case 91, WRAR, NA.

38. Ibid.

39. Ibid.

40. Internal Security, *Duty Manual*, 5; Judith Halberstam, *In a Queer Time and Place: Transgender Bodies, Subcultural Lives* (New York: New York University Press, 2005); "War

Relocation Authority, Internal Security Division, Rules and Regulations, May 1, 1943," series 13, folder 2, LC, UA; *DT*, 21 January 1944.

41. "Internal Security Case Report, Jerome Project," 13 September 1943, RG 210, entry 51, box 8, project case 91, WRAR, NA.

42. "Housing, Jerome Center, Monthly Report, for Month Ending Sept. 30, 1943," part II, section 5, reel 138, JAERR, UCB. For pictures of Block 1, see RG 210, series G, items H431–H434, WRAR, SPB, NA. Peter Boag, *Same-Sex Affairs: Constructing and Controlling Homosexuality in the Pacific Northwest* (Berkeley: University of California Press, 2003). See also Anna Hosticka Tamura, "Gardens Below the Watchtower: Gardens and Meaning in World War II Japanese Incarceration Camps," *Landscape Journal* 23 (2004): 1–21.

43. "Imperial Japanese Government, Passport, No. 541306," stamped 12 December 1923; "Affidavit of Identity, State of California, City of San Francisco," 30 April 1969; "Will and Testament of Jiro Onuma," 30 January 1987; "Last Will and Testament," 17 March 1970; "Acme [Photo] Album" and loose photographs; all in OP, GLBTHS. See also Ken Kaji, "From the Past, a Gay Life," in "Gay and JA" special issue, *Nikkei Heritage* 14 (Summer 2002): 7.

44. *RO*, 10 February 1943; "Community Activities, Jerome Center, Monthly Report, for Month Ending 11-1943," part II, section 5, reel 139, JAERR, UCB; John Donald Gustav-Wrathall, *Take the Young Stranger by the Hand: Same-Sex Relations and the YMCA* (Chicago: University of Chicago Press, 1998); Howard, *Men Like That*; D. Michael Quinn, *Same-Sex Dynamics among Nineteenth-Century Americans: A Mormon Example* (Urbana: University of Illinois Press, 1996); *National Historic Landmarks of Arkansas: Rohwer Relocation Center* (Little Rock: Arkansas Historic Preservation Program, 1999).

Assertions of increased Japanese American juvenile delinquency during the war have been perpetuated in historical accounts, as seen with Smith, *War and Wartime Changes*, 72. Of the survey texts taking in lesbian history and sexual space, see Lillian Faderman, *Odd Girls and Twilight Lovers: A History of Lesbian Life in Twentieth-Century America* (New York: Columbia University Press, 1991); and Leila J. Rupp, *A Desired Past: A Short History of Same-Sex Love in America* (Chicago: University of Chicago Press, 1999).

45. Bérubé, *Coming Out Under Fire*; *Something Strong Within,* Nakamura, dir. On womanless weddings at Rohwer and elsewhere in Arkansas during the 1930s and 1940s, see William Brock Thompson, "The Un-Natural State: Exploring Same-Sex Desire and Gender Identity in Arkansas from the Depression through the Clinton Era" (Ph.D. diss., University of London, 2006), 58–81.

46. "War Relocation Authority, One-Day Trip Pass, Jack Yamashita, 9-7-F, August 2, 1943," and "War Relocation Authority, One-Day Trip Pass, Jack Yamashita, 9-7-4, 8/3/43," RG 210, entry 48, box 189, folder 19.702, WRAR, NA.

47. Mary Nakahara, "The Bordered World, Vol. I," entry dated 11 April 1942, JANM; Diane C. Fujino, "To Serve the Movement: The Revolutionary Practice of Yuri Kochiyama," in *Legacy to Liberation: Politics and Culture of Revolutionary Asian Pacific America*, ed. Fred Ho (San Francisco: AK Press, 2000), 257–59. See also Fujino's important book-length study, *Heartbeat of Struggle: The Revolutionary Life of Yuri Kochiyama* (Minneapolis: University of Minnesota Press, 2005).

48. Nakahara, "Bordered World," 11 April 1942. Other teenage girls in Arkansas wrote about their aspirations to become nurses in autobiographical essays submitted to English teacher Virginia Tidball. See Mary Aoto, "Autobiography of Mary Aoto," n.d.; and Haru Nakanishi, "The Next Step," 13 August 1943, in Tidball Student Essays, TC, UA.

49. Nakahara, "Bordered World," 5, 24, 30 April; 1, 2, 10 May 1942. For more on Dr. Sakaye Shigekawa, midwifery, motherhood, and health care in the camps, see Susan L. Smith, *Japanese American Midwives: Culture, Community, and Health Politics, 1880–1950* (Urbana: University of Illinois Press, 2005), 159–83.

50. Nakahara, "Bordered World," 12, 22, 23, 26 April, 2, 10 May 1942.

51. Ibid., 4, 6, 24 April, 5 May 1942; *Rafu Shimpo*, 10 July 1946; Mary Nakahara, "The Bordered World, Vol. II," entry dated 11 September 1942, JANM.

52. Nakahara, "Bordered World," 13 May 1942; *Revolutionary Worker*, 13 December 1988; *East Bay Express*, 13 March 2002.

53. Nakahara, "Bordered World," 18 May 1942.

54. Rankin quoted in Lester E. Suzuki, *Ministry in the Assembly and Relocation Centers of World War II* (Berkeley, CA: Yardbird, 1979), 292. Not only Rankin but also many others in the United States and Japan viewed the conflict as a race war. As the foremost historian of the Pacific War writes, "The Allied struggle against Japan exposed the racist underpinnings of the European and American colonial struggle. Japan did not invade independent countries in southern Asia. It invaded colonial outposts which the Westerners had dominated for generations, taking absolutely for granted their racial and cultural superiority over their Asian subjects. . . . At the same time, the Japanese themselves dwelled at inordinate length on their own racial and cultural superiority, and like their adversaries, who practiced discrimination while proclaiming they were 'fighting for democracy,' they too became entangled in a web of contradictions: creating new colonial hierarchies while preaching liberation; singing the glories of their unique Imperial Way while professing to support a broad and all-embracing Pan-Asianism." John Dower, *War without Mercy: Race and Power in the Pacific War* (London: Faber and Faber, 1986), 5, 8.

NOTES TO CHAPTER FIVE

1. Margaret Sorenson, letter to Mary Tsukamoto, 26 May 1943, RG 210, entry 48, box 62, folder 67.011, WRAR, NA; *RO*, 5 May 1943.

2. *CSR* 5 May 1943; *RO*, 1, 5 May 1943.

3. *RO*, 21 April 1943; *PC*, 15 April 1943.

4. Allan Bérubé, *Coming Out Under Fire: The History of Gay Men and Women in World War Two* (New York: Free Press, 1990).

5. James W. Loewen has used this phrase to summarize the condition of Chinese Americans living in the Delta: *The Mississippi Chinese: Between Black and White* (Cambridge, MA: Harvard University Press, 1971). One of the most recent and most perceptive accounts of southern racial segregation is Grace Elizabeth Hale, *Making Whiteness: The Culture of Segregation in the South, 1890–1940* (New York: Pantheon, 1998).

6. David K. Yoo, *Growing Up Nisei: Race, Generation, and Culture among Japanese Americans of California, 1924–1949* (Urbana: University of Illinois Press, 2000), 1–3.

7. Ulys A. Lovell, untitled speech given at the University of Arkansas, Fayetteville, AR, c. 1944, folder 1, item 29, LUC, UA.

8. Leave procedures were spelled out in United States War Relocation Authority, *The Relocation Program: A Guidebook for the Residents of Relocation Centers* (Washington, DC: GPO, 1943). Interestingly, the pass system was not mentioned, though its stipulations were repeatedly circulated and argued among WRA personnel. Because the historical literature rarely addresses the Arkansas camps, the fluidity of camp boundaries is poorly understood. The congressionally mandated study of 1982, for example, perpetuates the notion of camps as sealed compounds: "For a long time, no evacuee could leave the center, except for emergency reasons, and then only in the company of someone who was not of Japanese ancestry. . . . By the end of 1943, evacuees were sometimes allowed to leave the grounds. . . ." United States Commission on Wartime Relocation and Internment of Civilians, *Personal Justice Denied: Report of the Commission on Wartime Relocation and Internment of Civilians* (Seattle: University of Washington Press, 1997), 172, 177. As I demonstrate below, prisoners passed in and out of the camps unaccompanied for any number of reasons, from the very beginning in 1942.

The few accounts that do discuss Arkansas often prove erroneous, especially as regards interactions with locals. For example, in *The Great Betrayal: The Evacuation of the Japanese-Americans during World War II* (London: Macmillan, 1969), 218–19, Audrie Girdner and Anne Loftis describe "a sense of isolation, a feeling of being forsaken [that] pervaded all the camps." Locked up in the "swampy *low*lands of Arkansas," inmates there had little contact, they assert, with "the Caucasians who lived nearby, the *hill* people [*sic*]." Emphasis added. They further assert that the "evacuees never went to" Little Rock.

9. Paul A. Taylor, letter to E. B. Whitaker, 25 June 1943, RG 210, entry 16, box 388, folder 65.100 #3, WRAR, NA; Internal Security Office, "Daily Trip Passes," 19 July 1943, RG 210, entry 48, box 189, folder 19.702, WRAR, NA; Nat. R. Griswold, memorandum to Ray D. Johnston, 1 May 1944, series 2, folder 11, GC, UA. Emphasis in the original. For instances of leave with and without passes, see Jack S. Curtis, letter to Robert A. Leflar, 30 January 1943, series 2, folder 2, LC, UA; Robert A. Leflar, memorandum to E. B. Whitaker, 12 October 1942, series 2, folder 4, LC, UA; Robert A. Leflar, letter to Philip M. Glick, 17 October, 1942, series 2, folder 1, LC, UA; and *DT*, 18 May, 15 June 1943. For lists of dozens of individuals—both white and Japanese American—authorized to sign "Daily Evacuee Passes, Form WRA-X-54," see W. O. Melton, memorandum to Captain Cooper, 5 July 1943; and W. O. Melton, memorandum to Captain Peterson, 24 January 1944, RG 210, entry 48, box 189, folder 19.701-A, WRAR, NA.

10. *DT*, 8 October 1943; Thelma Chang, *"I Can Never Forget": Men of the 100th/442nd* (Honolulu: Sigi Productions, 1991), 126; Hawaii Nikkei History Editorial Board, *Japanese Eyes, American Heart: Personal Reflections of Hawaii's World War II Nisei Soldiers* (Honolulu: University of Hawaii Press, 1998), 373; Arvarh E. Strickland, "Growing Up Black in Wartime Mississippi," in *Remaking Dixie: The Impact of World War II on the American South*,

ed. Neil R. McMillen et al. (Jackson: University Press of Mississippi, 1997), 156. See also Franklin Odo, *No Sword to Bury: Japanese Americans in Hawai'i during World War II* (Philadelphia: Temple University Press, 2004), 230–31.

11. Chang, *"I Can Never Forget,"* 111; Vernon Miki Uyeda, Clarence Louie, and Nelson Nagai, *The Other Side of Infamy* (Stockton, CA: Stockton Record, 1983); Mike Masaoka, with Bill Hosokawa, *They Call Me Moses Masaoka: An American Saga* (New York: William Morrow, 1987), 143; Thomas Taro Higa, *Memoirs of a Certain Nisei/Aru Nisei No Wadachi, 1916–1985* (Kaneohe, HI: Higa Publications, 1988), 50; *Heart Mountain Sentinel*, quoted in *PC*, 19 February 1944.

12. Paul Taylor, "A Message from Paul Taylor"; John C. Baker, "Outside Relocation Program"; Eddie Shimano, "Letter from New York"; M.M., "Beyond the Fence"—all in *DM*, April 1943, 1, 3, 9, 17. See also Charlotte Brooks, "In the Twilight Zone between Black and White: Japanese American Resettlement and Community in Chicago, 1942–1945," *Journal of American History* 86 (March 2000): 1655–87. For historical examples of ethnic minority attempts at upward social mobility via anti-black racism, see Noel Ignatiev, *How the Irish Became White* (New York: Routledge, 1995); and Vijay Prashad, *The Karma of Brown Folk* (Minneapolis: University of Minnesota Press, 2000).

13. Robert Alan Mossman, "Japanese-American War Relocation Centers as Total Institutions, with Emphasis on the Educational Program" (Ed.D. diss., Rutgers University, 1978), 130; Joseph B. Hunter, letter to Jimmie Woodward, 18 October 1943, RG 210, entry 48, box 251, folder 17.300, WRAR, NA.

14. Nobuko Lillian Omi—a Nisei Christian from Santa Ana, California, incarcerated at Jerome—described mobility in this way: "I was president of the camp YWCA so I had access to the outside." Shizue Yoshina, ed., *Nisei Christian Journey: Its Promise and Fulfillment*, vol. 1 (Sunnyvale, CA: Nisei Christian Oral History Project, 1988). On administrators' attempts to ensure hospitality for Japanese American traveling companions, see Nat R. Griswold, letter to Louis Ederington, 17 May 1944; letter to Manager, Lafayette Hotel, 18 May 1944; and letter to J. H. Wright, 23 May 1944, series 1, folder 5, GC, UA. On the Girl and Boy Scout outings, see *RP*, 1943.

15. Lucy M. Cohen, *Chinese in the Post–Civil War South: A People without a History* (Baton Rouge: Louisiana State University Press, 1984), xi; Loewen, *The Mississippi Chinese*, 61; William T. Schmidt, "The Impact of the Camp Shelby Mobilization on Hattiesburg, Mississippi, 1940–1946" (Ph.D. diss., University of Southern Mississippi, 1972), 100–101; Sen Nishiyama, *Pearl Harbor to Nikkei-jin: Nichibei Yuko to Byodo eno Michi* [Pearl Harbor and the Japanese Americans] (Tokyo: Simul Press, 1991); Arthur A. Hansen and Nora M. Jesch, eds., *Japanese American World War II Evacuation Oral History Project, Part V: Guards and Townspeople* (Munich: K. G. Saur, 1993), 300–301. See also Robert Seto Quan, *Lotus among the Magnolias: The Mississippi Chinese* (Jackson: University Press of Mississippi, 1982).

Also, as Robert O'Brien noted, "by 1944, 53 colleges and universities in the South, together with 29 in Missouri and 5 in Maryland, had admitted over 320 Nisei, thus setting a definite stamp of approval on the second generation as belonging on the 'white side' of the segregation line. . . . Among the southern colleges and universities registering evacuees were: Tulane, Vanderbilt, Baylor, Emory, Wake Forest, Rice, Goucher, Lynchburg, and the Universities of North Carolina, Texas, Louisiana, Missouri, Maryland, and Florida." "Selective Dispersion as a Factor in the Solution of the Nisei Problem," *Social Forces* 23 (December 1944): 147. See also O'Brien's book-length study, *The College Nisei* (Palo Alto, CA: Pacific Books, 1949).

16. Robert A. Leflar, letter to Philip M. Glick, 14 November 1942, series 2, folder 1, LC, UA.

17. Ibid.; Robert A. Leflar, letter to Philip M. Glick, 23 November 1942, series 2, folder 1, LC, UA; Robert A. Leflar, letter to Philip M. Glick, 14 December 1942, series 2, folder 2, LC, UA; *AG*, 11, 14 November 1942; *DC*, 17 November 1942.

18. WRA, *The Relocation Program*, 10; *DC*, 17 November 1942.

19. Robert A. Leflar, letter to Philip M. Glick, 4 December 1942, series 4, folder 29, LC, UA; Philip M. Glick, letter to R. A. Leflar, 9 December 1942, series 2, folder 2, LC, UA; *DC*, 8 December 1942; J. B. Cook, reports dated 2 and 4 December 1942, RG 210, entry 48, box 204, folder 65.100, WRAR, NA; Paul A. Taylor, teletype to E. B. McMenamin, 27 March 1943, RG 210, entry 48, box 179, folder 19.120. The Brown, Person, and Wood assaults are also described in William Cary Anderson, "Early Reaction to the Relocation of Japanese in the State," *Arkansas Historical Quarterly* 23 (Autumn 1964): 204–6.

20. Jacquelyn Dowd Hall, "'The Mind that Burns in Each Body': Women, Rape, and Racial Violence," in *Powers of Desire: The Politics of Sexuality*, ed. Ann Snitow et al. (New York: Monthly Review Press, 1983), 328–49; Joel Williamson, *A Rage for Order: Black-White Relations in the American South since Emancipation* (New York: Oxford University Press, 1986).

21. In her op-ed piece, "A View from Behind the Wire," the daughter, Betty Hunter Adams, later remembered her being stood up as "a shock for me, . . . being on the receiving end of prejudice." *AG*, 22 May 2000. Paul R. Spickard, *Mixed Blood: Intermarriage and Ethnic Identity in Twentieth-Century America* (Madison: University of Wisconsin Press, 1989), 103–5. Notable among the revivalists was E. Stanley Jones. Some Buddhists and many who did not attend religious services at Jerome described Christian pastors there as "pro-administration." Lester E. Suzuki, *Ministry in the Assembly and Relocation Centers of World War II* (Berkeley, CA: Yardbird, 1979), 311.

22. Bob Kiino, letters to Virginia Tidball, 3 October, 7 November 1943, series 1, folder 1, TC, UA; Robert A. Leflar, letter to Philip M. Glick, 4 December 1942, series 4, folder 29, LC, UA.

23. *DT*, 20 April, 18 May 1943; "Bi-Weekly Report on Evacuee Opinion, [Jerome] Community Analysis Section and Document Section," 21 June 1943, RG 210, entry 48, box 207, folder 67.012, WRAR, NA.

24. *DT*, 11, 22 June 1943.

25. *DT*, 15, 22, 25, 29 June 1943, 30 May 1944; *RO*, 19 June 1943, 30 August 1944. On women as the ultimate rationales for and spoils of war, see the compelling work of Cynthia Enloe, particularly *Does Khaki Become You?: The Militarisation of Women's Lives* (London: Pluto Press, 1983). Also, on the racial and sexual politics of American women's war service, see her *Maneuvers: The International Politics of Militarizing Women's Lives* (Berkeley: University of California Press, 2000). The classic text on rape and warfare remains Susan Brownmiller, *Against Our Will: Men, Women, and Rape* (New York: Simon and Schuster, 1975).

26. *DT*, 25 June, 23 July 1943; *RO*, 14 April 1943; Diane C. Fujino, "To Serve the Movement: The Revolutionary Practice of Yuri Kochiyama," in *Legacy to Liberation: Politics and Culture of Revolutionary Asian Pacific America*, ed. Fred Ho (San Francisco: AK Press, 2000), 257–59; *Revolutionary Worker*, 13 December 1988. On family reunions, see *CSR*, 5 May 1943. Federal government officials' primary role in the dances and their objectification of Japanese American "girls" are perhaps best evidenced by Norman R. Gilbert, letter to [Rohwer] Project Supervisor, 30 March 1943, RG 210, entry 48, box 262, folder 67.011, WRAR, NA.

27. *RO*, 21 April, 7 July, 11 December 1943, 12 January 1944. Leave-clearance hearings—as part of the registration program—were repeatedly described by Arkansas officials, perhaps unconvincingly, as "not a trial nor inquisition." Those whose loyalty was called into question found it difficult if not impossible to get a pass or obtain short- or long-term leave. For one example, see "Transcript of Hearing for Mary Shigetome," 17 September 1943, series 6, folder 3, LC, UA.

28. United States War Relocation Authority, *The Evacuated People: A Quantitative Description* (Washington, DC: GPO, 1946), 165, 168; "Monograph on History of Military Clearance Program," 22, series 2, folder 1, CC, UA; Ho, *Legacy to Liberation*, 298. On resistance to the draft, see Eric Muller, *Free to Die for Their Country: The Story of the Japanese American Draft Resisters in World War II* (Chicago: University of Chicago Press, 2001).

29. Maxine Andrews and Bill Gilbert, *Over Here, Over There: The Andrews Sisters and the USO Stars in World War II* (Washington, DC: Kensington, 1993); Julia Margaret Hicks Carson, *Home Away from Home: The Story of the USO* (New York: Harper, 1946); Frank Coffey, *Always Home: 50 Years of the USO: The Official Photographic History* (Washington, DC: Brassey's, 1991), 5; L. F. Kimball, "Operation USO: Report of the President, February 4th, 1941–January 9th, 1948" (New York: United Services Organizations, 1948), 31. On headquarters' support for USO clubs in the Arkansas camps, see, for example, Ray Johns, letter to Edward B. Marks Jr., 16 February 1943, RG 210, entry 48, box 197, folder 61.100, WRAR, NA.

30. *CSR*, 11 March 1942; *Hattiesburg, Miss. Telephone Directory, July 1944*, Southern Bell Telephone and Telegraph Co.

31. *USOB*, especially 4 (November 1943): 3; 4 (January 1944): 3–4; 4 (February 1944): 3; 4 (March 1944): 2. Earl M. Dinger, "When Millions Migrate" (New York: United Services Organizations, 1945); Kimball, "Operation USO," 20; L. F. Kimball, "USO, Five Years of Service: Report of the President" (New York: United Services Organizations, 1946), 11; Gee Gee Lang, conversation with author, 17 November 2000 (Lang's parents first met at one of the Oregon dances); *Defense Morale: A Transcript of the Proceedings of the Defense Morale Conference of the United Service Organizations for National Defense, Inc., at Washington, D.C., April 17, 1941* (New York: United Services Organizations, 1941), 26.

Photographs of African American soldiers selected for the *USO Bulletin* tend to depict them singing; images of African American men and women—as no other—include captions filled with dialect and contractions: for example, "'Tween Train Service" and "Wot's Cookin'?"

32. *New York Herald Tribune*, 6 February 1944.

33. *DT*, 16 November 1943.

34. The Crusaders, letter to Dear _____, n.d. [November 1944], series 7, folder 3, GC, UA.

35. *DT*, 5 March 1943.

36. Crusaders, letter to Dear _____.

37. *CSR*, 5 May, 2 June, 18 August 1943, 30 March 1944; *PC*, 21 August, 23 October 1943, 15 January, 26 February 1944; Adria Imada, "Hawaiians on Tour: Hula Circuits through the American Empire," *American Quarterly* 56 (March 2004): 111–49. Among countless images of island women performing hula during the war years, a few photographs surface of white soldiers and sailors in Hawaii dancing hula and wearing grass skirts, sometimes explicitly cross-dressed as women. Jim Heimann, ed., *Hula: Vintage Hawaiian Graphics* (Cologne: Taschen, 2003). On earlier periods, see Dorothy B. Barrère, Mary Kawna Pukui, and Marion Kelly, *Hula: Historical Perspectives* (Honolulu: Bishop Museum, 1980).

38. *HA*, 30 March 1946; *PC*, 10 June, 19 July, 19 August, 16 September 1944, 3 March 1945. See also, *PM*, 12 September 1944. Hisako Yamashita, letter to Mark Santoki, 19 November 1999, in author's possession. For another account of Earl Finch's relationship to the Serenaders, see Odo, *No Sword to Bury*, 231–32.

39. Chester Tanaka, *Go for Broke: A Pictorial History of the Japanese American 100th Infantry Battalion and the 442nd Regimental Combat Team* (Novato, CA: Presidio Press, 1982), 61, 106, 110–11, 144.

40. Ibid., 67; Terry Shima Bukuro, "442nd Regimental Combat Team," n.d. [1945?], 8, box 1, MP, UW. On non-national servicemen naturalized as citizens, see as an example *CSR*, 8 September 1943.

41. Tanaka, *Go for Broke*, 61; Bukuro, "442nd Regiment," 8, MP, UW.

42. *RO*, 1 January 1944; Mary Tsukamoto, letter to Paul A. Taylor, 29 June 1943, RG 210, entry 48, box 197, folder 61.100, WRAR, NA. See also Mary Nakahara, letter to W. O. Melton, 28 July 1943, series 2, folder 2, USWRAJ, UA. To engender goodwill among the local community, the Rohwer USO and related camp organizations placed a full-page ad in the local paper about Japanese American soldiers and their families, sparking a related set of articles detailing those killed in action, awarded purple hearts, and other citations. *McGehee Times*, 15 March 1945.

43. *HA*, 27, 28 February, 4 March 1942; "The Charter of Incorporation of Mississippi, Camp Shelby Cooperative Association, January 1941," box 11, folder 2, CCR, USM; "Narrative Program Reports" for August 1942, March 1943, May 1943, "USO Club Operated by Army YMCA," box 1, folder 1, HUSO, USM.

44. Minutes of the Hattiesburg Community Council, 28 November 1943, box 11, folder 17, CCR, USM; *PC*, 5 February 1944; Yuri Kochiyama, interview with Mark Santoki, Oakland, CA, 2 February 2000.

45. "Narrative Program Reports" for March 1943, USO Club Operated by Army YMCA," box 1, folder 1, HUSO, USM; Dan Ogata, interview with Mark Santoki, n.p., July 2000; Masayo Umezawa Duus, *Unlikely Liberators: The Men of the 100th and 442nd* (Honolulu: University of Hawaii Press, 1987), 145.

46. *DHSC*, 1943; Mary Tsukamoto and Elizabeth Pinkerton, *We the People: A Story of Internment in America* (Elk Grove, CA: Laguna, 1987), 165; "Bi-Weekly Report on Evacuee

Opinion, [Jerome] Community Analysis Section and Document Section," 21 June 1943, RG 210, entry 48, box 207, folder 67.012, WRAR, NA; *DT*, 30 July 1943.

47. *DT*, 2 May 1944. Around the same time, "a Minstrel Show of thirty Negro entertainers was enjoyed by the [442nd Regimental] Combat Team" at Camp Shelby, sponsored by the Aloha USO. "The jive, jokes, and jitterbugging made a big hit." *CSR*, 22 April 1944. On the complexities of identification around minstrelsy, see Eric Lott, *Love and Theft: Blackface Minstrelsy and the American Working Class* (New York: Oxford University Press, 1995).

NOTES TO CHAPTER SIX

1. "Weekly Report, Week Ending Noon 10-31 1942, Jerome Relocation Center," part II, section 5, reel 138, JAERR, UCB; Mary Tsukamoto and Elizabeth Pinkerton, *We the People: A Story of Internment in America* (Elk Grove, CA: Laguna, 1987), 107, 115.

2. Tsukamoto and Pinkerton, *We the People*, 115.

3. Ibid., 116, 119–20; "Weekly Report, Week Ending Noon 12-26 1942, Jerome Relocation Center," part II, section 5, reel 138, JAERR, UCB.

4. On attendance at religious services, see "Weekly Report, Week Ending Noon January 23 1943, Jerome Relocation Center," part II, section 5, reel 138, JAERR, UCB.

5. *SAP*, 18 July 1942; *Community School Forum*, June 1943, series 3, folder 4, TC, UA. On Americanization and other aspects of instruction across the WRA camps, see Thomas James, *Exile Within: The Schooling of Japanese Americans, 1942–1945* (Cambridge, MA: Harvard University Press, 1987). See also Jan Fielder Ziegler, *The Schooling of Japanese American Children at Relocation Centers during World War II: Miss Mabel Jamison and Her Teaching of Art at Rohwer, Arkansas* (Lewiston, NY: Edward Mellen, 2005), 99–118.

6. "Denson Schools Hand Book, Jerome Relocation Center," series 4, folder 1, TC UA; "Report on Meeting in Project Director's Office, March 14, 1943," 38, box 2, folder 3, USWRAJ, UA; *DT*, 7 May 1943. On the history of the pledge, the schoolhouse flag, and other implements of Americanization, see Cecilia Elizabeth O'Leary, *To Die For: The Paradox of American Patriotism* (Princeton, NJ: Princeton University Press, 1999).

7. "Report on Meeting in Project Director's Office, March 14, 1943," 11, 39, box 2, folder 3, USWRAJ, UA.

8. *DHSC*, 1943; *DHSV*, 1943; "Commencement Exercises, February Class of 1944, Denson High School," series 4, folder 1, TC, UA.

9. *Community School Forum*, June 1943, series 3, folder 4, TC, UA; "Check List for Teachers," series 4, folder 1, TC, UA; Ziegler, *The Schooling*, 109.

10. *Community School Forum*, June 1943, series 3, folder 4, TC, UA.

11. The downplaying of racist exploitation and violence in such textbooks continues to this day. James W. Loewen, *Lies My Teacher Told Me: Everything Your American History Textbook Got Wrong* (New York: Touchstone, 1996).

12. Dillon S. Myer, "The Relocation Program," 7, box 1, folder 1, LC, UA.

13. John Edgar Hoover, memorandum for the Attorney General, 8 December 1942, box 1, folder 1, USFBI, UCB; Kenneth O'Reilly, *Hoover and the Un-Americans: The FBI, HUAC, and the Red Menace* (Philadelphia: Temple University Press, 1983), 87.

14. Dillon S. Myer, "The Relocation Program," 7, box 1, folder 1, LC, UA.

15. Tsukamoto and Pinkerton, *We the People*, 76. At least since the 1920s, Japanese immigrant intellectuals used the pioneer metaphor for their own ends. "By emphasizing Japanese development, the Issei challenged the Anglo-American monopoly of frontier expansionism, arguing for their own relevance to the settling of the West." Eiichiro Azuma, *Between Two Empires: Race, History, and Transnationalism in Japanese America* (Oxford: Oxford University Press, 2005), 91.

16. George Akimoto, *Lil Dan'l: One Year in a Relocation Center* (Rohwer, AR: Rohwer Outpost, 1943), 1, 3.

17. Ibid., 1.

18. Ibid., 5, 7, 13, 16, 25.

19. Ibid., 25.

20. Ibid., 6, 18, 19.

21. "War Relocation Authority, Internal Security Section, Total 1944 Cases," RG 210, entry 16, box 388, folder 65.100 #5, WRAR, NA; "Weekly Report, Week Ending May 22, 1943, Jerome Relocation Center," "Weekly Report, Week Ending June 12, 1943, Jerome Relocation Center," "Weekly Report, Week Ending June 19, 1943, Jerome Relocation Center," part II, section 5, reel 138, JAERR, UCB; Robert A. Leflar, letter to Philip M. Glick, 14 November 1942, series 2, folder 1, LC, UA; *DT*, 15 June 1943; Ulys A. Lovell, letter to Philip M. Glick, 17 June 1943, part II, section 5, reel 138, JAERR, UCB. On illegal alcohol distribution as a distinctive opportunity for women, see Mary Murphy, "Bootlegging Mothers and Drinking Daughters: Gender and Prohibition in Butte, Montana," *American Quarterly* 46 (June 1994): 174–94.

22. The two photos are cataloged as RG 210, series G, items E290 and I160, WRAR, SPB, NA.

23. Akimoto, *Lil Dan'l*, 24.

24. Deborah Gesensway and Mindy Roseman, *Beyond Words: Images from America's Concentration Camps* (Ithaca, NY: Cornell University Press, 1987), 26–27.

25. Kristine Kim, *Henry Sugimoto: Painting an American Experience* (Berkeley, CA: Heyday Books, 2000), 85, 90.

26. Ibid., 61, 63, 91. The Sugimoto paintings are cataloged as 92.97.139, 92.97.82, and 92.97.83, SC, JANM. Koji Yamamoto, *Senso to Nikkei America-jin* [Japanese Americans and World War II] (Tokyo: Kusanone, 1995), 73–77.

27. Denson Y.B.A., "Gathas and Services," [1943], part II, section 5, reel 139, JAERR, UCB; Lester E. Suzuki, *Ministry in the Assembly and Relocation Centers of World War II* (Berkeley, CA: Yardbird, 1979), 310.

28. Suzuki, *Ministry in the Centers*, 298–99.

29. Paul R. Spickard, *Japanese Americans: The Formation and Transformations of an Ethnic Group* (New York: Twayne, 1996), 29; Japanese American Curriculum Project, *Wartime Hysteria: The Role of the Press* (San Mateo, CA: Japanese American Curriculum Project, 1973), 1; Duncan Ryuken Williams, "Complex Loyalties: Issei Buddhist Ministers during the Wartime Incarceration," *Pacific World* 5 (2003): 259; *Denson Buddhist Bulletin*, 12 December 1943, part II, section 5, reel 139, JAERR, UCB.

30. Williams, "Complex Loyalties," 257. See also Duncan Ryuken Williams, "Camp Dharma: Japanese-American Buddhist Identity and the Internment Experience of World War II," in *Westward Dharma: Buddhism beyond Asia*, ed. Charles S. Prebish and Martin Bauman (Berkeley: University of California Press, 2002), 191–200.

31. *SAP*, 8 July 1942.

32. Williams, "Complex Loyalties," 266; Kyuji Hozaki, Candleholder, 91.26.1, BCAA, JANM; Allen H. Eaton, *Beauty behind Barbed Wire: The Arts of the Japanese in Our War Relocation Camps* (New York: Harper and Brothers, 1952), 126; "Souvenir Edition, Denson Young Buddhists' Association," 5, series 7, folder 3, GC, UA.

33. Tetsuden Kashima, *Buddhism in America: The Social Organization of an Ethnic Religious Institution* (Westport, CT: Greenwood Press, 1977), 57; "Souvenir Edition, Denson Young Buddhists' Association," 5, series 7, folder 3, GC, UA; *Denson YBA Bulletin*, 5 September 1943, part II, section 5, reel 139, JAERR, UCB.

34. "Sangha Brotherhood, Rohwer Y.B.A.," 1943, series 7, folder 3, GC, UA; Williams, "Complex Loyalties," 267.

35. Kashima, *Buddhism in America*, 47–68; "Community Christian Church, Jerome Relocation Center, Denson, Arkansas, the Junior Church, August 15, 1943," part II, section 5, reel 139, JAERR, UCB; *Rohwer Y.B.A.*, 30 January 1944, "Quarterly Report, January–March 1943, Religion," part II, section 5, reel 145, JAERR, UCB; Residents of Blocks 7, 9, 10, 11, 23, 24, 25, and 26, Petition, 9 February 1943, RG 210, entry 48, box 262, folder 68.010, WRAR, NA.

36. *Denson Buddhist Bulletin*, 12 March 1944, part II, section 5, reel 139, JAERR, UCB; "Souvenir Edition, Denson Young Buddhists' Association," 5, series 7, folder 3, GC, UA.

37. Williams, "Complex Loyalties," 268.

38. "Monthly Report, for Month Ending May 31, 1943, Reports Office, Jerome Center" and "Jerome Weekly Report #11, Covering Two Weeks' Period of April 18 to May 1, 1943, Reports Division, Documents Section," part II, section 5, reel 138, JAERR, UCB.

39. "New National Legion Commander Wants to Deport Japanese," n.d., Pamphlet Boxes of Materials on the Japanese in the United States during and after World War II, UCB; "Monthly Report, for Month Ending 7-31, 1943, Reports Office, Jerome Center" and "Office of Reports, Month Ending Jan. 31, 1943, Jerome Project," part II, section 5, reel 138, JAERR, UCB.

40. "Weekly Report, Week Ending March 20, 1943, Jerome Relocation Center," part II, section 5, reel 138, JAERR, UCB.

41. William Cary Anderson, "Early Reaction to the Relocation of Japanese in the State," *Arkansas Historical Quarterly* 23 (Autumn 1964): 206–7; "History of the Rohwer Federated Christian Church, Compiled by the English Secretary, Ministers' Council, on October 21, 1943," series 2, folder 6, GC, UA.

42. Audrie Girdner and Anne Loftis, *The Great Betrayal: The Evacuation of the Japanese-Americans during World War II* (London: Macmillan, 1969), 255.

43. "Monthly Report, for Month Ending April 30, 1944, Reports Office, Jerome Center," part II, section 5, reel 138, JAERR, UCB; *DT*, 25 July 1943. The Susu-Mago play is cited in "Bibliography on War Relocation Authority, Japanese and Japanese Americans, October

1942–July 1943," series 1, folder 4, LC, UA. For a concise, astute reading of Nakahara's play, see David K. Yoo, *Growing Up Nisei: Race, Generation, and Culture among Japanese Americans of California, 1924–1949* (Urbana: University of Illinois Press, 2000), 117–18.

44. "Jerome Christian Mission: Christ Is the Answer," series 4, folder 3, TC, UA; *DT*, 14, 21 May 1943; Anne Reeploeg Fisher, *Exile of a Race* (Kent, WA: F & T Publishers, 1987), 188–89. For a more flattering assessment of Jones and liberal Christians aiding Japanese Americans, see Robert Shaffer, "Cracks in the Consensus: Defending the Rights of Japanese Americans during World War II," *Radical History Review* 72 (1998): 84–120.

45. "The Christian Mission Week, Jerome Relocation Center, Community Analysis Section, May 26, 1943," Community Analysis Reports and Community Analysis Trend Reports of the War Relocation Authority, 1942–1946, microfilm publication M1342, reel 19, WRAR, NA.

46. Tsukamoto and Pinkerton, *We the People*, 160–61.

47. "Monthly Report, for Month Ending Dec. 31, 1943, Reports Office, Jerome Center," part II, section 5, reel 138, JAERR, UCB.

48. Evelyn Brooks Higginbotham, *Righteous Discontent: The Women's Movement in the Black Baptist Church, 1880–1920* (Cambridge, MA: Harvard University Press, 1993); Glenda Elizabeth Gilmore, *Gender and Jim Crow: Women and the Politics of White Supremacy in North Carolina, 1896–1920* (Chapel Hill: University of North Carolina Press, 1996).

NOTES TO CHAPTER SEVEN

1. *DC*, 22 January 1943; Robert A. Leflar, letter to Philip M. Glick, 22 January 1943, series 2, folder 2, LC, UA. Literary scholar Alan Wolfe argues: "To mention suicide and Japan"—or Japanese Americans, I would add—"in the same sentence is to bring to bear a set of stereotypes that continue to shape Western perceptions of non-Western cultures. . . . And yet, the prosaic facts of the matter are that suicide in Japan is essentially comparable as a sociological phenomenon to its manifestations in other advanced industrial societies." *Suicidal Narrative in Modern Japan: The Case of Dazai Osamu* (Princeton, NJ: Princeton University Press, 1990), xiii. Japanese American scholar Harry H. L. Kitano has written of "doubts about whether suicide is socially acceptable in the Japanese-American culture. . . . [S]uicide rates within this group are no higher than in the majority." *Japanese Americans: The Evolution of a Subculture* (Englewood Cliffs, NJ: Prentice-Hall, 1969), 100.

2. "Internal Security, Jerome Center, Monthly Report, for Month Ending Aug. 31, 1943," part II, section 5, reel 139, JAERR, UCB; "Report for Week Ending August 28 1943, Jerome Relocation Center," part II, section 5, reel 138, JAERR, UCB; "Internal Security, Jerome Center, Monthly Report, for Month Ending February [29,] 1944," part II, section 5, reel 139, JAERR, UCB; "Internal Security Case Report, Jerome Project," 8 February 1944, RG 210, entry 51, box 8, project case 108, WRAR, NA.

The other twenty-one boys and men were foreman Tom Matsumoto (age not specified), Hideo Doi (age 16), Michio Imashi (29), George Ishisaki (17), Ben Kawasaki (20), Mitsuru Matsumoto (16), Howard Matsumura (17), Tom Matsumura (19), Joe Minomiya (22), Yokoyama Motokazu (16), Hiroshi Okada (20), Noboru Sasaki (21), Yoshio Shinkawa (21),

Toyomi Shitanishi (25), Kiyonori Takamine (19), Minoru Tokumoto (20), Tadao Tsuneoka (22), James Yamagata (21), Johnie Yamagishi (22), Yukio Yamamoto (21), Masao Yoshida (20). "Internal Security Case Report, Jerome Project," 27 August 1943, RG 210, entry 51, box 8, project case 85, WRAR, NA.

3. "War Relocation Authority, Monthly Report, for Month Ending May 31, 1943, Reports Office, Jerome Center," part II, section 5, reel 138, JAERR, UCB; "War Relocation Authority, Jerome Relocation Center, Report on Meeting in Project Director's Office, March 14, 1943," Appendix No. 5: "Mess Operations, Number of Rations, Costs per Day, Sample Evacuees Menus," Appendix No. 8: "Quarters and Mess for Appointed Personnel," series 2, folder 3, USWRAJ, UA.

4. On the violence at Poston and the riots at Manzanar, see Arthur A. Hansen and David A. Hacker, "The Manzanar Riot: An Ethnic Perspective," *Amerasia Journal* 2 (Fall 1974): 112–57; Gary Y. Okihiro, "Japanese Resistance in America's Concentration Camps: A Re-evaluation," *Amerasia Journal* 2 (Fall 1973): 20–34; and Gary Y. Okihiro, "Religion and Resistance in America's Concentration Camps," *Phylon* 45 (1984): 220–33.

5. Edward H. Spicer et al., *Impounded People: Japanese-Americans in the Relocation Centers* (Tucson: University of Arizona Press, 1969), 95; "Weekly Report, Week Ending Noon, Nov. 21, 1942, Jerome Relocation Center," part II, section 5, reel 138, JAERR, UCB; *DC*, 20 November 1942.

6. Walter Goodman, *The Committee: The Extraordinary Career of the House Committee on Un-American Activities* (New York: Farrar Straus and Giroux, 1968), 153; Robert A. Leflar, letter to Philip M. Glick, 4 January 1943, series 4, folder 29, LC, UA; "Weekly Report, Week Ending Noon, Nov. 21, 1942, Jerome Relocation Center," part II, section 5, reel 138, JAERR, UCB; *DC*, 26 November 1942.

7. *DC*, 22 December 1942.

8. *DC*, 15 January 1943.

9. *DC*, 4 December 1942; Mary Nakahara, "The Bordered World, Vol. I," entry dated 16 June 1942, JANM.

10. "Weekly Report, Week Ending 12-19-1942, Jerome Relocation Center," part II, section 5, reel 138, JAERR, UCB.

11. Violet Kazue de Cristoforo, ed., *May Sky, There Is Always Tomorrow: An Anthology of Japanese American Concentration Camp Kaiko Haiku* (Los Angeles: Sun and Moon Press, 1997), 48, 81–85, 91, 97.

12. Ibid., 167.

13. Ibid., 97.

14. "Weekly Report, Week Ending 12-19-1942, Jerome Relocation Center," part II, section 5, reel 138, JAERR, UCB.

15. "Weekly Report, Week Ending 2-27-1943, Jerome Relocation Center," part II, section 5, reel 138, JAERR, UCB; Richard Drinnon, *Keeper of Concentration Camps: Dillon S. Myer and American Racism* (Berkeley: University of California Press, 1987), 17.

16. *DT*, 19 November 1943; "War Relocation Authority, Jerome Relocation Center, Report on Meeting in Project Director's Office, March 14, 1943," Appendix No. 12: "Agricultural Outlook—Crops, Acres, Yield," series 2, folder 3, USWRAJ, UA.

17. "Weekly Report, Week Ending 12-19 1942, Jerome Relocation Center," part II, section 5, reel 138, JAERR, UCB.

18. De Cristoforo, *May Sky*, 96, 153; Robert A. Leflar, letter to Philip M. Glick, 4 January 1943, series 4, folder 29, LC, UA.

19. "Statement of Witnesses," "Statement of Government Medical Officer or Physician Who First Examined Case," "Official Superior's Report of Injury," "Report of Termination," "Report of Death," 19 January 1943, series 2, folder 2, LC, UA. Relying on the accounts of camp officials, another historian describes the incident in this way: "Unaccustomed to cutting firewood and impeded by the persistent mud, the Japanese [*sic*] experienced great difficulty in sustaining adequate amounts of firewood for the large camp populations. At times, their inept efforts at felling trees resulted in many self-inflicted injuries, and in January 1943, the death of an internee, crushed by a falling tree. The WRA conscientiously worked to improve the living conditions at the camps. . . ." Russell Bearden, "The False Rumor of Tuesday: Arkansas's Internment of Japanese-Americans," *Arkansas Historical Quarterly* 41 (Winter 1982): 332–33.

20. *DT*, 15, 18 June 1943.

21. "War Relocation Authority, Jerome Relocation Center, Report on Meeting in Project Director's Office, March 14, 1943," Appendix No. 6: "Motorized Equipment," Appendix No. 11: "Agricultural Equipment—List and Description," series 2, folder 3, USWRAJ, UA; "Weekly Report, Week Ending April 24, 1943, Jerome Relocation Center," part II, section 5, reel 138, JAERR, UCB; Edgar C. McVoy, "Strike in the Motor Pool and Repair Section," 12 May 1943, Community Analysis Reports and Community Analysis Trend Reports of the War Relocation Authority, 1942–1946, microfilm publication M1342, reel 19, WRAR, NA.

22. "Weekly Report, Week Ending May 15, 1943, Jerome," part II, section 5, reel 138, JAERR, UCB; "Weekly Report, Week Ending May 22, 1943, Jerome," part II, section 5, reel 138, JAERR, UCB; *DT*, 14 May 1943; Paul A. Taylor, memorandum to All Division Chiefs, 12 May 1943; and Paul A. Taylor, memorandum to All Division Chiefs and Section Heads [file copy], RG 210, entry 48, box 178, folder 15.032-D, WRAR, NA.

23. Ulys A. Lovell, letter to Philip M. Glick, 11 May 1943, part II, section 5, reel 138, JAERR, UCB; "Jerome Weekly Report #11, Covering Two Weeks' Period of April 18 to May 1, 1943, Reports Division, Documents Section," part II, section 5, reel 138, JAERR, UCB.

24. "Weekly Report, Week Ending May 22, 1943, Jerome," part II, section 5, reel 138, JAERR, UCB; "Jerome Weekly Report #11, Covering Two Weeks' Period of April 18 to May 1, 1943, Reports Division, Documents Section," part II, section 5, reel 138, JAERR, UCB; "Final Report, W. O. Melton, Assistant Project Director in Charge of Operations, Jerome Relocation Center, July 25, 1944," series 2, folder 1, USWRAJ, UA.

25. "Weekly Report, Week Ending 12-19-1942, Jerome Relocation Center," part II, section 5, reel 138, JAERR, UCB; Robert A. Leflar, letter to Philip M. Glick, 4 January 1943, series 4, folder 29, LC, UA; Drinnon, *Keeper of Concentration Camps*, 276–77; "Weekly Report, Week Ending May 22, 1943, Jerome," part II, section 5, reel 138, JAERR, UCB.

For a history of the Corps of Engineers, see Todd Shallat, *Structures in the Stream: Water, Science, and the Rise of the U.S. Army Corps of Engineers* (Austin: University of Texas Press, 1994). From the period, see Staff of the Infantry Journal, *The Corps of Engineers of the United States Army* (Chicago: Rand McNally, 1943).

26. "Community Analysis Section, Jerome Relocation Center, Denson, Arkansas, May 31, 1943," part II, section 5, reel 138, JAERR, UCB; "War Relocation Authority, Monthly Report, for Month Ending July 31, 1943, Jerome Center," part II, section 5, reel 138, JAERR, UCB; *DT*, 2 July, 3 August, 15 November 1943; "Weekly Report, Week Ending May 29, 1943, Jerome," part II, section 5, reel 138, JAERR, UCB.

27. *DT*, 27 July 1943.

28. *DT*, 27 August, 5 October 1943; "Report for Week Ending September 11, 1943, Jerome Relocation Center," part II, section 5, reel 138, JAERR, UCB; "Internal Security Case Report, Jerome Project," 29 November 1943, RG 210, entry 51, box 8, project case 102, WRAR, NA. At Rohwer "three hundred junior and senior high school boys . . . agreed [*sic*] to spend their three-week summer vacation chopping wood for the community," as one camp publication put it. But the story seemed to subtly imply the coercion and physical strain, noting—with revealing quotation marks—that the "boys are 'having a wonderful time' two miles east of the center these days." Jan Fielder Ziegler, *The Schooling of Japanese American Children at Relocation Centers during World War II: Miss Mabel Jamison and Her Teaching of Art at Rohwer, Arkansas* (Lewiston, NY: Edward Mellen, 2005), 62.

29. Kiyoshi Hamanaka, "Voluntary Wood Crew Report," 9 October 1943, Community Analysis Reports and Community Analysis Trend Reports of the War Relocation Authority, 1942–1946, microfilm publication M1342, reel 19, WRAR, NA.

30. *PC*, 23 October 1943; Ulys A. Lovell, letter to Philip M. Glick, 23 October, 1943, part II, section 5, reel 138, JAERR, UCB; "Jerome Relocation Center, Weekly Report, October 16, 1943," part II, section 5, reel 138, JAERR, UCB. By this time administrators had to concede the dangers inherent in woodcutting, instructing so-called volunteers—via the newspaper—to first register at the employment office in order "to be covered for compensation in the event of injury." *DT*, 22 October 1943.

31. "Jerome Relocation Center, Weekly Report, October 23, 1943," part II, section 5, reel 138, JAERR, UCB.

32. "To Be or Not to Be—Suckers!! How the WRA Exploits You in the Wood Situation!!" part II, section 5, reel 138, JAERR, UCB.

33. *DT*, 22 October 1943.

34. "Internal Security Case Report, Jerome Project," 20 October 1943, RG 210, entry 51, box 8, project case 97, WRAR, NA; Ulys A. Lovell, letter to Philip M. Glick, 1 November 1943, part II, section 5, reel 138, JAERR, UCB; "Internal Security, Jerome Center, Monthly Report, for Month Ending Oct. 31, 1943," part II, section 5, reel 139, JAERR, UCB; *DT*, 29 October 1943; Ulys A. Lovell, letter to Philip M. Glick, 13 November 1943, part II, section 5, reel 138, JAERR, UCB.

As evidence of Paul Yokota's editorial autonomy, E. J. Friedlander, who interviewed Yokota in 1984, cites the "top-of-the-fold story" on the 19 November 1942 strike over "poor quality lunches"; he mentions no other strikes. He cites "hard news" coverage of the trailer accident but makes no mention of the death of Haruji Ego. He offers no rationales for Yokota's leaving the paper and the camp. "Freedom of Press behind Barbed Wire: Paul Yokota and the Jerome Relocation Center Newspaper," *Arkansas Historical Quarterly* 44 (Winter 1985): 308–9, 312.

35. "Jerome Relocation Center, Weekly Report, October 30, 1943," part II, section 5, reel 138, JAERR, UCB.

36. Ulys A. Lovell, letter to Philip M. Glick, 1 November 1943, part II, section 5, reel 138, JAERR, UCB; Ulys A. Lovell, letter to Philip M. Glick, 13 November 1943, part II, section 5, reel 138, JAERR, UCB; "Jerome Relocation Center, Weekly Report, November 13, 1943," part II, section 5, reel 138, JAERR, UCB.

37. *DT*, 19 November 1943; "Jerome Relocation Center, Weekly Report, November 20, 1943," part II, section 5, reel 138, JAERR, UCB.

38. U.A. Lovell, teletype to Philip M. Glick, 9:36 a.m., 21 June 1944, RG 210, entry 16, box 388, folder 65.100, #4, WRAR, NA; Ulys A. Lovell, letter to Philip M. Glick, 21 June 1944, series 1, folder 5, USJRC, UA; "Final Report, W. O. Melton, Assistant Project Director in Charge of Operations, Jerome Relocation Center, July 25, 1944," series 2, folder 1, USWRAJ, UA.

39. *DC*, 22 January 1943.

40. Ibid.; Robert A. Leflar, letter to Philip M. Glick, 22 January 1943, series 2, folder 2, LC, UA.

41. *PC*, 25 August 1945.

42. United States War Relocation Authority, *The Evacuated People: A Quantitative Description* (Washington, DC: GPO, 1946), 147–48; "Total 1944 Cases, Internal Security Section, War Relocation Authority," RG 210, entry 16, box 388, folder 65.100 #5, WRAR, NA; *PC*, 10 June 1944. See also Michi Nishiura Weglyn, *Years of Infamy: The Untold Story of America's Concentration Camps*, updated ed. (Seattle: University of Washington Press, 1996), 78, 126, 258.

NOTES TO CHAPTER EIGHT

1. Violet Kazue de Cristoforo, "A Victim of the Japanese Evacuation and Resettlement Study," 30 June 1987, 13, DP, UCB; Violet Kazue de Cristoforo, ed., *May Sky, There Is Always Tomorrow: An Anthology of Japanese American Concentration Camp Kaiko Haiku* (Los Angeles: Sun and Moon Press, 1997), 284; John Tateishi, *And Justice for All: An Oral History of the Japanese American Detention Camps* (New York: Random House, 1984), 124–40.

2. United States Commission on Wartime Relocation and Internment of Civilians, *Personal Justice Denied: Report of the Commission on Wartime Relocation and Internment of Civilians* (Seattle: University of Washington Press, 1997), 185–212, 224–26; Greg Robinson, *By Order of the President: FDR and the Internment of Japanese Americans* (Cambridge, MA: Harvard University Press, 2001), 192–94; "War Relocation Authority, Jerome Relocation Center, Report on Meeting in Project Director's Office, March 14, 1943," series 2, folder 3, USWRAJ, UA.

The registration program and other legalistic processes for ascertaining allegiances by a variety of federal bodies are examined in Eric L. Muller, *American Inquisition: The Hunt for Japanese American Disloyalty in World War II* (Chapel Hill: University of North Carolina Press, 2007).

3. Mary Tsukamoto and Elizabeth Pinkerton, *We the People: A Story of Internment in America* (Elk Grove, CA: Laguna, 1987), 126. On those who took advantage of long-term leave for university education, see Gary Y. Okihiro, *Storied Lives: Japanese American Students and World War II* (Seattle: University of Washington Press, 1999).

4. John Okada, *No-No Boy* (repr., Seattle: University of Washington Press, 1979). "Yes-yes" and "no-no" designations as markers of identity were not in widespread general use during the war. Years after the trauma, related to a newfound willingness to talk and write about these events, they began to be applied, not unlike the camp affiliations of parents and grandparents.

5. Etienne Balibar and Immanuel Wallerstein, *Race, Nation, Class: Ambiguous Identities* (London: Verso, 1991).

6. On internment camp appeals, see Louis Fiset, *Imprisoned Apart: The World War II Correspondence of an Issei Couple* (Seattle: University of Washington Press, 1997); "Leave Clearance Hearing for Isami Inouye," 7 July 1943; Leave Investigation Committee, memorandum and transcription to Ray D. Johnston [re: Masato Kamita], 2 September 1943; "Transcription of Hearing for Mr. Hirofusa Okumura," 17 August 1943; "Transcription of Hearing for Miss Kuniko Okumura," 17 August 1943; all in series 6, folder 3, LC, UA.

7. "Transcript of Hearing for Akira Oye," 17 September 1943; "Transcript of Hearing for Jimmy Toshikazu Kumamaru," 24 September 1943; both in series 6, folder 3, LC, UA. Here and elsewhere, I build upon concepts of the nation as an imagined community. See Benedict Anderson, *Imagined Communities: Reflections on the Origin and Spread of Nationalism*, rev. ed. (London: Verso, 1991).

8. James F. Rains, Edward B. Moulton, and Jack S. Curtis, memorandum to Ray D. Johnston, 18 September 1943; "Transcript of Hearing for Mary Shigetome," 17 September 1943; both in series 6, folder 3, LC, UA.

9. "Transcript of Hearing for Maseto Takemoto," 17 September 1943, series 6, folder 3, LC, UA.

10. "Transcript of Leave Clearance for Shoichi Yamada," n.d., series 6, folder 3, LC, UA; "War Relocation Authority, Jerome Relocation Center, Report on Meeting in Project Director's Office, March 14, 1943," series 2, folder 3, USWRAJ, UA.

11. Leave Investigation Committee, memorandum and transcription to Ray D. Johnston [re: Masato Kamita], 2 September 1943; Jack Curtis, memorandum to Ray D. Johnston [re: Yukiko Ota], 1 September 1943; both in series 6, folder 3, LC, UA; Lisa Lowe, *Immigrant Acts: On Asian American Cultural Politics* (Durham, NC: Duke University Press, 1996), 48–50.

12. "Transcription of Hearing for Miss Sachiko Tanaka," 17 August 1943, series 6, folder 3, LC, UA.

13. Ibid.

14. Lowe, *Immigrant Acts*, 103–4.

15. "Weekly Report, Week Ending March 13, 1943, Jerome Relocation Center," part II, section 5, reel 138, JAERR, UCB; "Final Report, W. O. Melton, Assistant Project Director in Charge of Operations, Jerome Relocation Center, July 25, 1944," series 2, folder 1, USWRAJ, UA; JRCL, 6, UA.

16. United States War Relocation Authority, *The Evacuated People: A Quantitative Description* (Washington, DC: GPO, 1946), 8, 120, 123, 165, 168, 196; Tokio Yamane, interview with author, Fukuyama, Japan, 28 July 2002; "Persons on Record as Desiring Repatriation, as of June 15, 1943, Jerome Center," 20; Paul A. Taylor, letter to Dillon S. Myer, 30 August 1943; E. B. Whitaker, letter to Dillon S. Myer, 3 December 1943; all in RG 210, entry 48, box 192, folder 36.310, WRAR, NA. Different methods yield different percentages. See Muller, *American Inquisition*; and Bruce Elleman, *Japanese-American Civilian Prisoner Exchanges and Detention Camps, 1941–45* (London: Routledge, 2006).

17. E. B. Whitaker, confidential letter to Dillon S. Myer, 17 March 1943, RG 210, entry 16, box 229, folder 31.007, WRAR, NA. Note that this confidential document seems out of proper sequence in the National Archives files, perhaps as a result of a subsequent process of declassification. Nonetheless, I cite the folder in which I found it.

18. "War Relocation Authority, Jerome Relocation Center, Report on Meeting in Project Director's Office, March 14, 1943," series 2, folder 3, USWRAJ, UA; Kristine Kim, *Henry Sugimoto: Painting an American Experience* (Berkeley, CA: Heyday Books, 2000), 86–87, 92–93; "Report for Week Ending August 28, 1943, Jerome Relocation Center," part II, section 5, reel 138, JAERR, UCB. A Japanese American Methodist minister seems to exaggerate the Yamazaki story as does Sugimoto, referring to the assailants as "hot-heads." He further, without supplying evidence, asserts that a Buddhist priest incited this "vicious opposition." Lester E. Suzuki, *Ministry in the Assembly and Relocation Centers of World War II* (Berkeley, CA: Yardbird, 1979), 293, 352.

19. Whitaker, confidential letter to Myer, 17 March 1943.

20. Ulys A. Lovell, letter to Philip M. Glick, 7 August 1943; "Report for Week Ending August 28, 1943, Jerome Relocation Center"; part II, section 5, reel 138, JAERR, UCB.

21. De Cristoforo, "A Victim," 9; Shiori Nomura, "Japanese Immigrant Women and the Idea of 'Home': Voices in *The Nichibei (Japanese American Daily)*, 1914–1924" (Ph.D. diss., University of Birmingham, 2006), 69, 74; Tateishi, *And Justice for All*, 130–32.

22. De Cristoforo, "A Victim," 9. For a discussion of the relationship between Violet Matsuda and Rosalie Hankey, see Violet Kazue de Cristoforo, "J'Accuse," "Further Clarification," "General Comments"; Rosalie H. Wax, "A Response"; George Yamada, "Two Letters to Rosalie Hankey Wax," all in *Rikka: Cross-Cultural Journal* 13 (1992): 16–37. See also Rosalie H. Wax, *Doing Fieldwork: Warnings and Advice* (Chicago: University of Chicago Press, 1971), 59–174.

23. Yamane, interview with author; Teruko Imai Kumei, "'Skeleton in the Closet': The Japanese American *Hokoku Seinen-dan* and Their 'Disloyal' Activities at the Tule Lake Segregation Center during World War II," *Japanese Journal of American Studies* 7 (1996): 71–72.

24. Barbara Takei and Judy Tachibana, *Tule Lake Revisited: A Brief History and Guide to the Tule Lake Internment Camp Site* (Sacramento, CA: T & T Press, 2001), 14–18; Tule Lake Committee, *Second Kinenhi: Reflections on Tule Lake*, 2nd ed. (San Francisco: Tule Lake Committee, 2000), 47–71; de Cristoforo, "A Victim," 15; *Personal Justice Denied*, 209.

25. Yamane, interview with author; Tokio Yamane, untitled handwritten statement, 6 April [1945?], trans. Takashi Ebina, in author's possession; de Cristoforo, "A Victim," 24–25; *Personal Justice Denied*, 210. ACLU and other accounts confirm the bloody broken bat.

26. Yamane, handwritten statement.

27. Ibid.; Yamane, interview with author; *Personal Justice Denied*, 247.

28. Yamane, handwritten statement.

29. Tateishi, *And Justice for All*, 115–17, 247; Yamane, handwritten statement; de Cristoforo, "A Victim," 18, 26, 61. Also on this period at Tule Lake, see Richard Drinnon, *Keeper of Concentration Camps: Dillon S. Myer and American Racism* (Berkeley: University of California Press, 1987), 81–116.

30. Tule Lake Committee, *Second Kinenhi*, 56; Kumei, "Skeleton in the Closet," 73–74, 78; *Personal Justice Denied*, 247–48.

31. Kumei, "Skeleton in the Closet," 74, 78; Yamane, interview with author; Takei and Tachibana, *Tule Lake Revisited*, 18–19.

32. Michi Nishiura Weglyn, "Preface to the Second Edition," in Tule Lake Committee, *Second Kinenhi*, iii; Michi Nishiura Weglyn, *Years of Infamy: The Untold Story of America's Concentration Camps*, updated ed. (Seattle: University of Washington Press, 1996), 147, 149, 230, 238, 245, 247; de Cristoforo, "A Victim," 92.

33. Kumei, "Skeleton in the Closet," 68, 82, 93; Yamane, interview with author.

34. Yoko Ota, *Cities of Corpses*, in *Hiroshima: Three Witnesses*, ed. and trans. Richard H. Minear (Princeton, NJ: Princeton University Press, 1990), 168, 181–82.

35. Ibid.; Tateishi, *And Justice for All*, 136; Yamane, interview with author.

36. "Hiroshima Testimony: The City Obliterated, the Aftermath," Hiroshima Peace Memorial Museum, Hiroshima, Japan, 1 March–10 July 2002; Sankichi Toge, "August 6," in *Poems of the Atomic Bomb*, in *Hiroshima: Three Witnesses*, ed. Minear, 306; John Hersey, *Hiroshima* (New York: Knopf, 1946), 182–83. See also Hiroshima Peace Memorial Museum, *The Spirit of Hiroshima: An Introduction to the Atomic Bomb Tragedy* (Hiroshima: Hiroshima Peace Memorial Museum, 1999).

37. David Serlin, *Replaceable You: Engineering the Body in Postwar America* (Chicago: University of Chicago Press, 2004), 57–110.

38. Ibid.; Hersey, *Hiroshima*, 9; Ota, *Cities of Corpses*, 155–56. American censorship continues, as with the congressional whitewashing of the Smithsonian Institution's *Enola Gay* exhibition in 1995; the Atlanta high school board cancellation of a presentation by four *hibakusha* in 2002; and the United Nations headquarters cancellation of a proposed exhibition on Hiroshima and Nagasaki later that year. Richard H. Kohn, "History and the Culture Wars," *Journal of American History* 82 (December 1995): 1036–63; *Asahi Shimbun*, 4 May, 16 July 2002.

39. Sankichi Toge, "When Will That Day Come?" in *Poems of the Atomic Bomb*, 363.

40. For insightful analysis of the work of Ota, Toge, and many others, see John Whittier Treat, *Writing Ground Zero: Japanese Literature and the Atomic Bomb* (Chicago: University of Chicago Press, 1995). On the American rationales for Hiroshima, see Mariana Torgovnick, *The War Complex: World War II in Our Time* (Chicago: University of Chicago Press, 2005), especially 4–7, 140–45.

41. Muffie Meyer and Ellen Hovde, dirs., *American Photography: A Century of Images* (St. Paul/Minneapolis, MN: Twin Cities Public Television, 1999); Edward P. Russell III, "Speaking of Annihilation: Mobilizing for War against Human and Insect Enemies, 1914–

1945," *Journal of American History* 82 (March 1996): 1505–29. On Korean women drafted into sexual slavery by the Japanese military, see Keith Howard, ed., *True Stories of the Korean Comfort Women*, trans. Young Joo Lee (London: Cassell, 1995), as well as Dean Spade and Sel Wahng, "Transecting the Academy," *GLQ* 10 (2004): 240–53.

42. *PC*, 16 February 1946; Yamane, interview with author.

43. De Cristoforo, "A Victim," 13; de Cristoforo, *May Sky*, 284; Tateishi, *And Justice for All*, 136–37.

44. De Cristoforo, "J'Accuse," 27–28.

45. Russell, "Speaking of Annihilation." Of 1,993 "family heads" at Jerome processed by their prefecture, territory, or state of origin, 491 claimed Hiroshima, 284 California, 191 Wakayama, 140 Kumamoto, 99 Yamaguchi, 94 Fukuoka, 81 Hawaii. *DT*, 6 June 1944.

NOTES TO CHAPTER NINE

1. Michi Nishiura Weglyn, *Years of Infamy: The Untold Story of America's Concentration Camps*, updated ed. (Seattle: University of Washington Press, 1996), 43–45; *The Commonweal*, 10 March 1944.

2. Mary Tsukamoto and Elizabeth Pinkerton, *We the People: A Story of Internment in America* (Elk Grove, CA: Laguna, 1987), 270.

3. "The Closing of the Jerome Relocation Center" and Rachel Reese Sady, "War Relocation Authority, Community Analysis Section, July 14, 1944, Summary of Closing Procedures," both in part II, section 5, reel 138, WRAR, NA; Mitziko Sawada, "After the Camps: Seabrook Farms, New Jersey, and the Resettlement of Japanese Americans, 1944–47," *Amerasia Journal* 13 (1986–87): 117.

4. *RO*, 2 June 1945. Here and elsewhere in this chapter, I am indebted to the work of Andrew King, a former undergraduate at the University of York. His first-class research essay, drawn from archival materials I provided, is entitled "Ambivalence and Uncertainty: Responses to Camp Closing at the Rohwer Internment Centre," autumn term, 1999.

5. Roger Daniels, *Prisoners without Trial: Japanese Americans in World War II* (New York: Hill and Wang, 1993), 82.

6. As previously noted, for a systemic reading and periodic translations of the Japanese-language sections of both the *Denson Tribune* and *Rohwer Outpost*, I am grateful to Sahori Watanabe.

7. See, for example, RG 210, series G, item H451, WRAR, SPB, NA.

8. *DT*, 28 September 1943; Lewis A. Sigler, "Solicitor's Memorandum No. 15," 10 July 1943, series 1, folder 2, JRCC, UA; Dillon S. Myer, "The Relocation Program," box 1, folder 1, LC, UA; Greg Robinson, *By Order of the President: FDR and the Internment of Japanese Americans* (Cambridge, MA: Harvard University Press, 2001), 218–22.

9. *American Legion Magazine*, June 1943; *New York Times*, 25 May 1943; *Common Ground*, Summer 1943; all cited in "Bibliography on War Relocation Authority, Japanese, and Japanese Americans, October 1942–July 1943," series 1, folder 4, LC, UA. Robinson, *By Order of the President*, 236–37; *DM*, April 1943, 3.

10. *RO*, 8 January 1944.

11. Thomas James, *Exile Within: The Schooling of Japanese Americans, 1942–1945* (Cambridge, MA: Harvard University Press, 1987), 112–39; "Denson Schools Hand Book, Jerome Relocation Center," series 4, folder 1, TC, UA; Earl M. Finch, letter to H. Rex Lee, 8 June 1945, RG 210, entry 16, box 489, folder 71.900H #2, WRAR, NA; H. Rex Lee, letter to C. C. Holloway, RG 210, entry 16, box 489, folder 71.900H #3, WRAR, NA.

12. Akiko Higake, "Resettlement," n.d.; Katsuto Nakano, "Relocation," n.d.; Clara Hasegawa, "Relocation," 12 August 1943; Michiko Odate, "Resettlement," 12 August 1943; all in Tidball Student Essays, TC, UA.

13. *RO*, 27 September 1944; Edgar Bernhard, letter to Ulys A. Lovell, 31 December 1943, series 1, folder 1, LUC, UA.

14. *RO*, 10, 20 January, 3 March, 7 April 1945.

15. Herbert Sasaki, interview with author, Hattiesburg, MS, 22 September 1999; interview with Mark Santoki, n.p., n.d. (1999–2000); interview with Mississippi Oral History Program, 23 October 1998; *Los Angeles Times*, 25 May 2005.

16. Kazu Iijima, interview with Mark Santoki, n.p., February 2000. This story is also told in Glenn Omatsu, "Always a Rebel: An Interview with Kazu Iijima," *Amerasia Journal* 13 (1986–87): 95.

17. William T. Schmidt, "The Impact of the Camp Shelby Mobilization on Hattiesburg, Mississippi, 1940–1946" (Ph.D. diss., University of Southern Mississippi, 1972), 100–101; Yuri Kochiyama, interview with Mark Santoki, Oakland, CA, 2 February 2000. On Kochiyama's later life and activism, see Diane C. Fujino, *Heartbeat of Struggle: The Revolutionary Life of Yuri Kochiyama* (Minneapolis: University of Minnesota Press, 2005), 110–311.

18. *DT*, 11 June 1943.

19. Tsukamoto and Pinkerton, *We the People*, 174–75; *RO*, 13 January 1945.

20. Tsukamoto and Pinkerton, *We the People*, 176–77.

21. Ibid., 178–79, 193, 275.

22. *PC*, 19 February 1944, 3 March 1945; Sawada, "After the Camps," 118; *DT*, 29 February 1944.

23. Tsukamoto and Pinkerton, *We the People*, 191–93.

24. Ibid. For another example of suicide in the wake of incarceration, see *PC*, 2 March 1946.

25. Tsukamoto and Pinkerton, *We the People*, xi, 197, 202.

26. United States War Relocation Authority, *The Relocation Program: A Guidebook for the Residents of Relocation Centers* (Washington, DC: GPO, 1943), 2, 4.

27. United States War Relocation Authority, *The Evacuated People: A Quantitative Description* (Washington, DC: GPO, 1946), 8; United States War Relocation Authority, *Administrative Highlights of the WRA Program* (Washington, DC: GPO, 1946), 6–7; United States War Relocation Authority, *They're Friendly in New England: What New England Newspapers Say about Japanese Americans* (Washington, DC: Department of the Interior, n.d. [1944]); Richard Drinnon, *Keeper of Concentration Camps: Dillon S. Myer and American Racism* (Berkeley: University of California Press, 1987), 60.

28. *RO*, 31 January, 14 February 1945; Roger Daniels, *Concentration Camps North America: Japanese in the United States and Canada during World War II* (Malabar, FL: Robert E. Krieger, 1981), 167.

29. "WRA Bulletin: Relocation Opportunities," 10 January 1946, RG 210, entry 16, box 489, folder 71.900H #3, WRAR, NA.

30. Ibid.

31. Ibid.; Gary Y. Okihiro, "Religion and Resistance in America's Concentration Camps," *Phylon* 45 (1984): 220, 229.

32. "WRA Bulletin: Relocation Opportunities," 10 January 1946, RG 210, entry 16, box 489, folder 71.900H #3, WRAR, NA. See Jeff Wiltse, *Contested Waters: A Social History of Swimming Pools in America* (Chapel Hill: University of North Carolina Press, 2007).

33. "WRA Bulletin: Relocation Opportunities," 10 January 1946, RG 210, entry 16, box 489, folder 71.900H #3, WRAR, NA.

34. Ibid. See Pete Daniel, *The Shadow of Slavery: Peonage in the South, 1901–1969* (1972; repr., Urbana: University of Illinois Press, 1990).

35. "WRA Bulletin: Relocation Opportunities," 10 January 1946; *Detroit Free Press*, 16 February 1943. On the protest statement by the Clarksville, Arkansas, branch of the American Association of University Women, see *AG*, 21 February 1943.

36. *DT*, 24 September 1943; D. S. Myer, memorandum to Project Directors, 13 December 1943, series 8, folder 3, LC, UA.

37. S. Muraoka, C. Sumida, and T. Takasugi, "Cooperative Colonization," 1 August 1944, part II, section 5, reel 145, JAERR, UCB; "War Relocation Authority, Jerome Relocation Center, Report on Meeting in Project Director's Office, March 14, 1943," series 2, folder 3, USWRAJ, UA. A rival plan at Rohwer proposed three colonies on new lands in Colorado, Nebraska, and Texas. Jan Fielder Ziegler, *The Schooling of Japanese American Children at Relocation Centers during World War II: Miss Mabel Jamison and Her Teaching of Art at Rohwer, Arkansas* (Lewiston, NY: Edward Mellen, 2005), 190.

38. Muraoka et al., "Cooperative Colonization."

39. C. Calvin Smith, *War and Wartime Changes: The Transformation of Arkansas, 1940–1945* (Fayetteville: University of Arkansas Press, 1986), 74–75.

40. Violet Kazue de Cristoforo, ed., *May Sky, There Is Always Tomorrow: An Anthology of Japanese American Concentration Camp Kaiko Haiku* (Los Angeles: Sun and Moon Press, 1997), 145. See also Anna Hosticka Tamura, "Gardens Below the Watchtower: Gardens and Meaning in World War II Japanese Incarceration Camps," *Landscape Journal* 23 (2004): 1–21.

41. De Cristoforo, *May Sky*, 95.

42. *RO*, 12 May 1945.

NOTES TO CHAPTER TEN

1. *HH*, 6 March 1946; *HSB*, 5 March 1946; *JDN*, 22 February 1946.

2. *HSB*, 5 March 1946.

3. *HA*, 7 March 1946; *HT*, 26 March 1946.

4. *HT*, 26 March 1946; *HSB*, 29 March 1946; [Kauai] *Garden Island*, 12 March 1946; *Maui News*, 9, 13 March 1946; *HH*, 29 March 1946.

5. *HSB*, 7 March 1946; *Times-Picayune Magazine*, 5 October 1947; *HT*, 6 March 1946; Masayo Umezawa Duus, *Unlikely Liberators: The Men of the 100th and 442nd* (Honolulu:

University of Hawaii Press, 1987), 144; *HA*, 12, 14 March 1946. Mark Santoki's excellent account of Earl Finch's first visit to Hawaii can be found in *The Earl Finch Story: One Man U.S.O.* (Honolulu: Seiji F. Naya, 2000), 24–35.

6. *HA*, 14 December 1946.

7. *HA*, 3, 16 February, 13 March 1950; *HSB*, 20 January, 8 February, 6, 25 March 1950; *Webster* [MS County] *Progress*, 2 March 1950.

8. *HA*, 23 December 1947, 21 February, 13, 18, 27 March 1952; *HSB*, 27 June 1950, 12 October, 9 November 1951; Tom Moffatt, interview with Mark Santoki, Honolulu, HI, n.d. (1999).

9. *HA*, 31 December 1951, 13 November 1953; *HSB*, 1, 16 December 1953, 23 January 1954, 7 July 1955.

10. *HA*, 31 December 1951; *HSB*, 1, 21 April 1952.

11. *HA*, 1 April, 27 May 1952; Seiji Naya, interview with author, Honolulu, HI, 11 January 2003; Seiji Naya, interview with Mark Santoki, Honolulu, HI, n.d. (1999). Hiroyuki Kaji, Naya's teammate on the Japanese boxing team, remembers first meeting Finch in Tokyo in 1950. Along with Naya's other friends, Kaji would take Finch out on his subsequent visits to Japan. Hiroyuki Kaji, interview with author (Tomomi Iino, interpreter), Tokyo, Japan, 11 June 2004.

12. Naya, interview with author; Naya, interview with Santoki; *HA*, 1 April 1952.

13. *HA*, 29 May 1952; *HSB*, 27, 29 May 1952; Naya, interview with author; Naya, interview with Santoki; Subject: Earl Finch, File Number: 105-3749, Federal Bureau of Investigation, Washington, DC; David K. Johnson, *The Lavender Scare: The Cold War Persecution of Gays and Lesbians in the Federal Government* (Chicago: University of Chicago Press, 2004).

14. Naya, interview with author; Naya, interview with Santoki; *HSB*, 12 October 1951, 25 February 1954; Kaji, interview with author; *HA*, 29 January 1978.

15. Roger Daniels, "Two Cheers for Immigration," in *Debating American Immigration, 1882–Present*, ed. Roger Daniels and Otis L. Graham (Lanham, MD: Rowman and Littlefield, 2001), 36; "Go for Broke 442nd Carnival, June 7–11, 1947, Official Souvenir Program, Honolulu Stadium," in files of author; *HA*, 30 April 1947.

16. Tom Moffat, interview with author, Honolulu, HI, 28 December 2005.

17. *HSB*, 26 April 1951; *HA*, 31 December 1951, 12 March 1955.

18. *HSB*, 9 November 1951, 22 March 1952, 1 December 1955, 20 February 1958; John Howard, *Men Like That: A Southern Queer History* (Chicago: University of Chicago Press, 1999), 226.

19. *PC*, 15 April, 27 July 1956. I am greatly indebted to historian Greg Robinson for locating these articles.

20. Howard, *Men Like That*, 163–65, 190–91.

21. *PC*, 25 August 1945. On any number of aspects of the occupation, see the essays collected in Carol Gluck and Stephen R. Graubard, eds., *Showa: The Japan of Hirohito* (New York: W. W. Norton, 1992).

22. Kobena Mercer's perceptive account of the pitfalls and dangers, the power differentials and colonial residues, in the white racial fetishization of black male bodies is applied

with particular force to the European American/Asian American context by literary scholar David L. Eng in *Racial Castration: Managing Masculinity in Asian America* (Durham, NC: Duke University Press, 2001), 220. As Richard Fung has bluntly stated about the feminizing and queering qualities of American racist representations: "Asian and anus are conflated." "Looking for My Penis: The Eroticized Asian in Gay Video Porn," in *How Do I Look?: Queer Film and Video*, ed. Bad Object-Choices (Seattle: Bay Press, 1991), 153. (On the other hand, Mercer's various discussions of Robert Mapplethorpe photographs have referenced Frantz Fanon to sum up another body of racist visual artifacts: "The Negro . . . *is* a penis." *Black Skin, White Masks*, trans. Charles Lam Markmann [New York: Grove, 1967], 170.) Mercer famously reconsidered his initial readings of Mapplethorpe in "Skin Head Sex Thing: Racial Difference and the Homoerotic Imaginary," in *How Do I Look?*

So, as David Eng tells us, rice queens tend to be much older than their partners—and uglier. We are left, then, with a whole host of scales, a matrix, of inequality that would seem to invalidate the rice queen's relationship, rendering it unsound: almost necessarily, perforce, socially unsanctionable. Continuing white privilege in the United States renders the rice queen racially and economically advantaged, in a position of power relative to the partner, who is at bottom, further, in the sexual sense. Left unelaborated by Eng are the inequities of age and beauty. While the forty-year-old rice queen fares much better than the partner half his age on wage and salary scales, Eng overlooks the power accruing to the young and beautiful in a dominant gay male culture even more ageist and looksist, if you will, than the mainstream. While racist norms of beauty and standards of desirability will continue to discount the allure of nonwhites of any age, youthful good looks nonetheless carry significant rewards. Still, "the common belief," writes Martin Manalansan in his powerful ethnography, "is that the rice queen preys on young Asian boys." In the view of many, he is indulging pedophilic urges with young, smooth, diminutive Asian males. *Global Divas: Filipino Gay Men in the Diaspora* (Durham, NC: Duke University Press, 2003), 84.

The denigration of rice queens, I believe, flows logically and historically from a legitimate, indeed crucial project of second-wave feminism. Promoting equality between women and men in heterosexual relationships entailed a more equitable distribution of household tasks, a joint commitment to paid labor outside the home, and a greater sharing of any number of gendered responsibilities and obligations, to offset the pernicious sexist biases, in global markets and in everyday life, that usually insured a significant power differential between the members of a couple. However, taken to its logical end, this reasoning would mandate that partners belong to the same economic class, have the same levels of educational attainment and other markers of status, be of the same race, age, and physical ability, and pursue sexual intercourse with equivalent standing. This reasoning was in fact taken to its logical end in the gay male realm when Charles Silverstein and Edmund White declared in *The Joy of Gay Sex: An Intimate Guide for Gay Men to the Pleasures of a Gay Lifestyle* (New York: Crown, 1977), 10–11, that the archetypal gay male couple might be "a 35-year-old lawyer in love with a 35-year-old doctor; they take turns fucking each other, they share expenses and household duties and they will stay together forever (or so they hope)." As a project of historical specificity, the authors contrasted this model with Athenian pederasty and further with a Victorian/Wildean aristocratic or bohemian "nineteenth-century homosexual, at least the figure we know about": "Wearing cloaks of secrecy, homosexuals [then] loved men of all ages, but almost never lived with another man." David Halperin helpfully critiques ancient, premodern, and modern temporal distinctions, insisting that "assertions of the essential modernity of [the twentieth-century model], of that ideology, produces invidious distinctions between" our couple of thirty-five years of age and "those unfortunates whose sexual or domestic lives still bore traces of" what Silverstein and White refer to as "one-sidedness." This couple, in both Silverstein and White's construction and Halperin's critique, goes unmarked as white, though Halperin quotes Cuban writer Reinaldo Arenas's disaffection from a dominant late-twentieth-century New York gay sexual reciprocity, to consider dominant sexual practices in contemporary "developing nations." In gay popular discourse, these get maligned as "pre-modern," "thereby perpetuating the hoary colonialist notion that non-European cultures represent the cultural childhood of modern Europe." David M. Halperin, *How to Do the History of Homosexuality* (Chicago: University of Chicago Press, 2002), 18–20.

23. Christopher Nealon, *Foundlings: Lesbian and Gay Historical Emotion before Stonewall* (Durham, NC: Duke University Press, 2001), 12; Halperin, *How to Do the History*, 17. Queer popular discourse acknowledges not only white men interested in black men with a particularly pernicious designation, dinge queen, but also black men given to partnering with whites: snow queens, or—seemingly in greater usage in the American South—dairy queens, after that section's popular fast-food chain. Potato queen is increasingly in use in the United States, even more so in the United Kingdom (with its very particular legacy of south, east, and southeast Asian imperialism) and, of course, in present-day east Asia. Inexpensive air travel means greater circulation not only for white Westerners between London and the former colonies, between New York and Tokyo, but also for postcolonial subjects moving between the homeland and the metropole. As Etienne Balibar puts it, "[Immigrants] appear [in the metropole] as the result of colonization and decolonization and thus succeed in concentrating upon themselves both the continuation of imperial scorn and the resentment that is felt by the citizens of a fallen power, if not indeed a vague, phantasmatic longing for revenge." Etienne Balibar and Immanuel Wallerstein, *Race, Nation, Class: Ambiguous Identities* (London: Verso, 1991).

If historical practice privileges the traditional written documents found in the wake of the famous and powerful, say, the rice queens of the fallen and not yet fully fallen powers, how do we accrue evidence of the potato queen? How might we get beyond conventional historical practice to speculate about the lives of potato queens, or about proto-potato queens, perhaps including Earl Finch's friends? Oddly, Eng's insightful book about masculinity and sexuality in Asian America doesn't even make reference to potato queens. Neither does Manalansan's, even as he rightly castigates accounts of rice queens that "construct the gay Asian man as devoid of agency." Unlike "rice queen," the term "potato queen" appears in neither index. If rice queens are "endemic," as Eng would have it, to mainstream gay communities, what about their partners? How might we return agency and subjectivity to potato queens? In other words, if it's incumbent upon us to historicize rice queens, how might we theorize potato queens? Manalansan, *Global Divas*, 85. Similar questions might be productively asked of Robert Aldrich's magisterial *Colonialism and Homosexuality* (London: Routledge, 2003).

24. Tom Moffatt, *Uncle Tom's Rock 'n Roll Scrapbook: Five Decades of Musical Memories in Hawaii* (Honolulu: Tom Moffatt, n.d. [1998]), 4, 52.

25. "Go for Broke 442nd Carnival, Souvenir Program"; *HA*, 12 December 1945; David J. O'Brien and Stephen S. Fugita, *The Japanese American Experience* (Bloomington: Indiana University Press, 1991), 86–88; Kaji, interview with author.

26. Moffatt, *Rock 'n Roll*, 6, 27; *HA*, 7 June 1957, 6, 29 November 1957.

27. Moffatt, *Rock 'n Roll*, 12, 27–31; *HA*, 8 February 1959, 6 June 1960.

28. Moffatt, *Rock 'n Roll*, 12, 30–33; *HA*, 27, 28 September 1960.

29. Moffatt, *Rock 'n Roll*, 8; *HA*, 14 February 1958, 26 January 1959, 16 July 1963.

30. *HA*, 14 August 1957; Ralph Yempuku, interview with Mark Santoki, Honolulu, HI, n.d. [1999]; Moffatt, interview with Santoki.

31. Hideo Sakamoto, interview with Mark Santoki, Aiea, HI, n.d. [1999].

32. Ibid.; Mark McLelland, *Queer Japan from the Pacific War to the Internet Age* (Landover, MD: Rowman and Littlefield, 2005), 78; Hideo Sakamoto, interview with author, Aiea, HI, 4 January 2006; Kaji, interview with author. As with Seiji Naya, press accounts then and now differ as to Sakamoto's age upon arrival in Honolulu—for reasons we might intuit. In an interview, Sakamoto told Mark Santoki he was eighteen. But based on his date of birth, as he reported it to me, I assert that he was twenty.

33. Yukio Mishima, *Forbidden Colors*, trans. Alfred H. Marks (New York: Knopf, 1968; Tokyo: Shinchosa, 1951), 106–7.

34. Sakamoto, interview with author; Sakamoto, interview with Santoki.

35. Sakamoto, interview with author; Sakamoto, interview with Santoki; Naya, interview with Santoki.

36. Sakamoto, interview with author; Sakamoto, interview with Santoki; *HA*, 14 August 1957, 21 July 1960.

37. *HA*, 21 June 1960; Sakamoto, interview with author; Sakamoto, interview with Santoki.

38. Hiro Higushi, letter to Hisako Higuchi, 7 April 1944, series 1 (digitized), HHP, UH. Regarding Sakamoto's use of the phrase "gay boys," as I have transcribed it, it is worth noting that "the word 'gay' . . . (*gei*) entered Japanese immediately after the war via gay men in the occupation forces, who referred to their Japanese partners as *gei bōi* or 'gay boys.'" Kazuhiko Kabiya, "Danshoku kissaten no jissō" [The person who christened "gay bars"], *Fūzoku kitan* (January 1962): 146–47. Cited in McLelland, *Queer Japan*, 104.

39. *HSB*, 20, 29 July 1953. Emphasis added.

40. *HA*, 30 August 1965; *Hawaii Hochi*, 30 August 1965; O'Brien and Fugita, *The Japanese American Experience*, 87.

41. *HSB*, 30 August 1965.

42. *HA*, 27 August 1965, 4 July 1966; *HSB*, 4 July 1966; Diane C. Fujino, *Heartbeat of Struggle: The Revolutionary Life of Yuri Kochiyama* (Minneapolis: University of Minnesota Press, 2005), 84.

43. *HSB*, 31 August 1965; *HA*, 27 August 1965; Yempuku, interview with Santoki; Sakamoto, interview with Santoki. Seiji Naya, interview with author, Honolulu, HI, 21 December 2005.

44. *HA*, 27, 28, 30 August 1965; *HSB*, 26, 27, 30 August, 1 September 1965; *Hawaii Hochi*, 27, 30 August 1965; Sakamoto, interview with Santoki; Tom Moffatt, interview with author, Honolulu, HI, 28 December 2005.

45. Sakamoto, interview with Santoki; Sakamoto, interview with author.

46. Mishima, *Forbidden Colors*, 149.

NOTES TO EPILOGUE

1. *DT*, 30 July 1943; "Report for Week Ending July 31, 1943, Jerome Relocation Center," part II, section 5, reel 138, JAERR, UCB.

2. *PC*, 8 December 1945: Chester B. Himes, "Democracy Is for the Unafraid," *Common Ground*, Winter 1944. Subsequent quotations are taken from this article.

3. On civil rights–era Mississippi, see John Dittmer, *Local People: The Struggle for Civil Rights in Mississippi* (Urbana: University of Illinois Press, 1994); and Charles M. Payne, *I've Got the Light of Freedom: The Organizing Tradition and the Mississippi Freedom Struggle* (Berkeley: University of California Press, 1995).

4. *Washington Evening Star*, 23 February 1945; *Clarion-Ledger*, 13, 28 February, 3, 4 July 1946; *JDN*, 27 February 1946; *Delta Democrat-Times*, 2 July 1946; *MCA*, 3 July 1946; David K. Johnson, *The Lavender Scare: The Cold War Persecution of Gays and Lesbians in the Federal Government* (Chicago: University of Chicago Press, 2004).

5. H.R. 5835, 80th Congress, 2nd Session, and H.R. 6519, 81st Congress, 1st Session, JRS, MDAH; John Rankin, "Let Us Not Imitate Nero's Fiddling While Rome Burned," 13 July 1950, JRS, MDAH.

6. *The Oprah Winfrey Show*, 31 October 2001, 7 June 2002.

7. Wesley McNair, *Mapping the Heart: Reflections on Place and Poetry* (Pittsburgh: Carnegie Mellon University Press, 2003), 165–66. Subsequent quotations are taken from these pages.

8. Gerda Lerner, *Why History Matters: Life and Thought* (New York: Oxford University Press, 1997), 116. For a helpful critique of these and other aspects of "reproductive futurism," as he calls it, see Lee Edelman, *No Future: Queer Theory and the Death Drive* (Durham, NC: Duke University Press, 2004).

9. "Report for Week Ending August 7, 1943, Jerome Relocation Center," part II, section 5, reel 138, JAERR, UCB.

Index

Page numbers in italic refer to photographs.